MW01036074

The Southeast's Best Fly Fishing

For my good friend Don Harp. Let's go fishing!

J— B—

8 99852 00111 8

The Southeast's Best Fly Fishing

PREMIER TROUT STREAMS
AND RIVERS OF
GEORGIA, NORTH CAROLINA,
TENNESSEE, AND KENTUCKY

including Great Smoky Mountains National Park

James Buice

HEADWATER
BOOKS

STACKPOLE
BOOKS

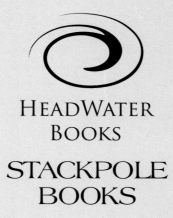

Published by
HEADWATER BOOKS
531 Harding Street
New Cumberland, PA 17070
www.headwaterbooks.com

STACKPOLE BOOKS
5067 Ritter Road
Mechanicsburg, PA 17055
www.stackpolebooks.com

Printed in China

First edition

10 9 8 7 6 5 4 3 2 1

Photography by the author, unless otherwise noted
Cover design by Wendy A. Reynolds

ISBN: 978-1-934753-02-6

Library of Congress Control Number: 2009923110

CONTENTS

ACKNOWLEDGMENTS

Writing has never been a chore for me, but it can become a job if you're not careful, especially when writing about something you love. When I began writing this book, it was evident that I was in way over my head, but thankfully, my friends, fellow guides, and colleagues in the fly-fishing community came to the rescue. With their help, this project was far from being a job. It was an excuse to visit and fish with friends, meet amazing people, and see some country that I had been away from for too long.

The list of people to thank for helping me is a long one, but somewhere near the beginning would have to be the guy who gave a young fishing guide a chance at an "indoor" job. Several years ago, I put on my best pair of flip-flops and sweet-talked Gary Merriman into giving me a job at his fly shop, The Fish Hawk, in Atlanta. Gary was instrumental in propelling me forward in the fly-fishing industry, offering advice and a good kick in the pants when needed.

For giving me a steady supply of writing assignments (and more than a few angry "motivational" phone calls), I'd like to thank Phil Monahan, along with Steve Walburn and Ross Purnell, for putting up with missed deadlines and letting me put together various manuscripts with words that are very easy to spell.

Jay Nichols gave me a shot writing for *Fly Fisherman* years ago, coming full circle and offering me a chance to do this book. His enduring patience and wisdom through e-mails and phone calls proved to be motivating pep talks. Jay is uniquely adept at telling you to "hurry up" while maintaining an extrinsically affable nature.

No book like this can be written without the help of those folks in the know. Guides and fly shop dudes are all part of a mix that resembles the angling version of the CIA in intelligence gathering for various watersheds.

Guiding for so many years myself, I know how difficult it is to put up with posing for photos, casting on cue, and trying to catch fish under pressure when you have a camera pointed over your shoulder. That said, a big thanks to fellow guides Guitou Feuillebois, Brad Barnes, Dane Law, Rocky Cox, David Hulsey, Henry Williamson, Ian Rutter, Charity Rutter, Chad Bryson, Chris Scalley, and the ever-patient Kent Klewein for letting me tag along and snap photos on your precious days off, as well as all the valuable information you were gracious enough to part with in an effort to make this book as accurate as possible.

Along with guides, fly shops provide links to the water, the good ones knowing their home waters and always offering a smile and a cup of coffee in the morning or a beer in the evening. I'd like to thank Jimmy, John, David, and Becky at Unicoi Outfitters, Kevin and Walker at Davidson River Outfitters, Than at Headwaters Outfitters, Byron and Daniel at Little River Outfitters, Jim and the gang at Fly South, Eddie at Fly Shop of Tennessee, Mac McGee at Choo Choo Fly & Tackle, Kenny at One Fly Outfitters, Cal at CR Outfitters, Kevin and "Hot Lauren" at Rolf Lanz Outdoors, along with all the folks at The Fish Hawk, Foscoe Fishing Company, Fly Box Outfitters, Mahoney's Outdoors, Smoky Mountain Fly Shop, Hunter Banks, Deep South Fly Shop, and Curtis Wright Outfitters for the coffee, information, flies, advice, and beer.

Photographs are such a special part of any book. They keep the imagination honest and animate the words on a page, breathing life into a book like this one. There is far more to it than simply shouting "Say cheeze!" and clicking a shutter. I feel very fortunate to call some of the finest photographers in the region my friends. They were all nice enough to contribute their art to the book. The eyes behind the best photos in this book belong to Louis Cahill, Zach Matthews, Ian and Charity Rutter, Chad McClure, and David Knapp. I owe you all big time.

Finally, thank you to everyone in my family and my close friends for putting up with me for the past year while I worked on the book. Dad. Joe. Let's go fishing.

INTRODUCTION

Stereotypes are present around the globe, and the South bears its fair share. I've been told we talk funny, and that we do things at a much slower pace. That *Deliverance* movie didn't help us out any. Our fisheries are likewise looked down on by those foreign to the Southland. Many believe the trout south of the Mason-Dixon Line are small, easily caught, and stocked.

This is true on some watersheds, but by and large, many of the high mountain streams and larger freestone rivers have large, self-sustaining wild

Large, wild brown trout are often loners and hunt in low light. Savvy anglers know bait-fish imitations are the way to go when looking for "the one." LOUIS CAHILL

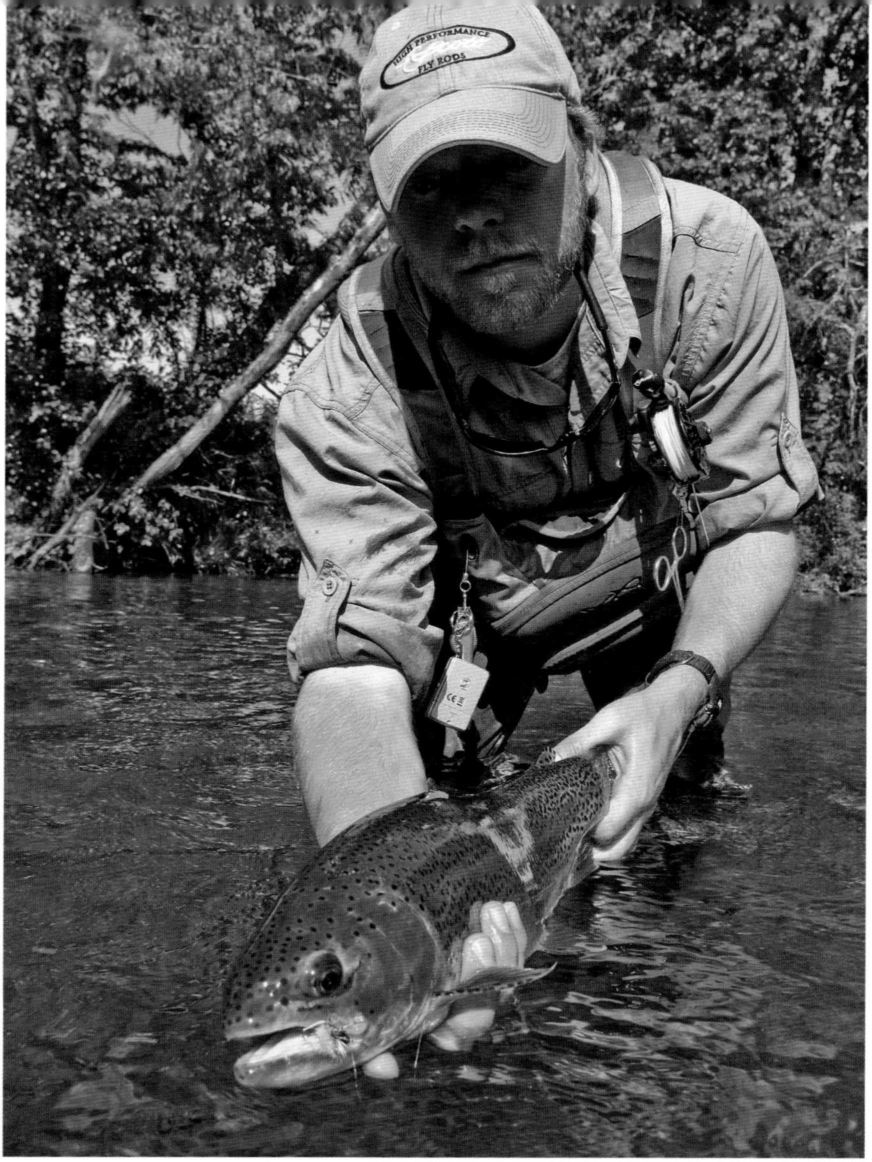

Some say the South is a land of small fish. Guides like Kent Klewein know better and prove it on a regular basis with hefty rainbows.

trout populations. The trout are not easy to catch by any stretch of the imagination. It seems everything in the country is trying to eat them, from herons, to raccoons, to otters. It's no wonder they spook sometimes at the flash of a bright fly line overhead or an angler's careless approach. When you do connect and bring one of these sparkling, spotted trout to hand, you have earned the chance to admire its brilliant colors.

Tailwaters add to the mix by providing what could arguably be the most consistent, prolific fisheries in the region. The cold waters downstream of the dams keep trout happy year-round and usually fortify a strong population of aquatic insects, resulting in larger trout and heavier hatches. Tailwaters are where large trout are consistently caught, save on the private stretches of freestone rivers where trout are fed to Godzilla proportions and people pay big money, as a guide friend of mine loves to describe, "to brag about getting laid in a whorehouse." Southern tailwaters have proven that, if managed properly, they can become world-class fisheries. This is assuming the powers that be provide enough water in the dire months to allow the trout and bug life to survive, regulations are enforced, and those along the banks are environmentally conscious.

Well over 10,000 miles of creeks, streams, and rivers course through the Southland. When I set out to write this book, it was decided that it would focus on the best fly fishing for trout in the region. But what exactly constitutes my version of "the best?" First, the river in question needed to be of a certain stature in the angling community, a watershed that for one reason or another had gained a following among anglers. It also needed to possess a certain intrinsic quality that set the river or stream apart from the masses. This covered a broad area, including but not limited to quality of fish, scenery, special regulations, insect hatches, and the amount of public access available. And the overall visceral experience of fishing a particular watershed was also taken into account.

I was not alone in this daunting task, enlisting the help of numerous fly shops, guides, and anglers from across the region in an effort to make the choices as egalitarian as possible. As you would expect, this led to a lot of discussion that spanned dozens of rivers and streams throughout the territory. In the end, we collectively assembled a list of what consistently have proven to be the region's best of the best. The waters listed in this book are by no means a complete representation of the grand trout-fishing opportunities to be had in the South. With so much water to cover, just because a particular river is not mentioned within these pages does not dictate a lesser-quality fishery. If you ask a hundred people from the Southeast to name their favorite trout waters, you will get a lot of different answers, but by the same token, you will get many that echo the same. The latter grouping is how we came to the list of rivers in this book.

A word about public access is in order, since the Southeast is suffering

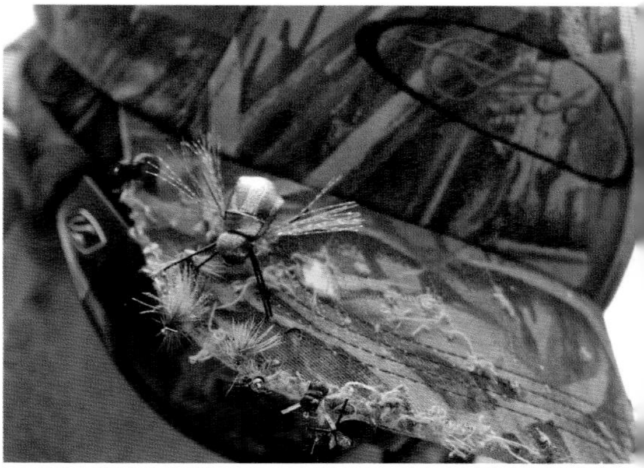

Terrestrials are an easy meal for trout on every river and stream during the summer. Carry a wide assortment of patterns, and don't be afraid to go big when looking to tempt large trout.

Hatches of large, robust mayflies such as Green Drakes are what draw anglers to many Southern freestone rivers in late spring. This hatch, if you can catch it, is perhaps the most heralded in the region.

from the same dilemma as much of the country. Landowners, for reasons ranging from the "mine, all mine" ideal to those who are tired of picking up trash after folks, are posting sections of rivers once open to the public. Oftentimes, the landowners are totally within their legal rights. For the most part, if a stream is considered navigable, anglers can float and wade the water, so long as they access it at a public point (i.e., boat ramp, bridge right-of-way, or public park). The property line is at the high-water mark, so anglers are within their legal rights so long as they do not exit the river onto private land. On smaller rivers and streams, landowners can post the riverbed as well as the banks. For instance, if a landowner owns a single bank, he or she is able to post to the center of the river. Should both banks fall into private hands, the entire stretch can be posted, disallowing any traffic in or out of the water.

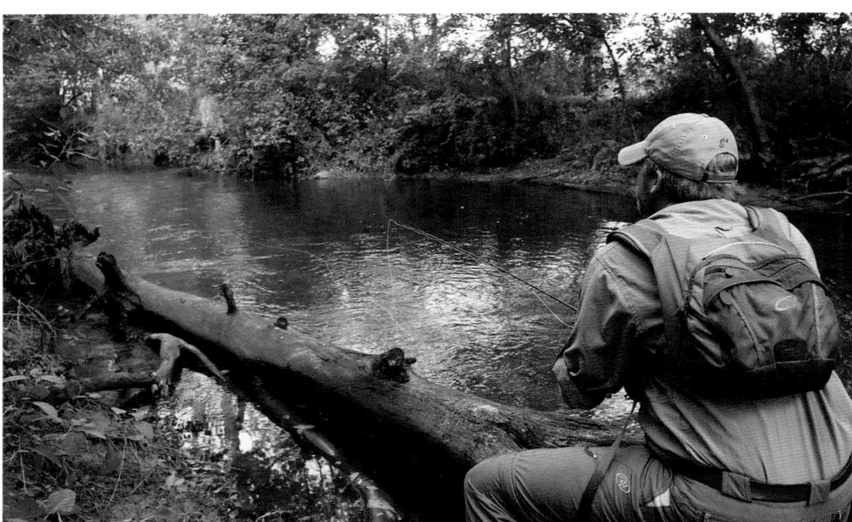

Small streams encompass the essence of Southern trout fishing. Stalking a trout, keeping a low profile, and blending in to your surroundings with dark clothing are tactics used by veteran small-stream anglers.

Anchoring during a float is legal on most southern tailraces, but the practice is being challenged by a few landowners. If a confrontation arises, it is best to take the high road and push off. There's always great fishing around the next bend.

Some tailwaters in the South are being confronted with issues of private ownership, most notably the Toccoa River in Georgia and the South Holston River in Tennessee, both of which are listed in this book. Although both rivers have historically been open to fishing and recreational floating, landowners—mostly those new to the region—have begun claiming rights to the center of the river. This has sparked much controversy, especially on rivers with high float traffic. There are two sides to every story, and from the looks of things, the issue will soon wind up in litigation, with the final decision handed down from a high court. Popular opinion suggests that anglers would eventually win out, but many have their reservations and are nervous about the battle. For now, it's best to push off if a confrontation arises. There's a lot more water to fish, and the view from the high road is always better.

When reading this book, remember that the waters listed are in the top echelon, but to confine yourself to fishing only these rivers and streams would do both you and the entire Southern trout fishery system a great disservice. Many other rivers and streams could have easily found their way onto these pages, but we decided early on that certain watersheds would not be named due to their delicate and fragile nature. There are too many of these to count, most scattered in the high mountains of Georgia, Tennessee, and North Carolina. They remain hidden gems, crooked needles in a haystack of blue lines that require nothing more than the time and opportunity to reach. If you fish the region long enough, you're bound to find your own personal "best of" list.

THE SOUTHEAST'S
PART I

For big trout in Georgia, concentrate your efforts on the Toccoa and Chattahoochee tail-races as well as the quality water on Dukes and Noontootla creeks. These areas are known for consistently producing larger than average trout, and they offer miles of water to explore. LOUIS CAHILL

BEST FLY FISHING GEORGIA

Being about as far south as most respectable trout are willing to travel, Georgia has over 5,000 miles of trout streams. Nearly 3,000 miles of these waters support wild trout populations whose brown, brook, and rainbow trout all reproduce outside of hatchery raceways. Many of these rivers and streams flow through public land, giving the angler countless opportunities to explore the Peach State.

Recently, Georgia has adopted the delayed-harvest program, currently including parts of the Chattahoochee River and Smith Creek, along with the Amicalola and Chattooga rivers. Outside of these seasonal fisheries, sections of Dukes and Waters creeks both have catch-and-release, barbless hook regulations, making for technical fisheries that test anglers' skill and patience.

Most of Georgia's trout streams are mountain freestoners, the majority being found in the northcentral to northeastern side of the state. Luckily, this puts many of these watersheds within the boundaries of various wildlife management areas, as well as the Chattahoochee National Forest. A single angler could explore this vast fishery for a lifetime and still not cover every nook. I have a friend who is desperately trying to fish as many as he can, and he is doing a fine job at it. I've fished with him since we both were in our early teenage years, and he will be the first to tell you that after fishing so many of these mountain waters, they are most certainly not all created equal. Low nutrient levels plague many of Georgia's streams, making for small trout that live short lives. The state counters this with a healthy stocking program—some of these plantings live on for a few seasons; others find their way to the dinner table, of either man or beast. Wild trout waters are normally difficult to access, especially creeks with native brook trout. Brook trout have a foothold, albeit a tenuous one, in 140 or so miles of water.

In addition to the countless mountain freestone creeks and rivers, Georgia has two first-class tailwater fisheries. The Toccoa and Chattahoochee

Georgia Fly Shops and Guides

Toccoa River

FLY SHOPS AND GUIDES

The Fish Hawk
3095 Peachtree Road
Atlanta, GA 30305
(404) 237-3473
thefishhawk.com

Choo Choo Fly & Tackle
17 Cherokee Blvd.
Chattanooga, TN 37405
(423) 267-0024

Unicoi Outfitters
7280 South Main Street
Helen, GA 30545
(706) 878-3083
unicoioutfitters.com

Unicoi Outfitters
490 East Main Street
Blue Ridge, GA 30513
(706) 632-1880
unicoioutfitters.com

GUIDES ONLY

Kent Klewein
(770) 330-7583
kent-klewein.com

Henry Williamson
(706) 746-5631

Southeastern Anglers
(866) 55-TROUT
southeasternanglers.com

rivers are perhaps the most popular fisheries in the state, partially due to their ease of access and the numbers of trout in their waters. They also remain much colder than even the highest freestone creeks during the warmer months that seem to be expanding their balmy grip. These tailwaters are not the places you go for solitude, although it can occasionally be found. In more places than not, the calls of the chickadee are being drowned by the mating call of the McCulloch chainsaw, and the only deer you see are green ones who like to be called John. Landowners beleaguered with apathy or ignorance scorch the banks right to the water, affording them an unimpeded view of the water they paid for so dearly.

This is not confined to the tailraces, as freestone rivers and creeks sit on a far more precarious fulcrum of environmental hazard. A delicate balance of natural order has preserved these waters for centuries, but it only takes a single snowflake to start an avalanche. As William Blake wrote, "Great things are done when men and mountains meet. This is not done by jostling in the street."

Studies by state and federal officials have found that development and rapid expansion into these areas are the largest threats to this and other states' coldwater fisheries. Poor land use, such as clearing past the 50-foot riparian buffer mandated by state law, causes sediments to wash into the river, suffocating the riverbed, and removes the shade trees that cool the river during the warmer months. The lack of county and state enforcement is upsetting, and if these contemptible practices carry on, every watershed adjacent to private land is at immediate risk.

Since Georgia lies farther south than any state in this book, it should be of no surprise that the warmwater fisheries are almost as popular as some of the state's trout fishing destinations. Shoal bass are a sought after prize among anglers, and the state has no shortage of options. The Flint River located south of Atlanta is one of the premier fisheries in the region for shoal bass and the lower Chattahoochee below Morgan Falls Dam is supporting a healthy population of the fish along with its trout population, the latter being more prolific during the delayed harvest season.

Striped bass have found their way into the upper Chattahoochee trout waters below Morgan Falls as well, having been a staple farther south along the Georgia-Alabama border for years. Both of these bass species have become widely popular with fly anglers in recent years with a great deal of credit going to folks like Kent Edmunds, a veteran guide to the bass fisheries on the Flint and lower Chattahooche rivers.

The rivers and streams of northern Georgia offer a diversity seen in few states. Tiny mountain brookie streams, picturesque freestone rivers, and cold flowing tailraces create a bounty of trout angling destinations. Add in the warmwater alternatives and you have more than ten lifetimes of water to explore. You'd better get started.

Chattahoochee River

FLY SHOPS AND GUIDES

Fly Box Outfitters
840 Ernest West Barrett Parkway
Kennesaw, GA 30144
(866) 460-2507

The Fish Hawk
3095 Peachtree Road
Atlanta, GA 30305
(404) 237-3473
thefishhawk.com

Unicoi Outfitters
7280 South Main Street
Helen, GA 30545
(706) 878-3083
unicoioutfitters.com

GUIDES ONLY

River Through Atlanta Guide Service
(770) 650-8630
riverthroughatlanta.com

Chattahoochee River Outfitters
(770) 402-7883
chatriveroutfitters.ccom

Chattooga River

FLY SHOPS AND GUIDES

Unicoi Outfitters
7280 South Main Street
Helen, GA 30545
(706) 878-3083
unicoioutfitters.com

Brookings Outfitters
3 Chestnut Road
Cashiers, NC 28717
(828) 743-3768
brookingsonline.com

Highland Hiker
601 Main Street
Highlands, NC 28741
(828) 526-5298
highlandhiker.com

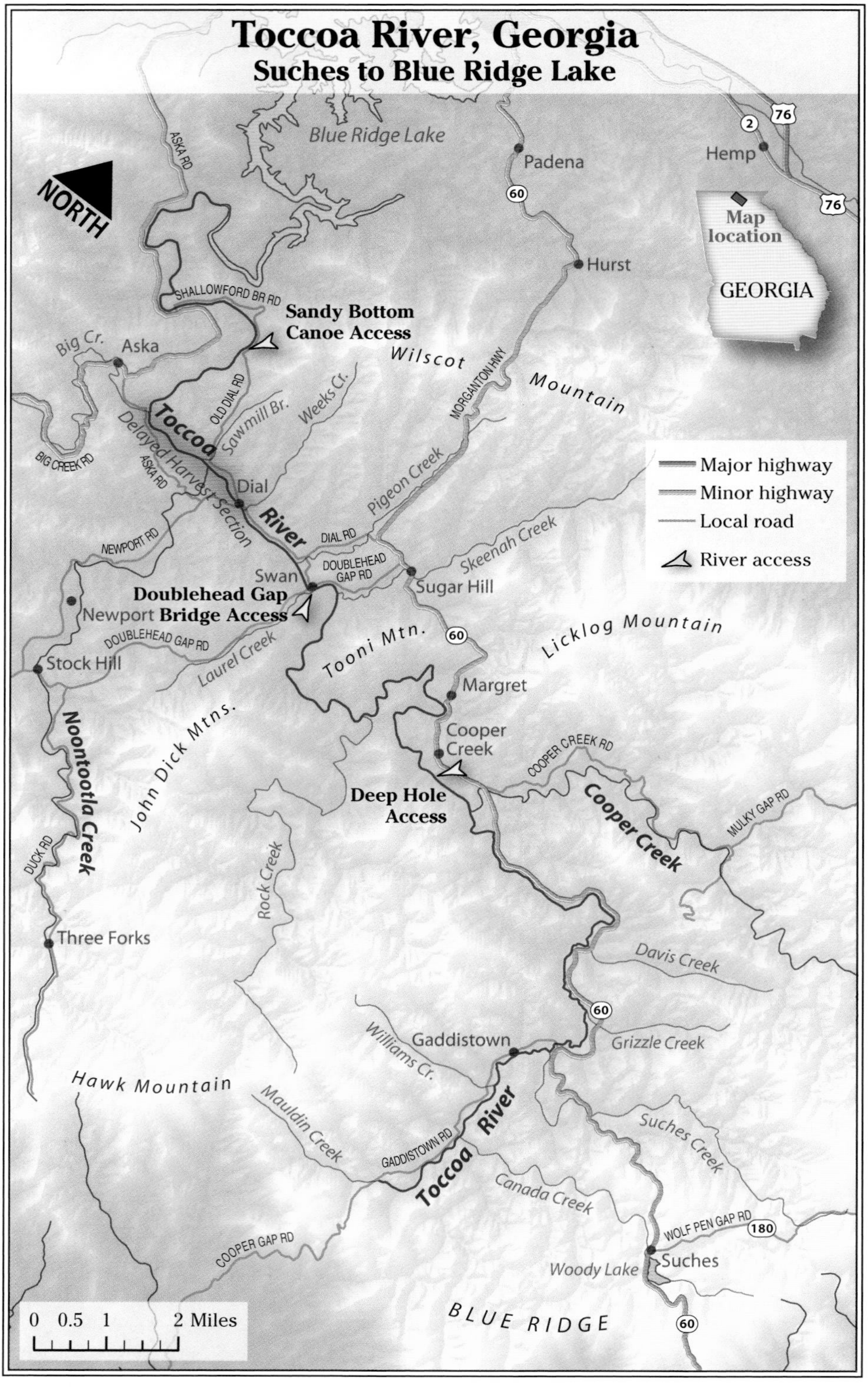
Toccoa River, Georgia
Suches to Blue Ridge Lake
NORTH
Blue Ridge Lake
Padena
Hemp
Hurst
Map location
GEORGIA
ASKA RD
SHALLOWFORD BR RD
Sandy Bottom Canoe Access
Aska
Big Cr.
Wilscot Mountain
MORGANTON HWY
OLD DIAL RD
Sawmill Br.
Weeks Cr.
Toccoa River
Delayed Harvest Section
BIG CREEK RD
Dial
Pigeon Creek
NEWPORT RD
DIAL RD
DOUBLEHEAD GAP RD
Skeenah Creek
Swan
Sugar Hill
Doublehead Gap Bridge Access
Newport
DOUBLEHEAD GAP RD
Laurel Creek
Tooni Mtn.
Licklog Mountain
Stock Hill
Margret
Cooper Creek
COOPER CREEK RD
John Dick Mtns.
Noontootla Creek
Deep Hole Access
Cooper Creek
MULKY GAP RD
DUCK RD
Rock Creek
Three Forks
Davis Creek
Gaddistown
Grizzle Creek
Williams Cr.
Hawk Mountain
Mauldin Creek
GADDISTOWN RD
Toccoa River
Suches Creek
Canada Creek
WOLF PEN GAP RD
COOPER GAP RD
Suches
Woody Lake
BLUE RIDGE
Major highway
Minor highway
Local road
River access
0 0.5 1 2 Miles
2
76
60
180

CHAPTER 1

Toccoa River
including Noontootla Creek

From its headwaters in the mountains above Suches, Georgia, the Toccoa flows northwest 60 or so miles before crossing into Tennessee to become the Ocoee River. To nonanglers, the Ocoee is perhaps more notable than the Toccoa, as it has been a world-class whitewater paddling destination for decades and was the site of the 1996 Summer Olympic kayaking events. The stretch of river between Suches and McCaysville near the Georgia-Tennessee border receives the most attention from anglers.

I grew up near the Toccoa and consider it my home water. When my friends and I skipped school to fish, this is where we hid out. I began guiding on the river many years ago, and many of my friends still make their living rowing down the river, searching for the brightly colored rainbows and deeply hued browns that will still rise to a dry just as they have for years. The river has seen some changes—not all good—but for the most part it still remains the best dry-fly river in the state.

Headwaters to Lake Blue Ridge

High in the mountains near the Tennessee Valley Divide, the Toccoa River begins as a small trickle within the Chattahoochee National Forest. The diminutive flow soon leaves public land, flowing for a little over 10 miles through a picturesque valley near the mountain community of Suches. It would be best to concern yourself only with the 14-mile stretch between the Deep Hole Recreation Area downstream to Shallowford Bridge.

Perhaps the biggest issue surrounding the upper Toccoa, especially between Deep Hole and Rock Creek Bridge, is fishing access. At one time you could float and fish the entire stretch below Deep Hole. The few homes along the river were mostly owned by mountain folk who didn't mind a few people coming by and fishing. If they did take a notion of exclusive water rights, you would know it by their scowl and few harsh words, typically with a shot-

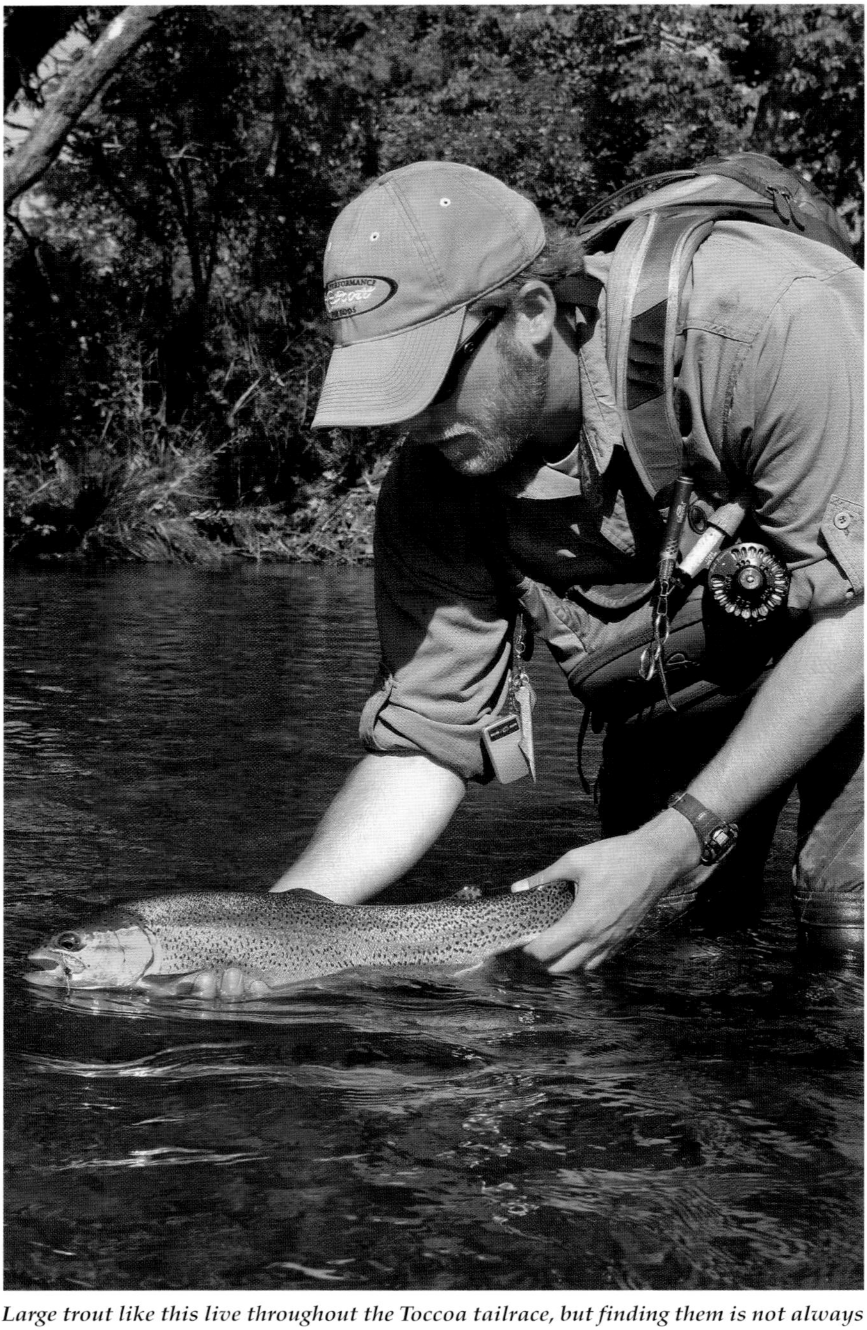

Large trout like this live throughout the Toccoa tailrace, but finding them is not always easy. You must pick your battles, passing up smaller trout in search of a trophy. The end result will not be as many fish, but quality will far outweigh quantity.

gun in tow. Now, the region surrounding the river has become popular with the well-heeled, nowadays armed with bureaucracy rather than buckshot (and far more liberal with its use).

Recreational floating is allowed from Deep Hole downstream (known as the Toccoa River Trail), so long as you obey the "No Fishing" signs posted along the riverbanks. Pods of trout, bulging and heavily fed, sit on the bottom of the large pools, looking rather out of place in a north Georgia river. It's tempting to flip a fly from the canoe when one of these oversize pigs rises to a dry, but it's best to keep things on an even keel and float on by.

A canoe is the best way to access the upper river from Deep Hole to Doublehead Gap Road. The narrow river is a mixture of long pools spliced together with short riffles and chutes, but no serious rapids encumber an otherwise lazy float. The best course of action is to fish where the river flows through National Forest land or nonposted private land and paddle through the posted water, hoping for new state regulations. Trout on this upper stretch are pretty much the same 8- to 10-inch variety found downstream; however, due to the supplemental feeding by some landowners, it is possible to hook into a larger-than-average rainbow or brown.

From Doublehead Gap Bridge downstream to Shallowford Bridge, the river is floatable, and for the most part nobody will give you a hard time for getting out and wading. Below Doublehead Gap Bridge, the river leaves the road, returning a little over a mile downstream alongside Dial Road. The float from Doublehead Gap Bridge to Dial Road will take you through some gorgeous rock gardens and gliding pools that are seldom fished by other anglers. This short stretch is perfect for a half-day trip. Below Dial Road Bridge, the river winds away from the road until it reaches Sandy Bottoms. It is possible to drop in a canoe or drift boat off one of the roadside pullouts on Dial Road, then float to Sandy Bottoms. It is not possible to take a drift boat out at the canoe launch. However, if you can thread the needle between two large hemlocks just downriver of the launch, a low spot on the bank and some elbow grease will make for an impromptu boat ramp. Below this, you'd best be pretty creative if you're going to get anything larger than a personal pontoon or light canoe out of the river before dropping over the rapids below Shallowford Bridge.

Recently, the state designated a small portion of the Toccoa under its delayed-harvest (DH) regulations. The delayed-harvest section stretches from around 450 feet above the Sandy Bottoms canoe launch downstream to a half mile above Shallowford Bridge. The stretch is only 1.3 miles long, but it encompasses some of the best water on the river. Large rock gardens, long riffles, and deep bends in the river make for an idyllic setting. During the delayed-harvest season, the trout, some stocked with holdover fish mixed in, are far more plentiful here than on any stretch of the upper river. Come June, the water begins to warm quickly and the trout push upstream, some seeking shelter in the larger tributaries including Cooper and Noontootla creeks.

Due to the unpredictable hatches on the upper Toccoa, nymphing or stripping a streamer is your best bet. Stonefly nymphs such as Ostenson's

The upper Toccoa and its tributaries flow through some of the most picturesque scenery in the state. The valley encompassing the mountain communities of Suches and Dial should be on every angler's "to visit" list. LOUIS CAHILL

Trout Retrievers, Stalcup's Rubber-Legged Stones, and Terminator Stonefly Nymphs (#8-12) in black, brown, and golden will work year-round in the deeper runs, usually tempting the larger trout. Other proven subsurface patterns include Lightning Bugs, Smith's Translucent Pupae, Copper Johns, Pheasant Tails, and *Hydropsyche* caddis larvae imitations (#14-18), along with UV Z-Midges, SLF Midges, Split Case BWOs, and Poison Tungs (#18-20).

When fishing nymphs, look for the tailouts leading into long pools, microseams in the deep water, and any fast water with enough depth and structure to create soft holding water. Use enough split-shot to get the fly down, and keep your indicator a tad over the depth of the water. Toccoa trout can be soft in their strikes, and you need to be connected to your fly at all times to detect even the most subtle take.

Streamer fishing comes in a close second to nymphing on the upper river. Crayfish patterns, along with baitfish imitations, match the meat hatch. Patterns such as Whitlock's NearNuff Sculpins, Wittmer's Shiela Sculpins, Sculpzillas, Bellyache Minnows, and trusty Woolly Buggers (#4-10) can be fished on either a floating or light sinking line. Some of the deeper holes may require a heavy sinking head to reach the depths, but on average, the river is relatively shallow, meaning a long, heavy tip will end up snagging bottom most of the time. Intermediate lines or short, 8- to 12-foot sinking heads (1.5 to 2.5 inches per second sink rate) are far better suited for probing the banks and around boulders. When you reach a deeper run and want to get down, stack-mend your sinking line to gain depth and allow it to swing down and across, keeping your rod tip low, retrieving with short, jerky strips. You may be surprised by what lives down there.

Hatches on the upper Toccoa can be broken down into winter Blue-Winged Olives (BWOs) and spring caddis. This is not to say that other bugs do not come off, but these are the two most reliable hatches and what the trout consistently key in on. Many of the river's lesser mayfly hatches can be matched with a simple Parachute Adams (#12-18), which is what most anglers tie on in blind faith.

November through March is prime time for the best Blue-Winged Olive hatches. Some of the better hatches occur downstream of Swan Bridge to the end of the delayed-harvest water. From late fall through the winter, Blue-Winged Olives hatch just about every day somewhere along the river. If you can find the particular stretch of water where the bugs are coming off, you will more than likely have your own private paradise full of rising trout. Some larger trout will often begin rising to these small mayflies, but you'll probably need to float away from the roadside access areas or fish in the delayed-harvest waters to get them. When you find the hatch, or it finds you, tie on a Harrop's CDC Biot Emerger, No-Hackle, or Brooks's Sprout *Baetis* (#20-24) to get your foot in the door.

Following the warming trends of late March, the caddis become active, and word quickly spreads among the angling community. When the fly bins that house caddis dry flies at the Unicoi Outfitters Blue Ridge shop begin looking particularly sparse, you know the hatch is on. Don't plan on being alone on the delayed-harvest (DH) section during the caddis hatch, but remember there's a lot more water upstream that can be just as good. A few bugs will come off from Deep Hole down to Swan, but the largest numbers will hatch from Swan downstream to Shallowford Bridge. Floating from Swan to Dial Road will put you in prime caddis territory, away from the crowds.

You will seldom need to stray farther than a tan or brown Elk-Hair Caddis or Mathews's X2 Caddis (#14-16). If things get techie, go with a Harrop's Fertile Caddis or CDC Caddis Emerger (#14-16). A favorite combo is an Elk-Hair Caddis trailing a Beadhead Soft-Hackle Pheasant Tail, Sparkle Pupa, or Stalcup's Bubble Caddis (#16-18). Dead-drift the meat of the run then allow the combo to swing around at the end of the drift. Many times, the trout will eat either fly on the swing after following it the length of the drift.

Caddis will continue until mid-May, around the end of the delayed-harvest season. Terrestrial fishing picks up after the caddis from the end of May until the river heats up, sometime around early July. Both cinnamon and black ant patterns (#16-18), along with Japanese beetles (#12-14) and grasshopper imitations (#8-12), will tempt a few trout on top, but for the most part, you're back to nymphing the deeper runs.

After the river begins heating up, fishing becomes especially tough. Early morning and late in the evening gives you a small window of decent fishing. Most folks prefer to hopscotch over Lake Blue Ridge and fish the tailrace where cooler water temperatures keep the game on through the heat of summer.

Tailrace

The Toccoa River tailrace is one of the most diverse fisheries in the region and arguably the best dry-fly destination in the state. Up until a few years ago, it was possible to catch over 50 fish in a day on the Toccoa, mostly on dry flies.

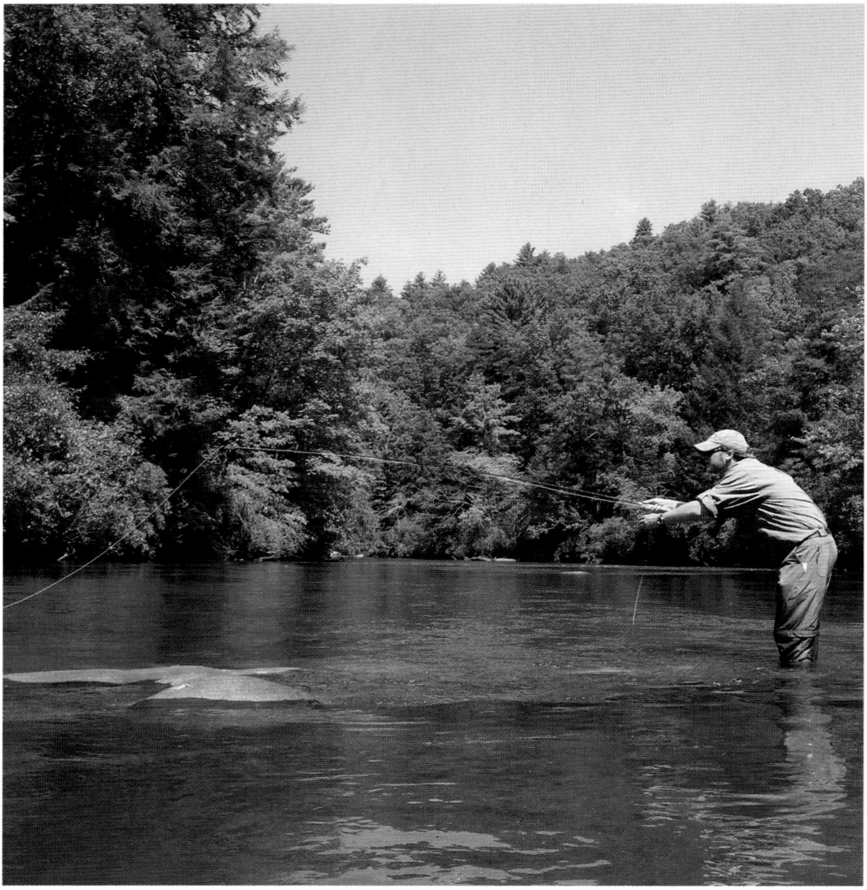

Wide, shallow expanses on the delayed-harvest water above Lake Blue Ridge give anglers plenty of room to spread out. Careful wading is a must here, as rock ledges drop off quickly into deeper water.

While these fish were not large, averaging 8 to 12 inches, they aggressively attacked dry flies and were not all that picky unless really keyed in on a specific hatch. In the last few years, increased pressure on the river has made fishing far more technical than it ever was. Large attractor flies with generic nymphs trailing behind have been replaced by tiny dry flies and midge larvae. Yes, the "easy" days on the Toccoa are long gone. Nowadays, even the standard 8- to 12-inch trout are not pushovers, and you'd best get ready to pay your dues if you want to step outside of the "average" box.

Fifteen miles of trout water flows below the dam downstream to the town of McCaysville near the Tennessee-Georgia border. Relatively narrow, around 40 to 60 feet wide in most areas, the Toccoa is an intimate fishery, not as intimidating as some of the larger tailraces in the region. Much of the river is bordered by private land, save for four access points that, despite offering a good deal of wade access, make up only a small part of the overall river. Most of the water is float access only, but this is no cakewalk. The river is rocky and shallow, running around 120 to 140 cubic feet per second (cfs) when the dam is not online. Scraps of paint and gelcoat from the bottoms of boats that have floated the river testify to the scrubbing, dragging, and bumping that go along with any float down the Toccoa. Factor in that the distance between the boat ramps is a minimum of 6 miles, and you have a pretty long day on the water. You may ask, is it worth it? It is.

Toccoa trout are feisty and strong. Even smaller wild fish have "shoulders" built from a lifetime of fighting the heavy-generation flows. Hatches on the river can be amazing, but you should bring a good selection of flies with you to properly match what the trout are eating, and don't be afraid to switch up patterns. What they're eating in one run may not be the same 100 yards downstream.

Generation on the Toccoa is either high or low, running at 1,600 to 1,800 cfs when the dam's only turbine is running. Not many folks venture on the river during periods of high water. Some guides on their days off, including me, will go out and try to coax a few trout to the boat. Really, this is more of a leisure float with friends than a serious angling expedition. In high water, streamers will get a few trout to eat, as will deep nymphing with large stonefly nymphs (#6-10) such as Kaufmann's Rubber-Legged Stones, Stalcup's Tungsten Stones, and Gabriel's Trumpets. Weight the flies heavily with at least three BB-size shots and run the indicator all the way up a 9-foot leader to get the fly down into the softer water on the bottom.

Low water, when the turbines are off and the minimum-flow gate is open, is when the Toccoa really comes into its own. Wading anglers will find several hundred yards of shallow, wadable flats between the dam and Tammen Park, as well as Curtis Switch TVA access and at Horseshoe Bend Park in McCays-

Small flies and light tippets will fool wary Toccoa trout. Going to a #20-24 fly fished shallow under an indicator is a proven tactic.

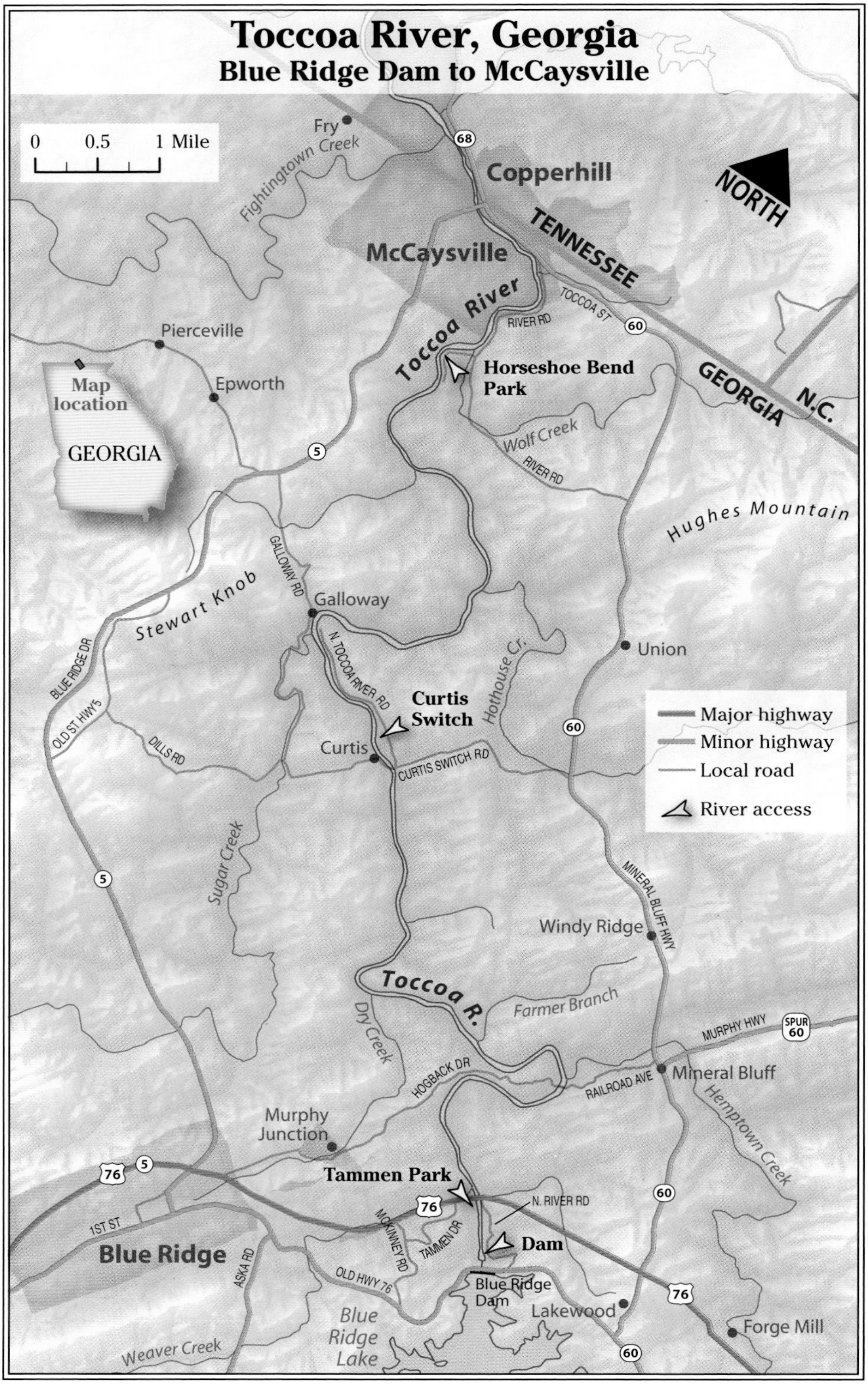

Toccoa River, Georgia
Blue Ridge Dam to McCaysville
0 0.5 1 Mile
NORTH
Fry
Fightingtown Creek
68
Copperhill
TENNESSEE
McCaysville
Toccoa River
TOCCOA ST
RIVER RD
60
Pierceville
Horseshoe Bend Park
GEORGIA
N.C.
Map location
GEORGIA
Epworth
Wolf Creek
RIVER RD
5
Hughes Mountain
GALLOWAY RD
Stewart Knob
Galloway
Union
N. TOCCOA RIVER RD
Hothouse Cr.
BLUE RIDGE DR
Curtis Switch
OLD ST HWY 5
60
DILLS RD
Curtis
CURTIS SWITCH RD
Major highway
Minor highway
Local road
River access
Sugar Creek
5
MINERAL BLUFF HWY
Windy Ridge
Toccoa R.
Farmer Branch
Dry Creek
MURPHY HWY
SPUR 60
HOGBACK DR
Mineral Bluff
RAILROAD AVE
Hemptown Creek
Murphy Junction
76
5
Tammen Park
60
76
N. RIVER RD
1ST ST
MCKINNEY RD
TAMMEN DR
Dam
Blue Ridge
ASKA RD
OLD HWY 76
Blue Ridge Dam
76
Lakewood
Forge Mill
Blue Ridge Lake
Weaver Creek
60

ville. These areas all offer parking and access to the river, as well as unimproved canoe launches. More on that later.

The wading opportunities may sound limited on such a long tailwater, but there is plenty of room to spread out, and anglers hardly ever trip over each other. Most anglers fishing near the dam seldom find trout over 12 inches, but they make up in quantity what they lack in size. A reverse dichotomy of many tailwaters, the Toccoa's smallest fish tend to be around the dam, due to the lack of a weir that would ease the scouring effects of water release. There is simply not enough biomass here to grow the large numbers of stocked and holdover trout to larger sizes.

Around 7 miles downstream, the Curtis Switch TVA (Tennessee Valley Authority) access gives you a shot at some larger trout, but again you'd best have your game face on to fool them. This popular access consists of a large flat directly in front of the launch that extends downstream to a small island. If you're not afraid of getting a little water over the top of your waders (the deepest water you'll have to wade through is 5 to 5 1/2 feet deep), it is possible to wade below the island and access a small riffle. Unaffected this far downstream by the scouring of the water releases near the dam, caddis and mayflies, along with a steady stream of midges, help maintain a healthy trout population and create some noteworthy hatches.

Horseshoe Bend Park marks the third and final public access point for wading anglers. Just upstream of the town of McCaysville, the park has plenty of parking and offers the greatest amount of wade access. Similar to Curtis Switch in bug life, Horseshoe Bend routinely gives up a few large browns and rainbows each year, some well over 20 inches.

As mentioned earlier, the three wade access points also have rudimentary canoe launches. Canoes, one-man pontoons, and other small, manageable watercraft are easy to launch at any of the access points. Larger drift boats and rafts are a bit more of a challenge. Over the years, folks floating in drift boats have gotten pretty creative launching and retrieving larger boats on the river. Boats are usually dropped down embankments alongside the canoe launches using a variety of winches, homemade slides, and plenty of elbow grease. When the day is over, boats are usually removed in an orchestra of pushing and winch cranking. Float times between any of the launches are an all-day affair, especially since it's hard to not stop and fish along the way.

Float fishing is the best way to see the river, and exceptional skills with a paddle or oar are not required. This makes the Toccoa a popular river with float anglers, especially on—you guessed it—the weekends. During the week, the river is all but vacant save for a few guide boats.

The Toccoa is known as a dry-fly river. Its shallow nature, combined with exceptional biomass, means the trout are often looking up. Hatches of mayflies, caddis, midges, and stoneflies keep the local fly shop busy selling Gink and Frog's Fanny. Blue-Winged Olives hatch throughout the year, the heaviest hatches coming on overcast days and winter evenings following a stretch of cold, snowy weather. Going down to at least 6X tippet with a

Brooks's Sprout *Baetis*, Harrop's BWO CDC Biot Emerger, or BWO Last Chance Cripple (#18-24) tied securely to the end matches the *Baetis* hatch anytime during the year.

In February, Little Black Stoneflies are the first heavy hatches of the year. This hatch lasts just a few weeks, but during this time North Fork Specials and Gabriel's Trumpets (#10-12) drifted deep near banks or large boulders will tempt trout watching for active stonefly nymphs crawling on the bottom of the river. Dry-fly fishing can be decent, but typically nymphs are far more effective for this early stonefly hatch.

There is no reason to fret about the lack of fishing on top, as dry-fly fishing is right around the corner. Sometime around the third of February to the first week of March, Blue Quills and Quill Gordons will begin coming off in numbers good enough to entice the trout. Traditional Catskill-style dry flies to match both hatches should be on hand, in #12-14 for the Quill Gordons and #18 for the Blue Quills. There are not enough bugs on the surface for the trout to become picky, and these are the first larger mayflies they've seen since the previous fall.

Closely following, occasionally overlapping this mayfly duo, Dark Dun/Black Caddis (*Chimarra* spp.) begin hatching, *usually* appearing in late February to early March. This is one of the favorite hatches of veteran river guide David Hulsey. "It's the first big hatch of the year, and the trout will eat just about anything that looks like a little caddis, so long as the color and size are right." Set up just below the riffles where the water begins to slow, and start looking for heads. David prefers using a dun-colored caddis imitation such as a Harrop's CDC Biot Emerger, CDC Bubble Back Caddis, and Elk-Hair Caddis (#16-18) to match the hatch.

Another fan of the early caddis is Henry Williamson, arguably one of the first true fly-fishing guides in the mountains of North Georgia. Henry's accent is as unmistakable as his fishing prowess. He fishes more days a year than most folks work and isn't afraid to share his opinions, when asked, in an unfiltered juggernaut free of ambiguity. Guiding a bit less now and spending more time in his workshop making gorgeous bamboo rods, Henry still catches fish on the Toccoa when the rest of us are scratching our heads. Henry loves fishing dry flies, but believes that swinging a soft-hackle caddis or Pheasant Tail through the riffles during this early hatch will produce larger trout than sticking exclusively with dry flies. Whatever the choice is, dry or wet, it would be hard to argue with either of these veteran guides' strategies.

Mid-April is a special time on the Toccoa and a time of torture for many of us sharing other outdoor interests. About the time the Hendricksons and March Browns begin hatching in mid-April, the wild turkeys are in the peak of their mating season. Flocks of wild turkeys can be seen in the fields alongside the river, the males gobbling and displaying for the hens. Along with the calls of the turkey, mayflies fill the air. Hendricksons and March Browns usually hatch for a week, maybe two, then it's all over save for a few stragglers. If the hatches are heavy, it is one of the best times to be on the river.

A Female Adams or Parachute Adams (#14-16) will cover you for the Hendrickson hatch. For the March Browns, which usually overlap the end of the Hendricksons, traditional wet and dry patterns (#12-14) will do the trick. Swinging traditional March Brown wet flies through the tailouts of riffles and braided runs is a great way to bring several nice trout to hand that may not be inclined to rise for the adults.

Overlapping the Hendricksons and March Browns, brown and gray caddis begin coming off in mid-April and continue through the end of May. This hatch can bring a lot of fish to the surface, especially scores of little 4- to 8-inch trout. Riffles seem to be exploding at times as these smaller trout swat at emerging caddis, but if you watch closely, you will find larger trout feeding along with the smaller fish. Surprises lie in nearly every riffle, but you must be observant and pick out the fish you want to cast to instead of "bunch shooting" among a dozen rising fish.

Fish high-floating dry flies such as Henryville Specials, Mathews's X2 Caddis, and Spotlight Caddis (#14-16) in the braided water, where an extremely visible fly is needed. In the slower waters, low-riding patterns such as Harrop's Fertile Caddis, Flatwater Parachute Caddis, and CDC Bubble Back Caddis (#14-16) are better suited for trout that may study the fly a little longer.

Fishing down and across riffles with a Soft-Hackle Pheasant Tail or Sparkle Pupa (#14-16) can be highly effective just before the caddis begin com-

Long, shallow stretches make floating the Toccoa a chore, both for small personal crafts and larger boats. Be aware that walking your boat through these shallows will increase float times when planning a trip.

ing off, or at the beginning of the hatch. Just like swinging a wet fly during the March Brown hatch, swimming an ascending caddis imitation through tailouts and braided water, as Henry suggests, will often hook larger trout, especially the browns.

As the heaviest hatches of caddis are winding down in late May, the mid-day and evening skies begin to be filled with little orange-yellow mayflies. Usually around 2 PM or so, Sulphurs *(Ephemerella invaria)* begin emerging. The hatches are heaviest on the brighter days and tend to last for several hours each day. The Sulphur hatch is one of the most popular with the anglers and the fish, but most folks get discouraged quickly, finding the trout not all that easy to fool. Another crackerjack Toccoa guide, Kent Klewein, notes that most anglers are discouraged because they are fishing flies that ride too high in the water. "Low-water patterns and cripples are my favorite patterns to fish," he notes. Kent looks for the river's more exceptional trout, especially on days when he's not on the oars guiding. "It takes a certain skill level to catch big Toccoa trout on a dry. You can catch a ton of 8- to 10-inch fish because that's what we have the most of here. The big trout need long, accurate casts and perfect drifts, usually under tight cover, and most folks just can't make the cast."

No matter what you're looking for (a big solitary trout or going after numbers with the smaller guys), keep plenty of Compara-duns, Last Chance Cripples, Harrop's Captive Duns, and A. K.'s Parachutes (#12-16) on hand. Using light tippets 6X, even 7X, and long leaders over 12 feet will help with wary fish in areas that are popular with anglers.

By mid-June, the *E. invaria* Sulphurs are replaced by *E. dorothea,* basically just a smaller version of the same bug, around a size 18. Along with the smaller Sulphurs—which are coming off in fewer numbers than their larger brethren—tan caddis, Light Cahills *(Stenonema canadense),* and Little Yellow Stoneflies begin showing up late in the evenings. The trout don't seem to pay a lot of attention to the Light Cahills, but the caddis will really turn some heads. In the evenings, tan-colored Elk-Hair Caddis, Hemingway Caddis, and Parachute Elk-Wing Caddis (#16-18) work well, especially when skated across the surface. Large yellow Kaufmann's Stimulators and Twisted PMX dry flies (#10-12) will work for imitating the yellow stoneflies that can be seen fluttering around all day. This is a great time to fish a Beadhead Pheasant Tail, Deep Six Caddis Pupa, or Translucent Pupa (#16-18) using a buoyant caddis or stonefly dry as an indicator.

The Golden Stones, which began hatching in late April, continue to hatch through July and much of August, but terrestrials offer far more consistent fishing. Ants, beetles, hoppers, and inchworms are high on the trout's diet during the summer. In years where Japanese beetles are clinging to nearly every leafy bush on the side of the river, Steeves's Japanese Beetle and Harrop's CDC Beetle (#12-14) can give you a day of fishing to rival any hatch of the year. Flying ants in black and cinnamon (#16-18), Monster Beetles (#10), and Rainy's Foam Hoppers and Bugmeisters (#8-14) will cover you during the summer doldrums.

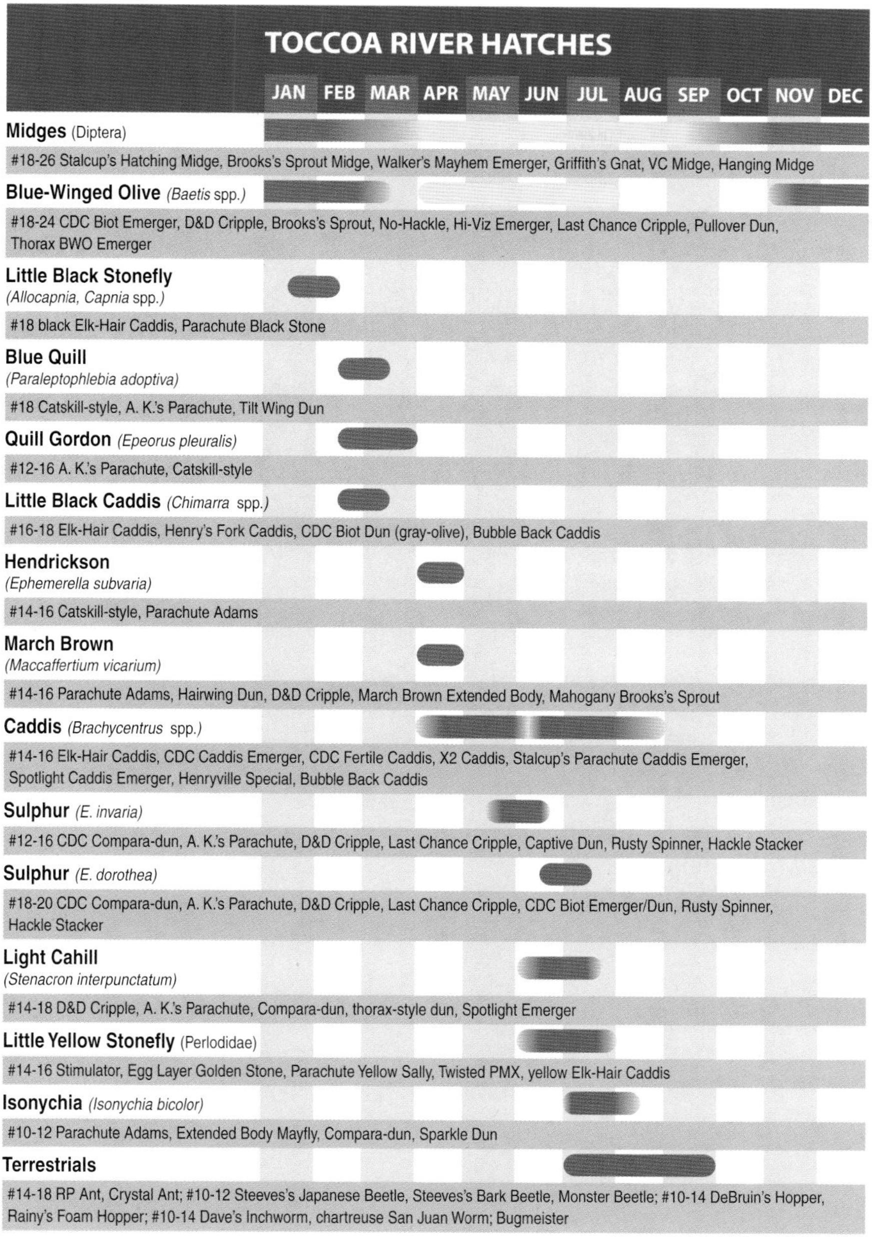
TOCCOA RIVER HATCHES
JAN FEB MAR APR MAY JUN JUL AUG SEP OCT NOV DEC
Midges (Diptera)
#18-26 Stalcup's Hatching Midge, Brooks's Sprout Midge, Walker's Mayhem Emerger, Griffith's Gnat, VC Midge, Hanging Midge
Blue-Winged Olive (Baetis spp.)
#18-24 CDC Biot Emerger, D&D Cripple, Brooks's Sprout, No-Hackle, Hi-Viz Emerger, Last Chance Cripple, Pullover Dun, Thorax BWO Emerger
Little Black Stonefly (Allocapnia, Capnia spp.)
#18 black Elk-Hair Caddis, Parachute Black Stone
Blue Quill (Paraleptophlebia adoptiva)
#18 Catskill-style, A. K.'s Parachute, Tilt Wing Dun
Quill Gordon (Epeorus pleuralis)
#12-16 A. K.'s Parachute, Catskill-style
Little Black Caddis (Chimarra spp.)
#16-18 Elk-Hair Caddis, Henry's Fork Caddis, CDC Biot Dun (gray-olive), Bubble Back Caddis
Hendrickson (Ephemerella subvaria)
#14-16 Catskill-style, Parachute Adams
March Brown (Maccaffertium vicarium)
#14-16 Parachute Adams, Hairwing Dun, D&D Cripple, March Brown Extended Body, Mahogany Brooks's Sprout
Caddis (Brachycentrus spp.)
#14-16 Elk-Hair Caddis, CDC Caddis Emerger, CDC Fertile Caddis, X2 Caddis, Stalcup's Parachute Caddis Emerger, Spotlight Caddis Emerger, Henryville Special, Bubble Back Caddis
Sulphur (E. invaria)
#12-16 CDC Compara-dun, A. K.'s Parachute, D&D Cripple, Last Chance Cripple, Captive Dun, Rusty Spinner, Hackle Stacker
Sulphur (E. dorothea)
#18-20 CDC Compara-dun, A. K.'s Parachute, D&D Cripple, Last Chance Cripple, CDC Biot Emerger/Dun, Rusty Spinner, Hackle Stacker
Light Cahill (Stenacron interpunctatum)
#14-18 D&D Cripple, A. K.'s Parachute, Compara-dun, thorax-style dun, Spotlight Emerger
Little Yellow Stonefly (Perlodidae)
#14-16 Stimulator, Egg Layer Golden Stone, Parachute Yellow Sally, Twisted PMX, yellow Elk-Hair Caddis
Isonychia (Isonychia bicolor)
#10-12 Parachute Adams, Extended Body Mayfly, Compara-dun, Sparkle Dun
Terrestrials
#14-18 RP Ant, Crystal Ant; #10-12 Steeves's Japanese Beetle, Steeves's Bark Beetle, Monster Beetle; #10-14 DeBruin's Hopper, Rainy's Foam Hopper; #10-14 Dave's Inchworm, chartreuse San Juan Worm; Bugmeister

In the fall, brown trout begin looking for a fight as their prespawn blood rises. Beldar Lemon Drops, Zonkers, and Galloup's Fatheads (#1/0-6) will get chases from some of the largest browns in the river. Go heavy on your tippets, and fish short, sinking-tip lines between 10 and 15 feet in length with sink rates between 2 to 4 inches per second. These tips get the fly down where you need it, but allow you to fish the more shallow stretches without hanging up on the bottom too often. Don't go to the river thinking you're going to catch a 10-pound brown trout. It's not an everyday occurrence, and it is possible to go an entire season without ever seeing one of these legendary browns. They are in the river, and folks do catch them, but browns from 12 to 16 inches are far more common during the fall and should be considered trophies in their own right.

The Toccoa has been through many changes over the years, both in the upper reaches above the lake and in the tailrace below. People have built homes along the river's banks, not always adhering to the state's riparian buffer, and local officials seem to have either turned a blind eye or simply lack the manpower to enforce environmental regulations. Runoff from scorched banks and increased siltation can cover gravel bars and muddy the water after a hard rain. Compounding the problem, many riverside homeowners wishing to see large trout are wrecking the fragile ecosystem, tossing food pellets into the river to ensure that they have large trout. This artificial influx of easy food pulls trout from hundreds of yards away, pooling dozens upon dozens of trout in large pods near private homes. Aside from increasing disease among the fish, these covens of trout concentrate anglers near homes whose owners feed heavily, making for some tense moments between landowners and anglers, as river ownership is still a hot point of contention between the two.

Luckily, the positive far outweighs the negative. The Toccoa is fishing as well as ever, and there are plenty of places you can go to get away from the crowds.

Noontootla Creek

Noontootla Creek is the largest of the Toccoa's tributaries. Flowing from the high mountains within the Blue Ridge Wildlife Management Area (WMA), Noontootla is an unforgiving, downright tough creek to fish. It runs alongside Forest Service Road 34 downstream from Three Forks near the heart of the WMA to its boundary. For nearly its entire length, Noontootla is classic pocketwater fishing, save for a few deep slicks and pools. The creek is managed under special regulations, mandating artificial lures only, and only one trout over 16 inches may be kept. You would think that with the special regulations the creek would be teeming with larger than average trout, but that is not the case. Poaching keeps trout numbers down and makes the larger trout all that much harder to catch. Don't let this dissuade you from a trip up

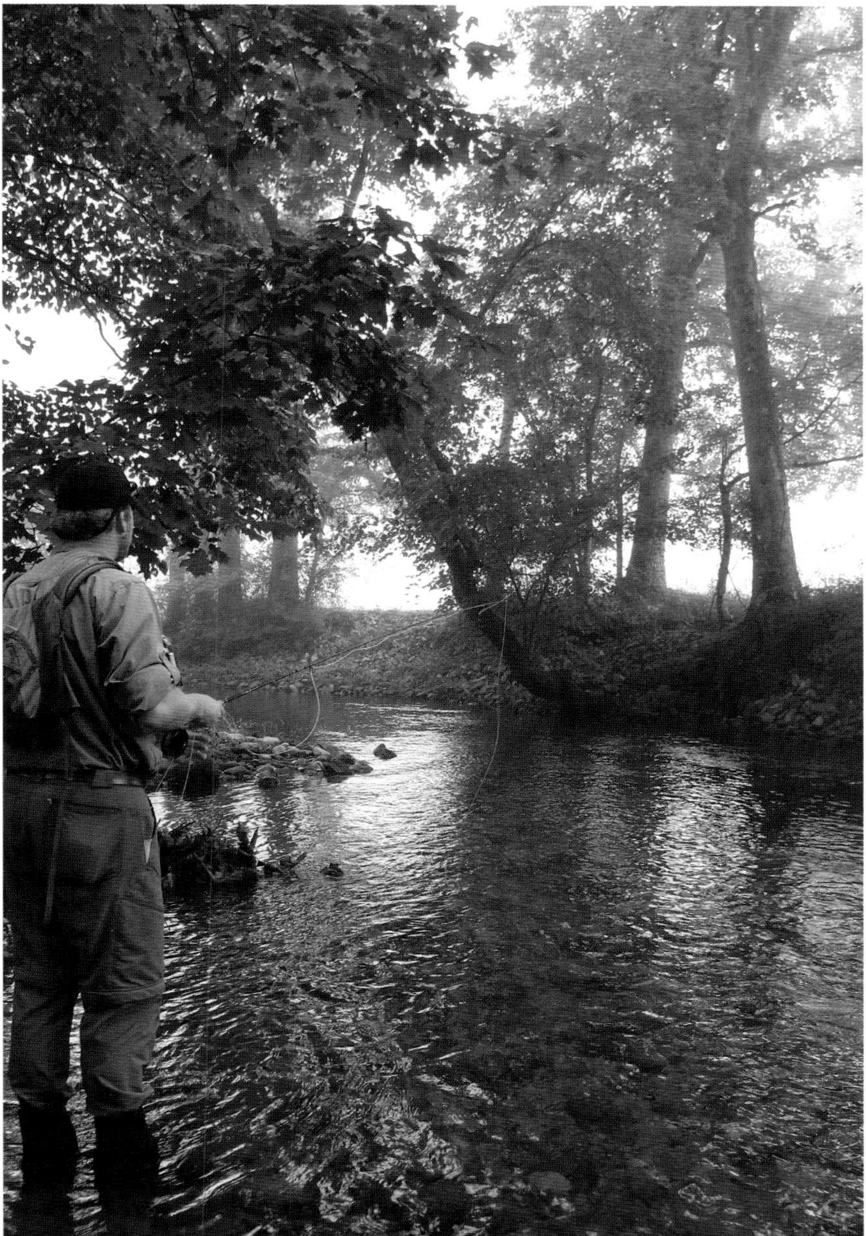

The private water on Noontootla Creek managed by Noontootla Creek Farms allows anglers to fish for trout on two miles of managed water. This stretch is known for very large, sometimes difficult, trout.

the gravel road to the creek, because even if the catching is off, Noontootla Creek is arguably one of the prettiest creeks in the mountains.

Downstream of the WMA boundary, Noontootla Creek flows through private land for several miles before it empties into the Toccoa River downstream of Dial Bridge. Some of the river is managed by Noontootla Creek Farm, a private pay-to-fish refuge that takes a limited number of anglers on its 4 miles of water. The trout here are large and plentiful, but come with a price. Not more than a mile downstream of the public water, some of these larger brown and rainbow trout find their way into the public water, surprising anglers with thoroughbred runs in the narrow creek.

For the most part, trout in Noontootla's public stretch are on the smaller side, usually 6 to 10 inches long, but some nice brown trout poke their noses out on occasion, and enough trout in the 12- to 16-inch range keep things interesting. This is not an easy creek to fish. The trout are spooky, and approaching them in such a narrow, overgrown stream is nearly impossible. But it can be done if you slow down and approach every likely spot as if it is home to a big trout . . . because many are.

Nymphing with a tandem rig consisting of a stonefly pattern such as a Stalcup's Rubber-Legged Stone, Mercer's Epoxy Stone, or Kaufmann's Stonefly (#10-12) along with a Pheasant Tail, Tellico, or Hare's Ear Nymph (#16-18) trailing closely behind is far more effective than other methods in this high-gradient mountain stream. Leave the bright indicators at home, or better yet, don't use an indicator at all. The trout are ultrasensitive and will spook at the slightest notion that something is amiss. Learning to nymph without an indicator will pay off in spades here.

Dry-fly fishing is relegated to the spring and early summer, occasionally slipping into August if the water levels are decent. Unlike other mountain creeks in the area, Noontootla draws from a large aquifer that keeps the creek running a bit higher and cooler than surrounding streams in the summer doldrums.

Come April, a few caddis are fluttering around on the river, along with the occasional Hendrickson or March Brown. Tan or brown Elk-Hair Caddis (#14-16) and the Catskill versions of the latter two mayflies (#12-16) will suffice. The hatches are not rock steady and can disappear in just a few days.

What the trout here seem to remember, even before the bugs begin hatching in June, are the Golden Stoneflies. From the onset of warm weather until the end of summer, Golden Stone parachute patterns and Stimulators (#10-14) can be fished with confidence.

Terrestrials are indispensable between July and late September. Wood beetle patterns such as Steeves's Bark Beetle and Tiger Beetle (#12), inchworm patterns such as Whitlock's Inchworm or a chartreuse San Juan Worm, and Steeves's Fireflies (#12-14) should be fished under overhanging bushes along deep cuts in the river's rocky bottom. For one reason or another, large, animated terrestrial imitations such as Schroeder's Parachute Hoppers, Chernobyl Ants, and Taylor's Fat Alberts (#8-12) will provoke strikes from larger

Brooks's Sprout *Baetis*

Hook: #18-24 Daiichi 1130
Thread: Olive 8/0
Tail: Brown Z-lon
Body: Olive goose biot
Post: White foam
Thorax: Olive dubbing
Hackle: Dun saddle

CDC Caddis Emerger

Hook: #14-16 Daiichi 1180
Thread: Brown 8/0
Tail: Green CDC fibers
Body: Olive goose biot
Thorax: Olive dubbing
Wing: Dun CDC feather

than average trout, along with their smaller cousins. It is advisable to keep a few on hand just in case everything else isn't working. As my buddy and fishing guide Kent Klewein says: "You can never carry too many flies."

In the fall, after the leaves have fallen from the trees and the mountainsides, the waters on Noontootla begin cooling drastically along with the air temperature. Brown trout, some coming from the private waters down below, will move up into the public water in an attempt at spawning. If you can catch the river coming down after a fall rain, with the water still up but clearing, you are poised for big brown trout. Streamer fishing for these prespawn trout in higher water is not for everyone. Wading is treacherous and casting is tight, but putting a large streamer like a Beldar Bugger, Zoo Cougar, or Zonker (#4-8) in a pocket of soft water could be your ticket to a cool ride.

Winter all but shuts down the Noontootla, save for the occasional warm day. During the coldest days of the year, you're better off leaving the creek for the Toccoa tailrace just a short drive away. On warmer days, you may be lucky enough to have a few tan caddis coming off, tricked by the rise in temperature, and have the entire creek all to yourself.

Chattahoochee River, Georgia

Henson Creek to Helen

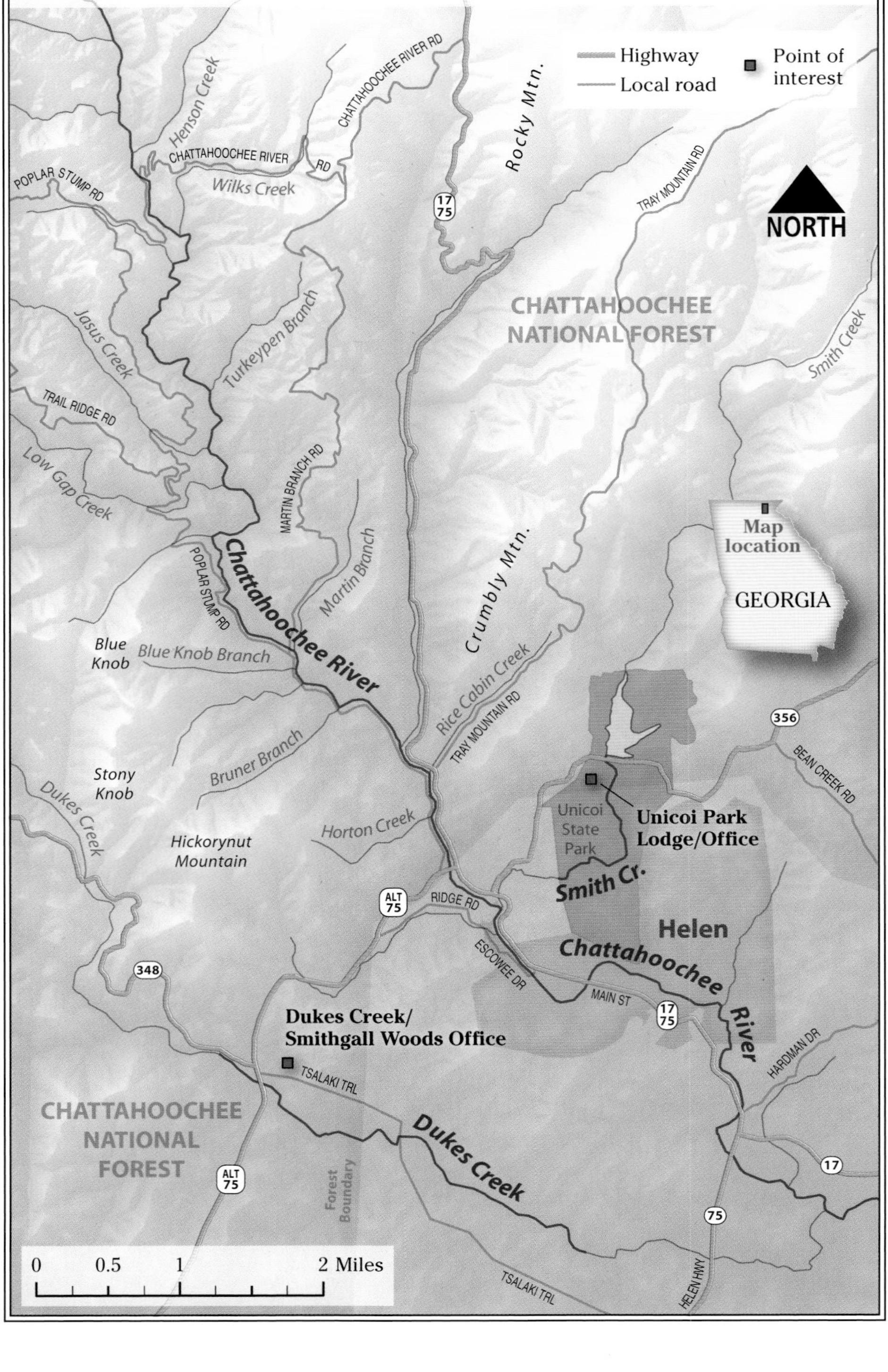

Highway
Local road
Point of interest
NORTH
Henson Creek
CHATTAHOOCHEE RIVER RD
Rocky Mtn.
POPLAR STUMP RD
Wilks Creek
TRAY MOUNTAIN RD
17
75
CHATTAHOOCHEE NATIONAL FOREST
Jasus Creek
Turkeypen Branch
Smith Creek
TRAIL RIDGE RD
Low Gap Creek
MARTIN BRANCH RD
Map location
GEORGIA
POPLAR STUMP RD
Chattahoochee River
Martin Branch
Crumbly Mtn.
Blue Knob
Blue Knob Branch
Rice Cabin Creek
TRAY MOUNTAIN RD
356
BEAN CREEK RD
Stony Knob
Bruner Branch
Dukes Creek
Unicoi State Park
Unicoi Park Lodge/Office
Hickorynut Mountain
Horton Creek
Smith Cr.
ALT 75
RIDGE RD
Helen
Chattahoochee River
ESCOWEE DR
348
MAIN ST
Dukes Creek/ Smithgall Woods Office
TSALAKI TRL
HARDMAN DR
CHATTAHOOCHEE NATIONAL FOREST
Dukes Creek
17
Forest Boundary
75
0
0.5
1
2 Miles
TSALAKI TRL
HELEN HWY

CHAPTER 2

Chattahoochee River
including Dukes and Smith Creeks

There is a small sign marking water with an arrow pointing down from Jack's Knob Trail near Chattahoochee Gap and Coon Den Ridge. Around 3,400 feet above sea level in the mountains of North Georgia the Chattahoochee River is born, little more than a trickle flowing through ferns, oak, and pine. Shortly downstream, creeks snaking through the Chattahoochee National Forest begin joining the flow, adding width, depth, and character to what the early Cherokee tribes called "Chota."

In the ancient valleys of the upper river, native Southern brook trout swim in the narrow, tumbling currents. In fact, the upper Chattahoochee and Henson Creek are possibly the most popular brook trout fisheries in the state—at least, the ones people talk about. If you're not familiar with native brookie fishing in the South, many of the creeks are closely guarded secrets, never printed and seldom talked about. In fact, most folks would have never heard of Henson Creek if it had not been brought into the proverbial spotlight when the Georgia Department of Natural Resources (DNR) placed a barricade on the creek's lower section as a barrier between the easily displaced brook trout and the nonnative rainbow and brown trout.

Both the uppermost Chattahoochee and Henson Creek are CQF, or "close-quarters fishing." You'll be doing more flipping and dapping the fly than actually casting. Remember, style points don't count when you're fishing tight cover. Though I'm not personally an advocate of rods shorter than 7½ feet, even on small streams, there are a lot of anglers who use brookie-specific sticks in the 5½- to 6½-foot range in 3-weight, all the way down to those sexy, ultralight boutique "0" and "00" weights. Niche rods such as these are kind of cool, and I've gotta admit, aside from being easier to carry when negotiating the tight, overgrown banks of these mountain creeks, the shorter rods give you a feel of seriousness the way specialized tools often do.

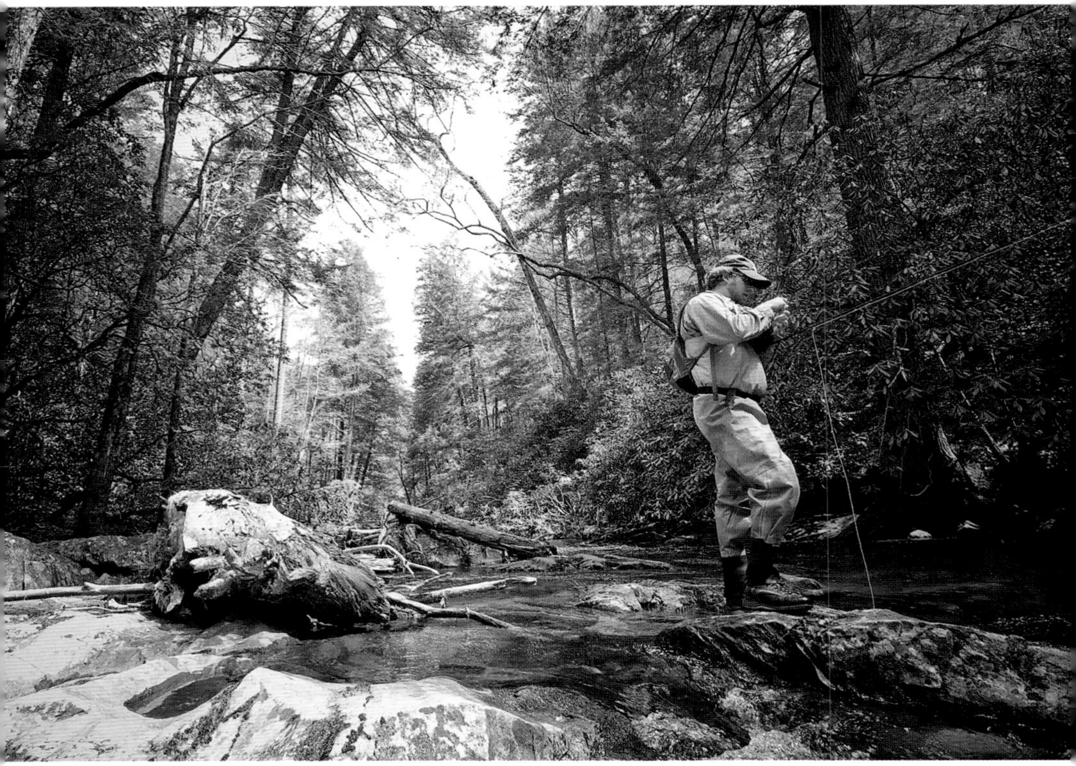

High in the mountains of North Georgia, the mighty Chattahoochee begins as a tiny mountain stream. LOUIS CAHILL

Fooling the little natives is often far easier than actually delivering the fly to the water, especially for those unaccustomed to small-stream fishing. Short leaders, 7½ feet tapered to 4X or 5X, are the norm. Like most of the anglers visiting these little creeks, I typically fish dry flies, figuring that when you're in the headwaters of such a mighty river, purity counts for something.

Downstream of the brookie water on the upper Chattahoochee, Low Gap Creek is the first feeder creek of significance to enter the river. This little creek, located off Forest Service Road 44, is worth exploring, as it holds rainbow and the occasional brown trout in the lower reaches, with brook trout farther upstream if you're willing to hike for them. A campground near the creek can serve as a base of operations during a multiday trip into the headwaters. Springtime and early summer are the best times, as you can tie on a bushy dry fly such as a Royal Wulff or Thunderhead and call it good.

From Low Gap Creek downstream to the Forest Service boundary, the Chattahoochee snakes away from the road several times, giving you the opportunity to fish roadside or hike a ways in search of solitude. Numerous roadside pullouts and campgrounds offer access to the river and many of its tributaries. Bushwhacking to the more remote stretches can be rewarding, with some larger trout inhabiting the deeper plunge pools away from the gravel road.

When it leaves the confines of National Forest land just upstream of GA 75 ALT, the river is a good-size flow of around 20 to 25 feet wide in some sections during normal water levels. Access here is limited until you reach the town of Helen, a Bavarian-themed tourist town complete with its own versions of Oktoberfest and Wursthauses. Through town, the river is stocked heavily, but also receives a great deal of fishing pressure. Weekdays are your best bet for missing the largest crowds, and some days you'll have the river all to yourself, but don't expect it. If you're not put off by crowded fishing and storefront scenery, the river through town is a gorgeous piece of tumbling water reminiscent of a perfectly sculpted mountain freestoner.

Below Helen, the Chattahoochee flows through private land, becoming a warmwater fishery before the next public access point. A notable stretch below is the water operated by Unicoi Outfitters at Nacoochee Bend. Here, stocked trout are grown to far larger than average size, some reaching double-digit weights. Big trout come with a price, with daily guided and nonguided day tickets available at the fly shop. This is pretty much Disneyland for trout anglers, somewhat artificial when compared with what the river naturally produces upstream, but you never hear anybody arguing when line is being peeled off by a huge, tail-walking rainbow cartwheeling its way to freedom.

The Nacoochee Bend water is open year-round, and the prime time is, as with most freestone rivers and streams, spring. March rides on the cusp of winter, a transitional time when snow is every bit as likely as 80-degree weather. From March until late June, the entire upper river from Helen to the headwaters fishes with reasonable consistency. The trout are active, temperatures are stable for the most part, and rains keep cool water coursing through the valley.

It's hard to argue that nymphing is the most productive fishing method here. Springtime hatches are sporadic at best, so going below the surface is necessary on most days. Use an attractor pattern such as a Stimulator, Royal Wulff, or Parachute Adams (#12-16) as an indicator over a Pheasant Tail, Copper John, or Prince Nymph (#14-18) if you don't see a decent hatch coming off. This method works well pretty much anytime from March through late September. Switching up your indicator dry to mimic the particular hatch that should be coming off at that time of year keeps you in the game, and even without bugs in the air, your dry fly will probably earn its keep.

Although the hatches are erratic, when the bugs do come off, the trout do not take long to notice. Following the first warming trends in March, Quill Gordons and Hendricksons in decent numbers begin hatching, but should not be depended on as daily providers of dry-fly action. Though these early hatches are not heavy, they are the first bugs of spring on the river and mark the time you should dust off your mountain dry-fly box. Traditional Catskill

Wild rainbow trout like this one call the headwaters of the Chattahoochee home and will readily attack a dry fly on warm days. Attractors such as Royal Wulffs, Stimulators, and Humpies are all good choices when prospecting the upper 'Hooch. LOUIS CAHILL

dry flies have a cool, retro vibe that really draws me to them, especially when fishing freestone rivers that hold trout that may not be all that picky. Quill Gordon (#12-14) and Hendrickson (#14-16) patterns should be at least a brace deep in your box.

As the trees fill out and the gray forests turn green, the first mayflies begin winding down and the caddis open shop. From the beginning of the hatch, sometime in mid-April, through the spring, a standard gray or brown Elk-Hair Caddis (#12-16) trailing a Soft-Hackle Pheasant Tail or caddis pupa pattern (#14-18) will consistently produce strikes.

Summer months find the water levels dropping, sometimes to levels dangerous to the trout. When the weather is sticky hot, rain has been absent for weeks, and the stream's trout are noticeably suffering, let them be, especially on the upper reaches where wild fish are present. Mortality can be high on stressed fish during these periods, the recreational benefit paling to the price paid by the trout. Luckily, these times are usually short-lived, as a summer rain will raise water levels quickly, giving the river a shot of life. Following a summer rain, trout will seem to appear out of nowhere ready to eat.

In the summer, prospecting with a terrestrial is a fun way to spend some time on the Chattahoochee. Wood beetles, ants, and inchworms are what the trout are used to seeing float by, and they know these helpless bugs are easy pickings. Dropping a Pheasant Tail or Prince Nymph off a buoyant foam terrestrial pattern just helps you provoke the stubborn guys. This late in the game, do away with the beadhead patterns, and drop your fly size down to a #18-20. The trout have seen it all by this time, and even the smaller fellas are not pushovers.

When the heat is on and the river is at its summer low, fish higher in the watershed above GA 75 ALT and into the headwaters where the water is cooler and oxygen levels are higher. This makes for better fishing and keeps from stressing trout in the warmer, lower reaches.

The nights begin growing cooler in the middle of September, marking the beginning of what is oftentimes a lull in fishing. Low water levels and temperature changes (sometimes rapid fluctuations) will put the trout into a funk that can last for a few weeks. Then the river stabilizes, usually following a few early fall rains and more consistent air temperatures. Around the end of September to early October, as the forest's green canopy slips into the colors of fall, trout once again begin feeding.

There are fewer trout now, especially rainbows—either caught and kept for the dinner table or victims of the natural world during summer's heat. Resilient brown trout in the lower river and brook trout in the upper reaches are ramping up for their spawn. Brilliantly colored in the clear waters, aggressive by nature and hormones, the browns will pounce on streamers, especially after a rain when the water is a bit off color. Sculpin patterns with lead eyes to get them down in the deeper pools help you knock on the right doors when looking for larger prespawn browns. Don't expect a "big brown" to be much larger than 12 inches—it's simply unrealistic. Although larger fish do call the river home, it would be a lofty, near futile expectation to catch a trout over 14 inches, even during this prime time for larger trout.

Winter is a dicey game. Snow, sleet, and freezing rain mark radical weather changes in the mountains. When the thermometer dips below 40 degrees F, don't even bother going. You may coax a trout or two into eating your nymph, but you have to hit them on the head with the fly, and they're not going to put up much of a fight. Bluebird winter days are the best. In north Georgia, a number of days from November through February usually find their way into the high 50s and slightly above. These are the times to head to the upper 'Hooch and wet a line. They are also prime days to fish one of the river's more noted tributaries such as Dukes or Smith creeks. Normally crowded in spring and early fall, these waters can be all but deserted in the winter months.

In the winter, nymph fishing is usually the only way to go. If you're lucky, a caddis hatch may kick into gear or enough midges will be on the water to make the trout look up for a short time. Dropping a stonefly nymph, such as Stalcup's Tungsten Rubber-Legged Stone or Tungsten Terminator Stone (#8-12), below an indicator and prospecting in deeper holes and plunge pools coax aggressive strikes from otherwise lethargic trout. Tie on a smaller Pheasant Tail, Cheeseman Emerger, SLF Midge, or BTS Nymph (#18-22) to up the ante.

Tailrace

Some of my first trout-fishing memories are on the Chattahoochee with my father. Spin or fly, he was an equal opportunity angler. We would float the upper river in an old boat he'd bought secondhand, usually fishing with my cousin Bill Bates. Back in the day, the access points were few and far between. Sometimes we would drop the boat in near Shakerag where the McGinnis Ferry Bridge crosses the river and float down to GA 20. Every morning we would fish, Dad would stop in at a local general store—the only one that was open in the predawn hours—and buy us the breakfast of champions: an RC Cola and a bearclaw.

Launching the old V-hull from a steep slide upriver of the equally difficult takeout didn't mean much to an eight-year-old kid. I was relegated to ferrying rods up the hill while he and whoever was with us dragged the boat several dozen yards up the slick, rocky banks to the truck. At the time, I was just along for the ride, but looking back now as my friends and I do on similar backbreaking floats on rivers lacking the amenities of civilization, I can understand the passion my father had for the sport.

Today, several concrete ramps allow easy access to most of the river, negating the backbreaking work of decades past. From Buford Dam down to

Wild brown trout populations on the Chattahoochee River tailrace are now flourishing. Catching fish like this one is becoming more common, especially in some of the more remote stretches.

Island Ford Park, then below Morgan Falls Dam to the Powers Island Recreation Area, anglers have no shortage of boating or wading access.

The tailrace of the Chattahoochee River begins at the base of Buford Dam, where the depths of Lake Lanier cool the waters, subsequently discharging the flow at around 42 degrees year-round. For more than 43 miles downstream, the river's cool waters hold rainbow and brown trout along pretty much every yard of water. During low flows, the average minimum discharge is around 600 cfs. This makes for easy wading in the wide, shallow shoals and a pleasurable float through the deeper water. When the sirens sound near the dam and the generators begin their chore, the river rises, with an outflow of around 8,000 cfs being produced from the dam. The waters quickly rise several feet, and the swift currents should be respected and avoided.

Trout were a by-product of Buford Dam, the fertile, rocky streambed creating an idyllic coldwater habitat. The first trout in the river were not stocked by state officials, but rather by a group of outlaw trout addicts who also just happened to be members of the Izaak Walton League. They bought several hundred trout from a hatchery and, in a clandestine mission, dumped them into the river. Risking prosecution, these men were the fathers of Chattahoochee trout fishing. Oddly enough, one of these covert operators turned out to become one of the top officials in the Georgia Department of Natural Resources (DNR) some years later.

Once planted, the trout took off on their own, forcing state officials to take notice, and not long thereafter, things were made official. The Chattahoochee was designated a trout fishery by the state and received some legislative juice to grease the wheels. Now, annual stocking (all rainbows) are somewhere in the neighborhood of 160,000 trout. As part of a study, brown trout stockings were halted in 2005 to see if the browns were indeed reproducing naturally in the river. In a recent survey, brown trout made up 70 percent of trout found in the river, despite all those stocked rainbows. The results speak for themselves about the river's self-sustaining brown trout population.

Much of the Chattahoochee's trout water lies within the boundaries of the Chattahoochee River National Recreation Area corridor. This means there are a lot of places you can wet a line without being chased out of someone's backyard. The river, for all its length, can be divided into two sections: Buford Dam to Island Ford Park and Morgan Falls Dam to Paces Mill Park.

Buford Dam to Island Ford Park

The section below Buford Dam is a year-round coldwater fishery supporting wild brown and rainbow trout in addition to the aforementioned hatchery plantings. Below Buford Dam to Island Ford, the river can be broken down further into three stretches, each having its own unique character.

Between Buford Dam and the GA 20 bridge lies a little over 3 miles of river. Here, the river bottom is heavily scoured by the massive releases from the dam and almost entirely devoid of mayflies and caddis. Midges and scuds

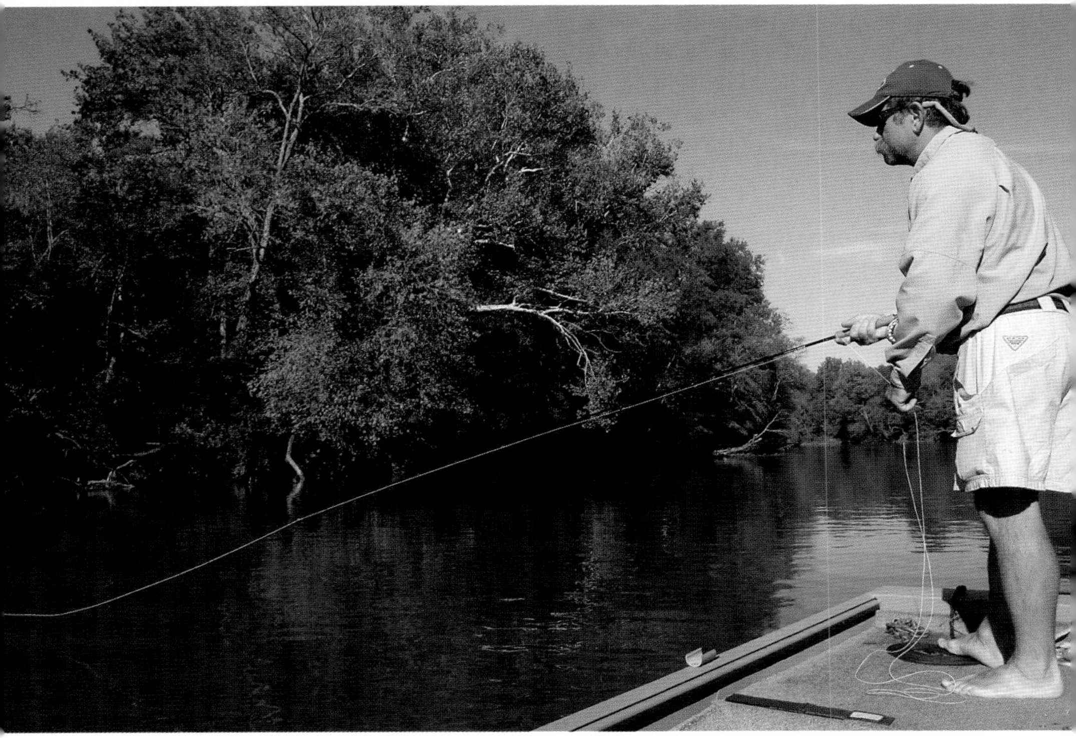

Rob Smith fishes the Chattahoochee from a small jet boat, the preferred method of accessing remote stretches of the tailwater. Casting streamers into structure while floating the river is the best way to connect with the river's larger brown trout.

make up the majority of invertebrate life. Directly below the dam, the river on the left side of Bowman's Island is softer and shallower than the right side. Anglers wishing to access the lower end of the island should use the hiking trail near the Buford Hatchery. From the parking lot just above the hatchery it is a short 30-minute walk to the river. Steep banks cut away by years of high water during generation can be difficult to descend, so take your time. Once you reach the water, you will be greeted with an expansive, wadable flat teeming with trout. It is well worth exploring the river on the left side of the island, because many folks never venture farther than a few hundred yards from the trail access.

Winding downstream from the dam, the river is strewn with boulders intersecting deeper pockets and long, deep pools. Midge fishing is by far the most effective way to catch trout in this upper stretch from the dam to GA 20. The trout seem to eat here at both ends of the thermometer, making the upper few miles of river popular during the dog days of summer and when winter's chill sets in. Most anglers find a small midge pattern fished under an indicator or small dry fly to be the best way to connect with trout. Small patterns such as UV Z-Midges, SLF Midges, Rojo Midges, and Zebra Midges (#20-24) along with a variety of pink, orange, and gray scuds (#16-18) will produce fish pretty much any day of the year. For dry flies, Griffith's Gnats, Walker's Mayhem Emergers, and Stalcup's Midge Emergers (#20-26) fished on 6X or smaller tippets can give you the same technical dry-fly fishing you'd find on any tailwater in the country. Although the trout here average on the smallish side—9 to 11 inches, with a few going 12 to 14 inches—fooling these guys with a dry during a midge hatch represents a significant accomplishment.

Fish will also take streamers year-round. Rolex Streamers, Zonkers, Sculpzillas, and Woolly Buggers in white, black, and green are all proven patterns. The water is fairly shallow, so you can fish any of these flies on a floating line, but an intermediate sinking-tip will help get the fly down just enough yet keep it off the rocks and underwater debris.

Below GA 20 downstream to Medlock Bridge, the river is managed under artificial-lures-only restrictions. This is also one of the most remote sections of river . . . well, it's remote in suburban terms. Several houses line the banks, some so large and extravagant you can almost hear Robin Leach's voice drifting over the water as you float by. Access is limited for wading anglers, with only a few small, wadable sections at Settles Bridge, Abbot's Bridge, and Medlock Bridge. Floating this stretch is the most popular and effective way to cover the best water.

There are only three access points here and the float times are long, especially if you're free-floating without a motor. Boat ramps capable of handling a trailer are available only at the Abbot's and Medlock access points, roughly 4 river miles apart. The float between the two is an all-day affair if you stop and fish along the way, and there are some gorgeous riffles that have caddis and mayfly hatches during the season.

The other option is to put in at Buford Dam and float to Abbot's, but you'd best pack breakfast, lunch, and dinner and not plan to stop along the way. The float is 13 miles long through some slow-moving stretches of water. If you can carry your boat to the river, Settles Bridge has a canoe launch that cuts the float in half, making for a far more leisurely excursion.

Most folks who fish the section between GA 20 and Medlock Bridge with regularity prefer to replace the oars with an engine and motor up from Abbot's or Medlock Bridge, then drift back to the ramp, fishing along the way. Things can get crowded on the weekends, so watch for other boats and anglers in the river. There are also several shallow, rocky stretches that will rip open a boat like a can of sardines if you are not extremely careful.

This section sees a few more insects than the area at the dam. This is especially true once the river gets into any shallow, rocky stretch. Settles Bridge sees one of the best caddis hatches on the river, but word spreads fast, and it can become overly crowded when the hatch is in full swing.

Chattahoochee River, Georgia
Buford Dam to Island Ford Unit

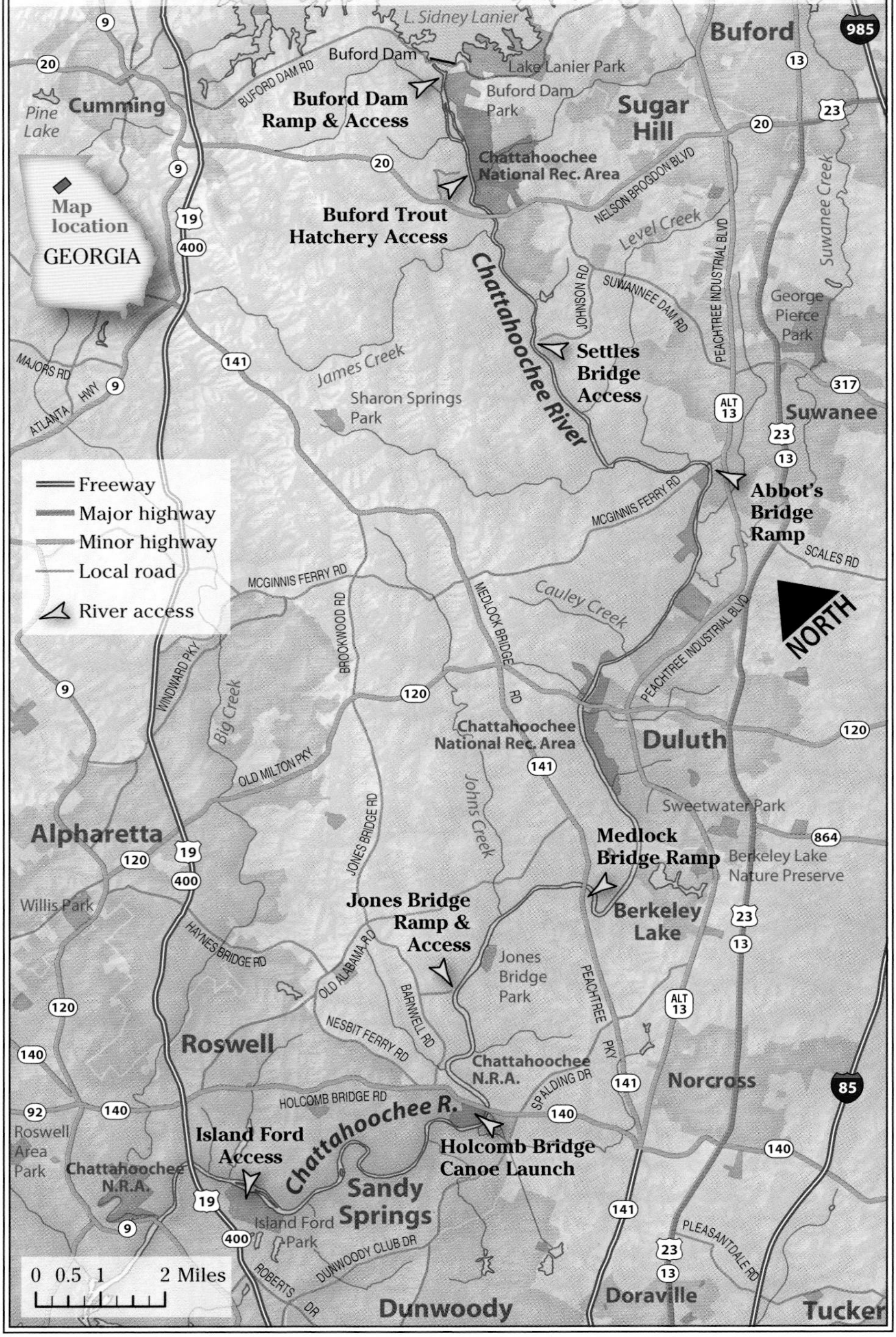

Between Medlock Bridge and Island Ford, the river is open once again under general state regulations. Access becomes easier than above, with Jones Bridge, Holcomb Bridge, and Island Ford all having plenty of wadable shoals nearby, and trails following the river as it winds through a mixture of private and National Park Service lands. The waters around Jones Bridge and Island Ford are perhaps the most popular destinations on the upper river, possibly with the exclusion of the area around Buford Dam.

Shallow shoals and high densities of trout, along with a healthy supply of biomass, all lend to the popularity of these areas. Mayflies, caddis, and midges are all well represented, and some surprisingly large trout rise during the spring's heavier hatches.

Improved boat ramps are present at Jones Bridge and Holcomb Bridge; however, large concrete pillars block trailers from backing down the ramp at Holcomb Bridge. Floating anglers can put in at Medlock and take out at Jones (making a float of around 3 miles) if the boat needs a proper ramp to launch from. If your craft can be easily carried, this opens up a float between Jones Bridge and Holcomb Bridge that is relatively short, about $2^{1}/_{2}$ miles, but numerous shoals and gravel bars let you wade some of the prettiest water on the river, easily taking up a full day. Below Holcomb Bridge it is $5\ ^{1}/_{2}$ miles to Island Ford, and takeouts require either a long walk up the trail at Island Ford or a long 4-mile paddle downstream to Azalea Park in Roswell. Neither of these options makes for a practical free-float down the river. Alternatively, jet boats or shallow-running Gheenoe-style boats are perfect for exploring this stretch.

Unlike the waters directly below the dam, the middle and lower reaches of the river have a diverse biomass. Fishing here varies from season to season and is dependent on the type of water you are fishing. The river between GA 20 and Island Ford varies little in width and flow, save for the wide expanses around Island Ford. Long, deep pools intersecting shallow shoals and gravel bars disperse trout in varying lies, calling for different tactics when fishing. As is to be expected, the shallower, rocky areas are best for drifting nymphs and finding the heaviest hatches. The long, slow pools beg to be fished with a streamer on a sinking-tip line.

Streamer fishing can be great year-round, but is especially good in the fall when the browns will pounce on baitfish imitations during prespawn. Deep green pools hold some of the river's largest trout, making sinking-tip fly lines imperative. You must get the fly down into the zone quickly to entice even aggressive trout. Deadfalls near the banks are prime trout lies, and this stretch has no shortage of them. Casting your fly deep into the tangles will bring strikes from some rather healthy brown and rainbow trout, but just plan on losing a few flies along the way. Consider it the cost of doing business.

Fly patterns such as Zonkers, Rolex Streamers, and big articulated patterns like Galloup's Sex Dungeons or Loop Sculpins in #1/0-8 should be tied onto at least 12-pound fluorocarbon tippet. When you get a trout to eat in the blowdowns, you've got to be able to turn it quickly before your line gets wrapped up in the mess.

Just outside the city limits of Atlanta, the Chattahoochee River's delayed-harvest stretch can provide reprieve from city life—though it can become crowded at times.

From the onset of cold weather in late November through early February, fishing with nymphs or catching a *Baetis* hatch is your best bet. Midges hatch throughout the year and add to the winter fare, but the trout are selective during the colder months, forcing anglers to drop down to 6X and smaller tippets to present #24-32 dry flies.

Cloudy days bring out the Blue-Winged Olives, and the hatches at Jones Bridge and Island Ford can be nothing short of spectacular. Keep some CDC Compara-dun *Baetis* along with Harrop's *Baetis* CDC Biot Emergers and Brooks's Sprout *Baetis* (#20-24) in your box anytime you head to the 'Hooch in the winter months.

While the heaviest hatches of *Baetis* may occur during the winter, these tiny mayflies continue to hatch throughout most of the year, especially in the evening. Rob Smith, longtime guide on the river, grew up on the banks of the Chattahoochee and has fished it since the early 1970s. It is a common belief that Rob derives his almost Samson-like angling ability from his profoundly large, Civil War–era mustache.

Unmistakable on the river, often referred to simply as "The Mustache," Rob can clean up on a *Baetis* hatch even when the fishing is tough. Rob believes that long, fine leaders of 12 feet or more, tapering down to 6X, are the key. He goes an extra step and greases his leaders so they sink just below the surface, eliminating the telltale tippet signature on the water's surface. Sure, it may sound extreme, but you don't want to argue with success . . . or The Mustache.

Wintertime nymphing requires rigging with a deep subsurface rig with a Lightning Bug, Copper John (#14-18), or Stalcup's Tungsten Rubber-Legged Stonefly (#10-12), then trailing a Rojo Midge, Split Case BWO, Pheasant Tail, or Mercer's Micro Mayfly (#16-22), a familiar task for most wintertime 'Hooch anglers. Getting the fly down in the deeper slots and along the edges of slow-moving pools is critical, especially on colder days. Look for microseams in otherwise flat currents. This is where the fish will be holding; if you find one, you can bet there are plenty more around.

In late February or mid-March, Little Black Caddis begin hatching, sparking a feeding frenzy among Chattahoochee trout. For about two weeks, sometimes less, these small caddis show up and drive the trout crazy from Island Ford all the way upstream to GA 20. The trout are not picky, eating the standard black Elk-Hair Caddis or a dun-colored Harrop's Flat Wing Caddis or Scalley's Cripple Caddis (#16-18).

Chris Scalley, the senior fly-fishing guide on the river and operator of River Through Atlanta Guide Service, is fiendish over the early caddis. "The number of trout that come up to eat the caddis is amazing. Even the larger trout will rise to this early hatch, which is atypical for the Chattahoochee." Scalley is on the water for well over a hundred days every year, guiding as well as helping spearhead the Chattahoochee Coldwater Fishery Foundation. The foundation is instrumental in studying the aquatic biomass found on the river, sampling individual sections to discern what bug life is present in the tailrace, and investigating the affects of pollution on the ecosystem.

Springtime on the Chattahoochee is without a doubt some of the best fishing of the year. As February gives way to March and the days grow longer, Gray Caddis, Hendricksons, and Quill Gordons begin showing up down low, working their way up to Settles Bridge. Around the second week of March, Quill Gordons are the first to show up in decent numbers, followed closely by Hendricksons. The hatches are usually light, but enough bugs are up to make carrying a few Quill Gordon A. K.'s Parachutes, Parachute Adams, and Last Chance Cripples (#12-16) a good idea.

Tan- and brown-colored caddis follow the first mayflies in late March and continue through April, but they can pop up anytime afterward through October in single-day to weeklong emergences. They flutter above the riffles like drunken moths, their dances driving the trout crazy. Fishing high-floating dry flies such as X2 Caddis, Elk-Hair Caddis, and Hemingway Caddis (#14-16) in the riffles and tailouts will draw splashing rises. If you find a trout

Use a tandem weighted nymph rig when fishing the many braided runs near the Paces Mill access. Don't be afraid to put on enough split-shot to get the fly down in the swift currents.

feeding in a section of slow water, fishing a low-riding pattern like Harrop's CDC Caddis Emerger or a Henry's Fork Caddis (#14-16) would be a good choice. Norris's Caddis Pupae in green and tan, Sparkle Pupae, and Stalcup's Bubble Caddis (#14-16) will all get the job done below the surface.

May is prime times for Sulphurs *(Ephemerella invaria)* and Light Cahills *(Stenacron interpunctatum)*. Sulphurs are the first to hatch in early May and continue to hatch for around two to three weeks. For this hatch, have plenty of Sulphur Compara-duns, Last Chance Cripples, and parachute-style Sulphur patterns (#14-16). They continue to hatch through June, sometimes into July. Later in the season, *E. invaria* is replaced by the smaller *E. dorothea*. In layman's terms this means simply a smaller Sulphur. Drop your patterns down to a size #18 by mid-June or once you begin seeing smaller Sulphur duns flying about.

The recipe for summertime in Atlanta and the surrounding suburbs is for blistering hot days and pressure-cooker high humidity. The river seems like the only reprieve from the heat, and luckily the trout are still eating. Summer is terrestrial time. From late June through September, June bugs, Japanese beetles, ants, inchworms, and grasshoppers can all be found near the river's edge, especially around brush-covered banks or near the lawns of riverside homes. Get on the water early or take advantage of the last few hours of daylight during the summer when fishing terrestrials. Otherwise, plan on nymphing deep with the standard fare of Crystal Pheasant Tails (a pattern similar to a Pheasant Tail but with more flash), Lightning Bugs, Mercer's Micro Mayflies, Split Case BWOs and PMDs (#14-18), and midges (#18-22).

In late September and early October, sulfides and metals in the lake become soluble and mix with the water at the bottom of Lake Lanier. In addition, due to pronounced stratification of the lake's water layers in the summer, lower oxygen levels are present in the deepest reaches. These two combined elements are discharged into the tailrace throughout most of the fall, pretty much wrecking the fishing for the first few miles below the dam. Oxygen quickly mixes with the water downstream, negating the lower dissolved oxygen levels in the water being discharged from the dam.

Morgan Falls to GA Highway 41

Downstream of Island Ford Park, the water warms rapidly and backs up into Bull Sluice Lake near Roswell. Bull Sluice Lake, impounded by Morgan Falls Dam, once held enough depth to create yet another coldwater tailrace downstream. The fishery below Morgan Falls was, without a doubt, the best fishery in Georgia and one of the best in the Southeast. Unfortunately, due to heavy runoff upstream, partially due to urban sprawl, silt filled the lake's bottom, destroying the thermocline and wrecking the year-round coldwater fishery below.

By the mid-1990s, the lower river's trout population was all but smothered during the hot summer months by the warming water temperatures

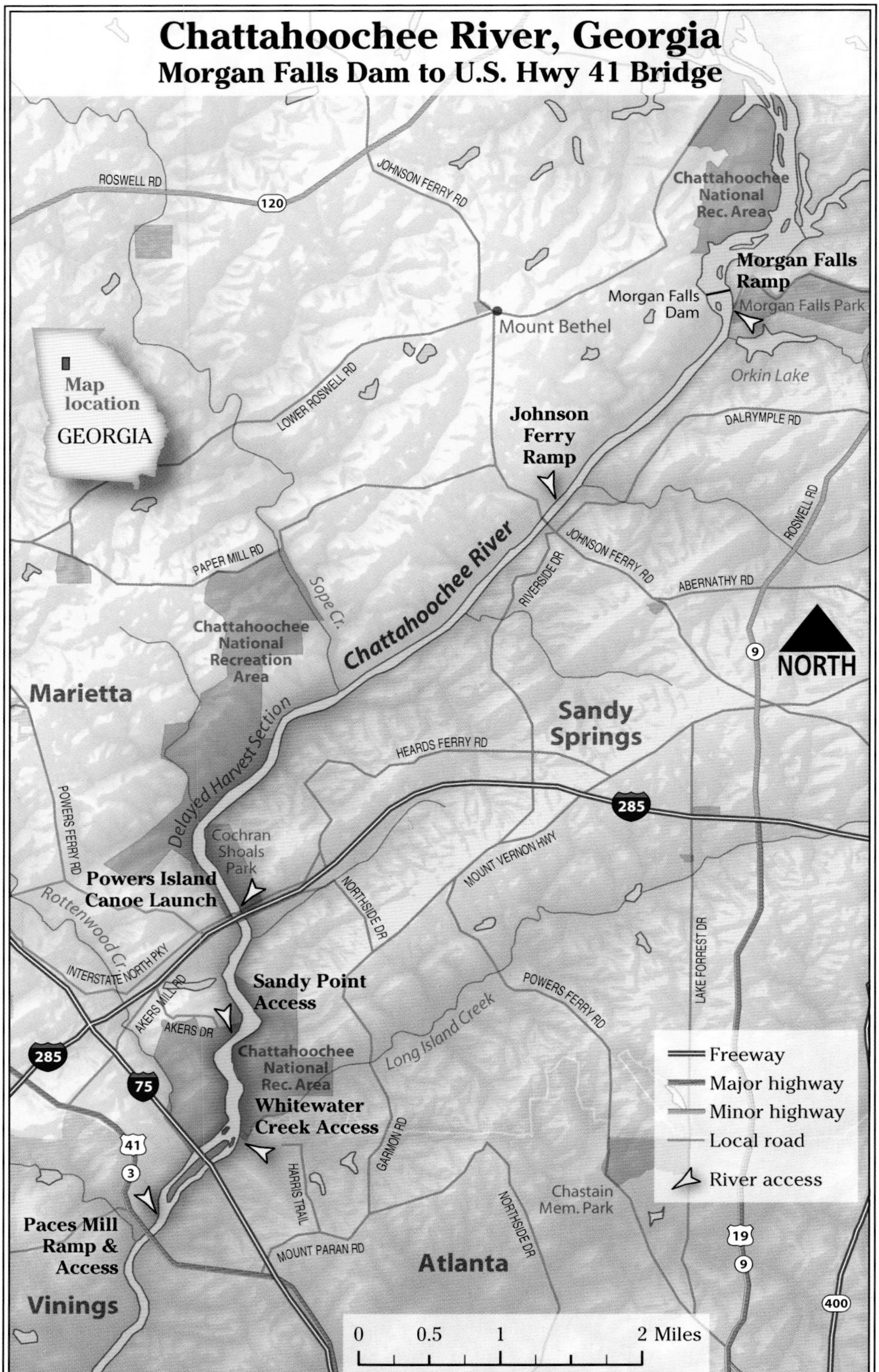
Chattahoochee River, Georgia
Morgan Falls Dam to U.S. Hwy 41 Bridge
ROSWELL RD
120
JOHNSON FERRY RD
Chattahoochee National Rec. Area
Morgan Falls Ramp
Morgan Falls Dam
Morgan Falls Park
Mount Bethel
Orkin Lake
Map location
GEORGIA
LOWER ROSWELL RD
Johnson Ferry Ramp
DALRYMPLE RD
ROSWELL RD
JOHNSON FERRY RD
ABERNATHY RD
RIVERSIDE DR
PAPER MILL RD
Sope Cr.
Chattahoochee River
Chattahoochee National Recreation Area
9
NORTH
Marietta
Sandy Springs
Delayed Harvest Section
HEARDS FERRY RD
285
POWERS FERRY RD
Cochran Shoals Park
Powers Island Canoe Launch
Rottenwood Cr.
NORTHSIDE DR
MOUNT VERNON HWY
INTERSTATE NORTH PKY
AKERS MILL RD
AKERS DR
Sandy Point Access
POWERS FERRY RD
LAKE FORREST DR
Long Island Creek
Chattahoochee National Rec. Area
285
75
Whitewater Creek Access
GARMON RD
41
3
HARRIS TRAIL
Freeway
Major highway
Minor highway
Local road
River access
Chastain Mem. Park
NORTHSIDE DR
Paces Mill Ramp & Access
MOUNT PARAN RD
Atlanta
19
9
400
Vinings
0
0.5
1
2 Miles

and a lack of dissolved oxygen. Nearly a decade later, the state reclaimed the tailrace as a viable trout-fishing destination, imposing delayed-harvest regulations between the mouth of Sope Creek and the Georgia Highway 41 (Cobb Parkway) bridge. The river was stocked with thousands of trout and practically overnight became the most popular fly-fishing destination in the entire state.

Even though a few trout may hold over and signs of natural reproduction have been found in one tributary creek, the lower 'Hooch is mostly a put-and-take fishery. Beginning on the first day in October and lasting until May 15, the lower river is managed under delayed-harvest regulations. The 5-mile stretch is stocked throughout the season with around 50,000 trout, giving the lower river roughly 10,000 trout per mile of water. Most of the trout are between 10 and 13 inches, however much larger fish do turn up, perhaps holdovers from seasons past.

Aside from the heavy plantings courtesy of the state, the delayed-harvest stretch also offers an abundance of public access sites from top to bottom. Numerous trails, parking areas, and long, wadable shoals allow anglers to reach most of the delayed-harvest water without a boat.

Powers Island Park sits near the upper reaches of the delayed-harvest section just off Interstate North Parkway. Parking areas and trails are present on both sides of the river, giving easy access to the area known as Cochran Shoals. There is over a mile of water accessible to the wading angler here, and plenty of trout. A canoe launch is on the main river side of the island, requiring you to carry a boat several hundred yards, over a side channel, then to the opposite side of the island. For this reason, trailered boats must launch upstream at the improved ramp off Johnson Ferry Road, around 4 miles upstream. This is not all bad, as the stretch between Johnson Ferry and the beginning of the delayed-harvest section receives far less pressure than the rest of the lower river.

About a mile and a half downstream, Thornton Shoals and the section known as Devil's Race Course mark the next wading areas with public access. There is a parking area at Sandy Point off Akers Drive where you must hike a short distance to reach the water. A quarter mile walk down the steep road that winds down the ridge to the river places you at the bottom of Devil's Race Course. The Race Course is a sluicing rapid created when a channel through rock ledges in the center of the river was dynamited to allow barges to float upstream early in the 1900s. It's not as ominous as the name suggests, and trout will hold in the slower water on either side of the Race Course and around the small island just downstream. A hiking trail leading downstream will place you at the head of Thornton Shoals. There is not much room to wade down here, and it is easy to step into a hole that will put water right over the top of your waders.

Whitewater Creek Park is the next access point, around a river mile below Sandy Point. Whitewater Creek allows anglers to reach Thornton

CHATTAHOOCHEE RIVER HATCHES

JAN FEB MAR APR MAY JUN JUL AUG SEP OCT NOV DEC

Midges (Diptera)

#18-26 Stalcup's Hatching Midge, Brooks's Sprout Midge, Walker's Mayhem Emerger, Hanging Midge, VC Midge

Blue-Winged Olive *(Baetis* spp.*)*

#18-24 CDC Biot Emerger/Dun, Last Chance Cripple, Captive Dun, Brooks's Sprout *Baetis*, No-Hackle, Hi-Viz Emerger, Thorax BWO Emerger

Little Black Stonefly
(Allocapnia, Capnia spp.*)*

#18 Elk-Hair Caddis, Bubble Back Caddis, Iris Caddis, Henry's Fork Caddis

Blue Quill
(Paraleptophlebia adoptiva)

#18 Catskill-style, A. K.'s Parachute, Tilt Wing Dun

Little Black Caddis
(Chimarra spp.*)*

#18 Elk-Hair Caddis, Hemingway Caddis, Henry's Fork Caddis, Iris Caddis

Quill Gordon *(Epeorus pleuralis)*

#12-16 A. K.'s Parachute, Catskill-style

Gray Caddis *(Brachycentrus* spp.)

#14-16 Elk-Hair Caddis, X2 Caddis, CDC Fertile Caddis, CDC Caddis Emerger, Spotlight Caddis Emerger, Scalley's Cripple Caddis

Hendrickson
(Ephemerella subvaria)

#14-16 Catskill-style, Parachute Adams

March Brown
(Maccaffertium vicarium)

#14-16 Parachute Adams, Hairwing Dun, D&D Cripple, March Brown Extended Body

Tan/brown caddis
(Brachycentrus spp.)

#12-16 Elk-Hair Caddis, CDC Caddis Emerger, CDC Fertile Caddis, X2 Caddis, Stalcup's Parachute Caddis Emerger, Hemingway Caddis, Scalley's Cripple Caddis, Henry's Fork Caddis

Sulphur *(E. invaria)*

#12-16 CDC Compara-dun, A. K.'s Parachute, D&D Cripple, Last Chance Cripple, thorax-style dun, Hackle Stacker

Sulphur *(E. dorothea)*

#18 CDC Compara-dun, A. K.'s Parachute, D&D Cripple, Last Chance Cripple, Captive Dun, Hackle Stacker

Light Cahill
(Stenacron interpunctatum)

#14-18 D&D Cripple, A. K.'s Parachute, Compara-dun, thorax-style dun

Little Yellow Stonefly (Perlodidae)

#14-16 Stimulator, Egg Layer Golden Stone, Parachute Yellow Sally, Twisted PMX

Terrestrials

#14-18 RP Ant, Crystal Ant; #10-14 Steeves's Japanese Beetle, Steeves's Bark Beetle, CDC Beetle, Monster Beetle; #10-14 Dave's Cricket, DeBruin's Hopper, Rainy's Foam Hopper; #10-14 Dave's Inchworm, chartreuse San Juan Worm

Shoals and the lower end of Devil's Race Course, in addition to the more readily available Long Island Shoals. A pretty lengthy hike is required to reach the lower end of Devil's Race Course, but it places you on the other side of the river from the popular Sandy Point access. An easier alternative to reach this opposite bank would be to park at the lot off Indian Trail and hike down to the river. The trail leading to Thornton Shoals, however, is relatively flat, and not many anglers walk that far, even though it's only about a mile.

Long Island Shoals sits directly in front of the parking lot at Whitewater and is where the majority of anglers fish when using this access. A large, wadable shoal stretches from just upstream of the parking lot downstream nearly to the Interstate 75 bridge.

Just below I-75, the last access point sits at Paces Mill. This section is perhaps the most popular on the delayed-harvest water, partly due to the expansive shoals that run from the I-75 bridge downstream to GA 41. The last boat ramp trout anglers should concern themselves with sits within sight of both bridges. There is easy wading just off the boat ramp, with anglers standing in close proximity on weekend days when the fishing is good.

Fly choice for the lower river should consist of the standard delayed-harvest trout assortment. Flashy, bright flies, streamers, and egg patterns are what most anglers carry in their fly boxes. Tandem nymph rigs using a pink San Juan Worm, Y2K Bug, Lightning Bug, or Rook's Blueberry (#12-16) as the top fly, then dropping a caddis larva or mayfly nymph 6 to 10 inches behind the lead fly is standard procedure. Popular trailers are Stalcup's Bubble Pupa, Split Case BWOs, Split Case PMDs, and Crystal Pheasant Tails (#14-18), along with Brassies, SLF Midges, and UV Z-Midges (#18-20).

Skilled nymph anglers can bring several dozen trout to hand in a day of fishing. One such Chattahoochee angler who locally possesses near rock star fame on the river is David Winarski. Known around town as "Fish Dave," he floats the river in a one-man custom wooden dory of his own design and construction. Fish Dave is one of the best nymph fishermen on the river. His secret: "If you're not catching fish, use more weight." Part of Dave's uncanny ability to outfish most anglers on the water centers around a two-pronged approach: using enough weight to get the fly down quickly to the trout and fishing each drift with the intensity of an osprey on Ritalin. Dave believes that fly selection is not as important as the ability to get the fly down to the trout consistently and maintain a perfectly drag-free drift.

Anglers seeking dry-fly action will have no shortage. *Baetis* hatches can occur pretty much anytime during the season, but really peak on those textbook cloudy days of February and March. Oftentimes, small Blue-Winged Olives will cover the slower stretches near Cochran Shoals, Thornton Shoals, and Paces Mill. The trout can become selective, but Brooks's Sprout *Baetis*, Harrop's *Baetis* CDC Biot Dun, and Smith's Translucent Emerger (#18-22) will usually fool them.

The hallmark hatch most anglers anticipate begins in late March, when the Tan Caddis emerge. On some days, thousands of caddis will blanket the water, sending the trout into a frenzy of splashing rises, all in the shadow of some of the busiest interstates in the country. The caddis will hatch through April, usually spilling over into early May. Some of the better hatches occur around Powers Island and Paces Mill. Early on in the hatch, you need nothing much more than a brown or tan Elk-Hair Caddis or X2 Caddis (#14-16). These patterns fished in the riffles and braided water will cause you to—as they say in Georgia—"catch fish until your arm falls off." After a few weeks, the trout become pretty selective, and you'd best have a few Iris Caddis, Harrop's Fertile Caddis, and CDC Bubble Back Caddis (#14-16) if you want to fool them.

In addition to the caddis, Light Cahills begin emerging sometime in mid-April and continue until the end of the season in the delayed-harvest water. The Cahills will not bring up trout like the caddis; however, it is worth keeping a few dry flies in your box just in case you find a pod of fish eating the emergers or duns. Keep it simple with a few Compara-duns and Cahill parachute patterns (#12-16).

On May 15, the game is pretty much over. Bait anglers descend like locusts and pillage the river's bounty in just a matter of weeks. Blue worm cans and blister packs of Rooster Tails litter the river's edge near parking lots, but they can't catch all the trout, no matter how hard they try. A few will escape the carnage, especially in the more remote stretches unreachable by wading or bank anglers. The remaining trout will usually find a coldwater seep or spring, holding over until the water cools again in the fall.

Tributaries

Smith Creek

Smith Creek is a narrow, slow-flowing stream that runs for around 2 miles below Unicoi Lake through Unicoi State Park, then several miles downstream until it eventually empties into the Chattahoochee River near Helen, Georgia. The stretch of Smith below the lake downstream to the state park boundary is managed under delayed-harvest regulations. The public stretch is heavily stocked with 9- to 12-inch trout and a few 18- to 20-inch toads throughout the delayed-harvest season. Knowing this, many anglers flock to the small creek in hordes, quickly crowding the water. Although Smith Creek can quickly become crowded on the weekends, if you can get away during the week, your chances of finding peace and quiet multiply exponentially.

Smith Creek trout can be caught year-round, save on the coldest days of winter. Although the creek flows below a large dam, it is not technically a tailwater. Water is discharged from the top of the lake, making this creek's temperatures fluctuate like almost any other mountain stream.

Hatches are infrequent at best, and nymph fishing is the customary act among the creek's angling masses. Midges make up the dry-fly action through much of the year, save for a few months in the spring when caddis and a few Golden Stoneflies hatch.

From the onset of delayed-harvest season on October 1, the stocked trout are fairly easy to catch. This changes as the fall progresses into winter and the trout become more heavily pressured. Even with the state steadily pumping more trout into the stream, the combination of angling pressure and tight-lipped winter fish makes for tough angling in the winter, and educated trout come spring. Though it's not as difficult as Dukes Creek, which is just down the road a few miles, catching a trout on Smith Creek does require stealth when approaching the water and proper presentation of the fly once you are creekside.

Most folks visiting Smith Creek fish a tandem rig with a nymph suspended under an indicator, whether it is fall, winter, or spring. Fishing various patterns such as a San Juan Worm, Lightning Bug, Y2K Bug, or Green Weenie (#12-16) as the top pattern, then going with something a bit more natural, such as a Pheasant Tail, Hare's Ear, or Rainbow Warrior (#16-20), down below is routine on Smith Creek. When things get tough, some anglers drop down to smaller midge larvae, such as UV Z-Midges, Smethurst's Answers, or Zebra Midges (#20-22), especially in the spillway hole and run just below the dam.

In April, a few caddis begin coming off, giving the trout—and anglers—something to look forward to. From mid-April until the end of the delayed-harvest season, caddis hatch in decent enough numbers to make a dry fly worthwhile. Simple Elk-Hair Caddis (#16-18) will usually tempt enough trout to make fishing it as an indicator fly, or alone, enjoyable. In the slower pools, try an Iris Caddis or CDC Caddis Emerger (#16-18). Along with the caddis, Little Yellow Stoneflies begin coming off sometime around the end of April and yellow Stimulators and Parachute Yellow Stones (#12-14) are effective patterns to imitate them.

Following the end of the delayed-harvest season, the creek, like so many others, is pretty much fished to the point of exhaustion. A few trout may dodge the bait guys, but they are met with rapidly warming water, and most do not survive the summer months. Luckily, in the fall, state fisheries officials begin the ritualistic stockings, and Smith Creek is back on the books as being one of the state's top delayed-harvest streams.

Dukes Creek

A tributary of the Chattahoochee River, Dukes Creek falls from high in the mountains north of Helen, Georgia. This small stream, typical of the southern Appalachians, winds through laurel thickets and stands of conifers before emptying into the upper Chattahoochee. The public stretch of Dukes Creek flows entirely through Smithgall Woods Recreation Area, save a short section near the headwaters.

The Smithgall Woods Recreation Area section is split into four sections, or beats, totaling a little over 5 miles of water. Fishing is permitted only on Wednesday, Saturday, and Sunday, and strict barbless hook, catch-and-release regulations are in place to preserve the creek's bounty. From November through February, day tickets are available for anglers, allowing them to fish the river from 8 AM to 4:30 PM. From March 1 through October 30, the days are split into half-day sessions. Fifteen anglers are still allowed on the water for each half-day session, the first beginning from sunrise until noon, and the second beginning at 2 PM and lasting until sunset. Day passes are available on a first-come, first-served basis and are free, apart from a $2 parking pass that is required at all state parks. If you plan on fishing the creek, make sure to call ahead and make reservations, especially in the spring, as the limited number of slots fills up quickly.

Anglers can park at the area's headquarters off GA 75 ALT, rig up their gear, get the permits, and either walk to the beat or wait for the shuttle van to take them to the lower reaches. Section 1 is perhaps the most heavily fished, because it is within easy walking distance of the park office. Also, it tends to hold a few more fish, perhaps due to its proximity to the cool springs of the headwaters and heavy canopy. Section 1 is a mix of large plunge pools, shallow riffles, and pocketwater, and pretty much every likely run holds trout. Rainbows dominate the upper reaches, but occasionally a big brown trout can be spotted in the deeper runs.

Just downstream of GA 75 ALT, Section 2 begins and flows downstream for a bit before entering a clearly marked private stretch of land that has been retained by the Smithgall family. Downstream of the private stretch, Section 2 continues to the first bridge crossing. In this section the river begins to flatten out a bit, with long pools holding spooky trout. Luckily, every bend holds a nice, deep elbow butting up to an undercut bank. These areas tend to hold the largest trout, but catching them is never easy.

Below the first bridge, Sections 3 and 4 finish out the state lands. The river leaves the road several times through both stretches, but is never far away. Undercut banks, deep plunge pools, and long stretches of slow water typify both Sections 3 and 4. These are the most remote stretches of the public water, especially Section 4, where the river has gained a respectable size and hiking along faint riverside trails provides the only access. Brown trout rule the roost down low, enjoying the deep, slow nature of these sections.

If you visit Dukes Creek, just be ready to strap on a bib and eat some humble pie. It is tough and sometimes downright frustrating. In low water, the larger trout seek shelter under overhanging rocks and in the deepest holes, making it even tougher to catch them. Even when water levels are ideal, the trout are no pushovers. Dark-colored clothing, even camouflage, is worn by savvy Dukes Creek devotees, who know that spotting a trout before casting a line is far better than prospecting every run.

High water on the creek can be an angler's best friend, and larger trout are consistently caught when the creek is high and slightly stained, especially when the river is dropping after a heavy rain. Large Zonkers, Double Bunnies, and Beldar Buggers (#2-8) in brown, chartreuse, and black will tempt the large browns and rainbows when the water is up.

CHAPTER 3

Chattooga River

Some of my first fishing road trips when I was a teenager were to the Chattooga. Tucked in the extreme northeastern corner of the state, where the Carolinas and Georgia meet, the river sat on the skirt of a young man's ever-increasing concentric circles away from parents who said where he could go and where he actually went and what he got away with. In my younger days, my friends and I would ride several hours to fish for the day, then camp along the river, more than a few times lowering the bar of social debauchery in the way only teenagers can manage and still be fit enough to fish at daylight the following morning.

Many anglers see the Chattooga as the pinnacle of Southern fishing, a quintessential trout river tucked away in one of the most remote parts of the region. Rumors of large brown trout abound. Images of gaping white mouths devouring a fly before the hook slips or the line snaps haunt scores of anglers who have witnessed them firsthand. The water beckons, calling anglers from hundreds of miles away, if not to actually catch one of these legendary brown trout, then at least to experience the Chattooga.

The river begins its flow from the base of Whiteside Mountain near the town of Cashiers, North Carolina, flowing nearly 60 miles into Lake Tugaloo. From Georgia Highway 28, where the river crosses, forming the boundary between Georgia and South Carolina upstream to the Georgia–North Carolina boundary, it is one of the wildest trout rivers in the state. Below the GA 28 bridge, the river begins warming quickly, the major attraction being in the form of Class III and IV rapids that generate their own fanfare as the river drops quickly into Tugaloo.

The Chattooga was brought into the national spotlight when it was used as the backdrop for the motion picture *Deliverance*. For those of you living under a rock and not familiar with the movie, it was called the Cahulawassee River and it was along its banks where Ned Beatty had the famous "squeal like a pig" scene that remains a running joke among anglers visiting the Chat-

The backcountry water on the Chattooga near Burrells Ford holds some of the river's largest trout. The farther you hike in, the better the fishing becomes. LOUIS CAHILL

tooga to this day. It doesn't take a lot of looking to find a general store somewhere in the area that sells T-shirts with the words "Paddle faster, I hear banjo music" printed on the front. Although there are some colorful characters living in the mountains surrounding the river, I have yet to hear of any strange encounters with banjo-wielding psychopaths. You're safe for now.

From the state line downstream to the end of the trout water at GA 28, the river is wide, varying between 50 and 60 feet in the upper reaches and spanning 100 feet near the bridge. It tumbles over rock gardens, granite ledges, and around massive boulders as it descends the valley. Low water means easy wading for the sure-footed. High flows after a rain bring the river up to dangerous levels with swift rapids that rival some of the downstream hydraulics.

In 1974, Congress officially designated the Chattooga a National Wild and Scenic River, a distinction that recognizes only the most pristine free-flowing rivers and protects the natural character of the watershed. It ensures the Chattooga will remain as it has for decades, a prodigious sculpture carved by nature's hand.

Upstream from GA 28, the Chattooga is managed under the state's delayed-harvest regulations until Reed Creek enters the main flow. This stretch sees its fair share of fishing pressure, not all of it good. Due to the remote nature of the river, some anglers choose to ignore the catch-and-release regulations, quickly depleting the river of its fish stocks. Georgia and South Carolina game officials are working hard to stop this and are making a dent in the illegal activity, but a few poachers will always slip through the cracks. Nevertheless, the state keeps the section heavily stocked, and fly anglers have a ball catching trout from 10 to 14 inches on the delayed-harvest waters.

Upstream of the delayed-harvest section, the river winds through the backcountry of north Georgia, passing under the bridge at Burrells Ford Road off GA 28. From the bridge upstream to the state line, the river is managed as a wild brown trout fishery. The trout upstream from here to Ellicott Rock are skittish, wild, and brightly colored works of art.

There are no roads accessing the upper reaches of the river, save Burrells Ford, which bisects the National Forest land. The upstream portion of the Chattooga lies in the Ellicott Rock Wilderness Area, an 8,274-acre preserve encompassing parts of the Chattahoochee, Sumter, and Nantahala National Forests. The actual Ellicott Rock lies at the boundary of Georgia and North Carolina and was named for surveyor Andrew Ellicott, who in 1811 marked the rock as the boundary between the states. Anglers fishing above the rock must have a North Carolina fishing license and trout stamp, or face the wrath of the man in the green shirt.

Trails run alongside the river between Ellicott Rock and Burrells Ford, with numerous campsites dotting the floodplain. The hike is relatively flat,

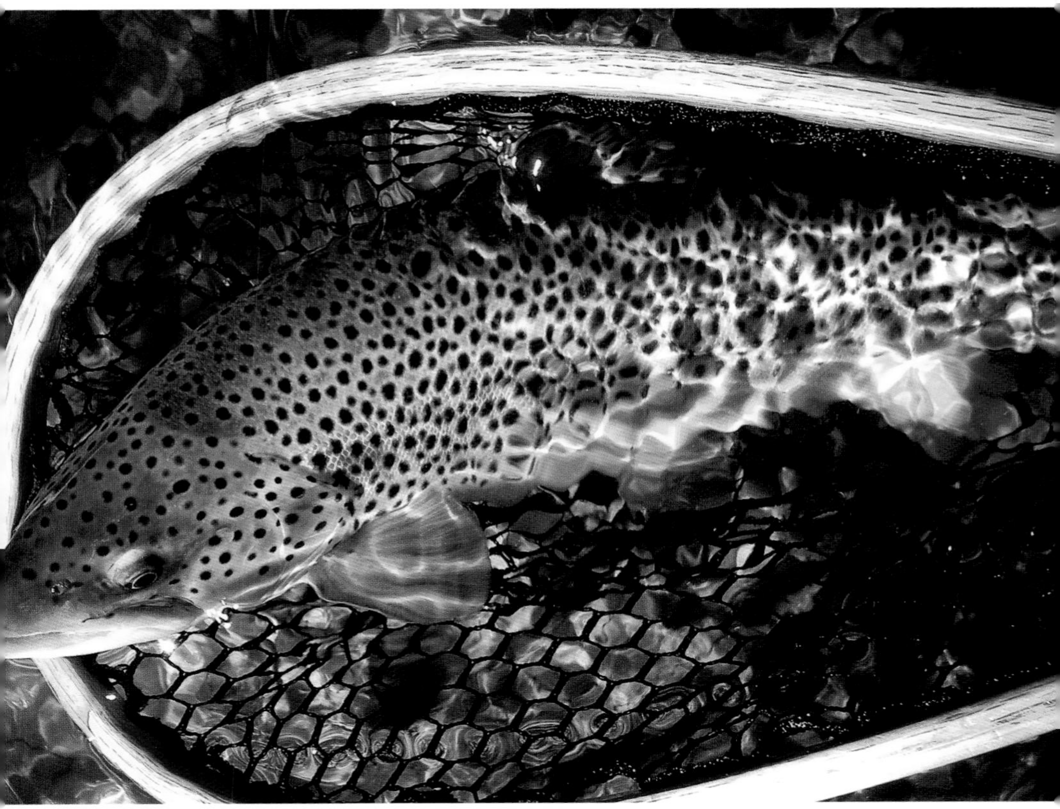

Above Burrells Ford, the Chattooga is known as wild brown trout water. Netting a big brown like this is a rarity, but the prospect of hooking a trophy keeps anglers returning to the river. LOUIS CAHILL

save for a few short climbs, making this a low-impact camping and fishing destination. You can bring all the comforts of home, more or less, but still get the feel of a wilderness camp and have first crack at the water before the day hikers arrive.

Fishing the upper section of the Chattooga requires stealth and accurate casting. Many anglers prefer using nymphs to probe the deeper runs and heads of pools. They cast a variety of nymphs, including Pheasant Tails, Thorax PMD Emergers, Prince Nymphs, and Rubber-Legged Hare's Ears (#14-16), in an attempt to coax trout off the bottom. Stonefly imitations should not be overlooked either, as the larger flies tend to correlate with larger trout. Tie on Stalcup's Tungsten Rubber-Legged Stones, 20-Inchers, and WMD Stoneflies (#8-12), add plenty of weight, and probe the deepest, darkest runs. The most consistent fishing, nymphing or otherwise, is during the spring and early fall. Summer months find the river bottom nearly naked save for a few deep sections, and the winters can be brutally cold, sending the trout into a near hibernation. If you are lucky enough to be on the river during a warm winter day, this all changes as the trout literally come back to life—and they are hungry.

Spring brings an array of hatches that don't seem to follow the calendar very closely. As with most mountain streams, weather temperatures and water levels dictate emergences, so keep that in mind when visiting the Chat-

Fickle fish make changing flies on the Chattooga an expected ritual. Just because a fly works well in one run may not mean that same fly will work in the next. Caddis and stoneflies make up the staple biomass, so experiment with variations of those until you find what the fish like. CHAD MCCLURE

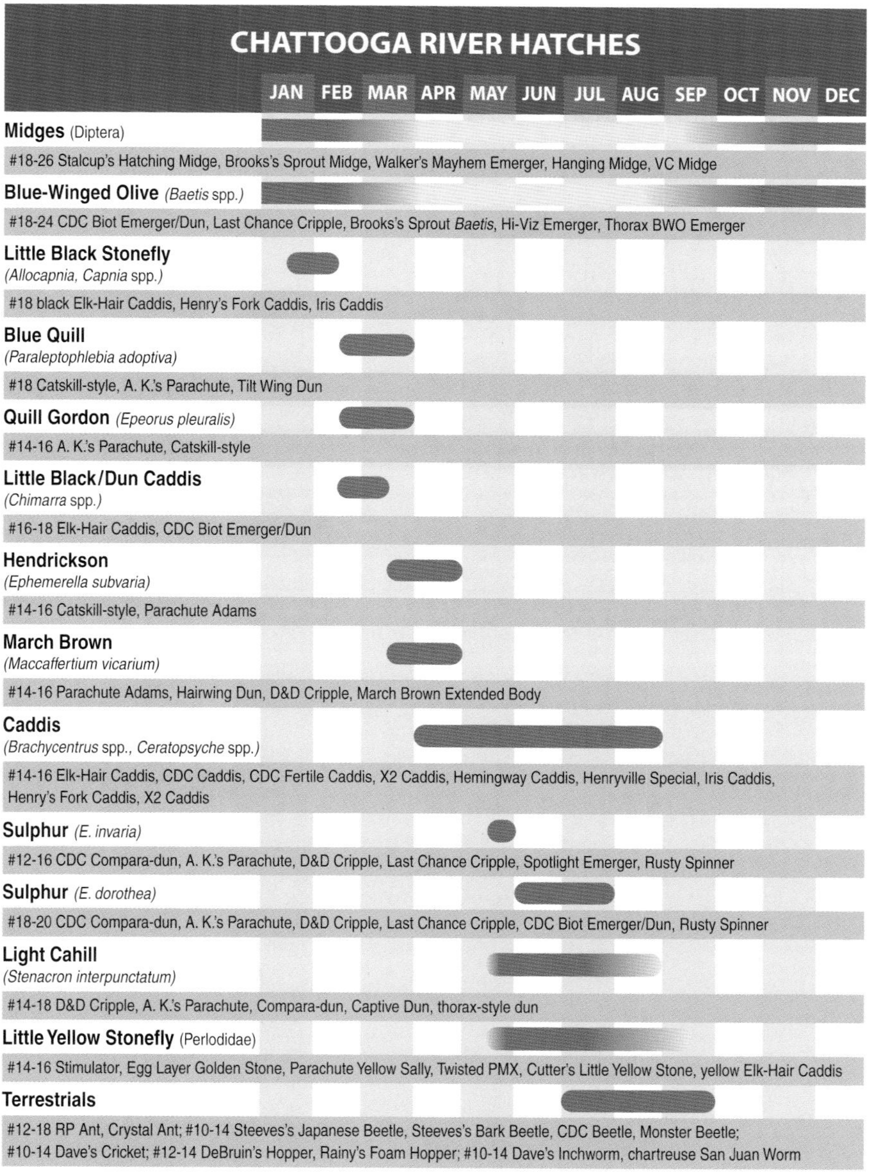
CHATTOOGA RIVER HATCHES
JAN FEB MAR APR MAY JUN JUL AUG SEP OCT NOV DEC
Midges (Diptera)
#18-26 Stalcup's Hatching Midge, Brooks's Sprout Midge, Walker's Mayhem Emerger, Hanging Midge, VC Midge
Blue-Winged Olive (Baetis spp.)
#18-24 CDC Biot Emerger/Dun, Last Chance Cripple, Brooks's Sprout Baetis, Hi-Viz Emerger, Thorax BWO Emerger
Little Black Stonefly (Allocapnia, Capnia spp.)
#18 black Elk-Hair Caddis, Henry's Fork Caddis, Iris Caddis
Blue Quill (Paraleptophlebia adoptiva)
#18 Catskill-style, A. K.'s Parachute, Tilt Wing Dun
Quill Gordon (Epeorus pleuralis)
#14-16 A. K.'s Parachute, Catskill-style
Little Black/Dun Caddis (Chimarra spp.)
#16-18 Elk-Hair Caddis, CDC Biot Emerger/Dun
Hendrickson (Ephemerella subvaria)
#14-16 Catskill-style, Parachute Adams
March Brown (Maccaffertium vicarium)
#14-16 Parachute Adams, Hairwing Dun, D&D Cripple, March Brown Extended Body
Caddis (Brachycentrus spp., Ceratopsyche spp.)
#14-16 Elk-Hair Caddis, CDC Caddis, CDC Fertile Caddis, X2 Caddis, Hemingway Caddis, Henryville Special, Iris Caddis, Henry's Fork Caddis, X2 Caddis
Sulphur (E. invaria)
#12-16 CDC Compara-dun, A. K.'s Parachute, D&D Cripple, Last Chance Cripple, Spotlight Emerger, Rusty Spinner
Sulphur (E. dorothea)
#18-20 CDC Compara-dun, A. K.'s Parachute, D&D Cripple, Last Chance Cripple, CDC Biot Emerger/Dun, Rusty Spinner
Light Cahill (Stenacron interpunctatum)
#14-18 D&D Cripple, A. K.'s Parachute, Compara-dun, Captive Dun, thorax-style dun
Little Yellow Stonefly (Perlodidae)
#14-16 Stimulator, Egg Layer Golden Stone, Parachute Yellow Sally, Twisted PMX, Cutter's Little Yellow Stone, yellow Elk-Hair Caddis
Terrestrials
#12-18 RP Ant, Crystal Ant; #10-14 Steeves's Japanese Beetle, Steeves's Bark Beetle, CDC Beetle, Monster Beetle; #10-14 Dave's Cricket; #12-14 DeBruin's Hopper, Rainy's Foam Hopper; #10-14 Dave's Inchworm, chartreuse San Juan Worm

tooga hoping to catch some dry-fly action. Your best bet is to call Unicoi Outfitters in Helen, Georgia, as many of their guides fish the Chattooga and readily share information about river conditions.

Look for Blue Quills, March Browns, and Hendricksons to come off anytime from March through early April. Their numbers will not be great, but the trout will find the dry flies irresistible. Keep a good selection of these patterns in standard Catskill ties in case you run across the hatch. There's nothing worse than being in the middle of nowhere surrounded by rising trout with not a fly in your box to match the hatch.

April and May bring with them caddis, which bring even some of the larger browns up to feed, especially late in the evening. Brownish-tan Elk-Hair Caddis (#14-16) work well in the braided, faster water, but you'd best have a few "stealth" patterns in your box for the larger pools that seem to move slower than a snail on Oxycontin. Slow-water patterns should include Harrop's Fertile Caddis, Iris Caddis, and Henry's Fork Caddis (#14-16).

If the trout are having none of your dry-fly offerings at this time of year, try nymphing with a Sparkle Pupa, Rockworm Caddis, or Graphic Caddis (#14-18) in the faster runs and braided water. Sometimes you can find trout you would have never dreamed were there by going deep during caddis season.

Late spring also brings another flurry of mayflies, with the Light Cahill being the predominant hatch. If you see a few of these bugs in the air, reach for an A. K.'s Parachute or Compara-dun (#12-16). Along with the Cahills, *Isoperla* stoneflies will come off from late May through July, necessitating a few yellow Stimulators and Parachute Yellow Sallies (#12-14) in your dry-fly box.

If the summer heat isn't too hot and the water levels have not dropped to dismal levels, terrestrial fishing can be good. If the water is down and the area

The upper Chattooga is one of the most picturesque rivers in the South. Even if the fishing is off, the scenery is always well worth the hike in. LOUIS CAHILL

X2 Caddis

Hook:	#12-16 Daiichi 1180
Thread:	Tan 6/0
Tail:	Olive Z-lon
Body:	Olive Crystal Dubbing
Rib:	Flashabou, one strand
Wing:	Elk hair
Underwing:	White poly yarn
Head:	Dubbing to match body

is in the middle of a dry spell, look for fishing elsewhere. The river, even its upper reaches, can warm quickly and you're liable to make a long hike in for nothing. If the rain dances work, the river will fish well through the summer. Black and cinnamon ant patterns (#14-18), Steeves's Bark and Tiger Beetles (#12-14), and both sinking and floating inchworm patterns will find some use on the Chattooga, especially early and late in the day.

November through February can produce some great *Baetis* action, the tiny mayflies convincing trout that coming to the surface is a worthwhile prospect. You can take advantage of this by lengthening your tippet and tying on a Brooks's Sprout *Baetis* or Smith's Translucent Emerger (#18-22). Fish will also rise to midges. VC Midges, Griffith's Gnats, and Walker's Mayhem Emergers (#18-22) will typically fool Chattooga trout without going to the much smaller variations.

The delayed-harvest stretch above GA 28 has become one of the more popular delayed-harvest waters in the state, coming in maybe a close second to the Chattahoochee River. Anglers make the long, winding drive across Goble Gap on Warwoman Road, many traveling several hours just to fish for the day. The trout are plentiful, just as they are on any delayed-harvest water, but the scenery is the best of any in the state. Narrow, well-worn paths lead anglers to a place where everyday life is swallowed by the water and the hemlocks.

If you make the drive across the mountains to fish the Chattooga, be sure to bring along the customary delayed-harvest fare, including Y2K Bugs, pink San Juan Worms, and Green Weenies. Drop a smaller nymph like one you'd use on the wild trout water and call it good. Stonefly nymphs also work well in the tumbling currents, especially when fished in tandem with the brighter delayed-harvest patterns.

No river in the state can challenge the Chattooga in a contest of innate beauty on a scale so grand. A true destination among so many gems in the mountains of southern Appalachia, the river has coursed its way into becoming a fixture among Southern anglers.

THE SOUTHEAST'S
PART II

Large trout do not come easy in North Carolina. While they are plentiful on some rivers, such as the Davidson, streamside approach and presentation are key. Large trout like this will give you one chance—if you blow it, game over. LOUIS CAHILL

BEST FLY FISHING NORTH CAROLINA

For quality freestone fishing in the South, it would be almost impossible to beat North Carolina. Along the western border of the state, over 3,000 miles of trout streams are open to anglers. The state also leads the region in the madly popular delayed-harvest program. More than 20 designated trout waters in 14 counties provide catch-and-release, artificials-only regulations from October to June. The state plants around 240,000 trout each year, a staggering number of fish from one of the most prolific hatchery programs in the South.

When considering delayed-harvest waters, there are many to choose, and each is guaranteed to have good numbers of trout swimming around during the season. Perhaps this assurance is what drives anglers to the delayed-harvest waters from fall to early summer. The majority of these fisheries are harshly seasonal. The trout flourish during the mild-weather months; but if not caught following the end of the delayed-harvest program, they meet a grim fate once the water warms in midsummer. Other stretches of delayed-harvest water have "outs" for the trout, coldwater refuges where the trout can escape the lethally warm water, holding out until the following autumn. Either way, anglers flock to every section of water managed under the delayed-harvest regulations, planning vacations around the forays and happily catching trout in Tarheel country.

Outside of the delayed-harvest program, the state has myriad fishing opportunities ranging from heavily stocked hatchery-supported waters to highly technical catch-and-release stretches of river. Names like Davidson, Nantahala, Tuckaseegee, and North Mills are spoken regularly in fly shops across the region. Some backcountry waters are never mentioned, and for good reason—if you found paradise, you'd want to keep it for yourself, too.

Falling within the physical borders of North Carolina lies the last eastern vestige of the Cherokee Nation. The Qualla Boundary, commonly called

North Carolina Fly Shops and Guides

Davidson River/ North Mills River

FLY SHOPS AND GUIDES

One Fly Outfitters, LTD
112 Cherry Street
Black Mountain, NC 28711
(828) 669-6939

Curtis Wright Outfitters
5 All Souls Crescent
Asheville, NC 28803
(828) 274-3471

Headwaters Outfitters
(828) 877-3106
headwatersoutfitters.com

Davidson River Outfitters
26 Pisgah Highway
Pisgah Forest, NC 28768
(828) 877-4181
davidsonflyfishing.com

Hunter Banks
29 Montford Ave.
Asheville, NC 28801
(800) 227-6732

Brookings Outfitters
3 Chestnut Road
Cashiers, NC 28717
(828) 743-3768
brookingsonline.com

Highland Hiker
601 Main Street
Highlands, NC 28741
(828) 526-5298
highlandhiker.com

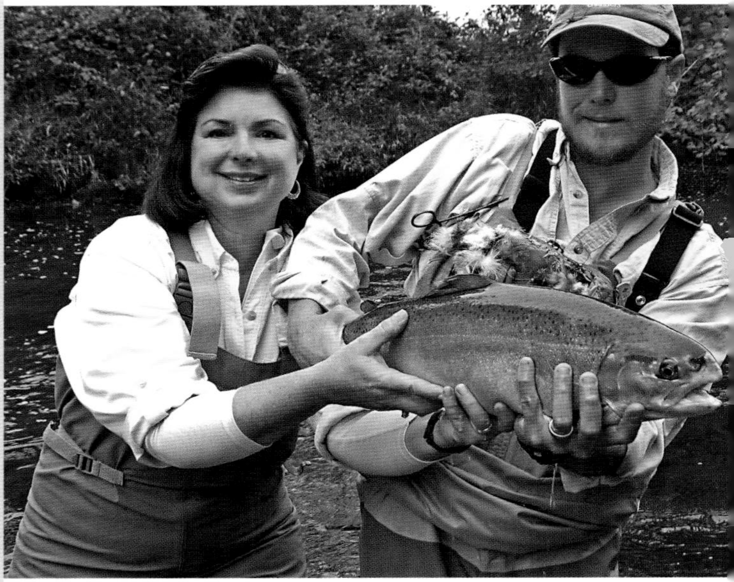

Oversize trout like this rainbow held by Davidson River Outfitters guide Walker Parrott are common on the Davidson. In North Carolina, it would be hard to beat the "Big D" if you're looking for a photo op with a hefty trout.

the Cherokee Indian Reservation, sits alongside the Great Smoky Mountains National Park between Bryson City and Maggie Valley. The reservation has its own rules and regulations set forth by tribal leaders and requires a permit separate from a state license to fish the waters. Much of the accessible water is alongside the road, so if you're looking for backcountry solitude, this is not the place. However, the trout you catch here are more than likely going to be larger than average and plentiful in numbers. The tribe maintains its own hatchery and stocks brown, rainbow, and brook trout, including more exotic strains such as Donaldson rainbows and golden trout.

Brook trout abound in the North Carolina high country and the state lays claim to one of the greatest native brook trout fisheries in the world, Big Snowbird Creek. As with most brook trout fisheries, getting to the best water is no easy task, but sweat and aching muscles seem a cheap price when releasing one of these brightly colored pieces of natural history.

Along with the overwhelming trout-fishing opportunities in the state, North Carolina's warmwater options extend the angler's scope to include the French Broad, Nolichucky, Hiwassee, and Little Tennessee rivers. Many of the popular trout destinations will also hold warmwater species such as smallmouth bass in the lower reaches where the temperatures become marginal for trout. In these transition zones, it is possible to catch trout and bass on the same float, adding a little spice to your trip. The Tuckaseegee is one of these rivers where trout and smallmouth co-exist, especially as the river nears Fontana Lake.

Warmwater species are too often overshadowed by trout in North Carolina, some anglers going so far as to shun the thought of pursuing anything but trout. Personally, this has never made sense to me. For those who have seen a smallmouth bass rise to inhale a popping bug or a 40-inch muskie chase a fly, the thrill is every bit equal to anything in the realm of trout. Fly fishing does not mean "trout only," especially in North Carolina.

The future of North Carolina angling is a bright one. Anglers continue to stream in from bordering states, a few travel even farther, to fish Tarheel country. Even if the delayed-harvest waters and the more known rivers are the main draw, don't forget the backcountry blue lines on the topo map and the state's numerous warmwater destinations.

Tuckaseegee River, Nantahala River, Big Snowbird Creek, Cherokee Reservation

FLY SHOPS AND GUIDES

Appalachian Outfitters
104 Tennessee St.
Murphy, NC 28906
(828) 837-4165

CCS Fly Fishing Outfitters
472 Haywood Rd.
Dillsboro, NC 28725
(828) 586-6212

Hunter Banks
29 Montford Avenue
Asheville, NC 28801
(800) 227-6732

One Fly Outfitters, LTD
112 Cherry Street
Black Mountain, NC 28711
(828) 669-6939

Curtis Wright Outfitters
24 North Main Street
Weaverville, NC 28787
(828) 645-8700

Headwaters Outfitters
(828) 877-3106
headwatersoutfitters.com

Davidson River Outfitters
26 Pisgah Highway
Pisgah Forest, NC 28768
(828) 877-4181
davidsonflyfishing.com

Davidson River, North Carolina

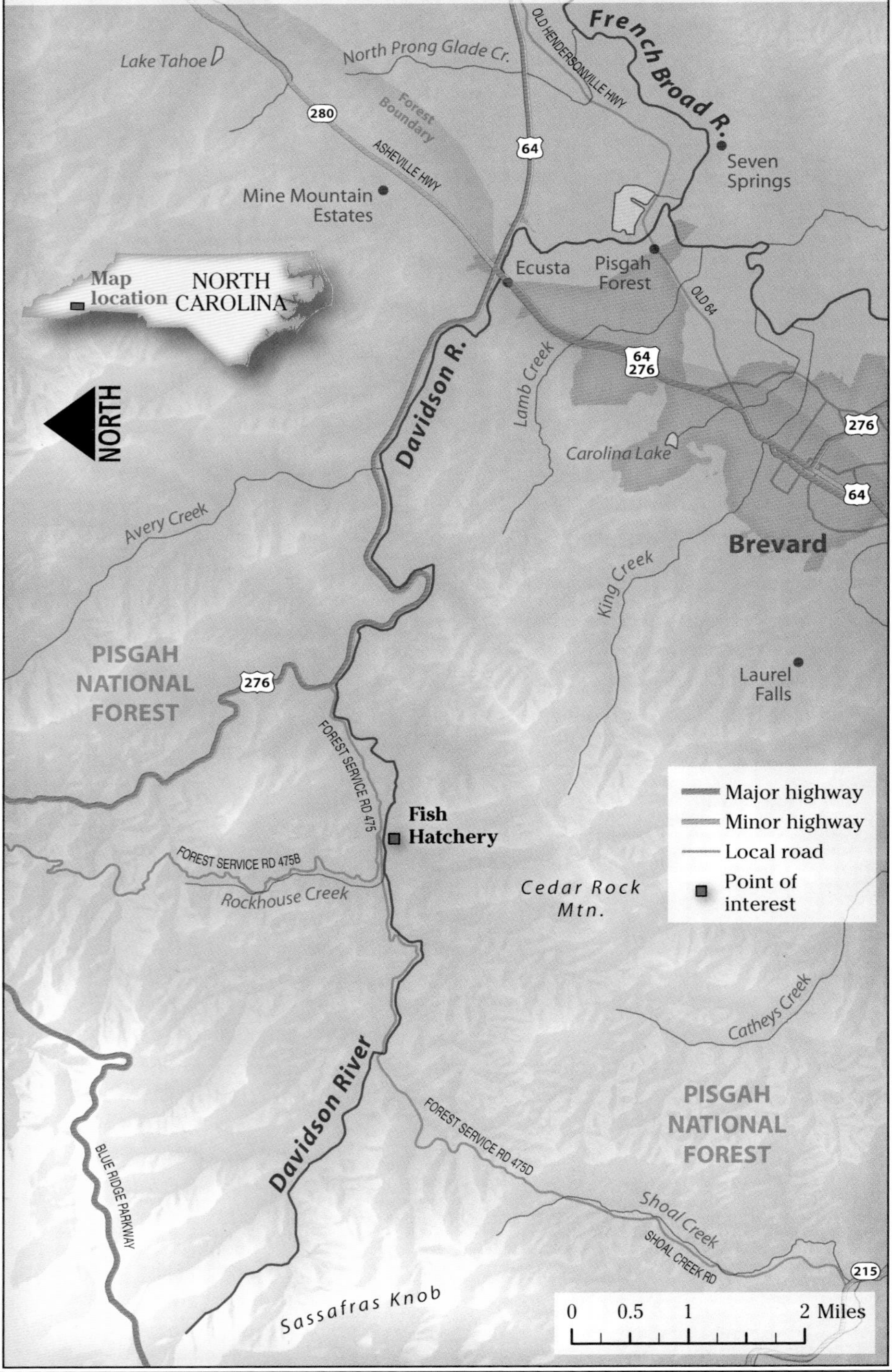

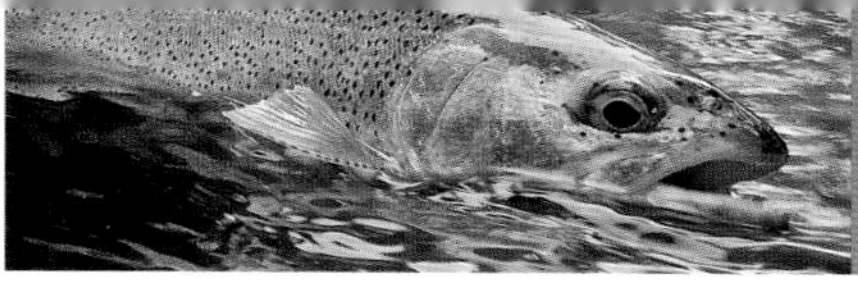

CHAPTER 4

Davidson River

When you walk into the back room of Davidson River Outfitters, the local fly shop in Brevard, a sign just above the lavender scooter and next to the refrigerator reads, "If you are '0' then you buy the beer." The postscript continues, "This means a case, not a six pack JEB!" I am told that beer is not often bought, but when some of the best guides in the region are chanced with a skunk, then you get the idea of just how hard the Davidson can be.

Don't let this discourage you, but know that on some days, a realistic expectation on the river could be a single fish. Then, on other days, the fish are cooperative and you actually wind up catching a few. There is a lot involved with fooling Davidson River trout, and nothing beats local knowledge and time on the water. If it is your first time on the Davidson, it is advisable to hire a professional guide to bump your learning curve. It can take several trips on your own before you figure out where the fish are holding, especially when exploring water not adjacent to the hatchery outflow.

The Davidson begins as a small stream high in the Pisgah National Forest near the town of Brevard. From the headwaters downstream to the hatchery, the Davidson is not fished that heavily. It's small, and with the exception of a stray, does not routinely hold the large trout the Davidson is so well known for. It does have a good population of smaller (6 to 10 inches) rainbows and browns that will sometimes save you from the dreaded skunk. But remember, it is the Davidson, so big trout can be anywhere. In the deeper pools of Davidson River Gorge, some nice trout wait for anglers willing to make the trek down to find them. It is a tough hike down, but you will be rewarded with fewer anglers and a dramatic backdrop.

Below the bridge at the hatchery the river widens a bit. However, from the hatchery bridge downstream for about a mile, the added breadth is quickly taken up by anglers. Standing on the bridge looking downstream, it is not uncommon to see a half dozen anglers fishing in relatively close proximity to one another. To someone who is not accustomed to the river, this

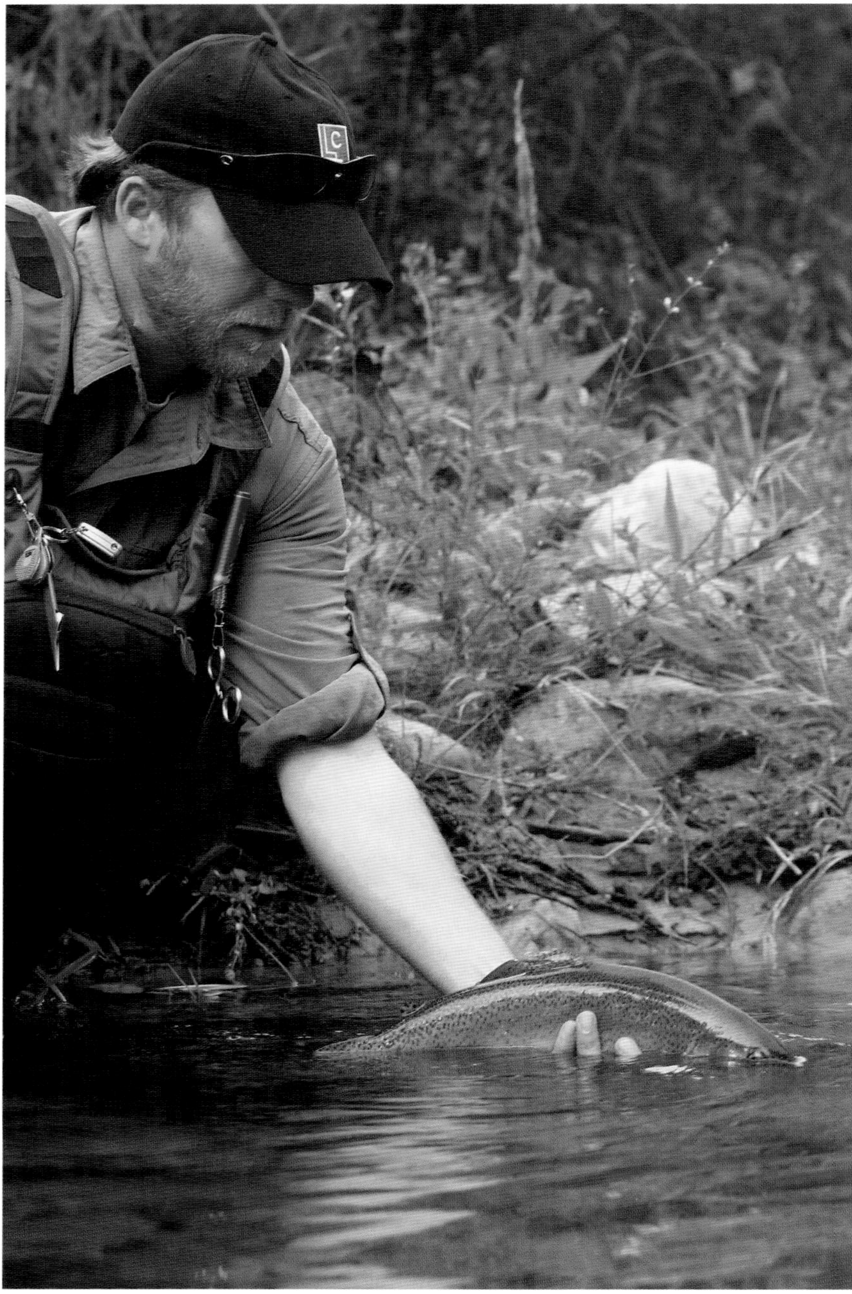

Anglers often overlook terrestrial patterns on the Davidson, instead opting for small midges fished subsurface. But, as this angler has proven, terrestrial patterns will bring trout to the surface during the warmer months.

would seem overly crowded, though that is not entirely true. Like the anglers, trout—big trout—stack up in this short stretch of river. Some of these trout are huge, seeming out of place in such a narrow confine. Built on the nutrient-rich discharge supplied by the hatchery's outflow, both directly and indirectly, their shoulders grow wide and become the very thing much of the Davidson's reputation is based on.

After the first mile or so below the hatchery, the Davidson flattens out into an area known as Horse Cove. From here nearly to the mouth of Looking Glass Creek, the river leaves the road, but several pullouts provide access to trailheads that lead to the river, usually just a few hundred yards away. This stretch is a mix of deep pools, shallow tailouts, and short stretches of pocketwater. The Horse Cove stretch is ideal streamer water, especially early in the day or late into the evening. It can also be rewarding during the warmer months when the terrestrials are most active.

Below Looking Glass Creek downstream to the end of the catch-and-release water at the mouth of Avery Creek, the river flows alongside North Carolina Highway 276. During the summer months, even when the river is just a trickle, this section can get crowded on the weekends and holidays. Not with anglers, but with tubers floating downstream. It is a nuisance, but a necessary evil of the Davidson that you can either suck up or avoid, coming back when the peak season is over.

This lower section of the catch-and-release stretch receives its fair share of angling pressure, but it is by no means as crowded at the hatchery stretch. Anglers have a tough time even spotting fish here. As I said, they are spooky. There is a lot of good-looking water here, but not every inch of it will hold fish. Finding trout is a matter of experience and patience. Fishing the river a lot will help you figure out where the fish usually lie in a particular run or pool. Sure, it's easier to head to the hatchery, where you know the trout are stacked up like cordwood, but as my friend and Davidson River guide says, "Man, there's 15 miles of water on the river, why would you want to fish the hatchery every day?" I couldn't agree more.

Below Avery Creek, the river is operated under hatchery-supported regulations and receives heavy plantings of trout. Visitors to this section looking for table fare make good use of this. The lower reaches below the catch-and-release water see excruciatingly high pressure from spin and fly anglers alike, but also receive one of the heaviest stocking regimens of any stretch of river in the entire state.

The waters below the hatchery section receive a good deal of pressure, but the larger trout are fewer and farther between. They are far less accepting of pressure, unlike the fish in the "hatchery pool." The big trout in the hatchery pool have grown as accustomed to anglers as trout can. Instead of hightailing it at the sight of a human form, they just sit there, being highly selective in their diets. When you leave the immediate vicinity of the hatchery, it becomes a game of stealth and good presentation. I've seen veteran guides on this water sneaking around the wooded shoreline as if they were stalking

Big trout love structure. Slow pools littered with downed trees are prime lies for some of the river's largest brown trout. Here, guide Walker Parrott tries to coax a large brown from structure in the Horse Cove section of the Davidson.

a whitetail buck, peering through bushes and around trees, sometimes crawling, just to try to spot a big fish holding.

Weather and water levels greatly affect the way the Davidson fishes. If the weather is mild and flows are between 80 and 150 cfs, the river fishes as well as it ever will. This range marks near-perfect flows for all types of fishing, especially if you want to fish a dry. Much lower and things get pretty sketchy; higher and you're going to find streamer fishing or casting a large, weighted fly far more in tune with the river's attitude.

When the water gauge gets over 350 cfs, the river becomes all but unfishable. Higher water means a lot of the fish will be displaced, and traditional dry-fly and nymphing techniques will not work quite as well. However, streamer fishing during these high-water, even near flood, times can work well. At the other extreme, during low water, the river can flow at a puny trickle. Anything less than 60 cfs is considered low, below 20 cfs can be deadly. If the river is running at or around 40 to 65 cfs, then going to small midges and fishing early and late in the day during the summer is really the only way to go.

Fly selection on the Davidson is as much a matter of personal preference as what rod brand you use, but some things float to the top of every angler's fly box. If you ask ten anglers to name their top three patterns on the Davidson, you would probably get twenty different answers, but ten would echo the same: midges.

Midge fishing is by far the best method of consistently fooling Davidson River trout, especially up near the hatchery where most folks seem to fish. Anglers use 6X and smaller tippets on long leaders to sight-fish to feeding trout. Walker Parrot and Kevin Howell, both of Davidson River Outfitters, prefer to add a little meat to their midge platter, especially in sections of braided and deeper water. Both have guided, fished, and lived in the area for the better part of their lives. Kevin's father and uncle were local legends in

North Carolina fly-fishing circles. Walker and Kevin also teamed up to win the Fly Fishing Masters in 2006. It's safe to say these guys know what they're talking about.

Both Walker and Kevin like to fish a large stonefly pattern such as a Kaufmann's Rubber-Legged Stone, Kevin's Stone, or Stalcup's Tungsten Rubber-Legged Stone (#8-12), with Craven's Jujubee Midge, BTS Nymph, or Zebra Midge (#18-24) trailing behind. Fishing this rig under an indicator shorter than the "industry standard" of one to one and a half times the water depth, along with enough weight to get the fly down quickly seems to be the way to go. Something along the lines of water depth or three-quarters depth tends to work better, especially in the fast water. Big fish hold in this faster water, but most folks cannot see them, so they get passed up. This rig will get the flies down to those fish quickly and allow you to detect a strike nearly the instant the fish takes.

Midges are another common denominator in another veteran angler's fly box for the Davidson. Than Axtell, guide and manager of fly fishing at Headwaters Outfitters in Rosman, North Carolina, fishes pretty much the same midge patterns as Walker and Kevin. However, his rigging methods differ, and he prefers to replace the heavy stonefly with a #24-28 midge pattern, particularly when fishing up near the hatchery. Than prefers long leaders with little weight, especially when prospecting the slower, more even flows, often sight-fishing to a spotted trout. A small indicator, if any, riding sometimes

Low water on the Davidson has always been an issue, especially during summer and fall. Target prime lies and cover lots of water to find willing fish when the water table is down.

twice the water depth tracks the progress of the tiny flies. Although Than's techniques differ greatly from those of Walker and Kevin, the end result is identical: a big trout dancing at the end of the line.

Now don't go thinking that the only way to catch big trout on the Davidson is to watch an indicator all day long. Dry-fly fishing can be nothing short of amazing. Caddis, mayflies, midges, and stoneflies all inhabit the tumbling waters. Midges are present year-round, and every person coming to the Davidson should have a good supply of both midge adults and emergers in addition to the larvae. Make sure to carry some Brooks's Sprout Midges, VC Midges, and Walker's Mayhem Emergers (#18-26). Most of the better midge fishing is above Looking Glass Creek upstream to the hatchery, but the lower reaches have good hatches as well. Winter is an especially good time to see some of the best midge hatches on the river. From November through February, midges provide anglers with trout rising to tiny flies, and they will eat them.

In line with the small-fly parade, Blue-Winged Olives can hatch on any given day through the year. The Blue-Winged Olive hatches will bring some big trout to the surface and are not as technical as midge fishing. Blue-Winged Olive patterns such as Brooks's Sprout *Baetis,* Harrop's CDC Biot Emergers and Duns, and Last Chance Cripples (#16-24) will cover you throughout the year depending on the size of fly coming off. Look for trout to set up in feeding lanes and pick off these little mayflies along the seams of long pools and slicks.

Beginning in late February, Blue Quills and Quill Gordons hatch simultaneously. Davidson Quill Gordons begin small, then progressively increase in size. Early in the hatch, go with smaller (#16-18) patterns, then advance to the (#12-14) Catskill ties. The high-floating patterns work well in the riffles where the Quill Gordons typically hatch, says Axtell. Blue Quill parachute patterns and Tilt Wing Duns (#18) are the flies of choice when matching the Blue Quill emergence.

From late March to early April, Black Caddis make their first appearance on the river, hovering above the Davidson for a few weeks before the hatch finally peters out. A black or dun-colored CDC Caddis Emerger (#14-16) fished in the riffles and tailouts will match the naturals being taken by the trout. The riffles above Avery Creek to the lower end of Horse Cove will hold trout feeding on the caddis, so it's best to concentrate your efforts there.

Larger March Brown mayflies begin showing up in late April, overlapping the early Black Caddis. Fly choices should include Parachute Adams, Hairwing Duns, CDC Compara-duns, and Harrop's CDC Biot Emergers (#12-14). The March Browns are big mayflies and don't really need to hatch in large numbers to get the attention of the trout. If you see a few mayflies flying around, tie on a dry and begin prospecting. If you can find a trout rising to this hatch, and if you can get your fly over the fish without spooking it, your fly is probably going to get eaten.

April through May is caddis time with a few carrying over through the summer. More predominant hatches are the Cinnamon Caddisfly *(Ceratopsy-*

che). Little Olive Caddisfly (*Cheumatopsyche*). and Great Gray Spotted Sedge *(Arctopsyche).* The Cinnamon Caddis is one of the first and the most prolific on the river. Dark tan Harrop's CDC Caddis Emergers, Fertile Caddis, and X2 Caddis (#12-16) are all good choices for the Davidson. Look for some amazing caddis hatches below Looking Glass Falls all the way to Avery Creek and below. This is a great time to explore the river below the hatchery stretch, where most people feel chained due to the numbers of trout visible when fishing.

Around Memorial Day, Sulphurs and Green Drakes start hatching, the latter being one of the most sought-after hatches on the river. Large, beefy mayflies hovering over the water cause anglers' hearts to race. Green Drake cripple and parachute patterns (#8-12) should always be in your spring fly box, especially when going to the Davidson. For the Sulphurs, which can hatch all summer long in some numbers, try CDC Compara-duns, Captive Duns, and various cripple patterns (#14-18). Finding a lone trout rising during either of these hatches will require skill in presentation, but once you hook up, take satisfaction knowing that you've just accomplished a milestone in your angling career.

June through August finds Little Golden Stoneflies and *Isonychia (I. bicolor)* hatching, the latter starting sometime in July. These large bugs, aside from being just plain fun to fish, will tempt trout even if they're hatching in fewer numbers than some of the other caddis and mayflies earlier in the year. During the early summer, keep a few Golden Stone parachute patterns and yellow Stimulators (#12-16) along with Compara-dun *Isonychias* and Parachute Adams (#10-14) tucked away in your box.

During normal water levels, the Davidson River runs clear, making long, fine leaders necessary. LOUIS CAHILL

Terrestrial fishing during the summer, from June through September, can be phenomenal. So many folks, thinking the hatches are all but over, will revert to throwing nymphs all day long. Sometimes all it takes to bring up a big trout is casting a Monster Beetle (#10), Steeves's Firefly (#14), or smaller ant pattern (#14-18) along a brushy, overhanging bank early and late in the day. These trout may not be noticeably feeding, but a big beetle floating overhead often proves to be too hard to resist.

From mid-September through October, the Davidson gets a decent hatch of October Caddis. These large caddis bring the trout up for one final hurrah

Eastern Green Drake

Hook:	#6-10 Daiichi 1130
Thread:	Green 6/0
Tail:	Moose mane
Body:	Dark olive dubbing
Rib:	Chartreuse 3/0 thread
Wings:	Black calf hair
Hackle:	Dark olive grizzly

before they're back to midges and *Baetis.* Robust, #8-14 orange Kaufmann's Stimulators or Spotlight October Caddis are good imitations for this late-season hatch. It can only last a short while, but the trout are active when the hatch is on, and you can close out the warmer months with some big dry-fly action.

Following a major rain, as the river is dropping back into shape, brown trout that would normally never eat a fly during daylight hours can be fooled with streamer patterns. Fishing a line with an 8- to 12-foot sinking tip and a meaty streamer can produce some large trout. There is a universe of distance between hooking and actually landing trout in the swift currents of the falling river, but fishing the Davidson just as it begins falling into shape is going to be your best option if big trout get your blood going. Beldar Buggers, Bellyache Minnows, and Shiela Sculpins (#2-6) are good choices when hunting for "the one." Use 3X fluorocarbon, as the trout will not be spooky in the turbid water, and you're going to need that extra strength to bring them to hand.

No matter whether you're fishing dry flies or nymphs, once the fish realize they're being fished to, they will get selective, stop feeding altogether, or just swim off. If you've taken all the time to get into position to cast to a large feeding fish, don't blow it by showing it the same fly over and over again until it realizes something is up. The general rule of thumb is five or six drifts, then change flies. If a trout sees the same pattern float by more than a half dozen or so times, you're going to "burn" him. It's best to trim tippet and dig a little deeper in the box rather than spook a happy trout with futile repetition.

Tuckaseegee River, North Carolina

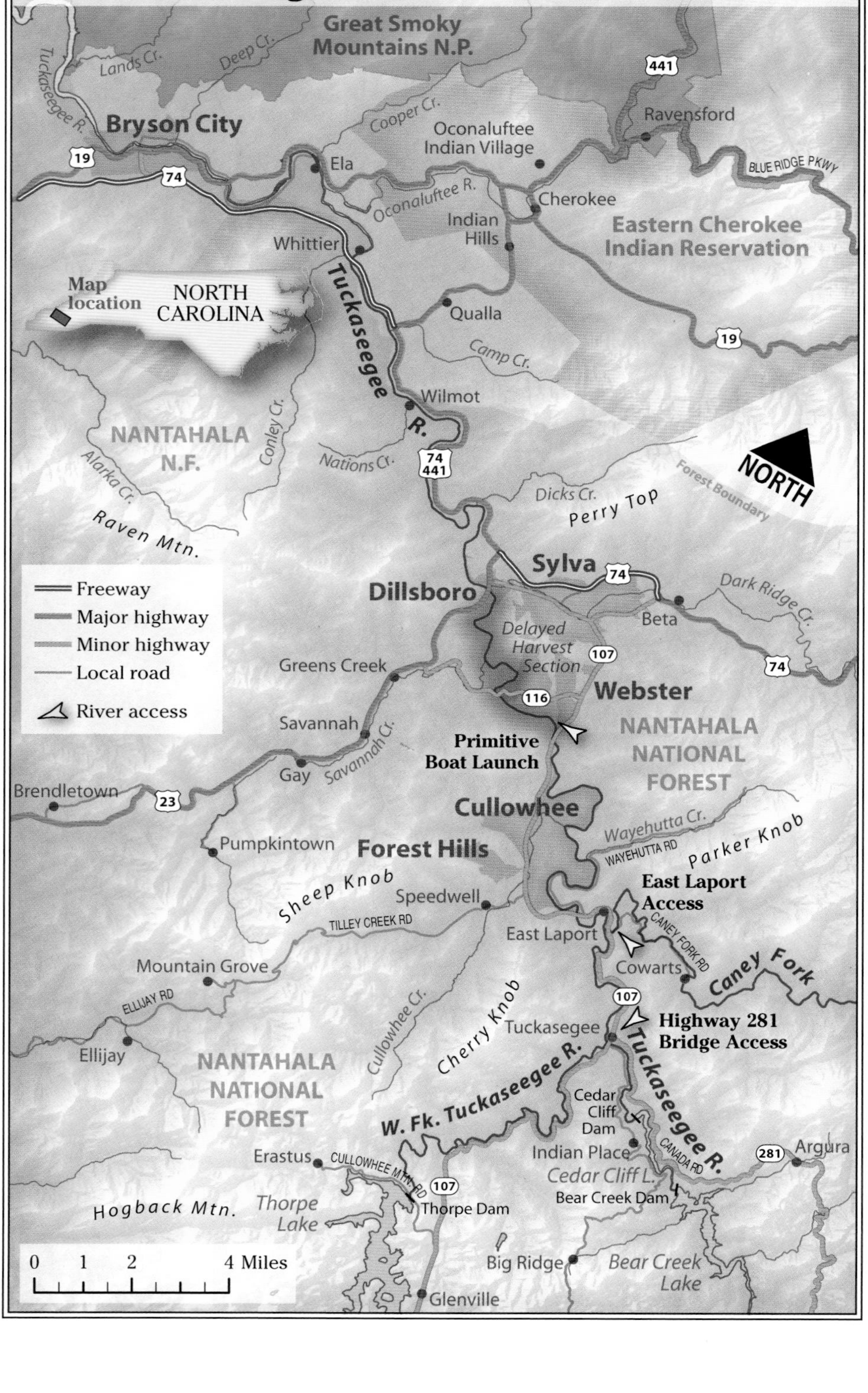
Great Smoky Mountains N.P.
Tuckaseegee R.
Lands Cr.
Deep Cr.
441
Bryson City
Cooper Cr.
Oconaluftee Indian Village
Ravensford
19
74
Ela
Oconaluftee R.
Cherokee
BLUE RIDGE PKWY
Indian Hills
Eastern Cherokee Indian Reservation
Whittier
Tuckaseegee R.
Map location
NORTH CAROLINA
Qualla
19
Camp Cr.
Wilmot
NANTAHALA N.F.
Conley Cr.
Alarka Cr.
Nations Cr.
74
441
Dicks Cr.
Perry Top
Forest Boundary
NORTH
Raven Mtn.
Sylva
74
Dillsboro
Dark Ridge Cr.
Beta
Delayed Harvest Section
107
74
Freeway
Major highway
Minor highway
Local road
River access
Greens Creek
116
Webster
Savannah
Savannah Cr.
Primitive Boat Launch
NANTAHALA NATIONAL FOREST
Gay
Brendletown
23
Cullowhee
Wayehutta Cr.
WAYEHUTTA RD
Pumpkintown
Forest Hills
Parker Knob
Sheep Knob
East Laport Access
Speedwell
TILLEY CREEK RD
CANEY FORK RD
East Laport
Mountain Grove
Cowarts
Caney Fork
ELLIJAY RD
107
Cherry Knob
Highway 281 Bridge Access
Tuckasegee
Cullowhee Cr.
Ellijay
NANTAHALA NATIONAL FOREST
W. Fk. Tuckaseegee R.
Tuckaseegee R.
Cedar Cliff Dam
Indian Place
CANADA RD
281
Argura
Erastus
CULLOWHEE MTN RD
Cedar Cliff L.
107
Bear Creek Dam
Hogback Mtn.
Thorpe Lake
Thorpe Dam
0 1 2 4 Miles
Big Ridge
Bear Creek Lake
Glenville

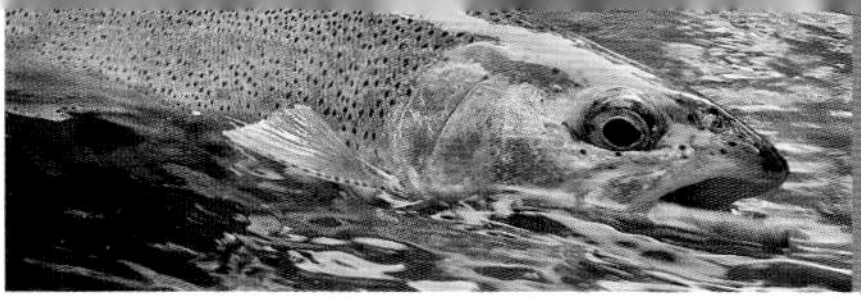

CHAPTER 5

Tuckaseegee River

Perhaps no stream in North Carolina is better known than the Tuckaseegee. The Tuck, as many call it, is one of the longest trout rivers in the state, flowing from its upper reaches above the small town of Cullowhee all the way downstream to Lake Fontana. Water levels are dictated by two dams upstream on the West and East forks. When neither is running, the river bottom is largely exposed. Expansive riffles and bedrock ledges litter the river upstream of Dillsboro, North Carolina. Below the low falls dam in Dillsboro, the river is a crazy quilt of rock gardens and pocketwater separated by long pools.

With the East Fork running water, the river rises only a foot or so, coursing a near perfect wading current around the rocks and boulders. The West Fork puts a bit more water into the river, making some areas a bit more technical when wading.

When either fork is running water, the river is wadable and there is enough water to float drift boats and other craft through the entire length. When both dams are pushing water, the river becomes off-colored and fishing becomes more difficult. Wade access becomes almost nonexistent, the swift currents being too high and dangerous for safe footwork. Floating is the only way to fish during these high flows. Anchors are necessary to stop along the way and fish the softer seams along the banks and ledges.

From the upper stretch below the East and West forks downstream to the mouth of the Oconaluftee River, roughly 18 miles, the Tuckaseegee holds brown, rainbow, and nonnative brook trout stocked by the state. Some trout hold over, growing upwards of 20 inches, but the average trout encountered in nonregulated water is typically 9 to 12 inches.

Access is plentiful the length of the river with North Carolina Highway 107, Wayehutta Road, South River Road, North River Road, and U.S. Highway 441 all running alongside the river for much of its length. Wading anglers should pay close attention to the generation schedules for both dams, and exit the water once it begins to rise noticeably.

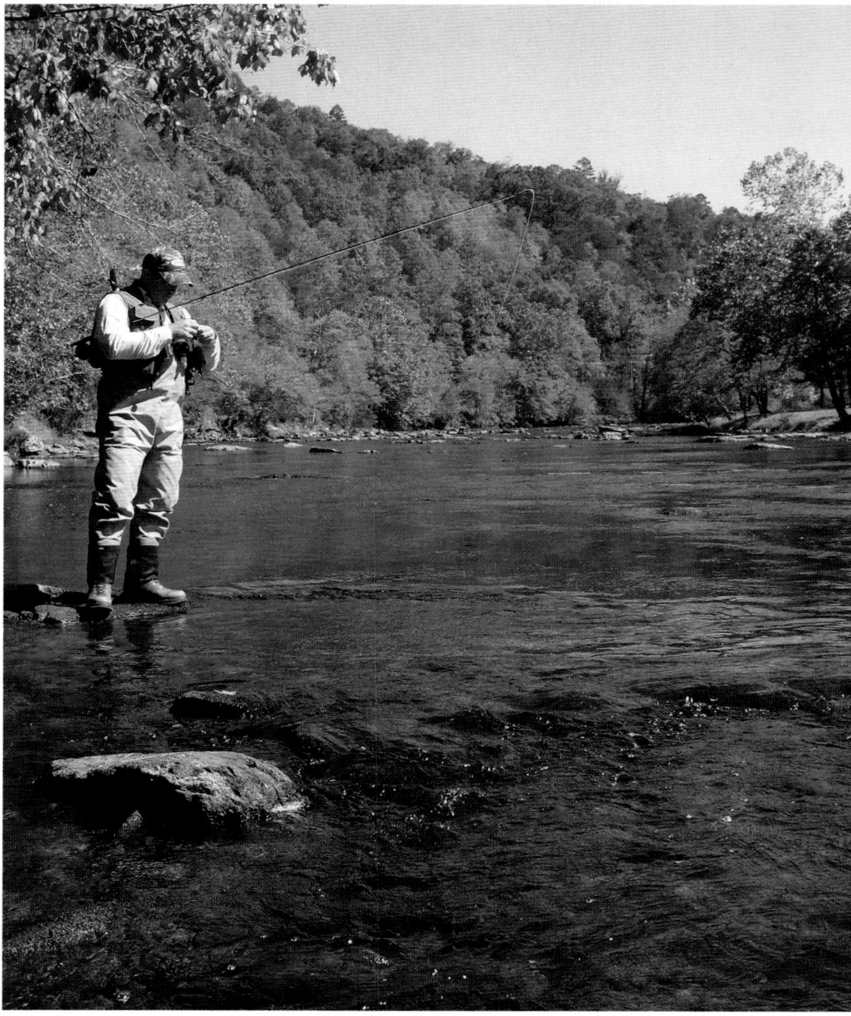

Lower water means easy wading for anglers and plenty of casting room on the "Tuck." It also means spooky trout, so be careful when approaching prospective lies to avoid spooking entire pods of trout.

Floating anglers can put in near the mouth of the Caney Fork at the East Laport Park access or farther upstream at the NC 107 bridge just below where the West Fork enters the river. The float between these two points is just under 5 miles and given the nature of both points of access, canoes or other small, easily manageable watercraft are highly advisable.

Below the village of Cullowhee, home of Western Carolina University, South River Road leads off NC 107, giving boating anglers another launch just downstream of the bridge. From Laport to the NC 107/South River Road access, the river courses over 9 miles through the Carolina backcountry. Cutting a float down along this stretch is possible along Wayehutta Road, as there are several pullouts where a small craft could be hauled up the bank. The upper floats can be nice, since you'll see few other anglers floating, especially when the middle section of the river is in its delayed-harvest season.

Below NC 107, floating anglers need to get creative about taking out larger boats, as the riverbanks are steep, and pulling a drift boat out is a difficult task. Smaller pontoon boats are a smarter option. When floating below NC 107, there is roughly 5 1/2 miles of water until a small impoundment in Dillsboro and, more important, a small dam that you don't want to go over. Floating anglers should take out along North River Road, which runs along the river just above Dillsboro.

From Dillsboro downstream to the end of trouty water, there are no good access points from which to launch a drift boat, and even smaller boats can be tricky. It's best to wade this stretch, pulling off along US 441 and walking the steep bank to the river. There are numerous "posted" signs along the US 441 corridor so honor them and you shouldn't find yourself in any trouble.

With so much water to cover, it is amazing that the short 5 1/2-mile section between NC 107 and Dillsboro receives the majority of pressure from anglers. The state manages this stretch under delayed-harvest regulations and stocks it heavily. Stocked trout consist mostly of rainbow and brook trout, with a healthy number of holdover rainbows and browns thrown into the mix. Some

A typical rainbow from the Tuckaseegee. The river boasts a higher fish per mile ratio than any river its size in the state.

large browns over 20 inches show up every season, especially in the fall. It is thought they run upstream from the lower reaches of the river to spawn. Large and aggressive, they bear little resemblance to the 10- to 14-inch rainbows and brookies that make up the average catch. Since we're on the subject of rumors, it is also thought that a run of lake-run rainbows comes up the river in the spring. While this is unlikely, according to biologists, an influx of large rainbows seeming to be holdover fish do turn up on the ends of many anglers' lines during this time. Who knows if it's true, but it is fun to think about the possibilities.

From below Dillsboro to the confluence with the Oconaluftee River, the rocky maze holds some nice brown, brook, and rainbow trout. With a mixture of stocked and holdover trout, this section is managed under the state's hatchery-supported regulations. Most of the trout here average 9 to 11 inches, with a few going much larger—and the chance at a nice smallmouth bass never hurts. They should not be expected, but I've seen several browns caught in the lower reaches that pushed 20 inches. The plus side of things is that the lower river is another wade option when the delayed-harvest section is crowded, or if you want to buy another hour or so of fishing before the water rises from power generation.

Above the delayed-harvest water, the Tuck is managed under hatchery-supported regulations. Whether you're wading or floating, this stretch can be the best on the river, especially during the summer when the water below NC 107 begins warming and the trout become far less active. Many of the trout left after the close of delayed harvest will migrate upstream in search of cooler water, leading to a healthy population of trout from June through September in the upper reaches. This is not to say that the upper reaches do not get pummeled by the summer's heat. Fishing early and late in the day is your best bet during those hot weeks.

Fly selection for the Tuck should begin with a well-stocked nymph box. Along with more specialized patterns, make sure to include a smattering of the usual suspects. Prince Nymphs, Hare's Ears, Pheasant Tails, and Tellicos (#14-18) are not too generic. These along with Lightning Bugs, Copper Johns, Split Case BWOs, Rockworm Caddis Larvae, and Whitlock's Red Squirrel Nymphs (#14-18) will get you well on your way. Add in a few larger stonefly patterns such as Stalcup's Rubber-Legged Stones (#10-12), and you're in business.

Your nymph choice shouldn't change throughout the length of the river. Any of the above nymphs will catch trout on any given day on the Tuck, but presentation is important. Getting the fly down with weight and using an indicator will help you get into the zone and detect strikes. When either of the river's forks is running water, you've got to break out some split-shot and get the fly down. A beadhead pattern is not enough.

Dry-fly fishing on the Tuck consists of a lot of midges, Blue-Winged Olives, and a few caddis. Everything else is pretty much window dressing. Sulphurs and Yellow Sallies are present, but not in significant enough numbers to warrant a full-blown assortment of patterns. Parachute-style Sulphur

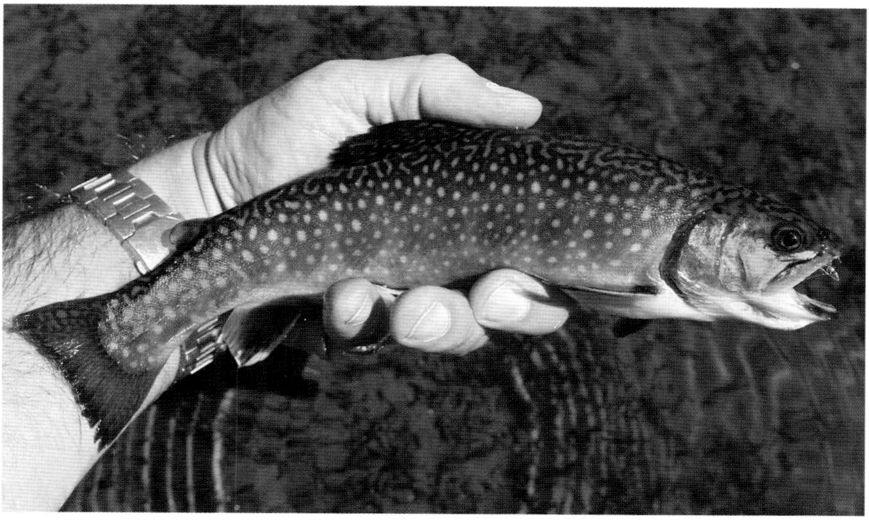

Brook trout like this one are common on the Tuckaseegee. Because they love bushy dry flies, dry/dropper rigs work well during the entire delayed-harvest season.

patterns (#14-18) along with a few yellow Stimulators (#10-12) should be somewhere in your fly box just in case.

Midge patterns such as Walker's Mayhem Emergers, Brooks's Sprouts, and Griffith's Gnats (#18-22) should be kept in good supply. Although the larger trout will seldom rise to a midge dry, they will eat nymphs, making a midge larva dropped behind one of the larger nymphs mentioned above a good insurance policy.

Blue-Winged Olives hatch in the heaviest numbers from late October through early March. Trout will key in on these tiny mayflies and drive you insane trying to find the right pattern. Once you find it and catch a few trout, they'll begin snubbing you again and it's back to square one. Usually, you can find something in your box that works, but on some days, a few fish is all you're going to get on a Blue-Winged Olive dry. That's just the way it goes.

Start out with a Blue-Winged Olive parachute, Brooks's Sprout *Baetis*, or CDC Loop Wing Emerger (#18-22), then try switching to something like a No-Hackle, Harrop's *Baetis* CDC Biot Emerger, or Captive Dun (#20-24). Floating nymphs olive-dun in color like Mayhems or Foam Back BWOs (#20-24) round out a few more options, but feel free to add to the list. If you get really frustrated, drop a Split Case BWO, Thorax Bead BWO, or Mercer's Micro Mayfly (#18-22) under a small indicator to exact some sort of retribution for your failed dry-fly efforts.

From mid-April through June, mottled brown and gray caddis begin hatching on the Tuck. The caddis hatch extends from the upper reaches nearly all the way downstream to Fontana Lake. Trout chase caddis all day long,

When the generators are off or only one fork is pushing water, the Tuckaseegee is wadable in most areas. However, when the dams on both the East and West forks come online, the swift currents cannot be waded safely. Keep an eye on the water level to ensure you are not caught off guard by an unscheduled release.

splashing at emergers, adults, and egg layers, attempting to ingest as many as they can before the emergence ends.

A few select patterns for the caddis are gray or brown X2 Caddis, Hemingway Caddis, CDC Fertile Caddis, and Spotlight Caddis Emergers (#14-16). Most anglers drop a beadhead caddis emerger or Soft-Hackle Pheasant Tail a foot or so behind the dry in an effort to tempt the trout that are stuck in limbo. Caddis time is crowded, with guide boats, wading anglers, and one-man pontoons covering what seems to be every square yard of water. If you can come on a weekday, the crowds are lighter, but don't expect to be alone in the delayed-harvest water.

A word here about the delayed-harvest stretch, as it doesn't fall exactly into the schema of the majority of the river. The fish are aggressive, partly because they are mostly newbies to the real world and haven't been all the

TUCKASEEGEE RIVER HATCHES

	JAN	FEB	MAR	APR	MAY	JUN	JUL	AUG	SEP	OCT	NOV	DEC
Midges (Diptera)												
#18-26 Stalcup's Hatching Midge, Brooks's Sprout Midge, VC Midge, Griffith's Gnat, Hanging Midge												
Blue-Winged Olive *(Baetis* spp.*)*												
#18-24 Brooks's Sprout *Baetis*, CDC Biot Emerger/Dun, CDC Compara-dun, D&D Cripple, Last Chance Cripple, Loop Wing Emerger, Thorax BWO Emerger; Hi-Viz Emerger												
Caddis *(Brachycentrus* spp.*)*												
#14-16 Elk-Hair Caddis, X2 Caddis, CDC Caddis Emerger, Henry's Fork Caddis, Stalcup's Parachute Caddis, CDC Fertile Caddis, Hemingway Caddis												

Deep Six Caddis

Hook:	#14-16 Daiichi 1130
Bead:	Black metal
Body:	Olive Ultra Wire
Dubbing:	Brown dubbing picked out
Hackle:	Partridge
Flash:	Krystal Flash

way around the block yet. That's not to say all the trout between the delayed-harvest boundaries are pushovers, since there are plenty of holdover trout, including some big browns, but on average it is possible to catch several trout without trying all that hard. Unless of course they get keyed in on a particular hatch, which makes them act like, well . . . trout.

On the Tuck's delayed-harvest waters, the nymphs and dry flies mentioned above work just fine, but sometimes it helps to add a bit of Liberace flare to your fly selection: pink San Juan Worms, Y2K Bugs, and egg patterns along with yellow, orange, and pink Lightning Bugs (#12-16). Bright and flashy is key on some days, especially if working with a tandem nymph rig. Go big and bright up top with something small and natural trailing behind; it's a proven setup that most folks swear by on the Tuck.

Streamer patterns should not be overlooked on the Tuck no matter where you are fishing. This is especially true in the fall and early spring, or on days when both forks are pushing water. For low-water work, a floating line is just fine. Use a 9-foot, 3X or 4X trout leader and smaller Woolly Buggers or Sculpzillas (#8-10). Some bigger trout will often come out of hiding when given the option of meat over a snack.

When the water is up from generation, leave the 4-weight at home and bring out the 6- or 7-weight rods along with fast-sinking 12- to 24-foot heads. Tie a Rolex Streamer, Beldar Bugger, Zoo Cougar, Bellyache Minnow, or Sculpzilla (#2-8) to a 36-inch section of 12-pound fluorocarbon, and get ready. There are some big browns and rainbows in the river, along with a few toad brook trout, and they are looking for a big meal. Going any lighter than 12-pound tippet will reduce your chances of landing a large fish in the swift currents, and when the water is up on two generators, they're not leader-shy.

The Tuck offers a lot of fishable water, so if one section is crowded, don't be afraid to explore some new water. Who knows, you may find something better than what you're used to. But you'll never know unless you try.

Oconaluftee River, North Carolina

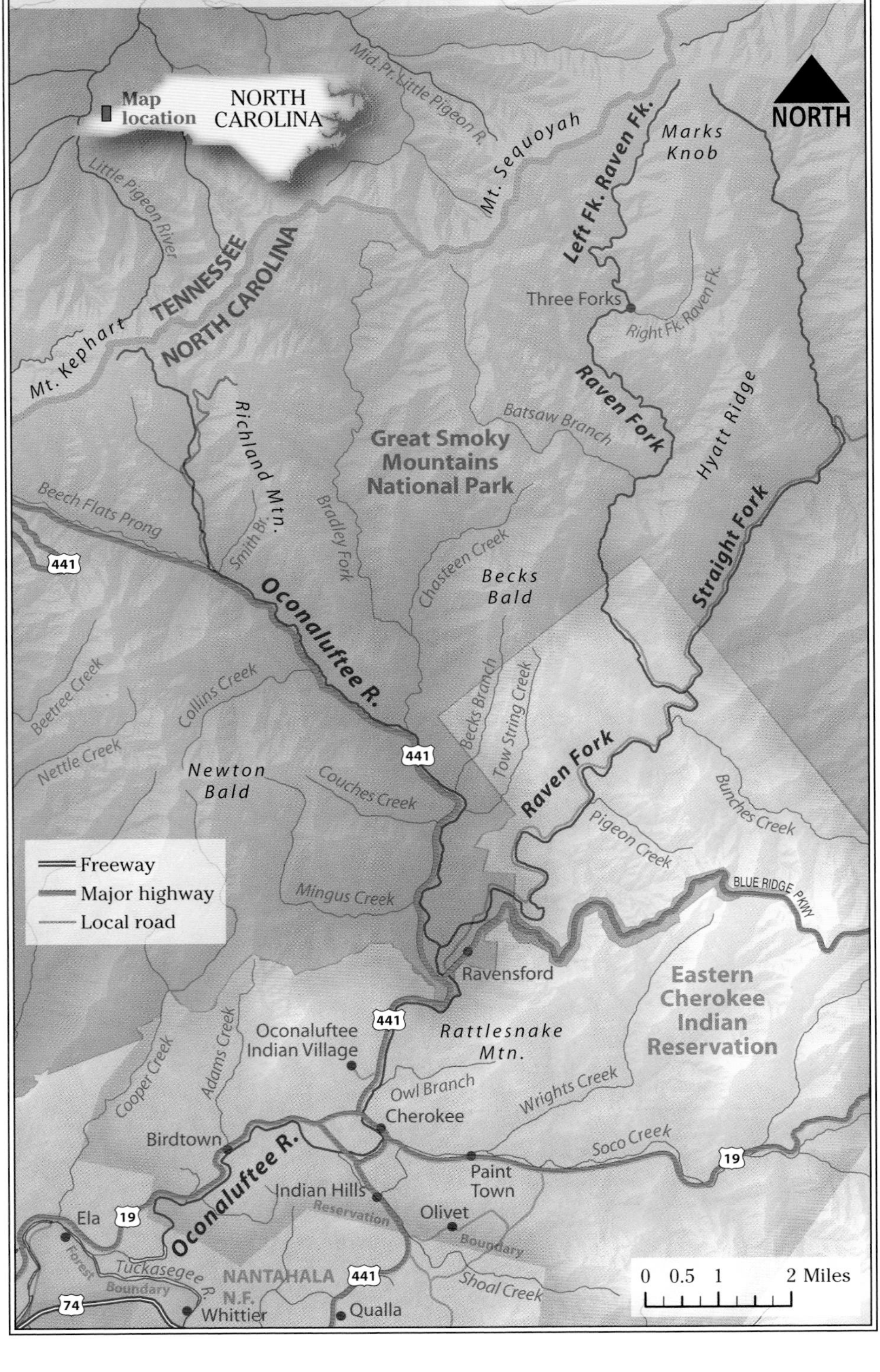

Map location
NORTH CAROLINA
NORTH
Mid. Pr. Little Pigeon R.
Mt. Sequoyah
Left Fk. Raven Fk.
Marks Knob
Little Pigeon River
TENNESSEE
NORTH CAROLINA
Mt. Kephart
Three Forks
Right Fk. Raven Fk.
Raven Fork
Batsaw Branch
Hyatt Ridge
Richland Mtn.
Great Smoky Mountains National Park
Straight Fork
Beech Flats Prong
441
Smith Br.
Bradley Fork
Chasteen Creek
Becks Bald
Oconaluftee R.
Beetree Creek
Collins Creek
Becks Branch
Tow String Creek
Nettle Creek
Newton Bald
Couches Creek
Raven Fork
Bunches Creek
Pigeon Creek
Freeway
Major highway
Local road
Mingus Creek
BLUE RIDGE PKWY
Ravensford
Eastern Cherokee Indian Reservation
Oconaluftee Indian Village
Rattlesnake Mtn.
Cooper Creek
Adams Creek
Owl Branch
Wrights Creek
Cherokee
Birdtown
Soco Creek
19
Paint Town
Indian Hills
Reservation
Olivet
Boundary
Ela
Forest
Boundary
Tuckasegee R.
NANTAHALA N.F.
Shoal Creek
74
Whittier
Qualla
0 0.5 1 2 Miles

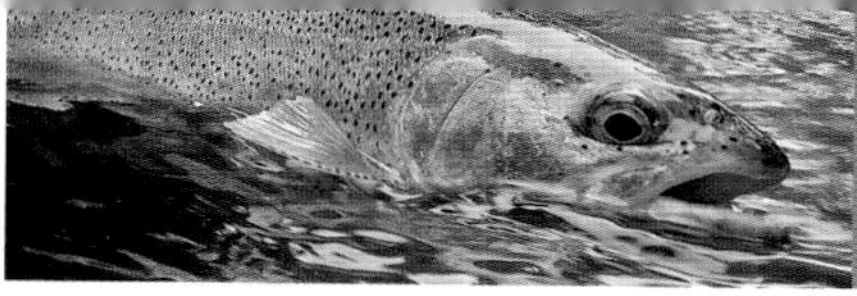

CHAPTER 6

Oconaluftee River and Raven's Fork

Some of my first memories of fishing around and in the Smoky Mountains are on the Cherokee Indian Reservation. Actually, the proper name for this is the Qualla Boundary, but most folks just call it the Rez. It consists of somewhere around 56,000 acres that have been set in trust for the Eastern Band of the Cherokee. Being part Cherokee, my father would always take us through the Rez on our family forays into the national park. Downtown Cherokee, the only major city in Qualla Boundary, resembles something along the lines of a Wild West show gone bad. Native Americans in full headdress regalia stand alongside teepees, plagiarizing their brethren of the plains, all within view of rubber tomahawks, T-shirts, and trinkets. There are a few cool attractions that you should check out, even if they're not currently on your fishing agenda: the play *Unto These Hills,* an epic about the Cherokees' history; and the Oconaluftee Indian Village, a true working replica of an ancient Cherokee village, complete with actors playing the parts of their ancestors.

Once you leave the town of Cherokee, you're back in the Smokies. Roughly 30 miles of water are open to the general public within the boundaries of the reservation. The most noteworthy of these are the Oconaluftee and Raven's Fork, both entering the Qualla Boundary from Great Smoky Mountains National Park. Outside the reservation boundaries, both streams are managed under Park Service regulations. It is well worth your time to explore both the Raven's Fork and the Oconaluftee inside the park, as both are beautiful streams in the upper reaches, teeming with wild rainbows and a few browns mixed in for good measure.

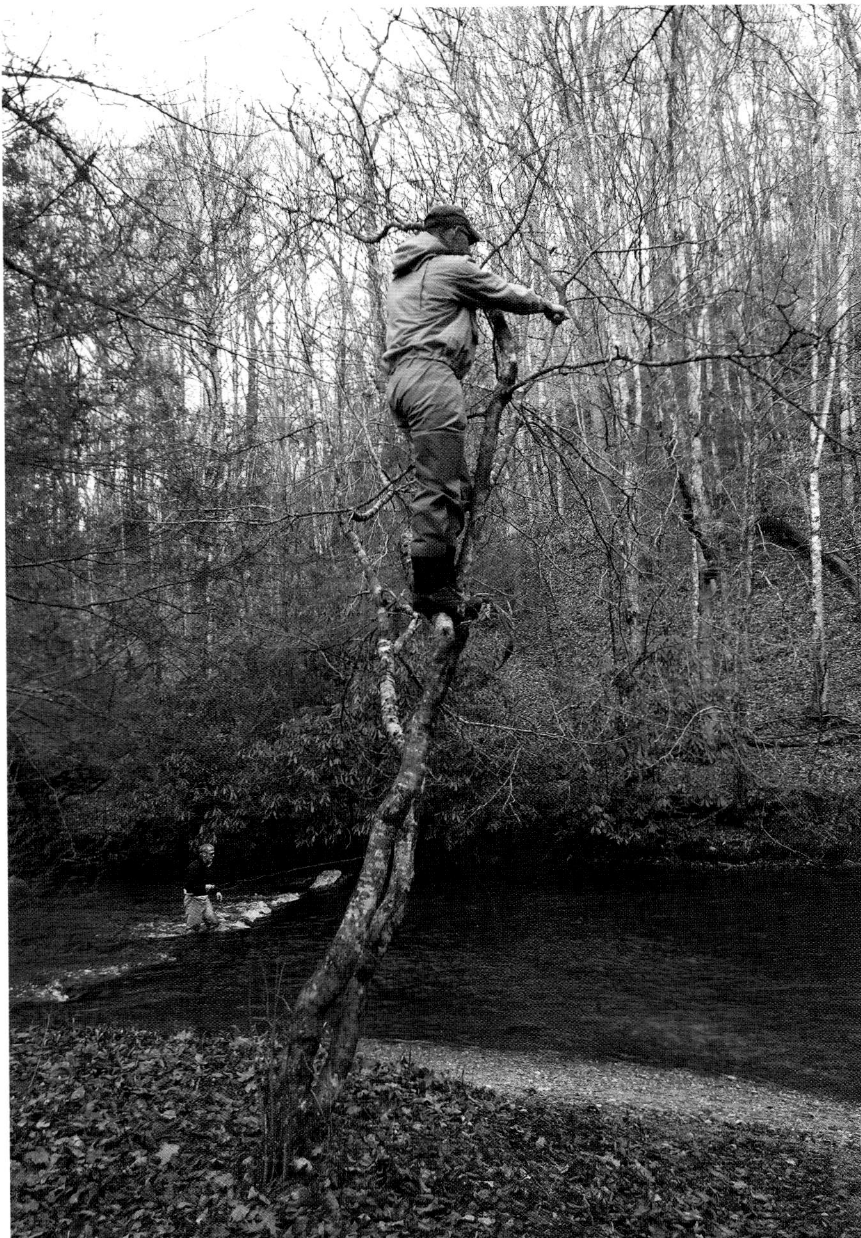

Spotting a large trout on the quality water before making your first cast is the most effective method of targeting these fish. Due to heavy fishing pressure, getting creative and working as a team, one angler fishing while the other acts as a spotter, can pay off big time. ZACH MATTHEWS

Inside the Cherokee boundary, both rivers support a healthy population of wild and hatchery fish. All rivers are open every day from the last Saturday in March through the end of the following February. A tribal permit is necessary to fish on native lands. Over 70,000 permits are issued annually, at $7 per daily permit, or you can spring for a season permit to the tune of $150. Unless you plan on fishing the reservation a lot, I'd just bite the $7 bullet on a daily basis.

Fly fishers used to flock to the reservation, finding the open waters in the Rez full of eager trout and the pressure usually low. In the last few years, almost coincidentally paralleling the opening of Harrah's Casino just outside of town, the trout fishing took a dive. Fish were hard to find, and the streams oftentimes seemed to be lacking the attention they once had before the casino overshadowed the fisheries program.

It didn't seem like things were going to get much better until Robert Blankenship, a progressive thinker who spent 19 years working for a nonprofit fisheries program in Alaska before returning to western North Carolina, was tasked with reviving the tribal hatchery and recreational fisheries. Under his guidance, Qualla Boundary's waters have rebounded in spades, and there's more good news to come. Blankenship, along with other tribal officials, has begun a massive effort to bring the waters inside the reservation into the spotlight as a true fly-fishing destination.

Tribal fishery authorities have begun efforts to increase the hatchery's production of rainbow and brown trout, along with a project to restore sicklefin redhorse, once a major food source of the Cherokee people. The reintroduction of native brook trout to the high mountain streams of the reservation is also on the docket. This type of progressive thinking is whittling away at the longtime notion that the waters on the reservation were mostly a put-and-take fishery.

Along with native fish restoration, tribal environmental officials have elected to place sections of the Raven's Fork and Oconaluftee River under catch-and-release, fly-fishing-only regulations. The section runs from the bridge on the Blue Ridge Parkway upstream to the Indian Valley Campground. Blankenship explains that this stretch of river consists of 2.2 miles of water with a possible expansion of this special-regulations umbrella in the near future. In addition to the standard license fee, a $20 special use permit is required to fish the catch-and-release water, but it will be well worth it.

The section that falls under this regulation holds large rainbow trout, as well as a few browns. Wild stocks mixed with hatchery plantings create a diverse fly-fishing destination, with some large trout holding in the reservation waters. While the fly-fishing-only water is new to the Cherokee, it is expected that it will become one of the most popular fly-fishing destinations in the region.

The Raven's Fork enters the Cherokee Reservation from the park, where it is considered an excellent, if difficult-to-access, wild brown and rainbow fishery. Once the Raven's Fork enters the reservation, a good part of its length

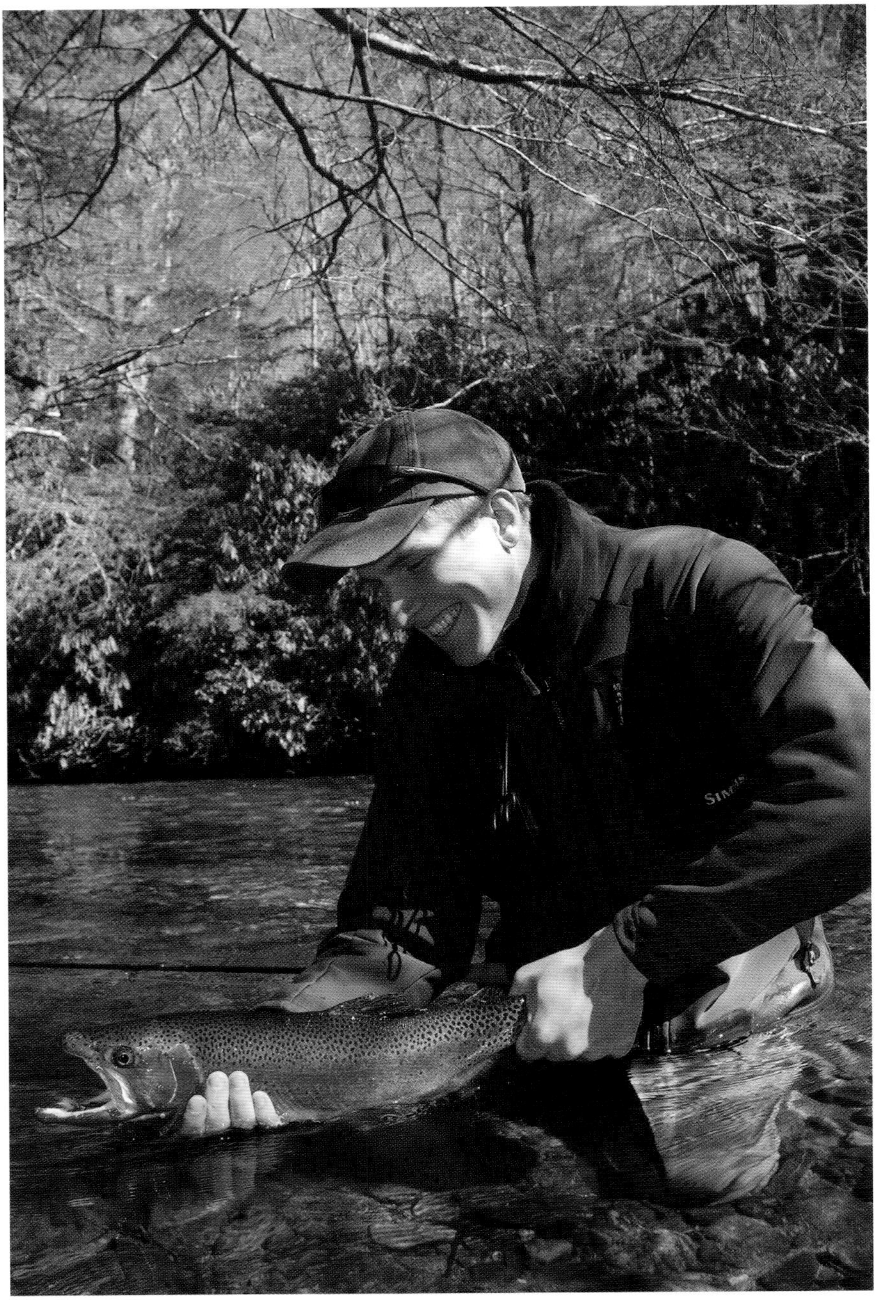

If you want to connect with a large trout like this, try fishing streamer patterns in the last hour or so before sundown. Concentrate on the larger pools and deeper runs to target the larger trout. ZACH MATTHEWS

runs parallel to Big Cove Road, which leads out of town and up into the more remote stretches of the Cherokee land. The river is a high-gradient stream just as it is in the park, becoming a whitewater paddler's dream when it rises after a spurt of heavy rain. During normal flows, the churning haystacks of water disappear and the river becomes wadable. You can park alongside Big Cove Road to access much of the Raven's Fork, but get there early if you want first crack at the water.

Through the center of town, the Oconaluftee River bisects the reservation after slipping in from the park. The Oconaluftee is a large river, especially in its lower reaches below where the Raven's Fork enters. Through town, the Oconaluftee is fishable during the fall and early spring, before it becomes warm enough to swim and play in. The tribe stocks the waters here, but the trout are usually caught quickly by spin and bait anglers. Below town, outside the reservation, the Oconaluftee flows downstream for several miles, then into the Tuckaseegee. Below the town of Cherokee, it warms quickly, keeping the trout holding farther north.

To catch trout consistently on the Raven's Fork or Oconaluftee, fish deep with a nymph rig. Large stonefly patterns work well in the tumbling, rocky riverbed. Probe the deep runs with Stalcup's Tungsten Rubber-Legged Stones, 20-Inchers, and Kevin's Stoneflies (#6-10). If the larger flies are not the ticket, try a Deep Six Caddis, Split Case PMD, Copper John, or Prince Nymph (#14-16), or something a bit smaller along the lines of a Brassie, Thorax BWO Emerger, or Pheasant Tail Nymph (#16-20).

Much as on any southern Appalachian freestone, hatches on both rivers appear with irregularity, but when the bugs come off it doesn't take long for the trout to key in and start poking their noses through the surface. Pretty much any cloudy day from October to June can see a fairly heavy *Baetis* hatch, especially on the Raven's Fork. Highly visible patterns like Hi-Viz BWOs and parachute-style BWOs with a bright foam or calf-hair post (#16-20) are needed when fishing the braided currents of these mountain rivers.

Trout of this size are not an uncommon occurrence on the new catch-and-release section provided by the Cherokee Nation. Larger trout are always a possibility, but they are extremely wary.

CHEROKEE INDIAN RESERVATION HATCHES

	JAN	FEB	MAR	APR	MAY	JUN	JUL	AUG	SEP	OCT	NOV	DEC
Midges (Diptera)	■	■	■	■	■	■	■	■	■	■	■	■
#18-26 Stalcup's Hatching Midge, Brooks's Sprout Midge , Walker's Mayhem Emerger, Griffith's Gnat, VC Midge												
Blue-Winged Olive (Baetis spp.)			■	■	■						■	■
#16-22 Compara-dun, CDC Biot Dun, Last Chance Cripple, A. K.'s Parachute, Hi-Viz Emerger, Thorax BWO Emerger												
Blue Quill (Paraleptophlebia adoptiva)			■									
#18 Catskill-style, A. K.'s Parachute, Tilt Wing Dun												
Quill Gordon (Epeorus pleuralis)				■	■							
#14-16 A. K.'s Parachute, Catskill-style, Quill Gordon spinner												
Hendrickson (Ephemerella subvaria)			■	■								
#14-16 Catskill-style, Parachute Adams, Last Chance Cripple												
March Brown (Maccaffertium vicarium)					■							
#12-16 Parachute Adams, Hairwing Dun, D&D Cripple, March Brown Extended Body, Brooks's Sprout Mahogany												
Light Cahill (Stenacron interpunctatum)						■	■	■				
#14-18 A. K.'s Parachute, D&D Cripple, Compara-dun, thorax-style dun												
Caddis (Ceratopsyche spp.)					■	■						
#14-16 Elk-Hair Caddis, X2 Caddis, Hemingway Caddis, Fertile Caddis, Translucent Emerger												
Little Yellow Stonefly (Perlodidae)						■	■					
#14-16 Stimulator, Egg Layer Golden Stone, Parachute Yellow Sally, Cutter's Little Yellow Stone												
Sulphur (E. invaria)					■	■						
#12-16 CDC and hairwing Compara-duns, A. K.'s Parachute, D&D Cripple, Last Chance Cripple, CDC Biot Emerger/Dun, Captive Dun												
Green Drake (Ephemera guttulata)						■						
#8-12 Green Drake Pullover Dun, Eastern Green Drake, Coffin Fly												
Sulphur (E. dorothea)							■	■				
#18 CDC Compara-dun, A. K.'s Parachute; D&D Cripple, Last Chance Cripple, Captive Dun, thorax-style dun, Spotlight Emerger												
Isonychia (I. bicolor)								■	■			
#10-12 Compara-dun, Sparkle Dun, Parachute Adams												
Terrestrials							■	■	■	■		
#10-12 CDC Beetle, Steeves's Japanese Beetle, Monster Beetle; #10-14 Rainy's Grand Hopper, DeBruin's Hopper; #14-18 RP Ant, Crystal Ant, Dave's Inchworm												

In early March, Hendricksons come off in decent numbers, and the large mayflies entice trout that would otherwise lie on the bottom. For the Hendrickson hatch, use Catskill and quill body parachute patterns (#12-16). They are not overly abundant, but they are important.

Throughout the spring and early summer, caddis, Sulphurs, and Light Cahills hatch from April through July, the latter two beginning in force sometime in June, making parachute and Compara-dun patterns to match the

An angler fishes the trophy section on the Raven's Fork in the Cherokee Indian Reservation. Smooth pools like this one can hold dozens of mammoth trout, so approach with caution. Often entering the pool from the head and fishing downstream and across will prevent spooking unseen fish.

mayflies and a good selection of brown and tan Elk-Hair Caddis and X2 Caddis (#12-16) a necessity. The hatches are unreliable, but trout will begin rising to dry flies if just a few of the bugs are emerging.

As the summer heats up, ants and beetles become standard fare, so pick up some Monster Beetles, Steeves's Bark Beetles, and Steeve's Tiger Beetles (#12-14) along with flying ant imitations (#14-18) to pick off bank feeders. Also, drifting a sunken inchworm such as a Green Weenie or chartreuse San Juan Worm under a dry fly or indicator can bring strikes from a few large trout, especially in a deep cut lying downstream from a large overhanging tree.

If you have never fished the Cherokee Reservation, or are one of those who did back in the day only to be frustrated, give the Qualla Boundary another look. The new regulations alone should be enough, but the beauty of the Raven's Fork and Oconaluftee River will keep you coming back.

Nantahala River, North Carolina

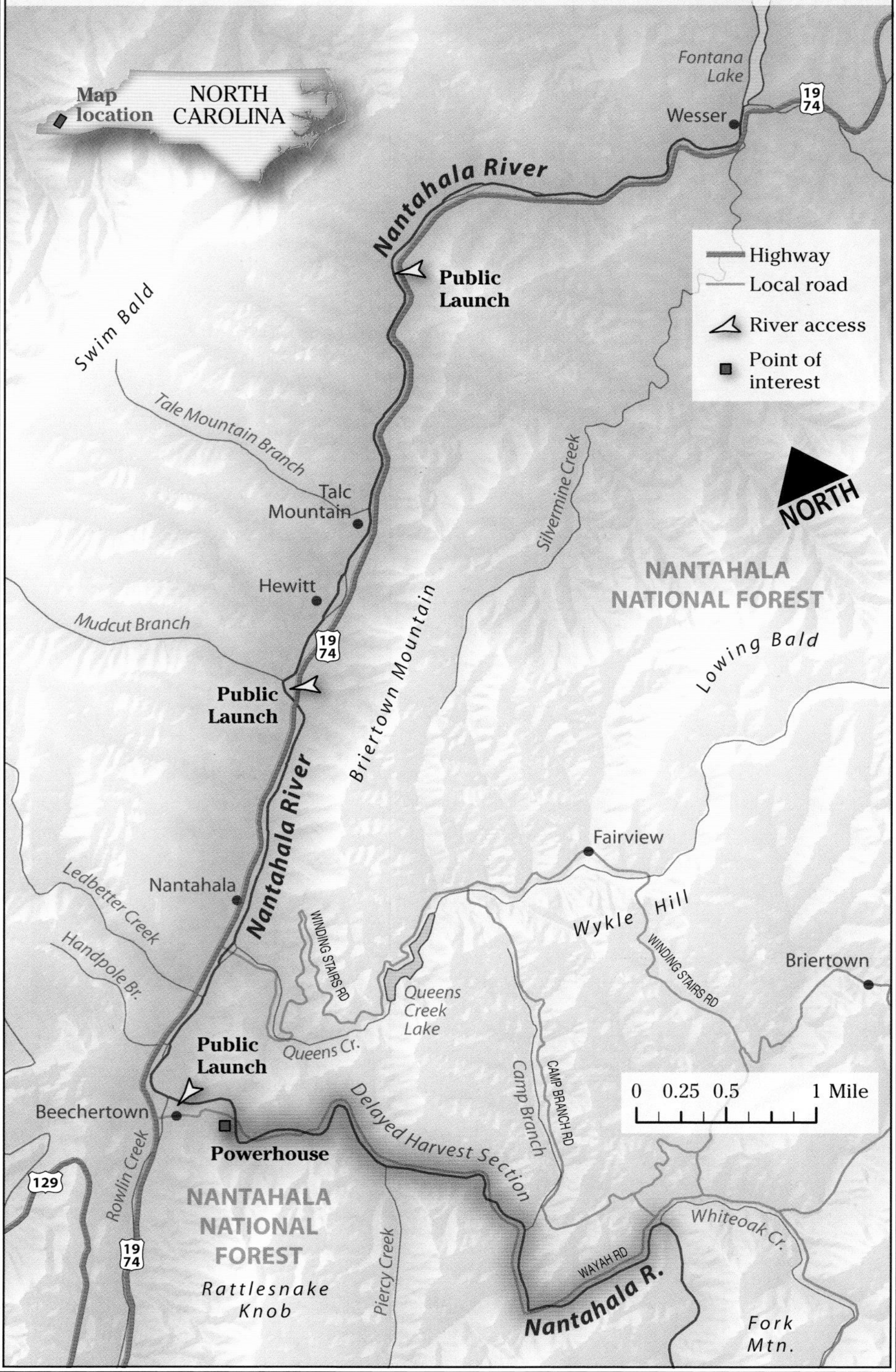

Map location
NORTH CAROLINA
Fontana Lake
Wesser
19
74
Nantahala River
Public Launch
Highway
Local road
River access
Point of interest
Swim Bald
Tale Mountain Branch
Talc Mountain
Silvermine Creek
NORTH
NANTAHALA NATIONAL FOREST
Hewitt
Briertown Mountain
Mudcut Branch
Lowing Bald
Public Launch
Nantahala River
Fairview
Ledbetter Creek
Nantahala
Wykle Hill
Handpole Br.
WINDING STAIRS RD
WINDING STAIRS RD
Briertown
Queens Creek Lake
Queens Cr.
Public Launch
Camp Branch
CAMP BRANCH RD
0 0.25 0.5 1 Mile
Beechertown
Delayed Harvest Section
Powerhouse
Rowlin Creek
129
NANTAHALA NATIONAL FOREST
Whiteoak Cr.
Piercy Creek
WAYAH RD
Rattlesnake Knob
Nantahala R.
Fork Mtn.

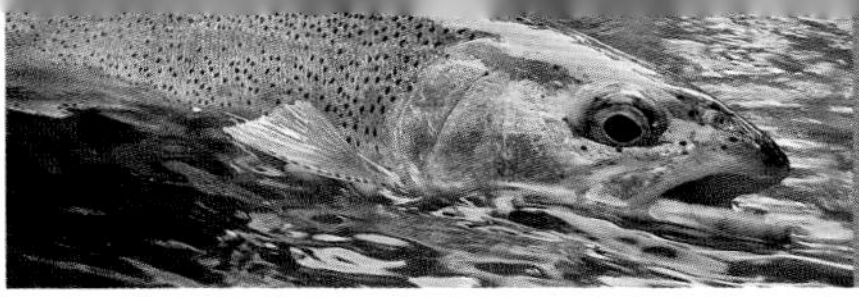

CHAPTER 7

Nantahala River

In a time before roads, when the valley was all but unmarked by man's progression, the native Cherokee people called the river Nantahala, meaning "Land of the Noonday Sun." In some places, the valley's walls tower 2,000 feet into the sky, the high rocky faces blocking out all but a few hours of direct sunlight. It was believed that hiding somewhere in the valley's long shadows lay the giant serpent *Uktena* and a liver-eating ogress, *Utlunta,* who preyed on those who ventured into this dark, primordial corridor.

Today, the river's name holds as true as it did a thousand years ago. Little sunlight reaches the valley floor, and the river exhales a cold breath into the air even on the warmest days. Falling from 4,000 feet near Doe and Rattlesnake knobs, the river begins as a small mountain stream high in the mountains of western North Carolina. The uppermost stretches of the river flow through Nantahala National Forest, the narrow, heavily canopied trickle hardly a destination for the fly angler unless he's looking for solitude. Just as the river widens to a fishable width, it enters private land, most notably flowing through the Rainbow Springs Club. This exclusive fishing club owns several miles of the upper river, restricting access to members only. Below the club, the river meanders through a patchwork of private land before entering Nantahala Lake. Although fishing the upper river is possible if you pay close attention to property boundaries, it is the river below the lake that is of the most interest to anglers.

The Nantahala below the lake can be divided into two distinct sections: the upper river from the base of Nantahala Dam downstream to the Nantahala Power and Light powerhouse, and the lower river from the powerhouse downstream to Fontana Lake. Unique in its makeup, directly below the dam the river is much akin to its counterpart upstream of the lake. It flows for several miles, tumbling and spilling over ledges and ancient rock formations before regrouping with the Nantahala Tunnel to form a coldwater tailrace.

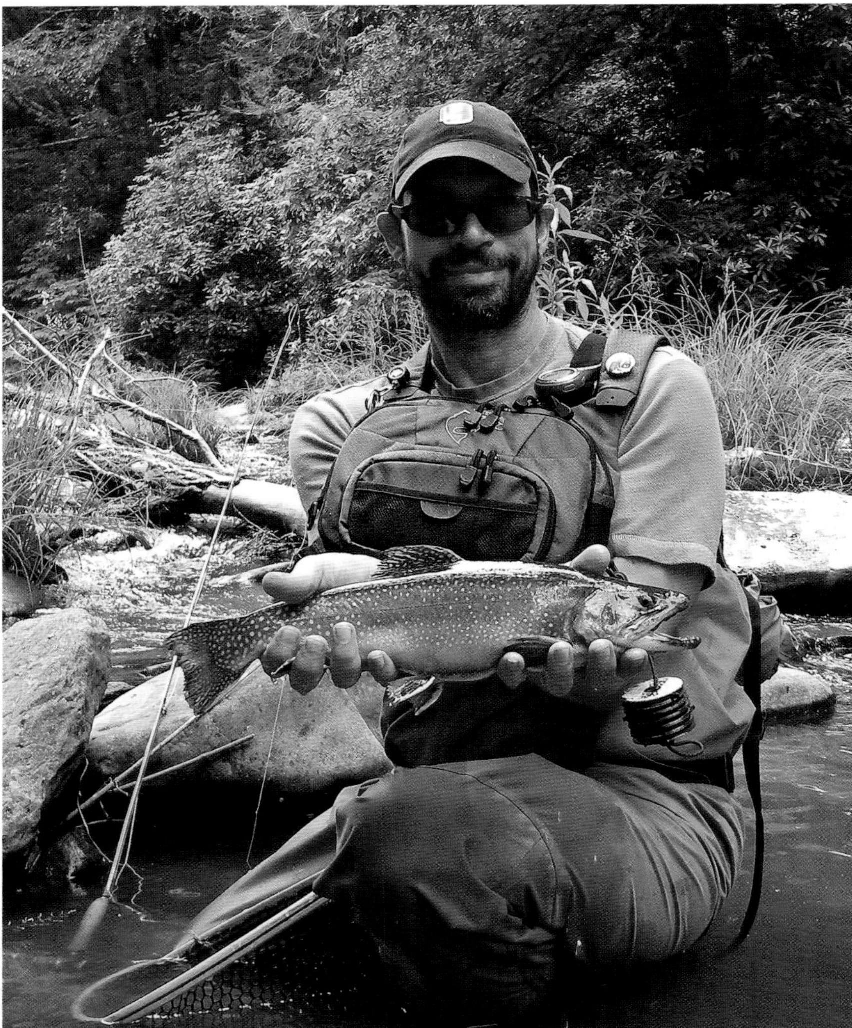

Photographer Louis Cahill proves large brook trout are more than just a myth in the upper Nantahala. Large trout like this typically call the deeper pools home and can be coaxed out of their lies with a variety of baitfish patterns. VICTOR VITEK

From the base of the dam to the mouth of White Oak Creek, the river is shallow, receiving only what water spills from a narrow pipe at the base of the dam. Managed under North Carolina's hatchery-supported regulations, this stretch warms quickly in the summer months and fishes only marginally well the rest of the year. There are several pullouts and camping sites on the upper stretch, however most fly fishers prefer to begin fishing below the confluence of White Oak Creek. It is below this cold-flowing creek that the Nantahala's reputation as one of the top trout-fishing destinations in the state truly begins.

From the mouth of White Oak Creek downstream roughly 4 miles, the Nantahala falls under North Carolina's delayed-harvest regulations. A narrow flow, averaging 30 to 40 feet wide, the river descends rapidly alongside Wayah Road the entire length of the delayed-harvest section. The waters of the Nantahala tumble and froth, giving the trout plenty of room to hide. Just downstream of White Oak Creek, the Nantahala flows through a small gorge. In high water, this section should be reserved for whitewater steep-creek paddlers, as the water is too fast to fish and too dangerous to wade. Even at regular water levels, a wrong step in this stretch could mean an uncertain ride through boulder-riddled whitewater chutes.

As expected, the gorge section does not receive as much pressure as the lower river, where roadside pullouts are just a few steps from the water's edge. A short, steep hike is required to reach the water here, but it is not difficult if you follow established paths and are careful on your way down. Dark, deep plunge pools tail out into shallow glides before narrowing and spilling through granite boulders. It is a quiet stretch, away from the road, and one of the most likely places you'll have water to yourself if the river is crowded. Getting from one plunge pool to another requires a bit of rock hopping, but the rewards are less harrowed trout and a chance at some of the larger rainbows in the delayed-harvest section.

An angler finds solitude on the Nantahala above the powerhouse. Fishing the upper Nantahala during the week is a good way to beat the crowds common on most weekends.
LOUIS CAHILL

In the delayed-harvest section, the Nantahala is a relatively small river, around 15 to 20 feet wide in most areas, but it lacks much of the canopy found on mountain streams of similar size, making for easier fly casting than on most other high mountain streams. This, combined with the ease of access along with heavy stocking by the North Carolina Division of Water Resources (DWR) from October through May, makes the Nantahala delayed-harvest season one of the most popular destinations in the state for fly anglers. On a good day, those who actually count every fish they catch report upwards of 50-fish days.

Following the first stockings in October, anglers begin to appear in the pull-offs along Wayah Road, rigging rods and donning waders. Now begins the parade. Weekends and holidays are by far the most crowded, but even during the week you should never expect to have the river to yourself. Etiquette is paramount when fishing these conditions, and you should always give your angling brethren a wide berth when visiting the river. A little courtesy goes a long way, as you may be the person who needs to be fished around in the next run.

Early in the delayed-harvest season through the end of November, usually following the first hard frosts, brown trout begin nosing upstream into the delayed-harvest waters. These browns, residents of the lower tailwater most of the year, enter the upper section above the powerhouse. Wearing the colors of fall, these fish—some pushing 20-plus inches—are cannibals, not to be swayed by a dry fly or small nymph. Most anglers never see these fish. They are skittish and will bolt at the sight of an angler moving near the river's edge. Stealth is paramount, so save the bright colors for the guys in the magazine photo shoots and dress down in neutral colors. Carefully approaching likely big-brown lies, such as undercut rock ledges, deep pools, and the edges of long, sweeping runs, will get you in the game.

If this talk of big brown trout gets your blood up, let me say this. To go looking for just prespawn browns on the river would sacrifice some good fishing, so it's best to approach every deep run or pool carefully and cast larger streamers only in the more likely spots. Flies 3 to 5 inches long are not too brazen for this type of work, and you will find that the larger brook and rainbow trout will attack these large baitfish patterns the same as a big brown.

December through February is a bit of a crapshoot. The hand of winter can set in for days at a time, locking the stream down, glassing over boulders with sheets of ice, and bringing heavy winds, sleet, and snow. Cold weather, aside from the obvious hazards when mixed with bad weather, will shut the fishing down until the system moves out.

Cold winter days will find you spoon-feeding the few trout that are even remotely interested in feeding. Clear water does little to cloak scores of trout holding in the deeper slots and pools, but no amount of coaxing will elicit a strike on the coldest days of the year. You are far better off watching for a break in the weather, when the temperatures rise above average levels, to make the drive.

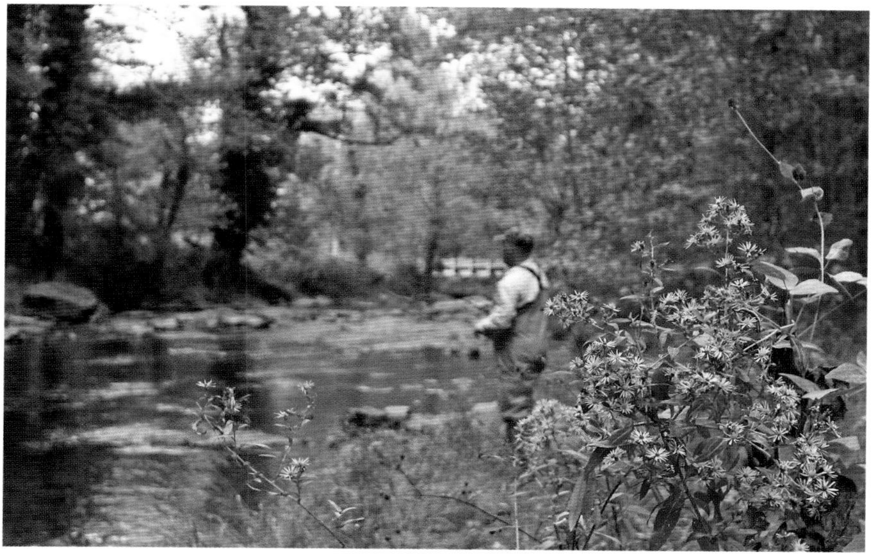

The Nantahala delayed-harvest section parallels the road for its entire length, but when you step into the water you feel miles away. The "DH" stretch is a good place to catch three species of trout in one day: brook, rainbow, and brown trout.

Warm winter days will put a bit of pluck in the fish and encourage a few bugs to hatch. Small cream midges and *Baetis* are sure to be out, if not in droves, then in numbers enough to give the trout something to look at. Small dry flies (#18-22) in the appropriate colors will pick up the risers. For the deeper runs or in the odd case that the trout are simply not rising, large Stalcup's Tungsten Rubber-Legged Stonefly nymphs (#8-22) trailing a midge larva such as a Smethurst's Answer, Egan's Rainbow Warrior, or Rojo Midge (#18-22) are all good bets.

March and April are fickle months in the mountains. It can be hot and sunny, or a fresh pack of snow can arrive overnight. The trout are beginning to transition out of their wintertime feeding periods and starting to look up with greater frequency. Hendricksons, Quill Gordons, and March Browns hatch erratically during this early spring transition. Matching the hatch is not as important as getting the correct size and profile. A good supply of Parachute Adams (#12-18) will fool almost any trout in the river during any of these hatches. Dropping a Beadhead Pheasant Tail off the back is a good insurance policy for those trout waffling on making the trip up to take the dry off the surface.

Later in the spring, the trees are laden with their spring coats, and the temperatures are consistently warm to downright hot. Most anglers have stowed their waders, and rain showers are a welcome sight. Starting in May Yellow Sallies and caddis turn the river into a dry-fly angler's dream. In fact, the river receives one of the best caddis hatches anywhere in the mountains, their drunken mothlike flights hovering over the river nearly every evening.

Make sure to have plenty of the tried-and-true Elk-Hair Caddis (#14-16) in tan and cream stuck in your box, along with some Stimulators (#10-14) and Sulphur A. K.'s Parachutes (#14-18). If you begin having trouble feeding rising trout, rigging a tandem dry-fly rig with a Yellow Sally or Elk-Hair Caddis as the point fly with a smaller midge or mayfly off the back will usually turn things around. For one reason or another, Nantahala trout are suckers for something small and floating, even when the little guys are not coming off.

Nymph fishing is good throughout the spring until the end of the season, but with such wonderful dry-fly action, I don't know why anyone would rather watch an indicator bob along. The exception would be after a rain, when the water is high and discolored. Heavy stonefly nymphs or weighted streamers will pry trout out of their high-water lies during these spring spates. Streamer patterns such as Beldar Buggers, Bellyache Minnows, and Whitlock's NearNuff Sculpins (#4-8) are all good bets when the water is dropping as well as in the last few hours of daylight when the river is flowing at normal levels. Swinging a baitfish pattern through some of the Nantahala's deeper runs may get you hooked up with trout you'd otherwise never see.

In June, the delayed-harvest season ends and the river is inundated with bait and spin fishers bound to bring home dinner. The trout are all but caught out, those surviving the carnage escaping to the lower tailwater downstream to weather the heat of the summer and hopefully survive for seasons to come.

Tailwater

Known more for its whitewater slalom course and rubber raft hatches, the tailrace of the Nantahala is something of an oddity. Located downstream of the delayed-harvest stretch, roughly 8 river miles below Nantahala Dam, the tailrace is formed by a unique flume that carries water from the dam, 6 miles across the mountains, and into the powerhouse. Here, the water is reunited with the riverbed via a short spillway, pumping an influx of cold 45-degree water into the system.

The spillway joins the riverbed just above the commercial raft launch on Wayah Road directly downstream of the delayed-harvest boundary. Downstream from the powerhouse to Wesser Falls, the river is open under North Carolina's hatchery-supported program. It receives a healthy stocking of rainbows throughout the year, and according to the regulations is closed the entire month of March. Brown and rainbow trout flourish here in the tailrace, some growing to impressive sizes thanks to the rich biomass sustained by the nutrient-laden water piped across the mountain from the lake.

When the turbines are silent, the lower Nantahala tailwater is a small stream flowing through the middle of a notably larger riverbed. High-water marks are clearly visible on the banks and boulders, reminding you of the awesome power that is housed behind those floodgates. The water is low and

Running the Class III rapids is half the fun when fishing the lower river, but when you can, pull off and nymph the good looking runs. High water calls for streamers fished on sinking-tip lines and heavily weighted nymph rigs to get down to where the big boys live.

clear as a sommelier's tasting glass, creating an angling environment rivaling a spring creek. The majority of fish here are on the smaller side, a mixture of wild and stocked fish in the 9- to 12-inch range. Don't let their diminutive size put you off, as they are wary for their age. These prodigious adolescents have adapted to their crystalline college of evolution and are working on their PhDs long before their older and larger cousins.

During low water, midges provide forage for the trout year-round. Keep a separate box full of midge dry flies, emergers, and larvae because chances are you're gonna need them. The cold water discharged from the powerhouse, combined with the scouring nature of the releases, makes the tiny midge king on this tailwater. Mayflies and caddis do show up, but they do not hatch in significant numbers.

Since you're fishing serenely calm water with tiny flies, long leaders—at least 12 feet, preferably 15 to 17 feet and tapering down to 6X—are a necessity. The trout spook at even the minuscule shadow of a thin leader passing

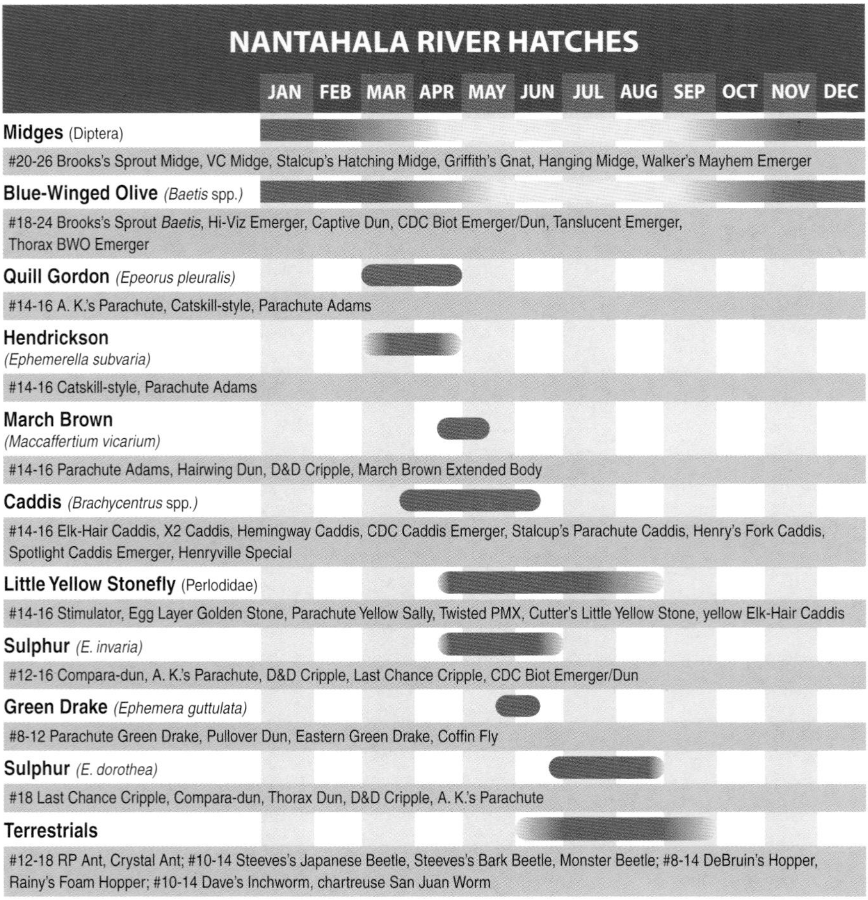
NANTAHALA RIVER HATCHES
JAN FEB MAR APR MAY JUN JUL AUG SEP OCT NOV DEC
Midges (Diptera)
#20-26 Brooks's Sprout Midge, VC Midge, Stalcup's Hatching Midge, Griffith's Gnat, Hanging Midge, Walker's Mayhem Emerger
Blue-Winged Olive (Baetis spp.)
#18-24 Brooks's Sprout Baetis, Hi-Viz Emerger, Captive Dun, CDC Biot Emerger/Dun, Tanslucent Emerger, Thorax BWO Emerger
Quill Gordon (Epeorus pleuralis)
#14-16 A. K.'s Parachute, Catskill-style, Parachute Adams
Hendrickson (Ephemerella subvaria)
#14-16 Catskill-style, Parachute Adams
March Brown (Maccaffertium vicarium)
#14-16 Parachute Adams, Hairwing Dun, D&D Cripple, March Brown Extended Body
Caddis (Brachycentrus spp.)
#14-16 Elk-Hair Caddis, X2 Caddis, Hemingway Caddis, CDC Caddis Emerger, Stalcup's Parachute Caddis, Henry's Fork Caddis, Spotlight Caddis Emerger, Henryville Special
Little Yellow Stonefly (Perlodidae)
#14-16 Stimulator, Egg Layer Golden Stone, Parachute Yellow Sally, Twisted PMX, Cutter's Little Yellow Stone, yellow Elk-Hair Caddis
Sulphur (E. invaria)
#12-16 Compara-dun, A. K.'s Parachute, D&D Cripple, Last Chance Cripple, CDC Biot Emerger/Dun
Green Drake (Ephemera guttulata)
#8-12 Parachute Green Drake, Pullover Dun, Eastern Green Drake, Coffin Fly
Sulphur (E. dorothea)
#18 Last Chance Cripple, Compara-dun, Thorax Dun, D&D Cripple, A. K.'s Parachute
Terrestrials
#12-18 RP Ant, Crystal Ant; #10-14 Steeves's Japanese Beetle, Steeves's Bark Beetle, Monster Beetle; #8-14 DeBruin's Hopper, Rainy's Foam Hopper; #10-14 Dave's Inchworm, chartreuse San Juan Worm

overhead. Ripples made when wading into position will also wreck your chances, so be overly cautious when you approach.

When the midges begin coming off, usually following the end of water release, tie on a small midge emerger such as VC Midge, Walker's Mayhem Emerger, or Brooks's Sprout Midge (#20-26) once you spot a pod of rising trout. Make a few passes through the trout and judge their response. If they shy away or refuse your offering several times but continue to rise, change flies. Showing them the same fly time and again will only put them down.

If no fish are spotted rising, try going subsurface with a tiny midge larva such as a Zebra Midge, Thread Midge, Smethurst's Answer, or UV Z-Midge (#20-26). Forget beadhead patterns here, folks, unless they have black beads or some other neutral color other than bright gold. Cast well above the trout, and use an indicator only if absolutely necessary. You are much better off greasing all but the last 6 or 7 feet of your leader and watching the line closely. If an indicator is necessary, use something small and white to mimic the bubbles floating on the river's surface. It's not easy work, but it can be rewarding.

As daylight fades, the valley becomes shrouded in the darkest of dark, the moon's rays having the same trouble as the sun. Fishing at night on the Nantahala requires some serious dedication. Being alone in the dark, the sound of the river drowning out everything around you, is an eerie feeling, especially when you know what the water looks like during the day when the turbines are on. I often find myself looking upstream in the darkness, thinking I hear the water getting louder as an unscheduled release of whitewater comes crashing down on me.

Night fishing on the river puts you at an advantage when chasing the big brown trout. A favorite way to fish for these bruisers is to cast a large mouse pattern against the opposite bank and retrieve it across the river, passing over deep runs and pools. You can't see well, but can detect the strikes by the unmistakable "sluuurrrrp" followed by a tight line and screaming reel. It doesn't happen often, but it happens just enough to keep you going back for more.

High water will make you think twice about fishing the lower Nantahala. During the late spring and summer months, rafts, canoes, and kayaks begin a steady parade downstream from the launch just below the powerhouse as soon as the river has reached full pool. This continues until the last commercial trips launch around 3 PM. The water is usually shut off around 5 PM each day, giving the boaters a few hours to play before the waters recede downstream and transform the raging torrent into a mild-mannered creek.

Wade access is available, but limited. It consists mostly of wading on narrow, shallow shelves where churning rapids dump into long pools. Accessing these areas off Highway 19 is relatively easy, as there are numerous roadside pull-offs with trails leading to the river's edge. Extreme caution should be taken when wading. The water is pushy and cold, and one wrong step could result in a bad trip downstream.

Although bugs come off in high water, the trout pay them little mind. Casting large attractor patterns to the banks can pay off, especially in the warmer months from May through early September. Chernobyl Ants, Wulffs, and Stimulators (#4-10) will draw explosive strikes, some trout rocketing up from the bottom and slamming the fly with unbridled aggression.

Wade anglers would be better served fishing heavily weighted nymph rigs under indicators, or streamer patterns on short, sinking-head lines. A large stonefly pattern such as a Delektable Stone or Stalcup's Tungsten Golden Stone (#4-10), trailing a Pheasant Tail, Prince Nymph, Copper John, or San Juan Worm (#12-14), especially in the slower pools, fished with several pieces of size BB split-shot make up a typical high-water Nantahala rig. The drifts are short, so getting the fly down quickly is necessary to hook up.

Streamers fished on a short, 10- to 15-foot type 6-8 sinking line can be difficult, but the payoff is well worth the tangled lines and snagged tree limbs.

Walker's Mayhem Emerger

Hook:	#20-24 Daiichi 1170
Thread:	Black 8/0
Tail:	White Z-lon
Body:	Tying thread
Rib:	Silver Ultra Wire (extra small)
Thorax:	Peacock herl
Wingcase:	Razor Foam

Stalcup's Tungsten Golden Stone

Hook:	#8-12 Daiichi 1730
Bead:	Gold metal
Thread:	Yellow 6/0
Tail:	Yellow goose biots
Body:	Yellow goose biot
Thorax:	Yellow ostrich herl
Legs:	Rubber
Wingcase:	Medallion Sheeting
Antennae:	Goose biots

Big brown trout call this water home, and there is no better way to feed them than with Galloup's Fatheads, Beldar Buggers, and Sculpzillas (#1/0-2). Keep the colors simple: black, yellow, and white. Yellow is by far my favorite streamer color on the river in the fall and early spring, but the color matters less than how the fly is fished. Cast directly across, maybe even a bit upstream in the faster runs, then mend the line staas it passes by to really get the fly down. As the line tightens, slowly strip the fly back, or simply let it swing much as in steelhead or salmon fishing. Just be ready for the tug, because you're going to need a quick hook-set to keep the trout on once it eats.

It is possible to float and fish during high water, but this is not for the ill-equipped or inexperienced boater. For most, negotiating the whitewater slalom of boulders and haystack rapids is enough, let alone trying to fish. Floating and fishing the lower river in high water is a two-person job—one rowing, one fishing. It is a state of controlled chaos, one angler casting quickly at targets zooming by while another pulls hard on the oars, trying to avoid rocks and other boats and to set up for the next chute.

When my friends and I float the lower river, we usually trade off, with one rowing and whoever is sitting in the front of the raft fishing. There are a few places to anchor up and fish, but mostly it's a partnership of logistics as we punch through standing waves and bounce off the occasional rock. Large rafts, preferably self-bailing and with fishing/rowing frames, are well suited for this type of work. My boat is an AIRE Super Duper Puma 14-foot self-bailing raft with a custom rowing/fishing frame. Keep spare oars and blades within easy reach and your life jackets cinched down tight.

If you're looking for an adventurous float and are either an experienced boater who doesn't mind rowing all day, or have a good friend with a boat who accepts bribes, the trip is one of the coolest floats in the South. Launching at the public raft/canoe launch just below the commercial ramp directly below the powerhouse, the float is about 7 miles in length. Plan on at least five hours to fish it well, covering as much water as possible. Ideally, floating anglers would want to launch just after the last commercial trips pass the ramp. This will let you miss the bulk of the daily flotilla and give you enough time to fish the water before it begins to bottom out.

In high water, you are looking for prime trout lies, just as you would in a river or creek following a high-water event. Look for any slow-moving water—tailouts of rapids, slack water near deep, rocky banks, and side channels should all be given special attention. Many of the larger trout we've seen have been holding in the large pools that dot the river between rapids. Unlike wading, you've got the entire river at your disposal, and many times you only get one shot at a prime lie. Pick your shots and have rods that will load quickly and put the fly out with minimal false casting.

From the boat, fishing streamers is far and away the most effective method. Bringing out the big guns—8-weight or even 9-weight rods with 300-grain sinking heads—gets you in the door. Now, you have to hit targets the size of a basketball with heavy lines and big flies, all without falling out of the boat in Class III whitewater. It's not for everyone, but for those of us who are crazy enough to try it, it is highly addictive.

The takeout for the lower river is located just upstream of Nantahala Outdoor Center in Wesser, North Carolina. Passing the Outdoor Center will put you in a whitewater slalom course, then over Wesser Falls. Both are bad mistakes. If you've never floated the river before, go with a guided whitewater float a few times to get a lay of the land.

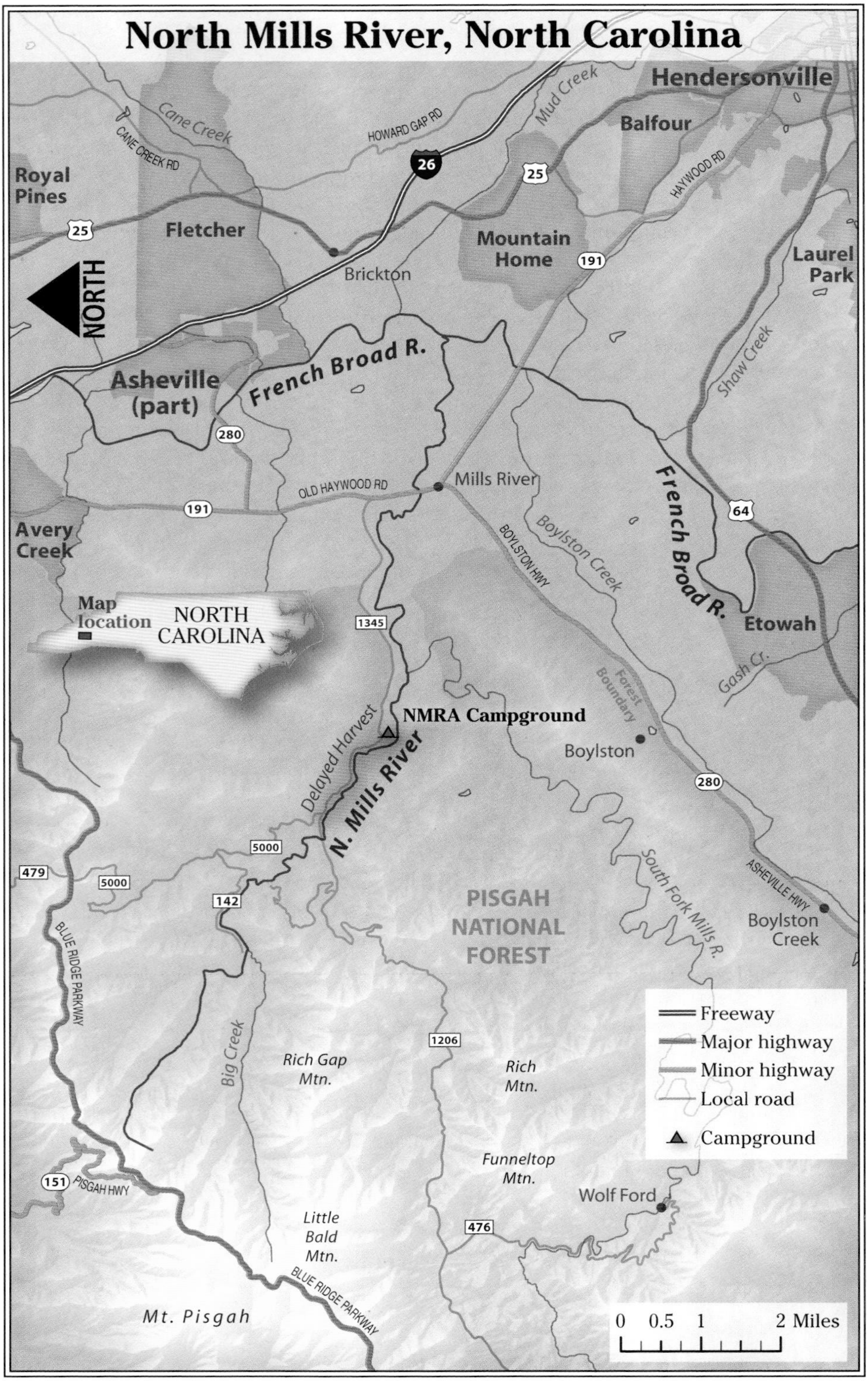
North Mills River, North Carolina
Hendersonville
Mud Creek
Cane Creek
HOWARD GAP RD
CANE CREEK RD
26
Balfour
25
Royal Pines
HAYWOOD RD
25
Fletcher
Mountain Home
191
Laurel Park
Brickton
NORTH
Shaw Creek
French Broad R.
Asheville (part)
280
Mills River
OLD HAYWOOD RD
191
French Broad R.
64
Boylston Creek
BOYLSTON HWY
Avery Creek
Etowah
Map location
NORTH CAROLINA
1345
Gash Cr.
Forest Boundary
NMRA Campground
Delayed Harvest
Boylston
N. Mills River
280
5000
479
5000
ASHEVILLE HWY
142
PISGAH NATIONAL FOREST
South Fork Mills R.
Boylston Creek
BLUE RIDGE PARKWAY
Freeway
Major highway
Minor highway
Local road
Campground
Big Creek
1206
Rich Gap Mtn.
Rich Mtn.
Funneltop Mtn.
151
PISGAH HWY
Wolf Ford
476
Little Bald Mtn.
BLUE RIDGE PARKWAY
Mt. Pisgah
0 0.5 1 2 Miles

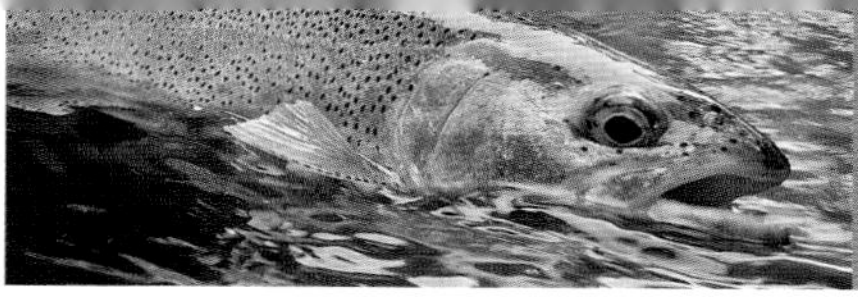

CHAPTER 8

North Mills River

Narrow and tumbling, the North Mills typifies a mountain stream. Fished more or less exclusively during the state's delayed-harvest season, the North Mills is second only to the Davidson in popularity in this neck of the woods. More of a creek than a river, the narrow, 4-mile stretch that falls under the delayed-harvest regulations can become crowded on weekends and holidays, but most folks understand the pressure, and working around fellow anglers isn't much of a hassle. The number of trout in the North Mills is the river's draw. During the delayed-harvest season, the state stocks roughly 2,000 fish per month into the stream. Many of these trout are around 12 inches, but many larger fish are planted as well. The North Mills is teeming with brook and rainbow trout, a few pushing 20 inches, and anglers can find eager fish pretty much from the lake downstream to the end of the delayed-harvest water.

Because the river is an easy drive from Asheville, even weekdays tend to see their fair share of anglers wading the North Mills. If the Davidson is not fishing well or is out of shape, figure on even more anglers descending on the narrow stream. Because of its numbers of fish and beauty, a lot of anglers flock to this small Tarheel stream.

The delayed-harvest water begins at the base of Hendersonville Reservoir's dam and extends downstream to just below the North Mills Recreation Area Campground. Needless to say, the area around the campground, extending upstream to the North Mills Road bridge, receives the most pressure. But with nearly 4 miles of water to explore, there is plenty of room to leave the crowds behind.

Upstream from the bridge to Hendersonville Reservoir, the river can only be accessed via a walking trail that runs the length of the upper river. A parking lot at the top just below the lake and downstream at the bridge offers a

There is no reason to cast more than a few feet of line on the North Mills. The most common mistake on this and other small streams is to cast too far when just a few feet will get you to the trout.

jumping-off point for anglers hiking upstream. The trail parallels the river and is an easy walk, but keep an eye out for snakes, since the region has a tendency to produce some large timber rattlers. Normally this is not something to be too concerned with, but it's always better to be safe than sorry.

The North Mills tumbles over the North Carolina backcountry, dropping from pocketwater runs into plunge pools that can hold dozens of trout. Much of the river is flanked by an overhanging canopy that makes casting a challenge, but there is not much need for more than a few feet of line to be out past the tip-top. Most anglers I see on small creeks and rivers like the North Mills try to cast too far. Fishing short, just as you should on any mountain stream of this nature, is going to serve you better than stripping line off the reel and going for yards. Even if the trout in the North Mills do not possess the near paranoid nature of those in the Davidson, they will still spook if line is slapped on their faces after a poorly executed cast.

At the beginning of the delayed-harvest season in October, the North Mills fishes best along the lower section and up near the lake. The entire fishery is based on state stockings, so for the first few weeks focus on areas where the state plants the fish. This sounds artificial and to an extent it is, but it is the reality of the North Mills, as with many seasonal delayed-harvest streams. Anglers visiting the river don't mind, and those who do are quickly dissuaded by the beauty of the setting where all this takes place. Pretty much anything will work for the first few weeks, but Y2K Bugs, San Juan Worms, and Lightning Bugs (#14-16) are good bets.

As the season progresses, the trout begin spreading throughout the watershed, and fishing is equally good from bottom to top. November through early March can bring some bitter weather or warmer than normal temperatures. Freezing weather will put even the most aggressive trout down, but if the mercury rises above 40, then game on. Stonefly patterns, midges, and tiny mayfly nymphs make up forage for the trout, so make sure your box has likenesses of all. In addition to the bright, flashy flies of the early season, Pheasant Tails, Copper Johns, and Split Case PMDs (#14-16) along with Kevin's Stone and Stalcup's Tungsten Rubber-Legged Stone (#8-12) and a variety of midge patterns (#18-20) are all complementary to the glitter flies commonly associated with delayed-harvest water. These nymphs will work all season long on the North Mills, and can be a lifesaver even on those rare spring days when you can't seem to raise a fish on a dry.

Spring brings sporadic hatches, but it only takes a few insects to get the fish looking up. The hatches on the North Mills closely mirror those on the Davidson, just a short distance over the mountain. Some anglers, frustrated by the fickle trout of the Davidson, will make the half-hour drive to the North Mills for "easier" fish.

From mid-March through the end of the delayed-harvest season, you should never be without a dry fly on the end of your leader on the North Mills unless there is high water. Even if you are just using the dry as a strike indicator for a nymph, the trout will fool you with how many times they slash at the dry. Even if the hatches are not as heavy nor as reliable as on the Davidson, the trout on the North Mills seem to be far more cooperative despite the small numbers of insects fluttering about.

Hendricksons and Quill Gordons begin hatching in late February or early March, but their numbers are few, and in some years a hatch may not even be recognizable. Usually, a few traditional Catskill-style dry flies

NORTH MILLS RIVER HATCHES

	JAN	FEB	MAR	APR	MAY	JUN	JUL	AUG	SEP	OCT	NOV	DEC
Midges (Diptera)	■	■	■	■	■	■	■	■	■	■	■	■
Blue-Winged Olive (Baetis spp.)	■	■	■	■	■	■	■	■	■	■	■	■
Blue Quill (Paraleptophlebia adoptiva)			■									
Quill Gordon (Epeorus pleuralis)			■									
Black Caddis (Chimarra spp.)					■							
March Brown (Maccaffertium vicarium)					■							
Caddis (Various spp.)					■	■						
Sulphur (E. invaria)						■						
Green Drake (Ephemera guttulata)						■						
Light Cahill (Stenacron interpunctatum)							■	■				
Yellow Sally Stonefly (Perlodidae)							■	■				
Terrestrials							■	■	■			
October Caddis (Pycnopsyche spp.)										■	■	

Midges (Diptera)
#18-26 Stalcup's Hatching Midge, Brooks's Sprout Midge, Hanging Midge, Griffith's Gnat, Walker's Mayhem Emerger, VC Midge

Blue-Winged Olive (Baetis spp.)
#16-24 Brooks's Sprout *Baetis*, CDC Biot Emerger/Dun, Last Chance Cripple, Translucent Emerger, CDC Compara-dun, Thorax BWO Emerger, Hi-Viz Emerger

Blue Quill (Paraleptophlebia adoptiva)
#18 Catskill-style, A. K.'s Parachute, Tilt Wing Dun

Quill Gordon (Epeorus pleuralis)
#14-16 A. K.'s Parachute, Catskill-style

Black Caddis (Chimarra spp.)
#14-18 Elk-Hair Caddis, CDC Caddis Emerger, X2 Caddis, Henry's Fork Caddis, Iris Caddis

March Brown (Maccaffertium vicarium)
#14-16 Parachute Adams, Hairwing Dun, D&D Cripple, Harrop CDC Biot Emerger/Dun

Caddis (Various spp.)
#14-16 CDC Caddis Emerger, CDC Fertile Caddis, X2 Caddis, Stalcup's Parachute Caddis Emerger, Henry's Fork Caddis, Hemingway Caddis

Sulphur (E. invaria)
#12-16 CDC and hairwing Compara-duns, A. K.'s Parachute, D&D Cripple, Last Chance Cripple, Spotlight Emerger, Sulphur Pullover Dun, Rusty Spinner

Green Drake (Ephemera guttulata)
#8-10 Parachute Green Drake, Eastern Green Drake, Pullover Dun, Extended Body Parachute, Coffin Fly

Light Cahill (Stenacron interpunctatum)
#14-18 D&D Cripple, A. K.'s Parachute, Compara-dun

Yellow Sally Stonefly (Perlodidae)
#14-16 Twisted PMX, Egg Layer Golden Stone, Parachute Yellow Sally, Cutter's Little Golden Stone, yellow Elk-Hair Caddis

Terrestrials
#14-18 RP Ant, Crystal Ant; #10-14 Steeves's Japanese Beetle, Steeves's Bark Beetle, Monster Beetle; #8-14 DeBruin's Hopper, Rainy's Foam Hopper; #10-14 Dave's Inchworm, chartreuse San Juan Worm

October Caddis (Pycnopsyche spp.)
#8-14 Pulsating Caddis, X2 Caddis, Stimulator

matching the early mayfly duo will be all you need, but the trout are just as likely to eat a Parachute Adams of a similar size to the hatching insects than a species-specific pattern. There's no reason to go crazy matching the hatch here, but it can be fun trying.

Later in the spring, Light Cahills, Yellow Sallies, and Sulphurs hatch on and off from around April through the end of the delayed-harvest season on June 1. As with the earlier mayflies, matching the exact fly isn't crucial, but you want to be in the ballpark. You can't go wrong with a good supply of Elk-

Hair Caddis (#14-16), parachute-style Light Cahills (#12-16), Sulphur Compara-duns (#14-18), and Parachute Adams (#12-18). Throw in a few Yellow Sally parachute patterns (#12-14) to round things out until the end of the season and call it good.

In addition to the mayflies, terrestrials are a staple for the trout on the North Mills. Crickets, inchworms, beetles, and grasshoppers all find their way into the river, and the trout capitalize on the helplessness of these insects, leisurely plucking them from the surface. Around the campground, hoppers can be seen floating in the river, but not for long before a mouth pops up from below and slurps down the wildly kicking bug. When you start to see hoppers in the grass or ants crawling around the mountain laurel blooms, tie on a Rainy's Foam Hopper (#10-12), Steeves's Firefly (#14), or flying ant imitation (#14-18). If you don't see a trout rising, don't worry. One of these flies will talk more than a few into coming up to say hello.

Rains are a heavy factor in the spring. Too little and the fish are stacked in the deeper pockets and pools like clowns in a circus car. A few may eat, but after you burn a pod, you'd better move on. Going to smaller flies, especially

Every piece of likely holding water in the North Mills probably holds a trout . . . or two.

midge larvae and mayfly nymphs (#18-22) is advisable during low water. Use a small, muted color dry such as a Parachute Adams, Quill Gordon, or Thunderhead (#16-18) as the indicator, trailing the smaller nymph off the back.

In low water, approach large pools with care, using the foliage and trees for camouflage. Do not wear brightly colored clothing. The trout will be skittish in low water, and there are several pairs of eyes watching for trouble. Keep your casts short and try not to line the trout. All it takes is one blown cast or a single trout spotting you to spook the entire pod before your fly ever touches the water.

Rain breathes life into the river, unless you're on the water just after the rain. The tumbling currents fill the streambed to the mountain laurel, displacing both fish and anglers until the levels drop back to a more manageable

The section below the lake downstream to the first bridge is a fine representation of an Appalachian trout stream. Laurel-choked banks make for tight casting, so practice your roll casts and bow and arrow casts to get the fly where it needs to be, which is on the water, not in the bushes.

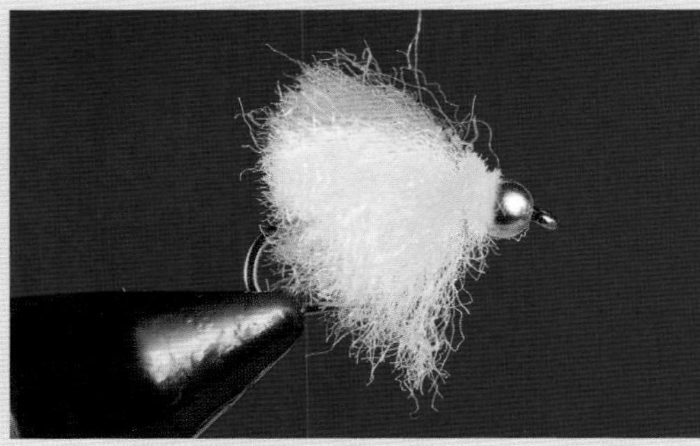

Y2K Bug

Hook: #10-12 Daiichi 1120
Bead: Gold metal
Thread: 70-denier Ultra Thread
Body: Pink and chartreuse Egg Yarn

level. Following spring rains, streamer fishing downstream and across pools and deeper runs is the most effective method. White and chartreuse Woolly Buggers, Beldar Buggers, Sculpzillas, and Zonkers (#6-10) will tempt trout, even in higher flows. When fishing higher water levels, make sure to watch your step. The North Mills can become a raging torrent quickly, and while its not particularly dangerous, a broken leg can seriously cut into fishing time.

It may be somewhat artificial, but hey, there's nothing artificial about admiring a gorgeous trout as it dances on the end of your line. Take it for what it is and have fun. Besides, a few trout on the North Mills can be just the ticket after getting your butt kicked on the Davidson.

Big Snowbird Creek, North Carolina

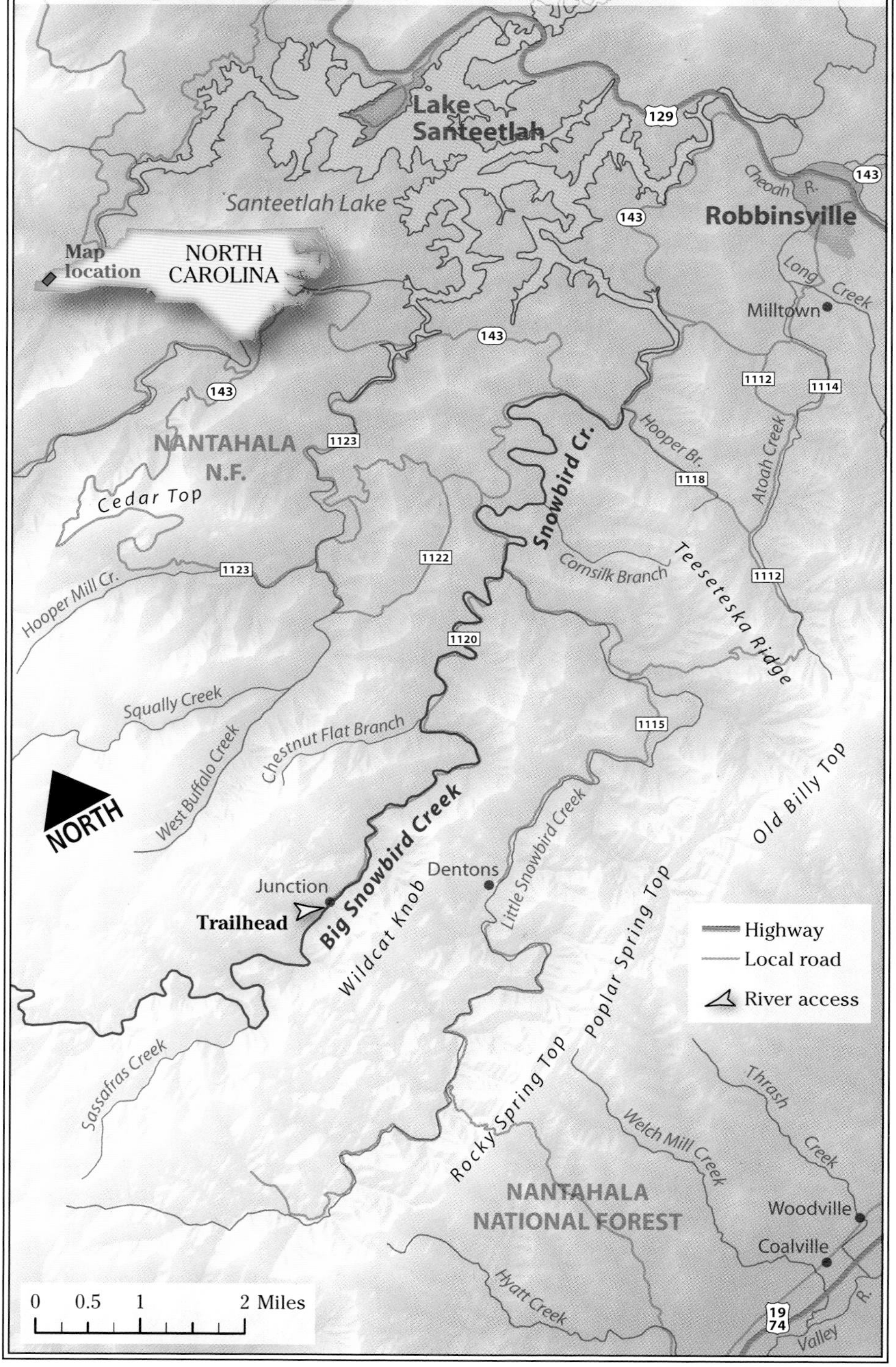

CHAPTER 9

Big Snowbird Creek

You work past burning legs, the lactic acid building as you pump away down the path. You think you've been walking forever. It's only been an hour, maybe more, but you're not even to the second falls, and tender feet are beginning to show wear. I'm not sure where a walk becomes a hike, but it becomes evident somewhere after the first blister wears through. Nothing in life worth having comes easy, and that makes Big Snowbird Creek a blessing for those of us who prefer a campfire to central heat.

Luckily the walk is not a steep one, mostly a gentle incline along an old railroad bed that leads you to this special place. The burden of a pack should be penance enough to ensure good fishing, but probably is not. It's a long walk, saturated by a green canopy that cups the trail. The sound of rushing water tempts from below, and in places the river gives you glimpses through the laurel, yet you press on. Not far enough. Keep walking. Finally, you're there, in the way back, a trip paid in full with stone bruises and sweat. You've bought brook trout the old-fashioned way. Get to work, you've still gotta make camp.

One of the last refuges for the Southern brook trout, Big Snowbird Creek is a mecca for spec chasers. The brookies here are larger than average, usually running around 7 or 8 inches in length. The dream of catching a true Southern brook trout over 10 inches is not out of the question. For those of you who may not know about the Southern brook trout, the average fish encountered is typically around 6 to 8 inches in length, maybe less, so a brook trout 10 inches or better is treated with the same revelry as a 22-inch brown trout caught on a dry using 7X tippet. Bring a camera.

The creek is not for the weary, requiring a 5-mile hike from the parking area at the Junction to the first set of waterfalls to reach the brook trout water. This is the minimum distance you must hike to expect to find brookies in

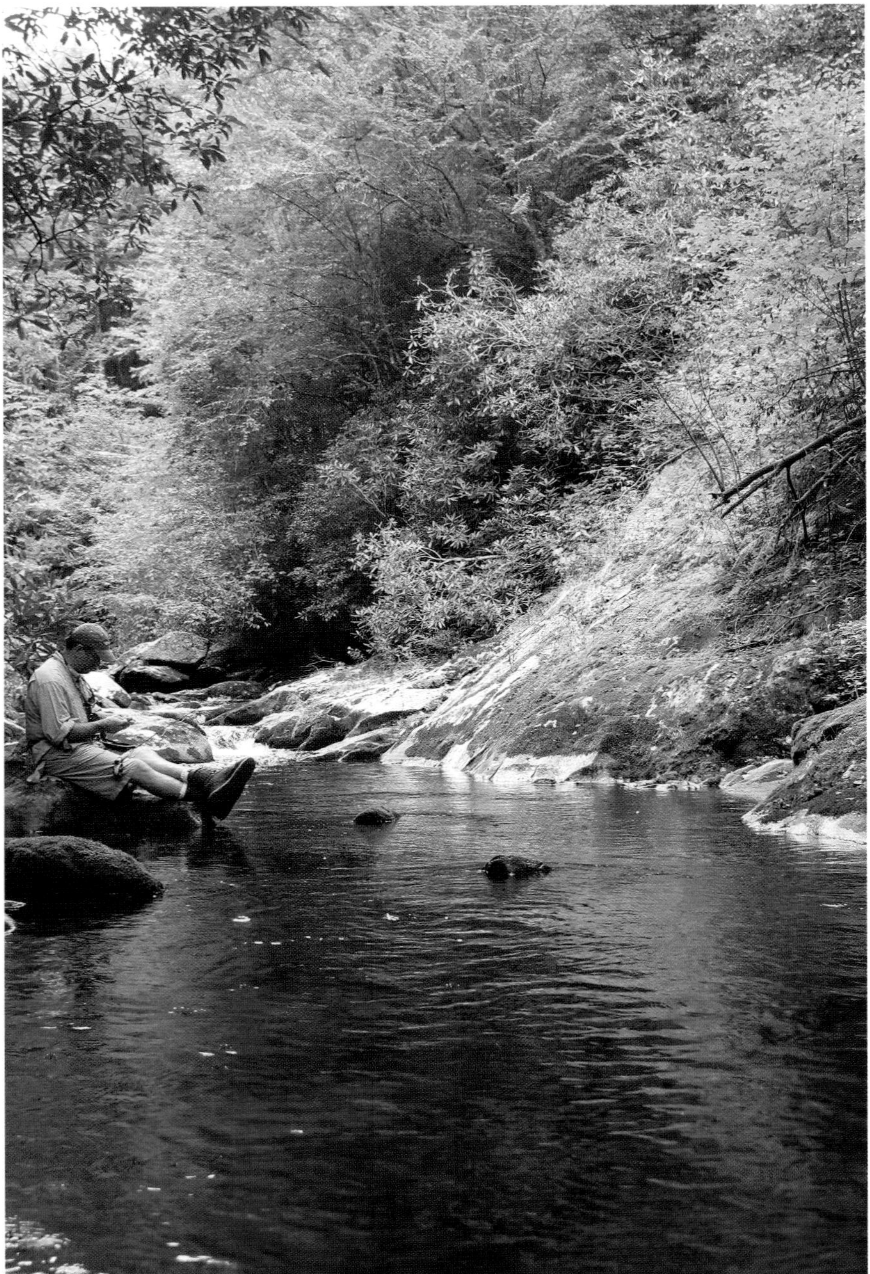

Plunge pools and long, deep runs often hold large numbers of trout. Once you catch a couple of fish, give the pool a break for a few minutes. The trout will settle down and you'll probably coax a few more into biting.

Brightly colored, wild, and pure Southern brook trout are what every angler coming to Big Snowbird is looking for.

good numbers. Below the falls, rainbows are the predominant species, giving way to larger brown trout as the water cascades down to Lake Santeetlah.

Fishing below the first falls (the line of demarcation separating brook trout from the rest of the lot) can be good, and there some large trout show up every season. Holding mostly rainbows from the first falls downstream to the Junction parking lot, the river winds through a maze of rock, making wading difficult. The rainbows are usually on the smaller side, but feisty. Once you get below the Junction parking lot, roadside access is abundant, and the mix of brown and rainbow trout begins to even out. Numerous camping sites are located on the lower river above the Junction of Little Snowbird.

When traveling up the river, past the campsites, you'll often see successful anglers cooking a few of their day's catch. Some anglers frown on this, believing that catch-and-release is always best with trout, but I am somewhat torn, lying in the no-man's-land of moral duress. There is something arousing about the smell of campfire smoke wafting through the hemlocks, the smell of a freshly cooked meal of trout and cornbread aromatically linking days gone by to the present.

From above the first falls to the headwaters, around 7 miles, brook trout find a life without the nuisance of the more invasive rainbow and the carnivorous brown. It is big water by brook trout standards, yet another anomaly of the watershed. Anglers who typically wedge 6-foot rods through tightly woven labyrinths of mountain laurel find longer rods and the necessity of a backcast welcome beneath the high canopy of oak trees and conifers.

From the first set of falls to the second, there are numerous existing camping sites, and you are free to make camp in a clearing of your own discovery so long as it is at least 50 feet from the water. The trail follows the creek for most of the way, but bushwhacking is necessary to get through the thick screen. Your best bet is to find a narrow trail leading to the river, then wade upstream until you can find another trail leading out, or backtrack to your point of entry. Otherwise, you can be crawling on your hands and knees and patching waders when you're back at camp instead of tying flies.

Once you reach the second falls, the trail begins to narrow and the creek shrinks to a size more recognizable among brook trout anglers. The fishing doesn't stop here, but the long walk required to reach this remote stretch keeps the pressure down. If you decide to make the walk up and fish the water between the second and third falls, you will find cold, spotted surprises in nearly every likely spot.

Big Snowbird is a magical place. A river so large teeming with wild brook trout so far removed from civilization could be seen as nothing different. In springtime, after the first thaw, the brookies of Snowbird will make you feel like the single best fly angler in the world. They rise to dry flies, and if you are so inclined, will take nymphs like a dog waiting on a well-deserved treat.

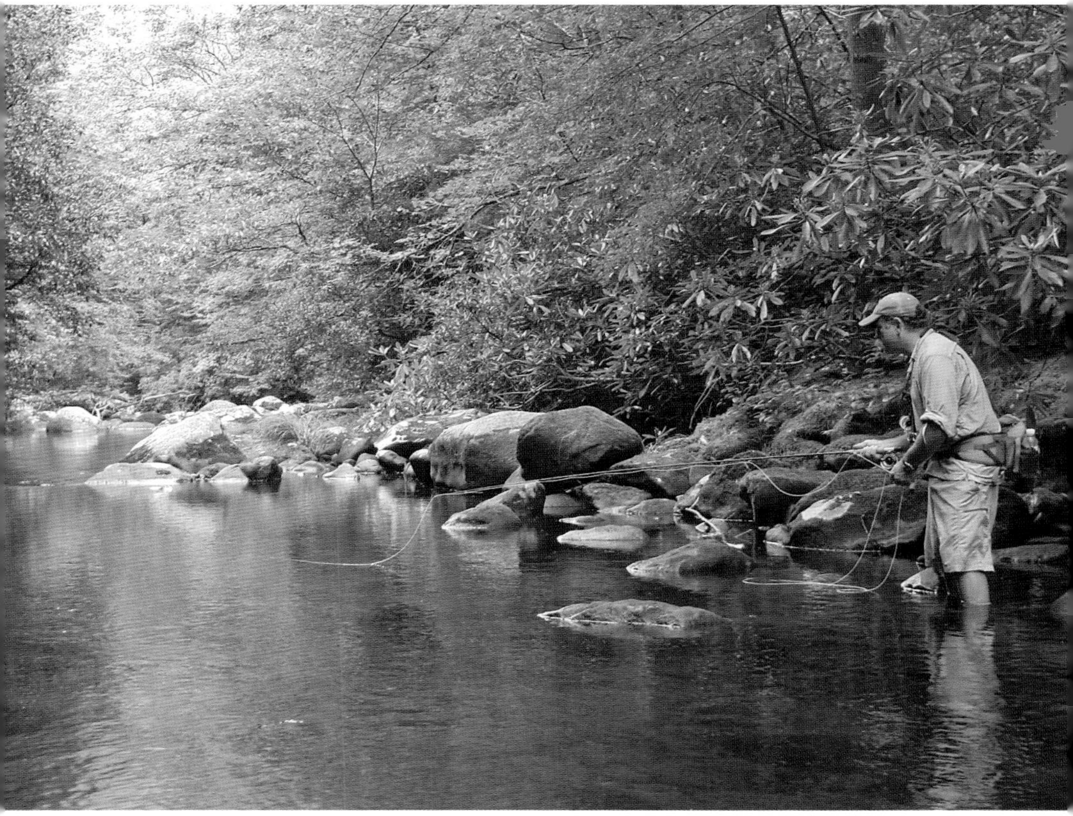

Big Snowbird is the largest of the Southern brook trout fisheries. This high-gradient stream offers plenty of room to cast a fly unlike the majority of brookie waters that are often just a few feet wide.

When fishing small water, your first cast to a trout is the most important. Think about where you're going to cast and how the current will affect your drift before putting the fly on the water.

The window is short, and it doesn't take long for the diminished capacity of the naive brook trout to change to paranoia. Things get tough quick.

Through early spring, when bluebird skies can easily give way to gray clouds burdened with snow, Big Snowbird can be the greatest brook trout fishery in the land. This is unless a bitter cold front sets in and forces the fish to relegate their active spirits to winterlike slumber.

Big Snowbird winds its way up from Lake Santeetlah into the wilds of North Carolina near enough to the Smokies that you wonder why they just didn't take this piece of land under the park's wing. It's a big, beautiful mountain river with everything you could want: long pools, pocketwater formed by large, flat rocks, and boulders eroded by enough water to fill the oceans three times over.

The dry fly coincides with the pulse of this backcountry water. Bushy dry flies such as Stimulators, Wulffs, Parachute Adams, and H & L Variants (#12-16) match the cadence of the trout and the water so perfectly that there is little reason to go with anything else. If you find your back to the wall, good ole standbys like Pheasant Tails, Prince Nymphs, and Hare's Ears (#12-16) fished beneath the surface work well. Another option is to throw stonefly patterns such as Stalcup's Golden Stone or Mercer's Epoxy Stone (#10-14) into the deeper, churning runs, both in the brook trout water and below the falls. There is a good population of stoneflies on Snowbird, and if the water is high, your chances of tying into a much larger than average trout are much better if you're throwing something with a little meat on its bones.

Keep a few parachute-style Yellow Sallies and yellow Stimulators (#12-16) in your box to match the Golden Stoneflies that hatch from late June through much of the early summer. Aside from this hatch, it would seem that pretty much any high-floating dry will work on the brook trout water, as well as the section of hatchery-supported river below the first falls. For the hatchery water, keep a smattering of San Juan Worms in red, pink, and brown in addition to Lightning Bugs, Copper Johns, and Gabriel's Trumpets (#14-18). Toss in a few streamers for the fall, just in case those rumors of lake-run fish are true, and you're in business for Snowbird country.

Fishing on Big Snowbird isn't overly technical. A few dry flies along with a few nymphs, and you're all good. Seasons are less dependent on the number and color of leaves on the trees than the temperature of the day. If it is over 60 degrees, throw nothing but a dry and raise your moral barometer. When the mercury falls much below, put on the training wheels and go back to the basics.

Put in the effort, and the time you spend on the trail will be rewarded exponentially. Brook trout could easily be adapted to an Aesop's fable; hard work and preparation pay off. If you're looking for a free lunch, you're more than likely going to go hungry.

THE SOUTHEAST'S

PART III

Slick water on the Clinch River below the weir dam means tough trout and long, fine leaders. Anglers who fish this tailwater know the benefits of cautious wading and accurate casts.

BEST FLY FISHING TENNESSEE

Decades ago, when the Tennessee Valley Authority (TVA) began its controversial damming projects across the Southeast, the last thing on anybody's mind was trout. A country in economic crisis and a region in need of power as well as jobs begat the medium for our modern-day Southern tailraces. Today, the great state of Tennessee has more trout-holding tailraces than any other Southern state. Not all Tennessee tailwaters are created equal; water quality, lake depth, and generation schedules combined with differing management programs by state and federal agencies all play a role in the end result.

In the past, the Little Tennessee tailrace was the region's premier fishery, one of the few true blue-ribbon trout fisheries in the South. Then, after further damming of the river, the very thing that created the fishery also destroyed it. Realizing the ability of tailraces to produce quality fishing, the state began putting more effort into managing various tailraces. Today, names like the South Holston, Hiwassee, Caney Fork, Watauga, and Clinch are synonymous with quality fly fishing. Anglers travel to fish these relatively new fisheries, at least when compared with the high-country freestone fisheries that have existed for a century or more.

When fishing tailwaters, anglers must pay close attention to generation schedules or risk being swept downstream. At the very least, it can wreck a day of fish-

Tennessee Fly Shops and Guides

South Holston and Watauga River

FLY SHOPS AND GUIDES

Hunter Banks
29 Montford Avenue
Asheville, NC 28801
(800) 227-6732

One Fly Outfitters, LTD
112 Cherry Street
Black Mountain, NC 28711
(828) 669-6939

South Holston Fly Shop
608 Emmett Road
Bristol, TN 37620
(423) 878-2822
southholstonriverflyshop.com

Curtis Wright Outfitters
Weaverville Store
24 North Main Street
Weaverville, NC 28787
(828) 645-8700

Fly Shop of Tennessee
102 Willmary Road
Johnson City, TN 37601
(423) 928-2007

Mahoney's
830 Sunset Drive
Johnson City, TN 37604
(423) 282-5413

Foscoe Fishing Company
8857 Hwy. 105 S
Boone, NC 28607
(828) 963-6556

(continued)

ing, especially after traveling a long way only to find high water and no place to wade. Anglers are not the only dependents on the water being pumped from the dam. Trout are the true beneficiaries below the dam. Too little water, and the temperatures rise and dissolved oxygen levels drop, a lethal combination for the fragile ecosystem downriver. Too much water at the wrong times, and precious trout eggs are washed downstream before the next generation is capable of fending for themselves. This is a delicate game and requires the constant monitoring of biologists to ensure the viability of each fishery.

Tennessee has created as good a balance as any Southern state in the arena of power generation for the masses versus downriver habitat preservation. The grim reality is that trout come second to power and sometimes third to lakeside landowners, who like to see their backyards full during the summer fun season. It may sound like trout are often placed on the back burner, but Tennessee officials see to it that many of the most viable waters have some type of regulatory program in effect to protect the trout downstream, thus preserving angling opportunities. Forward-thinking in many areas, state officials have closed sections of rivers during the spawn to let the fish breed, unmolested by unsavory anglers who insist on badgering trout in their most vulnerable state. In addition, slot limits are growing more and larger trout in tailraces where catch-and-keep ethics by the general masses would otherwise prove detrimental to trout populations.

Freestone rivers are limited to the extreme eastern portion of the state, primarily where the Great Smoky Mountains National Park drops across the North Carolina border. The limited geography of these high-country trout streams puts Tennessee behind North Carolina and Georgia in terms of overall miles of trout water; however, fishing quality is every bit as good. The Tellico drainage alone could be explored every day for months without ever fishing the same piece of water twice, so don't think the state's freestone opportunities are at all limited.

Along with trout, the warmwater contingency has established a firm foothold in Tennessee. Both striped bass and smallmouth can be found in many of the state's tailraces. Anglers fishing the Caney Fork, South Holston, Clinch, main stem of the Holston, and Hiwassee rivers should consider the warmer stretches

South Holston and Watauga River (continued)

FLY SHOPS AND GUIDES

Appalachian Angler
(828) 963-8383
appalachianangler.com

GUIDES

Watauga River Lodge
(828) 208-3428
wataugariverlodge.com

Mike Adams
(423) 741-4789
adamsflyfishing.com

High Country Angler
(704) 641-6815
highcountryangler.com

Justin Shroyer
(937) 308-9949

Guitou Feuillebois
(423) 483-6501

Hiwassee River

FLY SHOPS AND GUIDES

Choo Choo Fly & Tackle
17 Cherokee Blvd.
Chattanooga, TN 37405
(423) 267-0024

Reliance Fly and Tackle
588 Childers Creek Road
Reliance, TN 37369
(423) 338-7771
relianceflyshop.com

GUIDES

Southeastern Anglers
(866) 55-TROUT
southeasternanglers.com

Reel Angling Adventures
(866) 899-5259

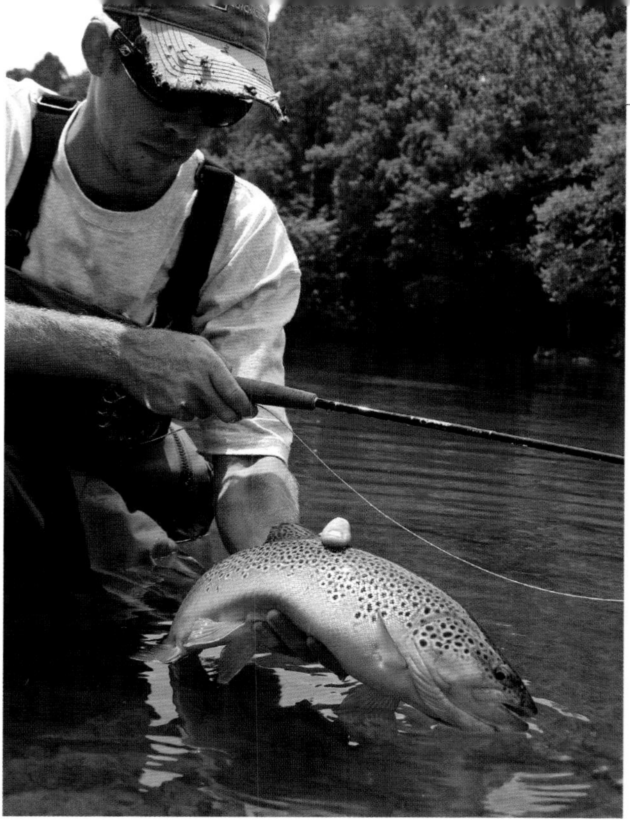

Thanks to special regulations, brown trout are allowed to grow shoulders on many tailwaters in Tennessee. Rivers like the South Holston, Caney Fork, Clinch, and Watauga are known for producing better than average fish.

downstream from the trout water. Stripers and smallmouth should be looked at as more than a side trip on a trout foray. While this book is geared toward the trout angling side of things, the warmwater option should never be off the table.

The popularity of alternative warmwater fishing opportunities could not be better represented than during the "Carp Tournament" put on by Fly South in Nashville. The monthlong tournament is widely popular and completely sheds the pretentious stigma occasionally associated with fly fishing.

From big brown trout to little brookies, stripers to carp, Tennessee has something for everyone. Along with tailraces that can rival famed western trout rivers; 20-pound striped bass, tailing carp, and smallmouth rising to popping bugs all cumulate to create a dynamic fisheries program.

Caney Fork

FLY SHOPS AND GUIDES

Fly South
1514 Demonbreun Street
Nashville, TN 37203
(615) 251-6199

Cumberland Transit
Nashville, TN
(615) 321-4069

Clinch River and Holston River

FLY SHOPS AND GUIDES

Rolf Lanz Outdoors
8039 Ray Mears Blvd.
Knoxville, TN 37919
(865) 690-3200

CR Outfitters
2830 Andersonville Hwy.
Norris, TN 37828
(865) 494-2305

Little River Outfitters
106 Town Square Drive
Townsend, TN
(877) 448-3474
littleriveroutfitters.com

GUIDES ONLY

Mike Bone
Knoxville, TN
(865) 494-0972
(865) 567-7138
clinchguides.com

Ian and Charity Rutter
(866) 766-5935
randrflyfishing.com

Southeastern Anglers
(866) 55-TROUT
southeasternanglers.com

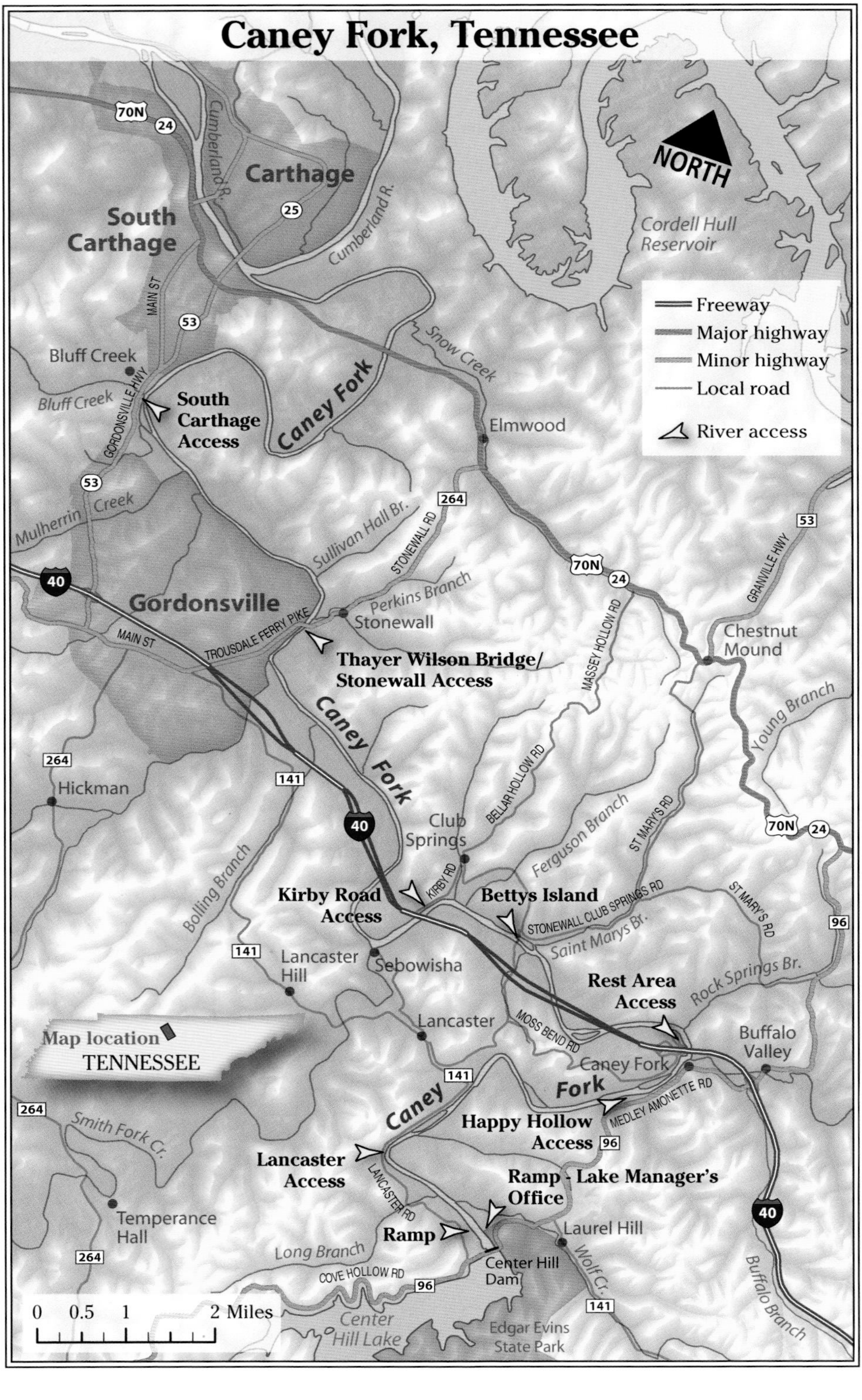
Caney Fork, Tennessee
NORTH
Freeway
Major highway
Minor highway
Local road
River access
70N
24
25
53
264
141
40
96
Carthage
South Carthage
Cumberland R.
Cumberland R.
Cordell Hull Reservoir
MAIN ST
Bluff Creek
Bluff Creek
GORDONSVILLE HWY
South Carthage Access
Caney Fork
Snow Creek
Elmwood
Mulherrin Creek
Sullivan Hall Br.
STONEWALL RD
Perkins Branch
Gordonsville
MAIN ST
TROUSDALE FERRY PIKE
Stonewall
Thayer Wilson Bridge/ Stonewall Access
MASSEY HOLLOW RD
GRANVILLE HWY
Chestnut Mound
Young Branch
Caney Fork
Hickman
BELLAR HOLLOW RD
Club Springs
Ferguson Branch
ST MARY'S RD
Bolling Branch
Kirby Road Access
KIRBY RD
Bettys Island
STONEWALL CLUB SPRINGS RD
ST MARY'S RD
Saint Marys Br.
Lancaster Hill
Sebowisha
Rest Area Access
Rock Springs Br.
Lancaster
MOSS BEND RD
Buffalo Valley
Map location
TENNESSEE
Caney Fork
Caney Fork
MEDLEY AMONETTE RD
Happy Hollow Access
Smith Fork Cr.
Lancaster Access
LANCASTER RD
Ramp - Lake Manager's Office
Temperance Hall
Ramp
Laurel Hill
Long Branch
Center Hill Dam
Wolf Cr.
COVE HOLLOW RD
Buffalo Branch
0 0.5 1 2 Miles
Center Hill Lake
Edgar Evins State Park

CHAPTER 10

Caney Fork

Some folks call it the "sad ditch," but those who label with such monikers surely fail to understand the cadence of water. The Caney Fork isn't sad; in fact, the river has a great sense of humor. How else can you explain how anglers dressed in the angling equivalent of their Sunday best can fish for hours with not so much as a tug, while the eight-year-old girl with her Snoopy pole just downstream lands a 22-inch brown on a Rooster Tail?

The Caney Fork tailwater was born in the late 1950s from the deep waters of Center Hill Lake. For nearly 28 miles, the cool waters of the Caney Fork flow northwest, then finally into the mighty Cumberland River. The river remained a put-and-take fishery for years, or so most of the region thought. Its fan club was derived from anglers residing mostly in the areas around Nashville and Knoxville, the latter group preferring their local Clinch River tailrace to the two-hour drive across to the Caney.

It was not until recent years that the Caney came into its own, rising to the top echelons of Southern tailraces. Special regulations imposed on the river dictating that only two brown trout may be taken, both of which must be over 18 inches, has helped the river become one of the most consistent producers of quality trout in the region.

Jim Mauries of Fly South has a more intimate relationship with the Caney than almost any other angler in the area. Jim was one of the first—if not *the* first—fly-fishing guides on the Caney. He's watched the river and studied its fish, hatches, and flows for several decades. Now his Nashville shop, Fly South, caters to anglers headed to the Caney as well as far more exotic locales.

Jim believes the river is one of the finest tailraces in the Southeast. "With the quality regulations, it is a 14- to 17-inch fish factory." Mauries feels that the Caney Fork, despite the quality regulations and water control efforts by the TVA, is literally being loved to death. "The kill rate is nauseating," he says.

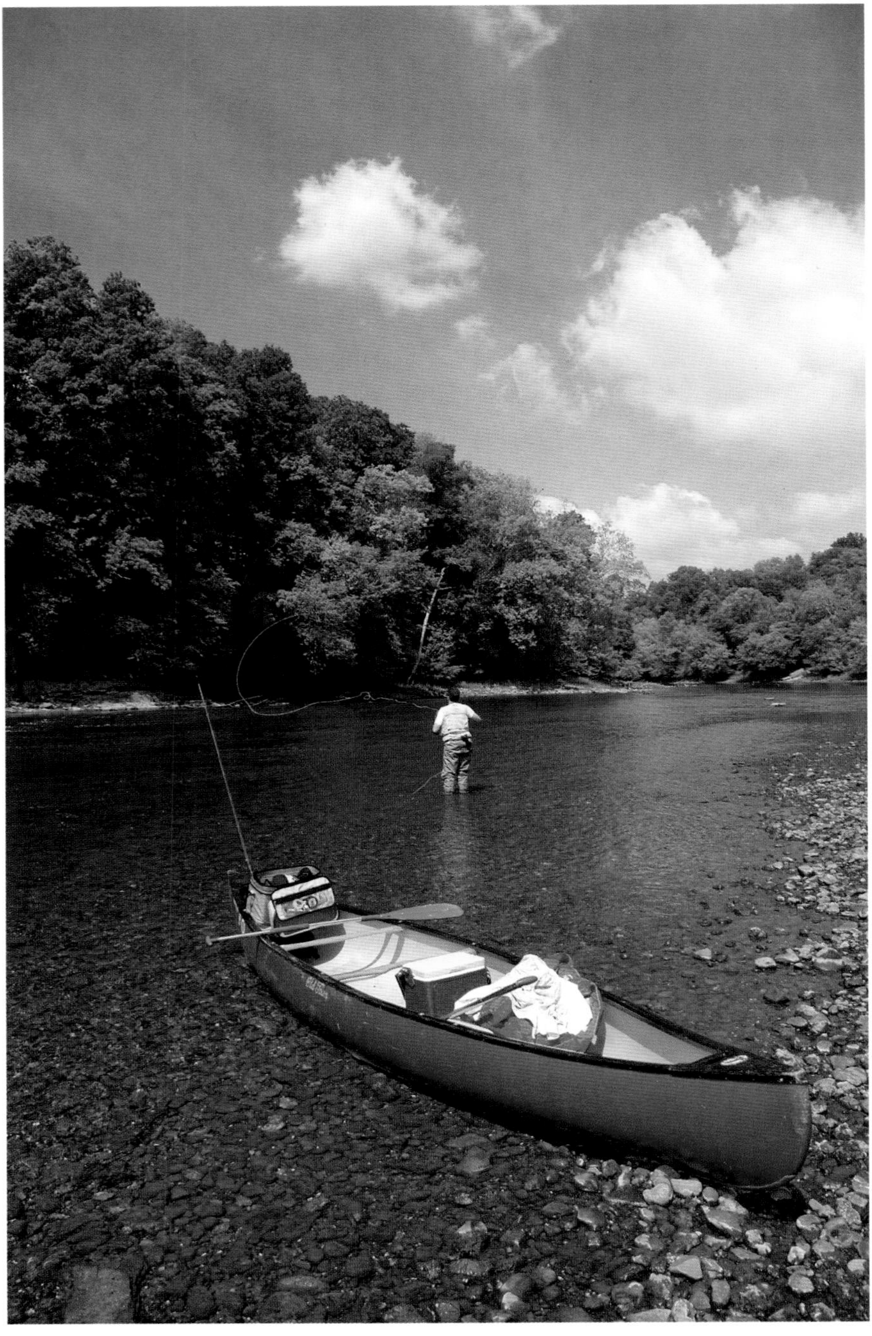

An angler fishes a seam on one of the Caney Fork's many gravel bars. Braided water and the edges of seams are prime lies for trout. ZACH MATTHEWS

I can attest to this firsthand, seeing single brown trout on stringers, most hovering around the 20-inch mark, being carried back to the parking lot. This is perfectly legal—however, the numbers of people fishing the river and the propensity for this watershed to produce trout of that quality mean that more and more of these fish are being taken, in all likelihood faster than they can be naturally replenished. It takes a long time for a trout to grow to that size and at the rate the larger browns are being caught and killed, the numbers of fish 20 inches and over are quickly shrinking.

The TVA dictates water flows, maintaining a minimum low-water flow of around 250 cfs. When running at minimum flow, the Caney meanders through the countryside at an excruciatingly slow pace. Long sections of flat water hopscotching long gravel bars and shallow shoals hold trout in areas you would never expect to find them. You must look for nondescript seams in the slow water, as this is where the trout, especially the larger ones, will hold. It is not always easy to discern a subtle seam when scanning a large expanse of seemingly featureless water, but if you look hard enough you will find these microcurrents within the main flow. Working these areas with your fly is the key to catching many trout on the Caney Fork.

When the turbines come online, the flow can fluctuate up to 5,300 cfs, especially when levels of dissolved oxygen drop below a certain level and the TVA sluices water to increase oxygen diffusion. When the turbines lie silent, much of the river is wadable and long gravel bars provide miles of access to the river's trout water. When the dam comes online, the river rises quickly, chasing off the wading masses and bringing drift boats and other forms of watercraft into play. Either way, the river can fish equally well, depending on the day.

Caney Fork anglers find no shortage of access, especially at low water. The first point of wading access extends from the dam downstream to access points along Lancaster Highway. Parking areas near the Center Hill Lake Resource Manager's office located at the base of the dam give you access to a variety of water, ranging from deep, slow pools to braided riffles that escape into deep, narrow slots as the water wedges itself between gravel bars and the river's high banks. You can either fish directly below the dam or hike downstream on one of the trails. On the opposite side of the river, Lancaster Highway parallels the Caney for a short time, giving anglers access to a large expanse of wadable water.

Below Lancaster, Happy Hollow access has a large flat directly in front of the gravel boat ramp extending upstream and down. This section and that around the island directly downstream let anglers spread out. Much like the area between the dam and Lancaster, long sections of flat water will test your skill here, especially when the trout are rising to tiny midges. Park at the lot up the hill from the large gravel bar. If the water starts coming up and you're parked on the gravel bar, you may come back to find out that Chevrolet does make a drift boat after all!

Downstream of Happy Hollow, just off Interstate 40 and west of Exit 268, there is a rest area where some anglers park and walk a short distance to the river. Exiting on the eastbound side of the interstate is best for accessing the river. Here you are around 5 1/2 miles below the dam, giving you a few extra hours to fish on days when the turbines are coming on later in the afternoon. There is plenty of wading, but watch your step, as the clear water is deeper than it looks.

Betty's Island is the next access point downstream. A large gravel bar extends into the river, visible in low water and a perfect spot to begin your fishing day on the Caney. This is the point where the Caney becomes even more interesting, as mayflies and caddis being cohabiting with the midges, scuds, and sow bugs present from the dam down. The access around Betty's is pretty easy to wade and a crapshoot on weekends—it gets crowded quickly when the fishing is good. Keep another access in your back pocket, just in case Betty's has a few more cars than you'd like to see.

Just over 10 miles below the dam, Kirby Road runs alongside the river providing access to a series of gravel bars and shallow, wadable flats. This is a favorite among anglers who fish the dam. Then, when the water hits, they hop in their cars and drive downstream to Kirby to extend the fishing day.

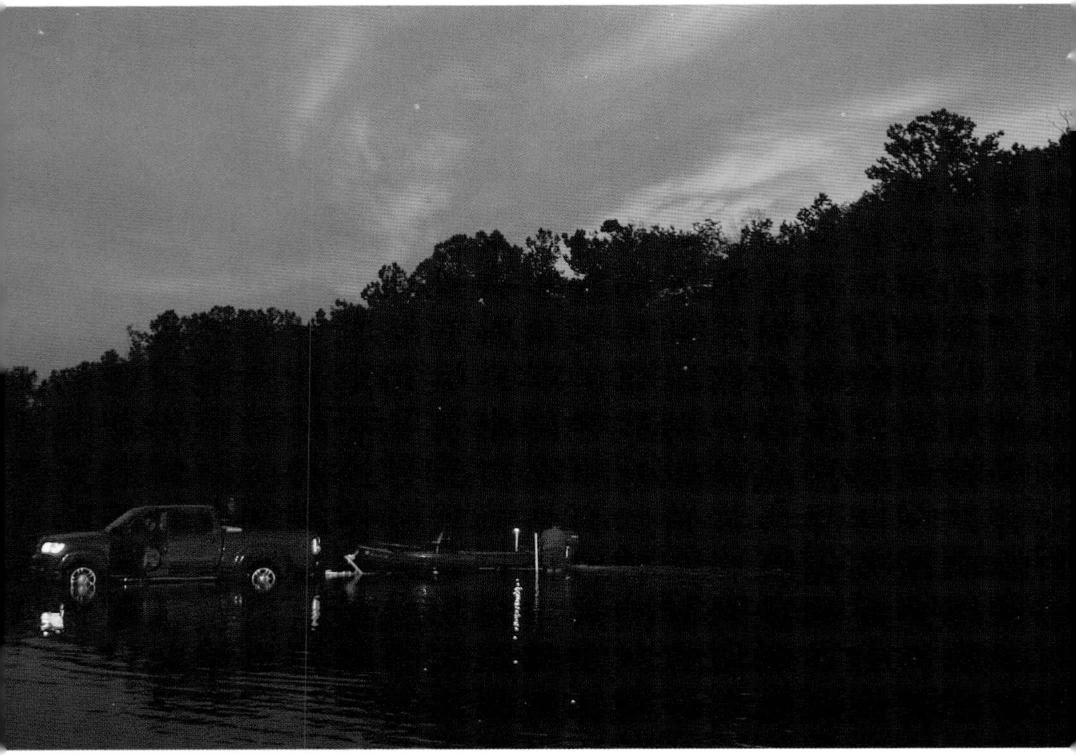

Pulling out on the Caney Fork at Happy Hollow "ramp" requires driving onto a large gravel bar in low water. It's not always the easiest way to get your boat out of the water.

The riffles around Kirby can see some of the river's heavier caddis hatches, so keep that in mind if you're thinking of bringing only your midge box riverside.

Thayer Wilson Bridge, which the locals sometimes call Stonewall, sits below the Kirby Road access where Tennessee Highway 264 crosses the river. Many consider this the lowest point from which wading anglers can access the river. For the most part, they are right, since the river gradually deepens and access becomes less prevalent as it snakes into the Cumberland. You can find a few spots to wade lower on the river, but with so much water around Thayer and upstream, there's little reason to head low looking for fish.

Floating anglers have an advantage because they are able to access much more of the river. Popular floats are from ramps on either side of the river at the base of the dam, the more heavily used being the one below the parking lot at the lake manager's office. From here, you can float a touch over 5 miles of river before arriving at the Happy Hollow access. The steep grade here and the gravel bar, which all but disappears at high water, can make extracting your boat a challenge. When the water is low, you're able to drive easily onto the gravel bar to snatch the boat from the water.

Floating downstream from Happy Hollow to Betty's Island takes you through about 4 miles of river, but don't let the distance fool you. There is enough trouty water here to keep you busy for days if you fish it properly. Like the stretch between the dam and Happy Hollow, the river winds through the Tennessee countryside and poses no real threat to even inexperienced boaters. Unlike the dam-to–Happy Hollow float, here you are not inundated with neon kayaks and rafts during the summer.

Below Betty's Island it is an 11-mile float to the ramp in South Carthage, then from there 6 more miles to the mouth of the Cumberland. Most folks favor a motor rather than oars in this stretch, preferring to launch from the South Carthage ramp and motor upstream in search of trout and striped bass. Down low, the river's trout can be large, but far fewer in numbers, causing most folks to spend their floating days on the river between the dam and Betty's Island.

Fishing the Caney for most consists of a basic rig involving a small midge, sow bug, or scud imitation tied on a few feet below a nondescript indicator. This is especially true of folks fishing from the dam downstream to Betty's Island. This stretch is predominantly a midge fishery, with scuds and sow bugs coming in a close second. Although hatching midges will bring trout up to the surface, this is tedious, oftentimes frustrating fishing. Long leaders, perfect drifts with small flies, and a lot of luck are required to feed a midging trout on top. There are just so many bugs hatching at any given time that figuring out a trout's rhythm and feeding it a midge pattern could take a long time.

Nymphing with a midge pattern is perhaps one of the most popular, and needless to say effective, methods employed on the river. For the length of the river throughout the year, Zebra Midges, Rainbow Warriors, UV Z-Midges (#18-24) and blackfly larvae imitations such as Black Cardinal Midges

Big trout do eat small flies on the Caney. This brown was fooled by a #22 Zebra Midge, one of the most popular flies on the river. Despite the widespread use of this pattern, Caney trout will still fall for it, oftentimes when all else fails.

and Black Beauties (#22-24) can probably be found tied onto at least 80 percent of anglers' tippets. Most anglers find a pattern that works and stick with it. You would think the trout would get wise after being fooled a few times by the same patterns, but this doesn't seem to be the case. Anglers continue to hook scores of trout on the same patterns over and over again.

Mauries notes that the Caney Fork scuds are not what you typically see, especially when represented in standard fly form. As he puts it, most scud patterns are short and fat, but this does not represent those found in the Caney. Thinner and stronger swimmers, the scuds in the Caney break the conventional mold. Mauries suggests using a thinner scud pattern than you typically see tied to better imitate those found in the Caney.

Swinging soft-hackles also works well on the Caney Fork. Try small soft-hackles such as the Red Ass, Pulsating Emerger, and Soft-Hackle Pheasant Tail (#16-22). Since these flies are swung across the current, similar to fishing for salmon or steelhead, some anglers are adapting the rods used for the latter two forms of angling and incorporating them for use on the Caney. With the recent surge of popularity in two-handed rods and the subsequent availability of more trout-friendly weights, two-handed (Spey) rods have been popping up on tailwaters around the South, the Caney included. Light 4- or 5-weight two-handers, 11 to 12 feet in length, are made for swinging flies on the Caney, adding a bit of extra excitement into the mix and allowing for longer casts as well as better line control during the swing. Some folks mock those who use two-handers on a trout river, but the basic physics of using a longer rod to fish a swung fly should overcome the doubters.

Below Betty's Island, the Caney begins to take on a new look, at least in terms of biomass. Stoneflies, caddis, and some mayflies begin showing up in good numbers here, dispelling the notion that the Caney is not a dry-fly river. Lacking the hatches of other tailraces in the South, the Caney still has some quality caddis and mayfly hatches, allowing anglers held hostage by the Zebra Midge to escape into the land of the dry fly.

A number of bugs hatch below Betty's Island, but the most important are the small green caddis that come off in mid-April, followed by the larger tan caddis in May and June. Jim Mauries explains that the caddis show up every year at around the same time, but their hatch is dictated by water levels and temperature. Some years, he explains, the hatch will last all the way through the summer. Other years, it comes in spurts, heavy for a few days, then dormant, then back on.

Fishing either hatch on the river requires the same presentation skill and stealth required when fishing subsurface, perhaps more. For the smaller

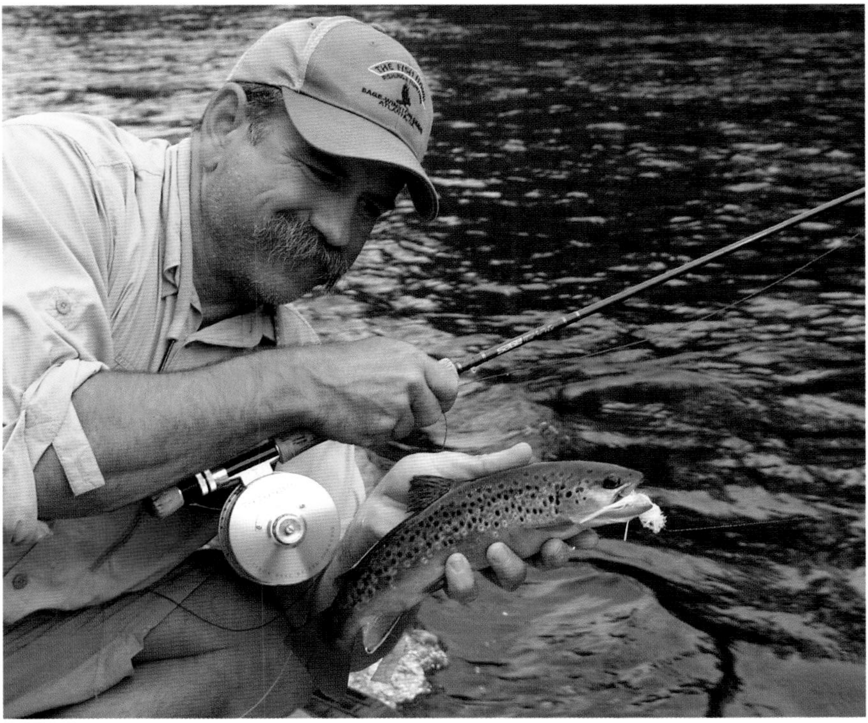

Give a kid a steak, and he'll try and finish it. Even smaller brown trout will attack streamers in high water. Shad patterns are highly effective on the Caney, especially during generation.

CANEY FORK HATCHES

JAN FEB MAR APR MAY JUN JUL AUG SEP OCT NOV DEC

Midges (Diptera)

#18-26 Stalcup's Hatching Midge, Brooks's Sprout Midge, Walker's Mayhem Emerger, Hanging Midge

Blue-Winged Olive (*Baetis* spp.)

#18-24 CDC Biot Emerger/Dun, Last Chance Cripple, Brooks's Sprout *Baetis*, No-Hackle, Hi-Viz Emerger, Translucent Emerger, A. K.'s Parachute, Thorax BWO Emerger

Caddis (Various spp.)

#14-16 Elk-Hair Caddis, CDC Caddis Emerger, CDC Fertile Caddis, X2 Caddis, Stalcup's Parachute Caddis Emerger, Hemingway Caddis, Henryville Special, Spotlight Caddis Emerger

Sulphur (*E. invaria*)

#12-16 CDC Compara-dun, A. K.'s Parachute, D&D Cripple, Last Chance Cripple, Spotlight Emerger, Captive Dun, Rusty Spinner

Terrestrials

#14-18 RP Ant, Crystal Ant; #10-12 Steeves's Japanese Beetle, Steeves's Bark Beetle, CDC Beetle; #10-14 Dave's Cricket, DeBruin's Hopper, Rainy's Foam Hopper; #10-14 Dave's Inchworm, chartreuse San Juan Worm

green caddis, try a Harrop's Fertile Caddis or CDC Caddis Emerger (#16-18) in the slow, smooth glides that typify the Caney. The tan caddis can be imitated with similar patterns in corresponding color, maybe adding a few Hemingway Caddis, Spotlight Caddis Emergers, or Henry's Fork Caddis (#14-16) for good measure.

Sulphurs *(E. invaria)* are one of the river's staple hatches, coming off in mid-May then continuing through September. Some days may not see big numbers of bugs hatching, but the trout will still rise to well-presented Sulphur dry flies, so prospecting isn't a shabby idea, especially if you run a small Beadhead Zebra Midge or Pheasant Tail dropper off the back.

Aside from the bug factory below Betty's, terrestrials can be found down the length of the river during the summer. Grassy banks hold ants and grasshoppers, while the overhanging trees and bushes drop beetles into the river at a steady rate. Working the banks with terrestrial patterns like Rainy's Foam Hoppers (#8-12), wood beetle patterns, Steeves's Japanese Beetles, CDC Beetles (#14-16), and flying ant imitations (#14-18) will find favor in the eyes of Caney trout. Presenting the larger beetles or hoppers with a heavy "plop" can be like ringing the dinner bell for trout looking out for these larger, more animated insects.

Once the turbines come online, Caney trout become susceptible to baitfish imitations fished on a sinking line. Lines with a fast sinking rate of 6 to 8 inches per second (ips) are going to get the fly down below the faster currents and into the "zone." During generation, stunned shad are discharged from the dam, a few eaten from the surface like large dry flies by big trout. The shad that do not float on top drift helplessly along beneath the surface, where they are picked off by marauding browns. Large white streamers 4 to 6 inches in length imitate the shad and can bring jarring strikes. Other streamer pat-

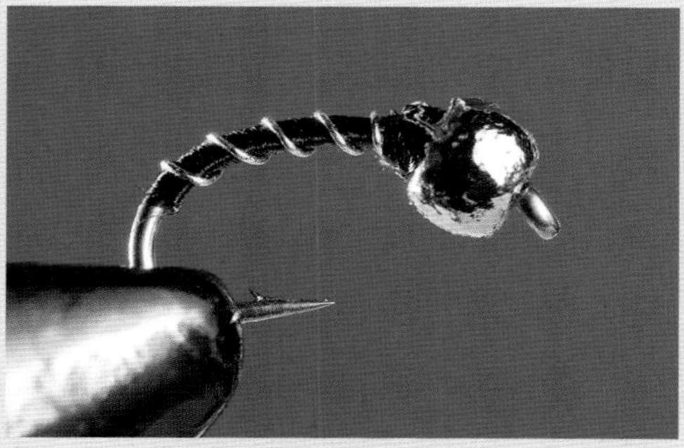

Zebra Midge

Hook: #20-24 Daiichi 1130
Bead: Silver, brass, or gold metal
Body: Black thread
Rib: Silver wire

Thorax Bead Soft-Hackle

Hook: #14-20 Daiichi 1130
Thread: Olive 8/0 Uni-Thread
Body: Olive goose biot
Thorax: Glass bead
Hackle: Brown hen hackle

terns such as Beldar Buggers, Sculpzillas, Zonkers, and Galloup's Sex Dungeons (#1/0-4) can prove equally effective. Just make sure your hooks are sharp and the gap is large enough to set firmly into the jaw of a large trout.

In the fall, browns stage on some of the gravel bars in an effort to spawn. Some anglers harass these trout while they are on the redds, wading through spawning gravel and destroying precious eggs. Although legal, this is widely frowned upon, and many anglers take the high road, not targeting the vulnerable browns during this time. Jim Mauries puts it best when he says: "Catching a trout on a redd is nothing to be proud of. Come back later in the season and catch the same trout when they are not spawning, and then you've really accomplished something." I could not agree more.

Things are indeed looking up for the Caney Fork. The trout are thriving in the cold waters, and with the help of state officials, the TVA, and conservation groups, they will continue to flourish. No longer a sleeper among Southern anglers, the Caney Fork is now a mainstay among many travelers, as well as the always loyal local angling crowd.

Hiwassee River, Tennessee

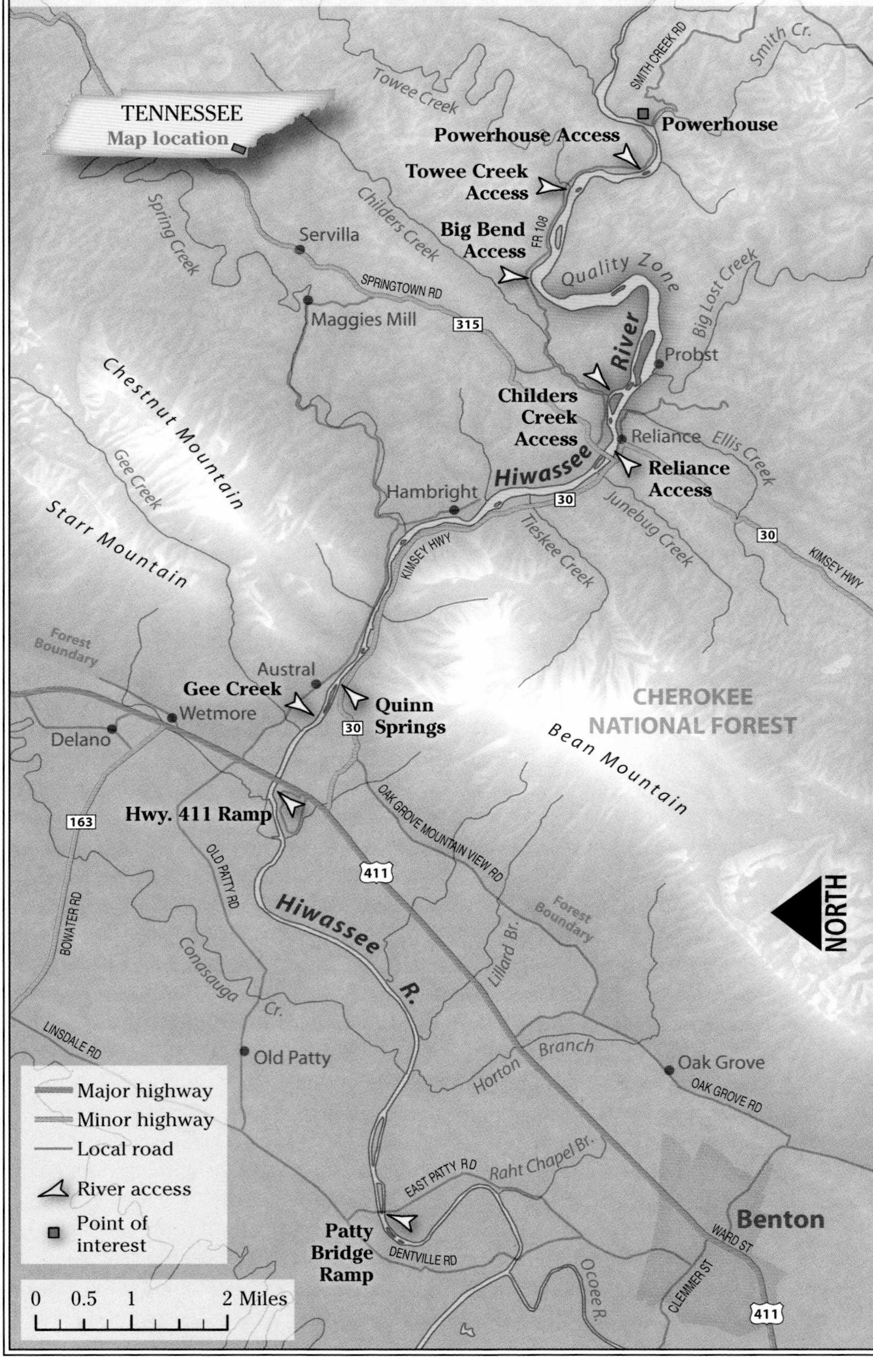

TENNESSEE
Map location
Towee Creek
SMITH CREEK RD
Smith Cr.
Powerhouse
Powerhouse Access
Towee Creek Access
Spring Creek
Childers Creek
Servilla
Big Bend Access
FR 108
Quality Zone
SPRINGTOWN RD
Maggies Mill
315
Big Lost Creek
River
Probst
Chestnut Mountain
Childers Creek Access
Reliance
Ellis Creek
Gee Creek
Hiwassee
Reliance Access
Hambright
30
Junebug Creek
Starr Mountain
KIMSEY HWY
Tieskee Creek
30
KIMSEY HWY
Forest Boundary
Austral
Gee Creek
Quinn Springs
30
Wetmore
Delano
CHEROKEE NATIONAL FOREST
Bean Mountain
Hwy. 411 Ramp
OAK GROVE MOUNTAIN VIEW RD
163
OLD PATTY RD
411
Hiwassee
NORTH
BOWATER RD
Forest Boundary
Conasauga Cr.
Lillard Br.
R.
LINSDALE RD
Old Patty
Branch
Horton
Oak Grove
OAK GROVE RD
Major highway
Minor highway
Local road
River access
Point of interest
EAST PATTY RD
Raht Chapel Br.
Patty Bridge Ramp
DENTVILLE RD
Benton
WARD ST
CLEMMER ST
Ocoee R.
411
0 0.5 1 2 Miles

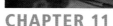

CHAPTER 11

Hiwassee River

Ronnie Hall was the first licensed outfitter on the Hiwassee River. That was back in 1983. Before that, he'd fished the river from the early 1970s on, using an old, single-lane dirt road to access the upper reaches near the Reliance Powerhouse. Not many folks were fishing the river back then, and the trout were, as Ronnie tells it, large and more than willing to rise to a dry fly. When Ronnie is expounding on the old days, I can almost hear Bob Dylan's voice in the background singing "The Times They Are A-Changin'."

Today, the Hiwassee is a shell of its former self, the river still churning a course through a rocky path, but the trout—ah, the trout—have indeed suffered. Gone are the days of 18-inch or better trout rising to inexhaustible hatches of mayflies and caddis. Now, fish in the 12- to 14-inch class are far more common, but larger trout are still caught, just not with expected regularity. The cause of this decline in not as clear-cut as some want to believe, but one contributing factor is for certain. The very thing that gave the Hiwassee life has also taken it away. Coldwater discharges from Hiwassee Lake formed the tailrace, but now recreation on the impoundment and in the backyards of the well-heeled is taking precedence over preservation of the downstream fishery. Years of drought, combined with the wishes of landowners in keeping the upstream lake as close to full pool as possible during the critical late spring and summer months, have forced the TVA to cut back on power generation. This has led to warmer downstream temperatures subsequently harming the aquatic biomass. Fewer bugs equal less food for the trout. What we are left with today is a gorgeous river with an amazing potential left unrealized by the powers that be.

All of this talk of gloom and doom may turn you off from the Hiwassee, but don't let it. Despite the negative facets, usually reserved for discussions among old hands on the river who actually knew what it was like "back then," the Hiwassee hovers in the top echelons of angling destinations among

Southern anglers. Perhaps the vast populations of large trout are a thing of the past, but the river's fish still fight as hard as ever, and there are enough big fish to keep things interesting. The hatches have fallen off, but mayflies and caddis still hatch in respectable numbers, bringing trout to the surface just as they did in years past. Nothing can remain the same forever, but anglers who visit the Hiwassee do far more than just make do with what they have left. Devoted anglers love the river for its beauty on a scale so grand that other rivers would blush if they ever saw it.

Viable trout water on the Hiwassee begins upstream from the town of Reliance, above the Hiwassee River Gorge, where the river flows through a virtually untouched wilderness area surrounded by the mountains of the Tennessee Overhill. From the powerhouse downstream to the bridge at U.S. Highway 411, the Hiwassee supports trout year-round. Wading anglers, as well as those who float with thighs securely locked into the braces of dories, fare well, casting a conglomeration of nymphs, dry flies, and streamers. Ever

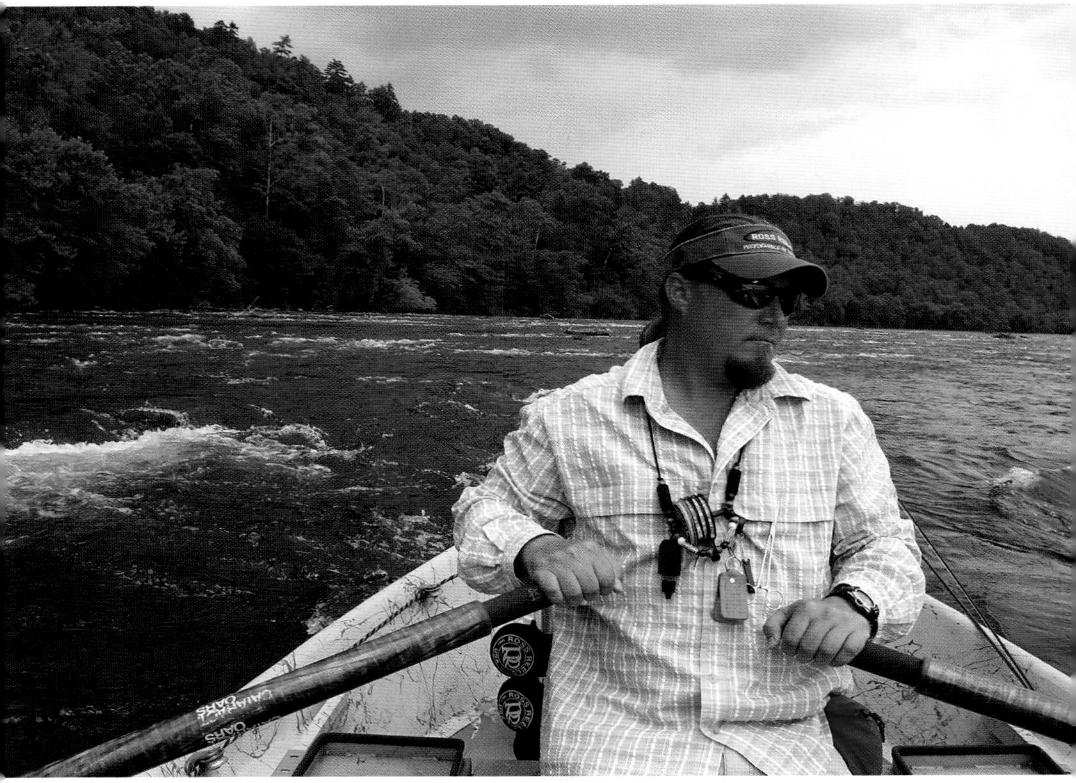

Guide Chad Bryson works the oars down the Hiwassee. The river is technical and not for novice rowers. Rapids like Stair Steps and Devil's Shoals have claimed drift boats from even experienced oarsmen.

hoping for the tug of a trophy fish, they ply the water in search of more than just a trout, but a connection to angling days past.

Below US 411, the river downstream to Patty Bridge becomes marginal during the summer, water temperatures spiking to near lethal levels on the hottest days. It's nice to think that the trout, resilient as they are, find a way to migrate upstream to cooler water. Below Patty Bridge, the trout are no more, a variety of bass and other warmwater species becoming kings of the water.

Access to the river is plentiful, especially between the powerhouse and the town of Reliance. The Hiwassee falls nearly entirely within the Cherokee National Forest, with a large portion designated as a National Wild and Scenic River. The options are limitless—so long as you're willing to hike in. From the powerhouse downstream to Big Bend, the river runs alongside Appalachia Powerhouse Road. Numerous pullouts and parking areas at the Powerhouse, Towee Creek, and Big Bend make accessing this upper section relatively easy. Improved boat ramps at the Powerhouse and Towee Creek let anglers launch everything from one-man pontoons to drift boats when the generators are running, further increasing the scope of angler access.

Downstream of Big Bend, the river flows into what is known as the Hiwassee Gorge. There are no roads, and the river looks, for the most part, just as it did back in Ronnie's day. Rapids such as Big Bend, Stair Steps, and Devil's Shoals mark obstacles for floating anglers. Even if you are handy on the oars, floating the river is still an adventure, with some runs offering only a single, complex line on which a drift boat must be rowed. Pick the wrong line and you could become pinned in the river's powerful current. Once you find yourself in this spot, there is a good chance the boat will swamp or you will need to get out and push, neither of which is a particularly attractive option in the cold, deep water.

Hike-in access to the remote Hiwassee Gorge section can be had via the John Muir Trail that runs between Big Bend Park and Childers Creek. From the trail, head from Big Bend Park downstream to the Stair Steps Rapid. It's not a long walk, and during low water this can put you on one of the best sections of the river.

Below the bridge at Reliance, where another improved ramp is located, the river flattens a bit, with huge boulders littering the riverbed and clearly visible during low water. Access points at Gee Creek and Quinn Springs give low-water anglers a jumping-off point to explore the braided channels and long pools. Another improved ramp at US 411 lets anglers floating from Reliance pull their boats from the water, but it doesn't really offer any viable wading options. From the US 411 bridge down to Patty Bridge, the river is deep, slow-moving, and accessible to the general public only by boat.

In contrast to the early years, many anglers now probe the Hiwassee's currents with a nymph, in both low and high water. The low water really concentrates the trout. With the current gone, they become more wary than when the TVA is pushing one or two turbines. Wading anglers will find the rocks to

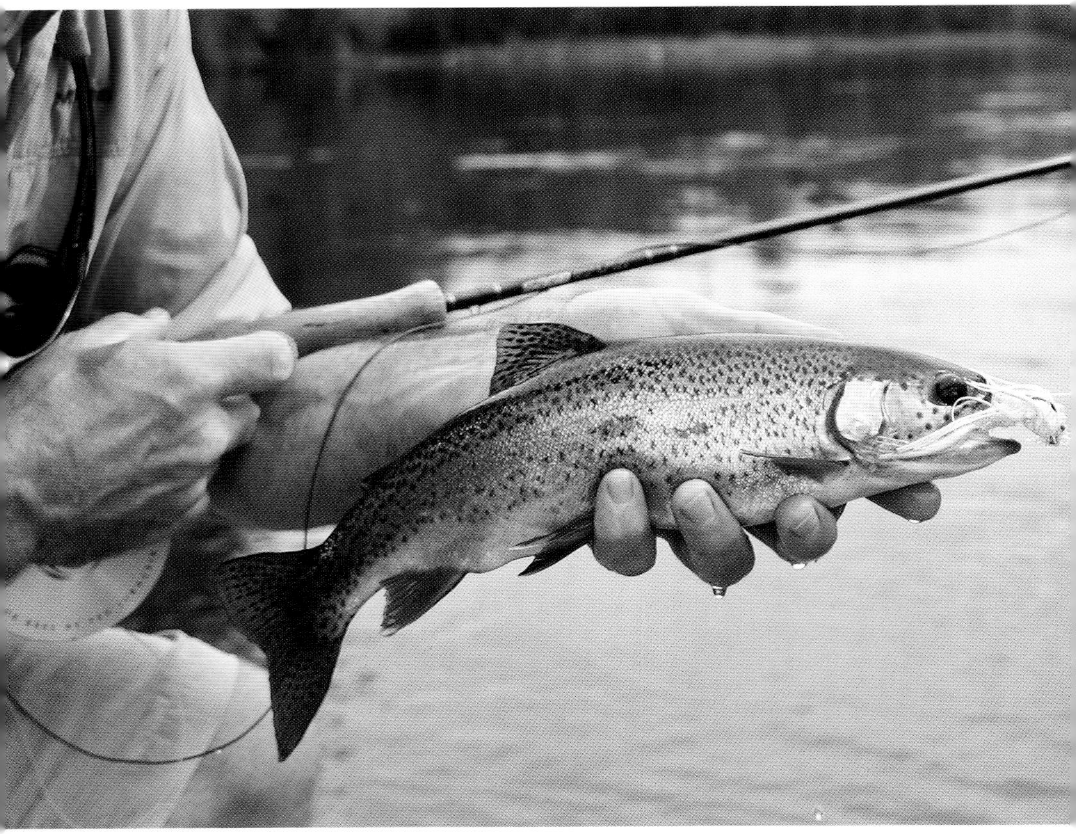

This rainbow proves that baitfish on tailwaters are a good choice when there are no hatches around. Forage fish, shad, and smaller trout all fall under the edible column.

be slippery with sharp edges. Bruised knees and torn waders are just facts of life up here. The depth of the water varies by the foot—one moment you're standing knee deep, and a step later you're in over your shoulders. A lot of anglers use wading staffs to aid in balancing on the slippery rocks and to probe the depths of the water.

In low water, you're best off going with a larger fly up top and trailing a midge close behind. Crystal Pheasant Tails, Psycho Mayflies, Norris's Caddis Pupae, and Split Case PMDs (#12-16) all work well as the top fly, with something like a Split Case BWO, UV Z-Midge, Mercer's Micro Mayfly, or Craven's Jujubee Midge (#18-22) dropped behind. Be prepared to move your indicator a lot, adjusting the depth to match the particular piece of water you are fishing.

Once the generators come online, floating anglers find the same patterns useful, occasionally adding a bit more meat to the top fly. Stalcup's Tungsten

Bead Stone, Kaufmann's Stonefly, and Tungsten Terminator Stonefly nymphs (#8-12) are a few patterns matching the larger bugs that may become dislodged during high water. Don't be scared of split-shot, as you're going to need to get down quickly to fish some of the faster runs. Work the edges of swift water and seams in long, smooth-flowing pools, as well as the tails of islands and grass beds. When you see the Hiwassee, this general description may seem to fit most of the river, but with enough time on the water, you'll find which sections hold fish and which look as if they should, but don't. A few guided trips can up your learning curve on the Hiwassee.

The guys at Southeastern Anglers make their living on the waters of the Hiwassee. Dane Law, head guide and owner of the operation, believes that anglers coming to the Hiwassee can catch fish on their own, but a guide knows where the trout live from day to day and how the often fluctuating water levels will affect their behavior.

Working a tandem nymph rig under an indicator gets more anglers hooked up nowadays than a dry, but that's not to say that dry-fly fishing is out of the question. Blue-Winged Olives can hatch in good numbers pretty much anytime from November through April, even coming off in decent numbers through the spring and summer on cloudy days. Small tippets are needed, even in high water, to fool the river's trout with these small bugs. Among others, Brooks's Sprout *Baetis,* Last Chance Cripples, Smith's Translucent Emergers, and olive Walker's Mayhem Emergers (#18-22 during the winter; #16-18 during March and April) are considered staples for the *Baetis* hatch. The beautiful thing about the *Baetis* hatch is the solitude afforded by the Hiwassee during the winter. Typically, the river is running low with the turbines silent through much of the late fall and winter. Fishing the expansive river in an intimate, serene setting makes you feel that you're the only one on the river.

In the spring, brown caddis begin hatching in April, blanketing the river on

What more do you need? Reliance Fly & Tackle is the last stop on the road leading to the still remote upper portion of the Hiwassee River tailrace. Remember, it is illegal to float with alcohol in the boat on the Hiwassee, so best save the toasting of that large trout for when you're back at camp.

some days. These caddis hatch through the end of May and provide anglers with some of the best dry-fly fishing of the season. Early in the hatch, you can swing a Sparkle Pupa (#14-16) through the riffles, forcing the trout to chase the ascending caddis and strike with jarring force. This technique works well both before and during the emergence. It is also a solid backup plan on days when the caddis are not coming off in good numbers, keeping the fish actively feeding on top.

Dry-fly caddis patterns for low water include brown Harrop's CDC Caddis Emerger, CDC Fertile Caddis, and Iris Caddis (#14-16). If you're wanting to fish a pupa below, try a pattern with more buoyancy such as Mathews's X2 Caddis or Hemingway Caddis (#14-16), trailing a Soft-Hackle Pheasant Tail, Deep Six Caddis, or Graphic Caddis (#14-16).

High water requires a pattern that will float higher in most circumstances. Standard Elk-Hair Caddis, X2 Caddis, or Hemingway Caddis (#14-16) supporting one of the trailing pupa imitations listed above is status quo on one or more generators. Look for pods of rising trout during the caddis hatch. Maneuver your craft into position and drop anchor. Oftentimes several fish can be picked off from the pod before the remaining trout wise up and drop down into the current.

In late May, the Sulphurs begin hatching in great numbers. Some days, especially when the sun is high on a bluebird day, the orange-yellow mayflies fill the skies and trout rise late into the evenings. CDC Compara-duns, Last Chance Cripples, and CDC Biot Emergers (#14-16) do the trick. High-water patterns include the above in soft, smooth stretches, as well as a few hairwing Compara-duns and parachutes for the rougher, braided water.

The **Isonychia** *hatch brings large trout like this one to the surface. Other times of the year, streamer fishing is your best bet for connecting with the big browns.*

Wading anglers can find plenty of water when the turbines are off. The low water concentrates trout in the deeper slots. Sometimes dozens of trout will hold in a very small area, but the skinny water makes them spooky and difficult to approach.

Anglers wait on the Mahogany Dun *(Isonychia bicolor)* mayflies to appear on the Hiwassee, as they have since the word first got out sometime back in the mid-1980s. These robust mayflies are known to bring "every fish in the river up" when the hatch is at its heaviest, says Dane Law. Included within this "every fish" umbrella are the larger trout that feed mostly subsurface, save this short, summer window. The *Isonychia* hatch brings anglers in from hundreds of miles away, and guides' books fill with trips during the month of July and into mid-August, when these mayflies typically hatch. Large Parachute Adams and *Isonychia* Sparkle Duns and Compara-duns (#8-10) are favorites when matching the *Isonychia* adult.

Since the *Isonychia* nymph is of the burrowing/swimming variety, fish the nymph imitations with some type of action. A slow retrieve or raising and lowering the rod tip during the drift will usually elicit strikes from trout as they key in on this active nymph. Another noticeable characteristic of the *Isonychia* is that it has a white stripe running the length of its back from head

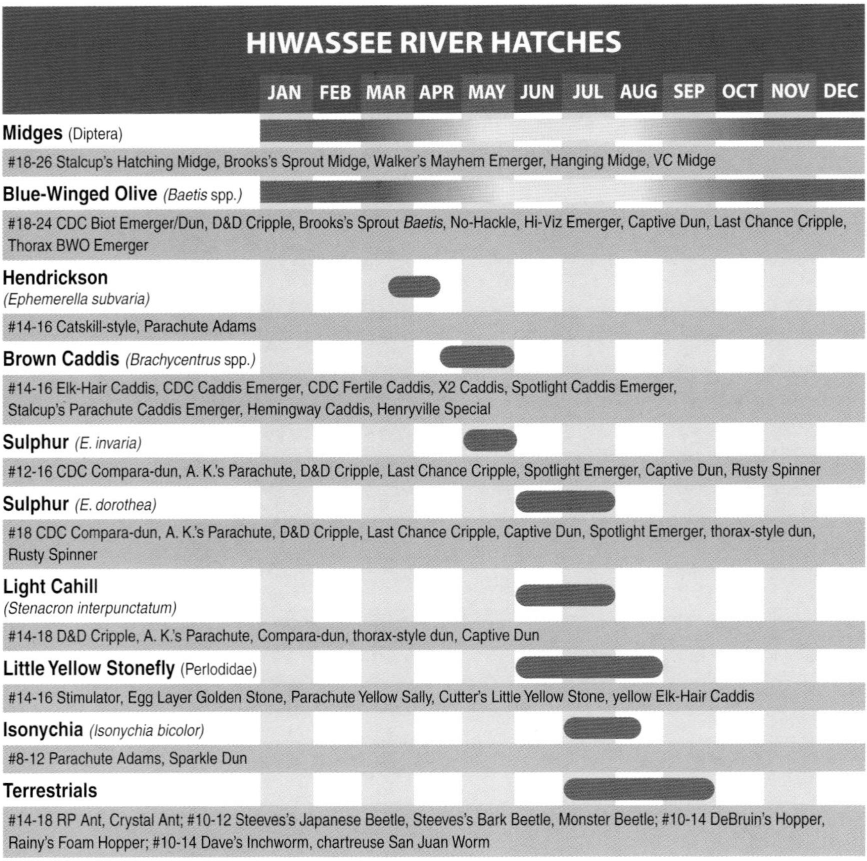
HIWASSEE RIVER HATCHES
JAN FEB MAR APR MAY JUN JUL AUG SEP OCT NOV DEC
Midges (Diptera)
#18-26 Stalcup's Hatching Midge, Brooks's Sprout Midge, Walker's Mayhem Emerger, Hanging Midge, VC Midge
Blue-Winged Olive (Baetis spp.)
#18-24 CDC Biot Emerger/Dun, D&D Cripple, Brooks's Sprout Baetis, No-Hackle, Hi-Viz Emerger, Captive Dun, Last Chance Cripple, Thorax BWO Emerger
Hendrickson (Ephemerella subvaria)
#14-16 Catskill-style, Parachute Adams
Brown Caddis (Brachycentrus spp.)
#14-16 Elk-Hair Caddis, CDC Caddis Emerger, CDC Fertile Caddis, X2 Caddis, Spotlight Caddis Emerger, Stalcup's Parachute Caddis Emerger, Hemingway Caddis, Henryville Special
Sulphur (E. invaria)
#12-16 CDC Compara-dun, A. K.'s Parachute, D&D Cripple, Last Chance Cripple, Spotlight Emerger, Captive Dun, Rusty Spinner
Sulphur (E. dorothea)
#18 CDC Compara-dun, A. K.'s Parachute, D&D Cripple, Last Chance Cripple, Captive Dun, Spotlight Emerger, thorax-style dun, Rusty Spinner
Light Cahill (Stenacron interpunctatum)
#14-18 D&D Cripple, A. K.'s Parachute, Compara-dun, thorax-style dun, Captive Dun
Little Yellow Stonefly (Perlodidae)
#14-16 Stimulator, Egg Layer Golden Stone, Parachute Yellow Sally, Cutter's Little Yellow Stone, yellow Elk-Hair Caddis
Isonychia (Isonychia bicolor)
#8-12 Parachute Adams, Sparkle Dun
Terrestrials
#14-18 RP Ant, Crystal Ant; #10-12 Steeves's Japanese Beetle, Steeves's Bark Beetle, Monster Beetle; #10-14 DeBruin's Hopper, Rainy's Foam Hopper; #10-14 Dave's Inchworm, chartreuse San Juan Worm

to tail. Some anglers believe the trout prefer flies with this stripe. Pheasant Tails with a section of white thread or wire tied along the length of the fly and large Prince Nymphs (#8-12) can all be fished as *Isonychia* nymphs.

Along with the *Isonychias,* terrestrials play a big part in the lives of Hiwassee trout. Beetles and ants are common along the summertime banks, easy pickings for trout once they hit the water. If you see a fish feeding along a bank, especially one with overhanging brush directly above or just upstream, you can bet that even if the trout is not rising with regularity, a terrestrial drifted overhead will usually draw a strike. Summertime anglers should keep a few Steeves's Japanese Beetles, Harrop's CDC Beetles, Steeves's Fireflies, (#12-14) and Monster Beetles (#8-10) on hand, along with a smattering of cinnamon and black ant imitations (#14-18).

Autumn brings fire to the valley and crimson and yellow glows on the surrounding hillsides. Even if the browns were not gearing up for their

Beldar Bugger

Hook:	#4-8 Daiichi 2220
Thread:	Black 3/0
Cone:	Tungsten
Tail:	Yellow and brown marabou
Body:	Crystal Chenille
Hackle:	Guinea
Legs:	Medium rubber

spawning ritual, which they are, just floating the river and taking in the sights would be enough. Anglers fishing from early fall through November should make sure to bring along a heavier rod to work streamers and sinking-head fly lines. This time of year is a two-rod deal. Bring a light rod for Blue-Winged Olives or maybe even the fall caddis—if you hit the lottery and the stars align—as well as a heavier 7- or 8-weight for the big browns.

Streamer patterns that are big and bright work well, as do natural-hued baitfish patterns. You really cannot go wrong fishing a Galloup's Fathead, Sculpzilla, or String Sculpin (#1/0-4) in yellow, white, and chartreuse during the fall. Sinking lines in the 150- to 300-grain realm will help get the fly down to where it needs to be.

The Hiwassee's future is unclear. The river is a fragile ecosystem, incapable of protecting itself or the trout that fin in its cold waters. Numerous elements have combined to dethrone the Hiwassee as the region's top dry-fly river, but there is hope of its recovering the crown. Closer flow regulation by the TVA and conservation efforts by Trout Unlimited and dedicated anglers are placing pressure on officials to further improve the fishery and restore it to the same standard seen in its golden years.

Holston River, Tennessee

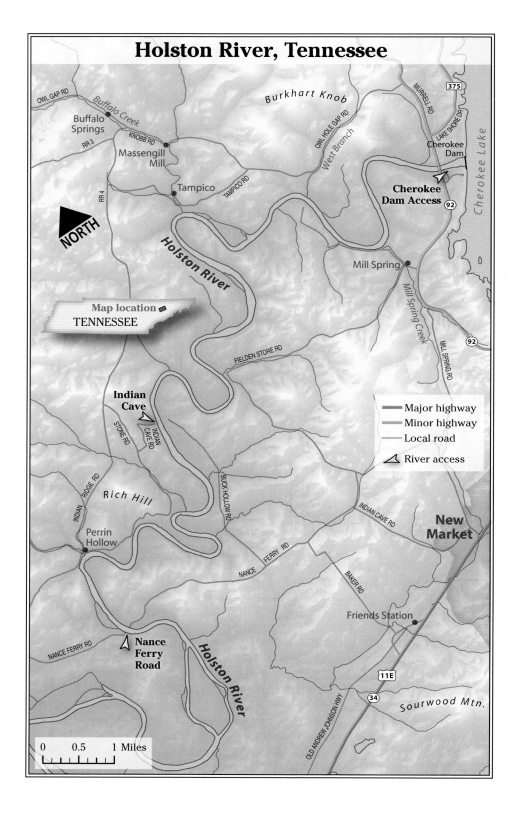

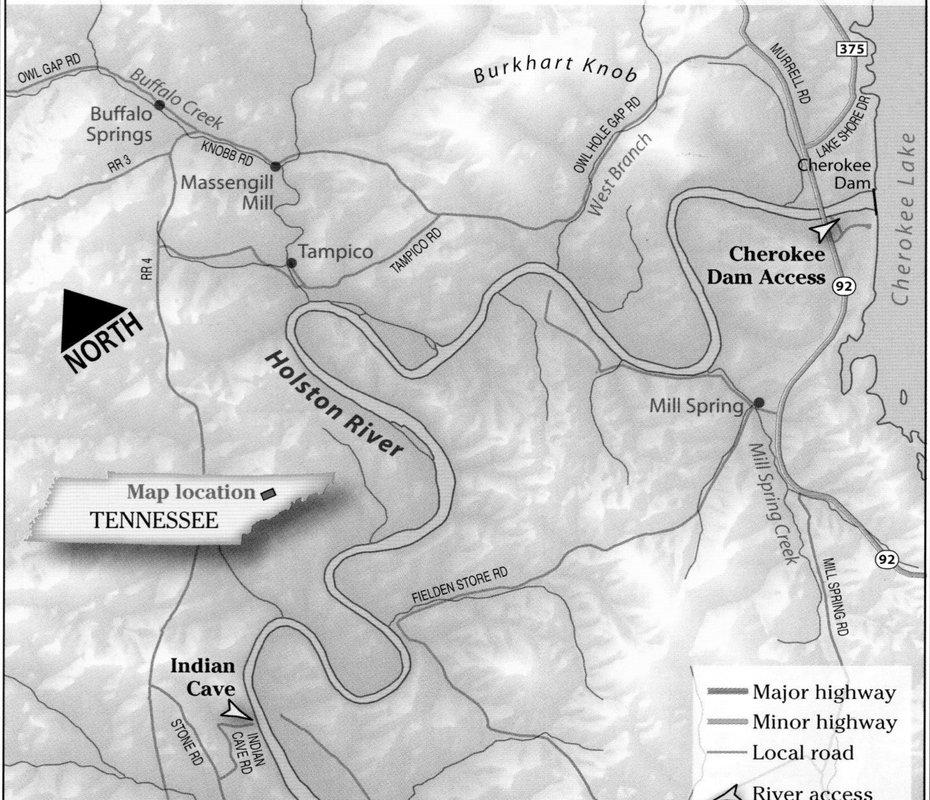
OWL GAP RD
Buffalo Creek
Buffalo Springs
KNOBB RD
RR 3
Massengill Mill
Tampico
TAMPICO RD
RR 4
NORTH
Burkhart Knob
OWL HOLE GAP RD
West Branch
MURRELL RD
375
LAKE SHORE DR
Cherokee Dam
Cherokee Lake
Cherokee Dam Access
92
Holston River
Mill Spring
Mill Spring Creek
Map location
TENNESSEE
FIELDEN STORE RD
MILL SPRING RD
Indian Cave
STONE RD
INDIAN CAVE RD
Major highway
Minor highway
Local road
River access
BUCK HOLLOW RD
INDIAN RIDGE RD
Rich Hill
INDIAN CAVE RD
New Market
Perrin Hollow
NANCE FERRY RD
BAKER RD
Friends Station
NANCE FERRY RD
Nance Ferry Road
Holston River
11E
34
OLD ANDREW JOHNSON HWY
Sourwood Mtn.
0
0.5
1 Miles

CHAPTER 12

Holston River

There was a time when the Holston River did not have a name—at least not a name that was uttered in public, especially in fly shops. The water below Cherokee Dam, just a half-hour drive from Knoxville, was overlooked by the majority of anglers, many favoring the nearby Clinch to the relatively unknown river just a short distance away. Those who were in the know would not dare utter the river's name, simply referring to the Holston as "River X." Well, sometime in the last few years, someone talked and word spread like wildfire. Now the Holston is on the map as one of the great sleeper trout-fishing destinations in the region.

Sometime in early 1999, the Tennessee Wildlife Resources Agency (TWRA) decided to stock 20,000 trout, give or take a few, in the waters below Cherokee Lake. The tailrace had been around since 1941, the massive concrete structure feeding cold water for more than 20 miles downstream. The trout took hold and are now flourishing, aided by continued stocking efforts from the TWRA.

Although the coldwater fishery carries 20 miles of water in the cooler months, the true year-round trout fishery lies more within the first 12 or so miles below the dam. During the summer, the water around Nance Ferry begins warming to lethal levels for trout, pushing the fish upstream in search of a more hospitable climate. In extraordinarily warm or dry summers, the river will fish well for only a few miles below the dam until the waters downstream begin cooling in the fall. Keeping an eye on the water temperatures and flows will let you know how far down you can expect to find trout.

Ideally, you want to be on the river during periods of nongeneration. The TVA maintains a minimum flow of around 300 cfs on the river when the turbines are silent. This level makes floating or wading the river an enjoyable and safe experience. Once the dam comes online, it can wreck fishing downstream, and makes for impossible wading conditions due to the high, swift water.

Cherokee Dam has the capability to generate over 15,000 cfs, but seldom does the dam run full tilt for very long. More common releases are "pulses," which are widespread on most TVA tailwaters. Pulsing simply means that the dam will come online, usually at a scheduled time every day, and run for a short period of time, typically a couple of hours or less. The water pushed from the dam will not affect the lower reaches of the river, the pulse dissipating after 6 or so miles, so long as it is not a heavy release. As a general rule, if you know the dam is pulsing and water is coming your way, keep an eye on the levels. If the water begins rising, head to the shore and wait it out. It may only rise a few inches, or it could come up several feet, depending on the dam's outflow. It is far better to be safe than sorry on any tailrace where generation levels are not always readily available to the public.

Very limited wade access and long floats keep many anglers off the Holston. Much of the land adjacent to the river is posted, but a few landowners will let you access their property, a couple offering a place to take your boat out for a nominal fee. Without securing landowner permission, float times

Floating the Holston will put you on water not accessible to many anglers, but be prepared for a long day on the water. IAN AND CHARITY RUTTER

between access points can make for a long day. Although the day may be long, the scenery and the fishing will help ease aching shoulders after many hours of rowing.

Much of the Holston River flows through a picturesque backdrop as it winds through the hardwood ridges of central Tennessee. Braided currents spill over large gravel bars to form long, green pools flanked by worn banks and scabrous outcroppings. Many shallow stretches make for easy wading, but most are far away from the parking lots. Floating is the best way to see the Holston, but wading anglers can also appreciate the river on a much smaller scale.

For those lacing up their wading boots rather than drawing on the oars, three access points can leave you with a good taste of the Holston. At the base of Cherokee Dam, the TVA Park will put you within striking distance of a few wadable sections downriver. Upstream, the riprap drops off quickly into deep water and isn't really suited for fly fishing on a practical or aesthetic level. On the downriver side, you can only wade a short stretch before reaching deep water.

Below the dam, the next access point is at Indian Cave, several miles downstream. The river is fairly deep here, making wading difficult save in a few places. Some anglers launch one-man pontoon boats or canoes here and head upstream during low water. The flows are slow enough that you can make good progress and access some wadable water just upstream of the launch.

The last access point is at Nance Ferry downstream. This section has the most wadable water, but typically fishes well only from late fall through the spring before the water temperature begins rising. During the prime season, however, the shallow shoals around the Nance Ferry access can be teeming with hungry brown and rainbow trout.

If you float the Holston, make sure to bring your lunch. The stretches are pretty long, and you'd best figure on being on the water all day long. This is unless you secure some private access to shorten the float—otherwise suck it up and enjoy the fishing.

Floating anglers can launch at the base of Cherokee Dam at the TVA Park. There is an improved concrete ramp here that makes launching a drift boat easy. That is where the easy part ends, as the next takeout is Indian Cave Park, which takes a minimum of eight hours to reach. It is a long, but beautiful float that takes you through the meat of the Holston trout fishery. Numerous gravel bars make for some classic riffle fishing that should not be passed up. Most anglers floating the river pull over around the shallow bars and ledges, hop out of the boat to fish, then row downstream to the next. It's easy not to get in a hurry, especially when you're catching fat rainbows and the occasional brown, but if you're not looking to float out in the dark, pushing through at a dedicated pace is necessary.

Below the Indian Cave access, a shorter, more manageable float to Nance Ferry is popular in the cooler months, when the trout are more active down

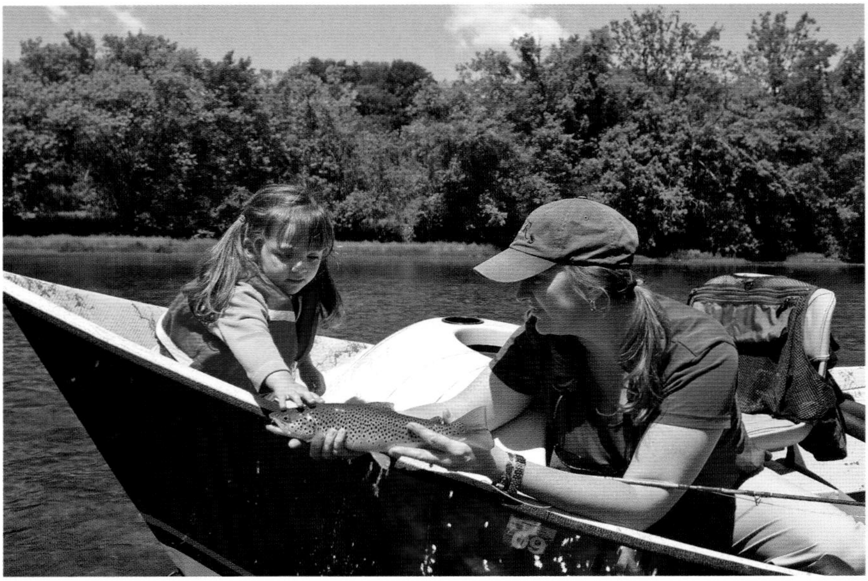

Willow Rutter makes a new friend on the Holston River. Rainbows like this are common on the Holston and will key in on the heavier hatches. Ian and Charity Rutter.

low. Just like the float from the dam to Indian Cave, there are several stretches where the river looks like more of a long, narrow lake. Pushing through the slow stretches and looking for prime trout water will help you find the fish and get off the river before the search parties are called out.

Trout on the Holston seem to enjoy a steady diet of biomass created by the higher than average pH levels in the water. The nutrient-rich water is created by a riverbed made up mostly of limestone, giving the bug life a jump start when compared with other tailraces in the region. The trout average 12 to 14 inches, with larger trout becoming more prevalent as the seasons pass. Midges, mayflies, and caddis make up the majority of trout food in the Holston, but don't overlook baitfish as a viable option in the slower, deeper water.

During the winter months, midges are king. The trout will rise to midges pretty much any day, and some nice fish will occasionally stick their beaks out. Small cream, black, and gray midge patterns such as Brooks's Sprouts, CDC Midge Emergers, and Walker's Mayhem Emergers (#18-26) are staple patterns for winter anglers. Going with a small tandem nymph rig is perhaps the most consistent bet for winter anglers. Tying a caddis larva or small mayfly such as a Split Case BWO, Pheasant Tail, Graphic Caddis, or thorax-style Blue-Winged Olive (#16-18) above a small midge pattern like a Zebra Midge or Disco Midge (#20-22) can move trout even on the coldest days.

Winter fishing on the Holston can be good, and quiet, especially if you're floating the river. Most anglers choose to avoid the long winter days on the water, and the river can be all but deserted, even on bluebird winter days. These are the days to get out, as the Blue-Winged Olive and midge fishing can be spectacular.

Throughout the year, nymphing will help you tie into more Holston trout than any other method. Anglers use a variety of flies, including Lightning Bugs, Copper Johns, Split Case PMDs, Deep Six Caddis, and Mercer's Micro Mayflies (#14-20) to name a few. Low water makes the current easy to read, and the trout lie just where you expect them to. Pulling up to a gravel bar and nymphing the deep water adjacent to the shallow, braided flow can yield dozens of fish at each stop.

Spring caddis on the Holston is what many anglers look for, considering it to be the best dry-fly fishing the river has to offer. Ian and Charity Rutter are two of these Holston caddis hatch devotees. Beginning in late March or early April, tan-gray caddis begin hatching on the Holston, the trout taking notice almost immediately. Ian and Charity, who operate R&R Fly Fishing out of Townsend, have been fishing the region for over a decade and were among

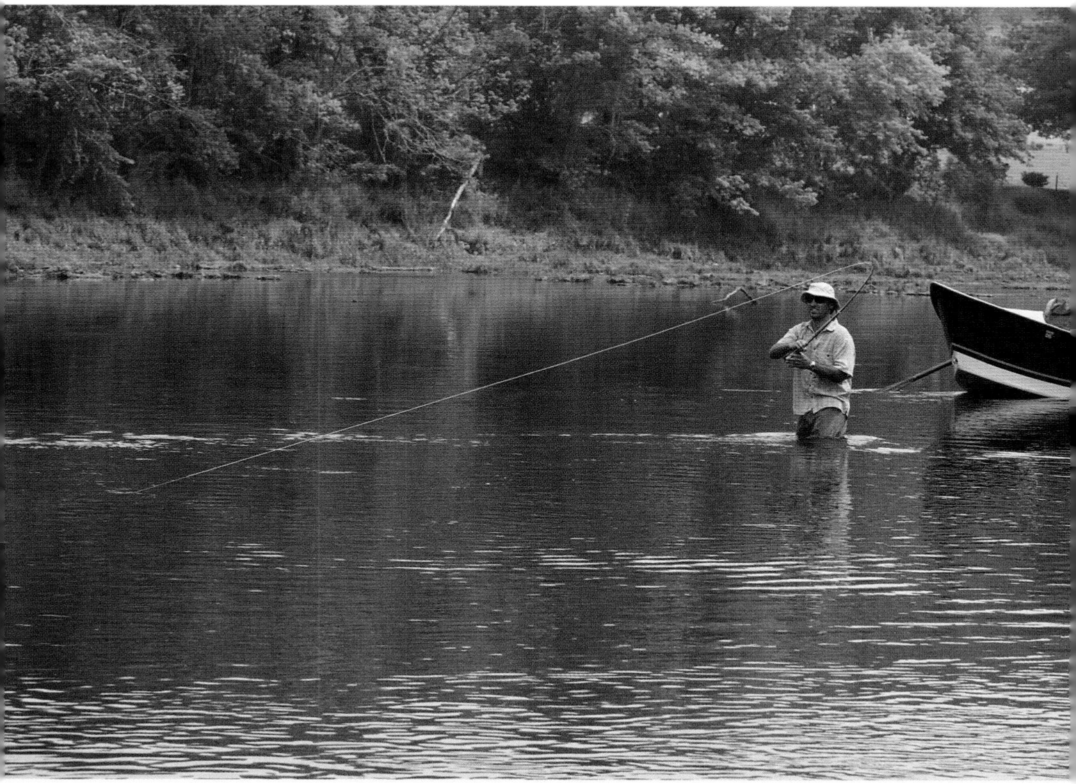

Large expanses of slow water below riffles should be explored carefully as large trout will often set up to feed in nondescript seams. IAN AND CHARITY RUTTER

HOLSTON RIVER HATCHES

	JAN	FEB	MAR	APR	MAY	JUN	JUL	AUG	SEP	OCT	NOV	DEC
Midges (Diptera)	■	■	■	■	■	■	■	■	■	■	■	■
#18-26 Stalcup's Hatching Midge, Brooks's Sprout Midge, Walker's Mayhem Emerger, Hanging Midge, VC Midge												
Blue-Winged Olive (*Baetis* spp.)	■	■	■	■	■	■	■	■	■	■	■	■
#16-24 CDC Biot Emerger/Dun, Last Chance Cripple, Brooks's Sprout *Baetis*, No-Hackle, Hi-Viz Emerger, Thorax BWO Emerger												
Little Black Caddis (*Chimarra* spp.)				■								
#18 Elk-Hair Caddis, Henry's Fork Caddis, Iris Caddis												
Tan Caddis (*Brachycentrus* spp.)					■							
#14-16 Elk-Hair Caddis, CDC Caddis Emerger, CDC Fertile Caddis, X2 Caddis, Stalcup's Parachute Caddis Emerger, Hemingway Caddis, Henryville Special, Spotlight Caddis Emerger												
Sulphur (*E. invaria*)					■							
#14-16 CDC Compara-dun, A. K.'s Parachute, D&D Cripple, Last Chance Cripple, Captive Dun, Spotlight Emerger, thorax-style dun, Pull Over Dun, Rusty Spinner												
Sulphur (*E. dorothea*)						■						
#18-20 CDC Compara-dun, A. K.'s Parachute, D&D Cripple, Last Chance Cripple, Captive Dun, Spotlight Emerger, thorax-style dun, Rusty Spinner, Pullover Dun												
Light Cahill (*Stenacron interpunctatum*)							■					
#12-16 D&D Cripple, A. K.'s Parachute, Compara-dun, thorax-style dun, Captive Dun												
Little Yellow Stonefly (Perlodidae)							■					
#14-16 Stimulators, Egg Layer Golden Stone, Parachute Yellow Sallie, Cutter's Little Yellow Stone, yellow Elk-Hair Caddis												
Terrestrials							■	■	■	■		
#14-18 RP Ant, Crystal Ant; #10-14 Steeves's Japanese Beetle, Steeves's Bark Beetle, CDC Beetle, Monster Beetle; #8-14 DeBruin's Hopper, Rainy's Foam Hopper; #10-14 Dave's Inchworm, chartreuse San Juan Worm												

the first operations to guide on the Holston. The duo prefers floating; enjoying the extended scope of water it allows you to access and the ability to escape the crowds.

For the caddis hatch, keep good supplies of both high- and low-riding patterns in your box, along with a smattering of emergers and larva imitations. Elk-Hair Caddis, Mathews's X2 Caddis, Harrop's Fertile Caddis, and Henry's Fork Caddis (#14-16), along with Graphic Caddis Pupae, and Norris Caddis Pupae (#14-18) will cover you when the caddis are coming off.

Around Labor Day, the Sulphurs (*E. invaria*) begin hatching. These seductive mayflies continue to hatch in good numbers through the end of June. Around 1 PM, the first bugs will begin punching through the surface film, the hatch steadily building as the evening wanes. Fishing a Compara-dun or parachute-style Sulphur (#14-16) is usually all it takes on the Holston, especially once you get away from the public access points. If the fish get picky, tie on a Last Chance Cripple or Harrop's CDC Biot Emerger or Dun (#16-18) to sway their vote in your favor.

Summer means warm water downstream of Indian Cave and slow fishing below this point. Fishing within the first 5 miles below the dam is your best bet for finding cold water and receptive trout. Nymphing with midge, caddis, and mayfly patterns is standard form on the Holston at this time of year, but don't overlook the terrestrial hatch. Japanese beetles, grasshoppers, and ants make up the trout's topwater forage. A summer dry box should include Rainy's Grand Hoppers (#8-12), DeBruin's Foam Hopper (#8-14), Steeves's Japanese Beetles and Fireflies (#12-14), and Monster Beetles (#8-10). This is prime time for running a hopper/dropper rig, doubling your chances at hooking up with a Holston trout.

If you are looking for large trout and the occasional smallmouth bass, try floating the river during periods of generation. The increased water levels speed up float times and take the edge off otherwise skittish trout. Long sinking lines tipped with Beldar Buggers, Bellyache Minnows, Zonkers, or Galloup's Zoo Cougars (#1/0-4), along with a number of general baitfish patterns, can turn a high-water float down the Holston into a successful fishing expedition.

The journey from an obscure, troutless tailwater to the mainstream spotlight was a short one for the Holston. Less than a decade has passed since this Tennessee river evolved from its juvenile fishery status. Because the Holston progressed from the clandestine destination of local anglers to one of the top trout fisheries in the South at breakneck speed, it is difficult to assess the future of the river. As it stands, the Holston is here to stay and is only getting better every year. One of the youngest tailwater fisheries in the region, the Holston has taken its place among the great fisheries of the Southeast, and from the look of things, it has no plans of fading.

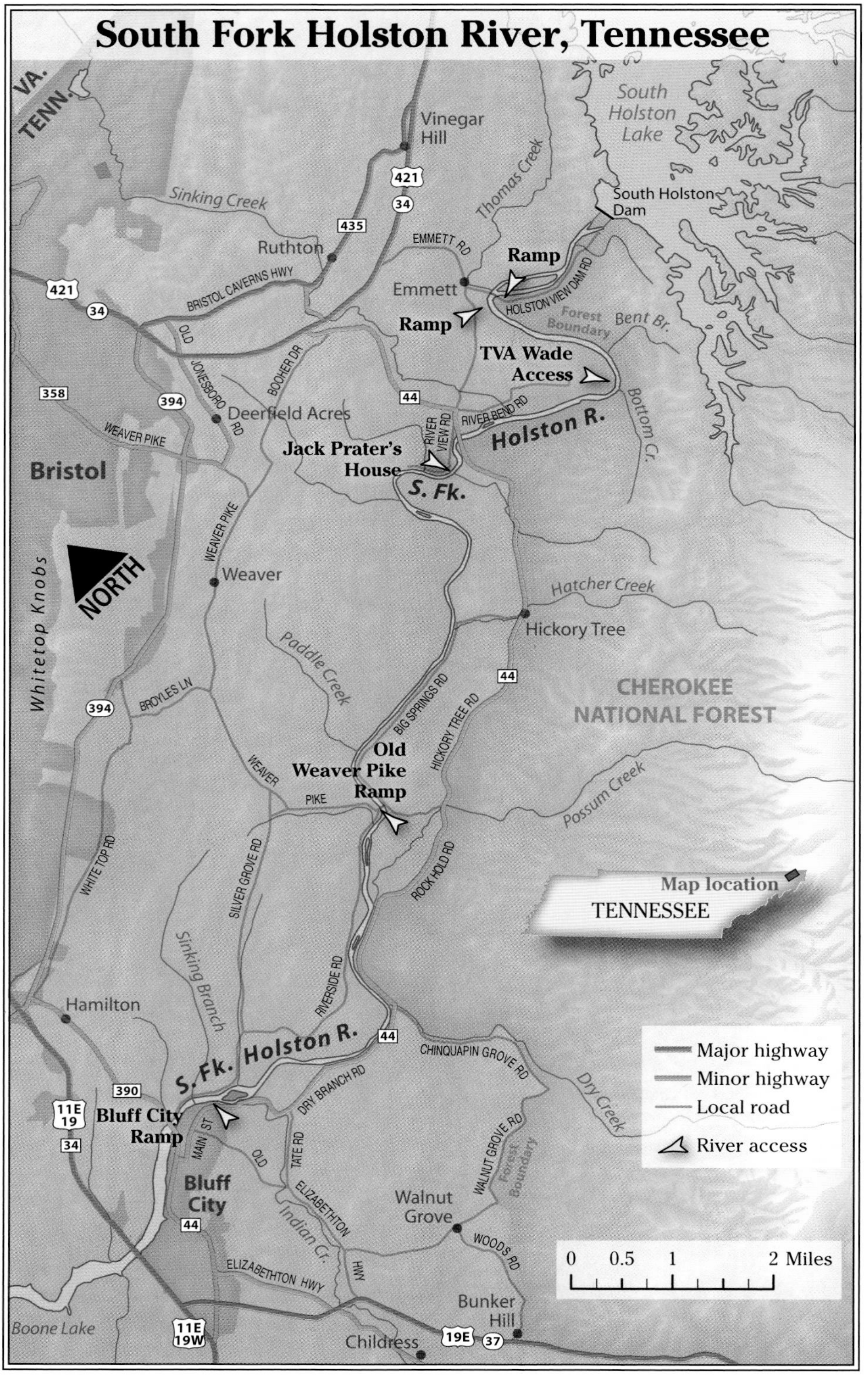
South Fork Holston River, Tennessee
VA.
TENN.
Vinegar Hill
421
34
435
Sinking Creek
Thomas Creek
South Holston Lake
South Holston Dam
Ruthton
EMMETT RD
BRISTOL CAVERNS HWY
Ramp
Emmett
Ramp
HOLSTON VIEW DAM RD
Forest Boundary
Bent Br.
TVA Wade Access
421
34
OLD JONESBORO RD
BOOHER DR
358
394
44
Deerfield Acres
RIVER VIEW RD
RIVER BEND RD
Holston R.
Bottom Cr.
WEAVER PIKE
Bristol
Jack Prater's House
S. Fk.
WEAVER PIKE
NORTH
Weaver
Whitetop Knobs
Hatcher Creek
Hickory Tree
Paddle Creek
44
394
BROYLES LN
BIG SPRINGS RD
HICKORY TREE RD
CHEROKEE NATIONAL FOREST
Old Weaver Pike Ramp
WEAVER PIKE
Possum Creek
WHITE TOP RD
SILVER GROVE RD
ROCK HOLD RD
Map location
TENNESSEE
Sinking Branch
RIVERSIDE RD
Hamilton
44
S. Fk. Holston R.
CHINQUAPIN GROVE RD
Dry Creek
390
DRY BRANCH RD
11E 19
34
Bluff City Ramp
MAIN ST
OLD ELIZABETHTON
TATE RD
WALNUT GROVE RD
Forest Boundary
Bluff City
44
Walnut Grove
Indian Cr.
WOODS RD
ELIZABETHTON HWY
HWY
Bunker Hill
Boone Lake
11E 19W
Childress
19E
37
Major highway
Minor highway
Local road
River access
0 0.5 1 2 Miles

CHAPTER 13

South Fork of the Holston River

This place is like *A River Runs Through It* on mescaline—a venerable cornucopia of long-hair hippie types, businessmen on holiday, backwoods mullets, and genuine east Tennessee country folk who cumulate to form an eclectic angling melting pot. You're just as likely to see a fellow who looks like he stepped fresh out of an Orvis Company catalog as you are an old, stumpy fellow smoking a cigarette, wielding a fine bamboo rod, and wearing an "I'm with Nietzsche" T-shirt, or a shirtless good ole boy sloshing around in overalls. They're all after a similar endgame, but travel different roads.

Folks come to the South Holston after hearing about it one way or another. They see photos of big trout and figure they'd like to see what all the fuss is about. Most find out quickly that the river doesn't just give up big fish, or any trout for that matter. Consistently catching trout, especially quality fish, on the South Holston is no easy task—sometimes it is downright unrealistic. The river is tough, period. It has been compared to the Henry's Fork and the Delaware in terms of selective trout, and maybe that is what makes it so popular with those who frequent the river. If you want easy, go somewhere else.

What makes the South Holston such an amazing river while so many other great rivers in the region have fallen from grace? Well, somehow the South Holston has managed to dodge the maladies that have wrecked many Southern rivers at one time or another. In the last few years, the river has received some favorable press, and a few fresh faces have shown up, but given the river's location, close to nothing, it has remained relatively untarnished.

The tailrace is born at the base of South Holston Dam, deep in rural northeastern Tennessee. Just below the dam, a labyrinth weir that acts much like a natural waterfall, adding oxygen to the waters below, improves the dissolved oxygen levels in the river. In addition to this, valved pipes at the base of the weir maintain a minimum flow on the river. As the pool drains during periods of no generation, the TVA releases water twice a day to refill the pool. These two efforts, combined with turbine venting, manufacture a nearly ideal trout habitat downstream, regulating dissolved oxygen and water levels.

When the turbines are silent, the South Holston is a wide, silky river, winding 18 miles through Tennessee farm country. Long, smooth glides are interrupted by shallow riffles and boulder-laced runs. In low water, the river is too shallow to float, but it is ideal for wading. Wading anglers should pay close attention to the water levels, marking a rock or some anchored object to judge if the water is stable or beginning to rise. Even if there is no scheduled generation, this doesn't guarantee that the TVA will not release water in extreme cases, such as to meet unforeseen power demands.

Once the dam comes online, the riverbed fills quickly and the large boulders that lie all but high and dry in low flows become catalysts for whitewater runs that, while not overly technical, can and do swamp boats. Like most other TVA tailraces, there is no rhyme or reason to the South Holston schedules; however, in the spring and summer, you can usually count on some type of midday generation, especially on weekdays. Keep an eye on the TVA generation schedule on this and other tailraces in the region by visiting their web site (www.tva.gov) or via the lake information hotline, (800) 238-2264.

Wading anglers have no shortage of access, but almost all require a bit of walking, typically over the river's slick rocks. Below the grate weir, several hundred yards of water downstream is accessible along a trail leading from

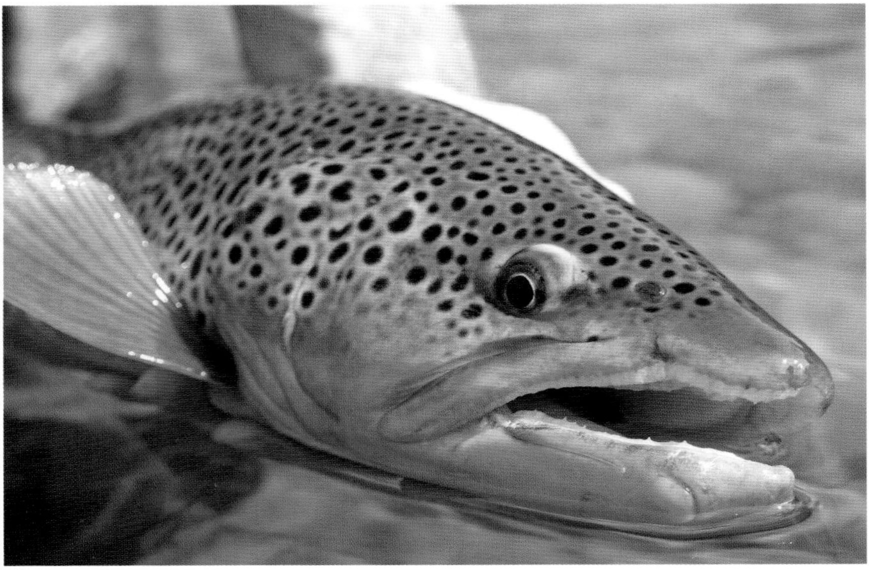

Big trout do eat small flies on the South Holston. Midges, blackfly larvae, and **Baetis** *nymphs fished on long, light tippets are the way of life on this Tennessee tailrace.*

the parking lot on river left downstream. The river is fairly shallow here, coursing over rocks and forming long riffles oftentimes flanking deeper slots near the bank, or dropping over low rock ledges and forming miniature plunge pools. Look for trout in any piece of water over a foot deep, as even large trout can surprise you in where they choose to lie.

Below the weir access, a single path leads downstream from a TVA access point off River Bend Road. There is little parking here and it doesn't take long for this access to become crowded. Riffles upstream and a long, glassy pool downriver give anglers their choice of water. The hike down to the river is not a long one, but if you're going in during the summer, keep a watchful eye on the trail, as copperheads really enjoy hanging out there.

Downstream of the TVA access, the water alongside Big Springs Road marks the last viable public access point for wade anglers. The road parallels the river for a few miles, with several pullouts for easy parking. Watch for the posted signs, and do not park in areas marked as private. The water down low is a hodgepodge of long, slick pools, braided riffles, and deep cuts, all holding trout. Trout in this section tend to pod up in the low water, making them extremely spooky. Instead of one pair of eyes, there are usually several dozen watching for fly line flashing overhead, flies splatting or dragging on the surface, and any other mistake you can think of. Even shadows of a fine leader floating over a pod of spooky trout can send them off in a flurry of tails and waking water.

Floating anglers are able to access the entire river, but the river is no longer as "readable" when the turbines increase the water flow. Evident lies are submerged under several feet of sweeping water, making intimate knowledge of the riverbed paramount when looking for trout in high water. Seams in the fast water are not always evident, and there can be a dozen prime lies stretched out over a hundred yards of water, but unless you know where they are, it is easy to miss the holding water. This is especially true when drifting nymphs. A few feet can make the difference between a bent rod with a nice trout dancing on the other end and a goose egg. This is where a good guide really earns his or her paycheck.

The South Holston can be divided into two stretches for floating anglers: the upper section from the weir dam at Osceola Island downstream to Jack Prater's house just below Old Hickory Tree Bridge, and the lower stretch extending from Jack's house downstream to the Old Weaver Pike bridge. Together they encompass the entirety of year-round trout water on the river. Below the Old Weaver Pike bridge, the river's flow flattens and slows. There are far fewer trout than in the upper reaches, and hatches are almost nonexistent.

If you're using a trailered boat, there are paved ramps on either side of the Holston View Dam Road bridge, just below the weir. There is ample parking at both, and the ramps are easily accessible. Some floating anglers launch above the weir, floating the upper stretch below the labyrinth weir and the grate weir. There are some large trout in this area, but it takes a lot of patience, skill, and luck to hook up.

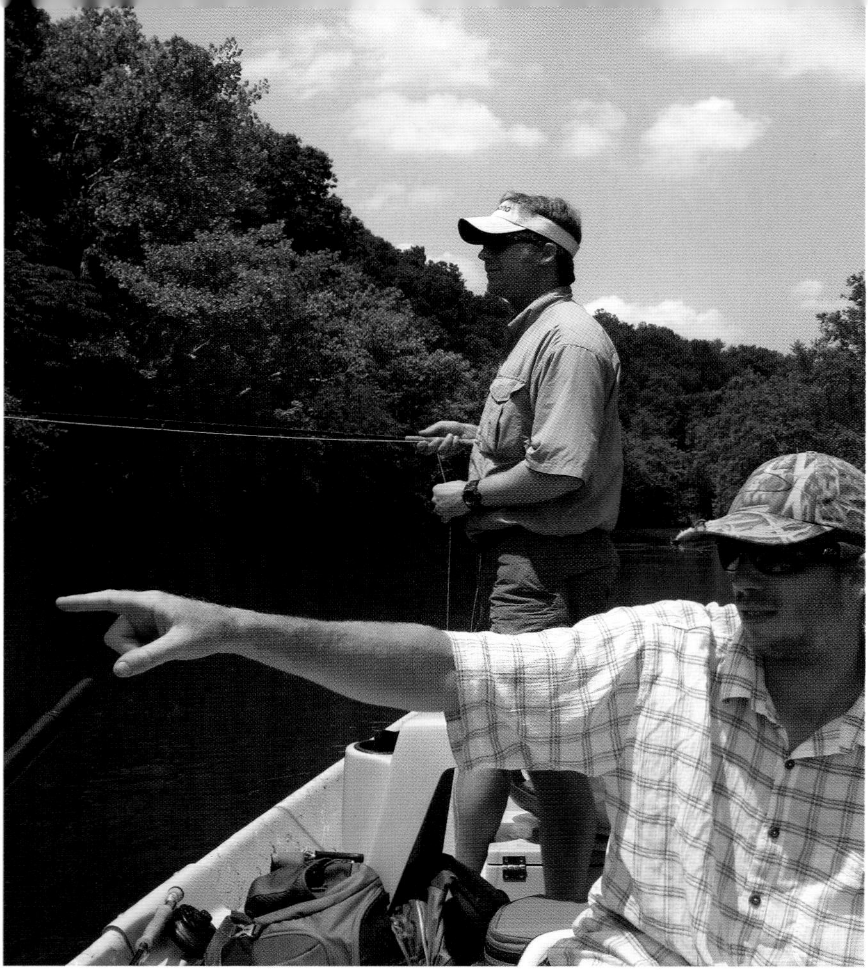

Guide Guitou Feuillebois points out a rising trout. Guides are well worth the price, especially if it is your first time to the river.

Below the weir, you have the option to float roughly 5 miles to Jack Prater's house just below the bridge on Old Hickory Tree Road, or continue downstream another 6 miles to the Old Weaver Pike bridge. Under the old bridge, there is a dirt ramp that is difficult to access, especially after a rain, due to the steep incline of the pullout. This ramp is small and primitive, requiring a bit of jockeying to get the trailer into position, but it marks the last boating access before the river empties into the lake at Bluff City.

The upper float, from the ramp near the weir off Holston View Dam Road to Jack's house on River View Road, is by far the more popular float. The stretch has the highest density of trout as well as the heaviest hatches, so there is little wonder why it is not uncommon to see a couple of dozen boats floating down during the spring and summer when the hatches are at their peak. On some days, Jack's house has more drift boat trailers parked on the grass than the ClackaCraft sales lot in Idaho.

Jack Prater is known as "the shuttle guy" on the South Holston River. Jack's home sits at what could be the perfect takeout point if you're floating down from the weir dam near Osceola Island, about 5 or so miles upstream. Few people are as genuinely nice as Jack, who always offers a smile and a wry, northeast Tennessee witticism along with a ride back to your rig. He is a fine representation of the other residents of the valley and one of the many reasons I enjoy trips to the South Holston. The region is unspoiled and natural, offering realism and a taste of true Americana that you can find only in a handful of places. Big brown trout rising to a dry fly don't hurt, either.

High-water and low-water fishing techniques differ from one another on the South Holston, each possessing its own set of challenges and requiring mutually exclusive skill sets from anglers. Low-water dry-fly fishing on the South Holston is a technical game, especially for the larger fish. The big boys do not tolerate mistakes. Bring your "A" game, or plan on getting an "F" from the trout. You're not going to catch big fish here by luck—it just doesn't happen. Sure, they can come along at unexpected moments, but they're not just gonna drop everything that has kept them alive this long to suck in your size 14 Parachute Adams as it tumbles past.

Perfect presentations combined with the river's most abundant food adds further to odds that continue to stack up against the angler. Midges are an abundant food source for the trout, making a selection of midge emergers, larvae, and dry flies necessary. Blackflies are also present, adding to the small-

Mind your speed around the takeout at Jack Prater's house. Jack is a fixture on the river and his property is a popular takeout for anglers floating the South Holston.

Low water on the South Holston means spooky trout. Careful stalking and accurate casting are required to connect with a big Tennessee trout.

fly medley. When nymphing, a number of midge patterns will work, but Zebra Midges, Smethurst's Answers, UV Z-Midges, Juju Midges, and Sidewinder Midge Larvae (#20-26) all consistently produce fish. Blackfly larvae can be imitated with black Poison Tungs, Miracle Midges, Jujubee Midges, BTS Nymphs, Black Cardinal Midges, and Black Beauties (#18-24).

Fishing these alone or in tandem under either a small, white indicator or an inconspicuous dry will allow you to detect strikes without spooking paranoid trout. Going down to 6X fluorocarbon tippet will stack another small advantage in your favor. Now it's up to you to get within casting distance of the trout without spooking them, present the fly perfectly, and set the hook when the ever so subtle take is detected.

For midge dry flies, take along a few Walker's Mayhem Emergers, Brooks's Sprout Midges, and VC Midges (#20-26), but get ready for some frustrating times. South Holston trout are extremely fickle when it comes to eating midges on top. Even if you do everything right, the trout sometimes simply refuse to eat your offering, if for no other reason that it doesn't fit into the erratic feeding pattern so often associated with midging trout on this river.

Aside from midges, dry-fly fishing on the South Holston can be had on nearly any day of the year, but just as it can be a near frenzy, it can be equally absent. The bugs are sometimes as fickle as the trout, emerging like crazy for a couple of days, then inexplicably going on strike like union workers. It's good to remember this when visiting the river. The reports you've heard or the hatch that's supposed to be coming off may not be there on a given day. Adapting to the conditions is the hallmark of a good angler, so don't try to force the issue. If the bugs are not coming off, then feed them what they're eating.

Blue-Winged Olives hatch from October through March, giving anglers something a bit larger to tie on. During a good Blue-Winged Olive hatch, even the large trout get in the game, rising to the tiny mayflies just as willingly as their 12-inch cousins. Presentation notwithstanding, Blue-Winged Olive patterns such as Brooks's Sprout *Baetis,* Harrop's CDC Biot Emergers and Duns, Last Chance Cripples, and Smith's Translucent Emergers (#18-24) can be used to tempt trout. During this time of year, Blue-Winged Olive nymphs also work well on days when there are no fish rising. Split Case BWOs, *Baetis* Thorax Nymphs, Mercer's Micro Mayflies, and Anatomic BWO Nymphs (#18-22) will all work as subsurface fare, especially when fished with one of the aforementioned midge larva patterns.

Perhaps the most prolific hatch on the South Holston is the Sulphur hatch. The hatch begins sometime in late May and continues through September, some years spilling into October. Guides promote the hatch in their literature the way Western shops do the Salmonflies. Floating and wading anglers alike can take advantage of this prolific east Tennessee hatch, but despite the fanfare, it can never really be counted on. It breaks down to a near day-to-day basis much of the season, with bugs coming off for days at a time, then inexplicably everything shuts down for a day, sometimes more, before regaining its momentum.

In high or low water, CDC Comparaduns, parachute-style Sulphurs, Last Chance Cripples, and Harrop's CDC Biot Emergers and Duns (#14-16) work well early in the season until mid-July. After the summer heat really sets in, smaller *E. dorothea* Sulphurs begin filing in behind the larger *E. invaria.* Fish the same patterns as above, but just drop down to a #18 Sulphur pattern to match these smaller variations.

Japanese beetles are a staple for trout on the South Holston and many other Southern rivers during the summer. Oftentimes a beetle plopped into the water under an overhanging tree or bush will bring up trout thinking they're about to get an easy meal.

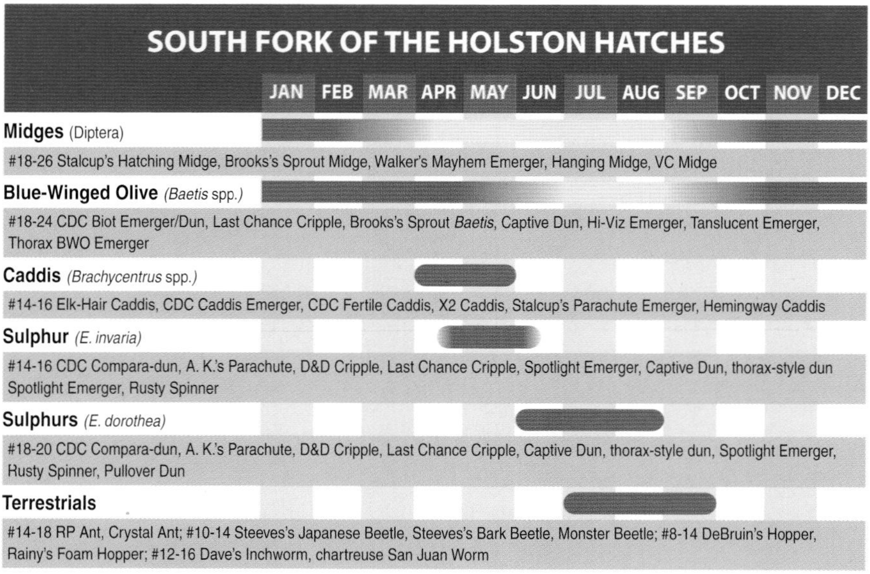
SOUTH FORK OF THE HOLSTON HATCHES
JAN FEB MAR APR MAY JUN JUL AUG SEP OCT NOV DEC
Midges (Diptera)
#18-26 Stalcup's Hatching Midge, Brooks's Sprout Midge, Walker's Mayhem Emerger, Hanging Midge, VC Midge
Blue-Winged Olive (Baetis spp.)
#18-24 CDC Biot Emerger/Dun, Last Chance Cripple, Brooks's Sprout Baetis, Captive Dun, Hi-Viz Emerger, Tanslucent Emerger, Thorax BWO Emerger
Caddis (Brachycentrus spp.)
#14-16 Elk-Hair Caddis, CDC Caddis Emerger, CDC Fertile Caddis, X2 Caddis, Stalcup's Parachute Emerger, Hemingway Caddis
Sulphur (E. invaria)
#14-16 CDC Compara-dun, A. K.'s Parachute, D&D Cripple, Last Chance Cripple, Spotlight Emerger, Captive Dun, thorax-style dun Spotlight Emerger, Rusty Spinner
Sulphurs (E. dorothea)
#18-20 CDC Compara-dun, A. K.'s Parachute, D&D Cripple, Last Chance Cripple, Captive Dun, thorax-style dun, Spotlight Emerger, Rusty Spinner, Pullover Dun
Terrestrials
#14-18 RP Ant, Crystal Ant; #10-14 Steeves's Japanese Beetle, Steeves's Bark Beetle, Monster Beetle; #8-14 DeBruin's Hopper, Rainy's Foam Hopper; #12-16 Dave's Inchworm, chartreuse San Juan Worm

Summertime brings out the dry-fly underground. Terrestrials including hoppers, inchworms, beetles, and ants become topwater temptations for fish. During years when the Japanese beetles are present, trout will gorge themselves on these insects, making it a necessity to have plenty of Steeves's Japanese Beetles and Harrop's CDC Beetles (#12-14) on hand. In addition, black and cinnamon flying ant patterns (#14-18), Dave's Inchworms (#12-16), and various hopper patterns (#8-14) should be well represented in a summertime South Holston box.

Dry-fly fishing can be epic on the river, but nymphing is what accounts for the most trout day in, day out. A variety of nymphs should be on hand including mayfly and caddis patterns along with scuds and the midges mentioned above. Some of the South Holston's usual suspects are Split Case PMDs, Pheasant Tails, and Copper Johns (#14-18), along with pink, orange, and gray scud patterns (#14-18), Norris's Caddis, Weedy's Drifting Caddis, and Sparkle Pupae (#14-18). These all work well in both high and low water. The rigging is a bit different, as plenty of split-shot needs to be added during high water to get the fly beneath the swift water, down into the softer currents where the trout are feeding.

High-water streamer fishing is another aspect of this river, as it is on almost all Southern tailraces. Pretty much year-round fishing can be had when stripping baitfish patterns on sinking lines. Some of the more savvy anglers on the river forgo the traditional trout weights and break out the big guns. Eight-weight, even nine-weight rods, seemingly better suited for a bonefish flat than a Tennessee trout river, are choice sticks for streamer work, the heavier weights

Harrop's *Baetis* CDC Biot Dun

Hook:	#18-24 Daiichi 1180
Thread:	Olive 8/0
Tail:	Wood duck
Body:	Olive goose biot
Thorax:	Olive dubbing
Legs:	Turkey flat
Wing:	Dun CDC

Steeves's Japanese Beetle

Hook:	#12-14 Daiichi 1170
Thread:	Black 6/0
Body:	Peacock herl
Back:	Foam and Swiss Straw
Legs:	Kreinik 1/8" ribbon

delivering sinking tips and large flies with less effort and an indispensable necessity when playing a large trout. Streamer patterns including Galloup's Zoo Cougars, Rolex Streamers, and a variety of big, burly baitfish imitations ranging in size from 3 to 6 inches in length can be used to tempt large trout, but don't expect to hook up every day. This is a search for "the one" and that can take some time, especially for novice South Holston anglers.

Fall is big brown trout time. There is much debate centering around fishing to spawning browns on the South Holston. Large sections of the river are closed for the spawn, but enough water is available for some anglers to target these vulnerable fish. State laws aside, the majority of anglers believe fishing for trout during the height of their spawn is unethical. A great deal of damage can be done to the spawning redds by anglers who insist on fishing during this period. Careless anglers who wade through active redds can have detrimental effects on future generations of wild fish. That said, it is best to leave the trout be during the peak of their spawn and concentrate your efforts on aggressive prespawn fish if you're looking for a trophy brown.

For the technical angler, the South Holston is one of the best in the South. For the novice, it is the epitome of frustration and heartache. The trout will test you, but in the end you will come out of the experience a wiser, more adaptive fly fisher.

Watauga River, Tennessee

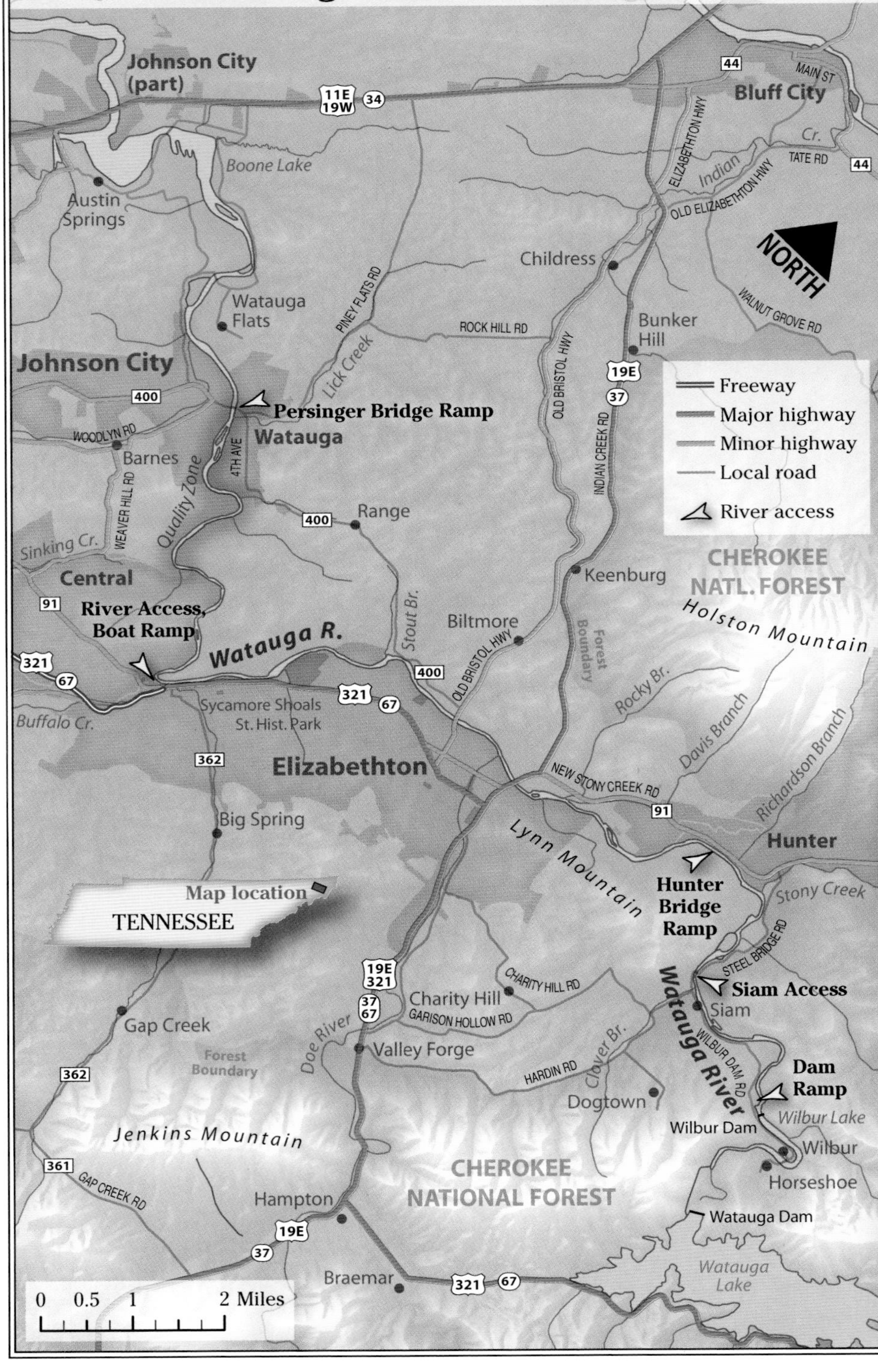

CHAPTER 14

Watauga River

When the TVA purchased Wilbur Lake in 1945, it is doubtful officials could have fathomed what would be created downstream. The Watauga sneaks through the mountains of North Carolina hiding in the shadow of its tailwater sibling. Near the town of Banner Elk, high in the mountains of North Carolina, the river is a jubilant freestone—one stretch is even managed under that state's popular delayed-harvest regulations. It is fished up there, but nobody is really making the trek up the mountain just for fishing. Angling on the headwaters is usually a by-product of another trip, usually involving the entire family.

Before any fanfare, the river must run its course through the North Carolina high country and drop into the valleys of east Tennessee. From there, the Watauga empties into Watauga Lake, then escapes by tunneling through the Iron Mountains, where it is finally impounded by Wilbur Lake. Below Wilbur Lake for 16 miles downstream to Boone Lake the river is full of 10- to 14-inch trout, with many trout in the 15- to 18-inch range, and more than a few well over 22 inches.

The Watauga has long been known as a blue ribbon trout fishery in the South, but its future was all but destroyed by a cataclysmic disaster in the first February of the new century. A fire at North American Rayon, a textile mill on the banks of the Watauga, precipitated a massive chemical spill. The spill entered the river, killing an estimated 24,000 trout from the mill downstream to Boone Lake. Nearly 10 miles of trout water were all but destroyed, and many thought the river would never make a full recovery.

Luckily, the naysayers were proven wrong. Following efforts by the TWRA, including massive stockings of brown and rainbow trout in the affected section of river, trout soon began thriving once again. Today, the river is a mirror image of itself from the old days, maybe even a little better. Big trout and a vast array of biomass inhabit the very waters declared dead less than a decade ago. This alone is testament to the river's resilient nature and near-perfect trout habitat.

For anglers wanting to fish the Watauga, there are plenty of options, from Wilbur Dam all the way downstream where the river flows into Boone Lake. Access is plentiful on the Watauga for wade and float anglers alike. Much of the river is open under the state's general harvest season, but the section between Smalling Bridge and just above Persinger Bridge near the town of Watauga is what concentrates the highest number of fly anglers. This is the Quality Zone, with only two trout 14 inches or longer legal for harvest per day. Some large trout swim in the Quality Zone, but miles of river lying outside this narrow scope can fish equally well.

Wading anglers can find access at the dam, the TVA access off Old TN 91, and along West Riverside Drive in Elizabethton. All these spots offer access to the river and ample parking. There are numerous wadable shoals in low water and stocked as well as wild brown and rainbow trout can get you away from the crowds on the Quality Zone.

The section of river flowing through Elizabethton is also popular among wading anglers, especially around the Sycamore Shoals area. This can be accessed from either side of the river, at Sycamore Shoals Recreation Area or directly across at Joe LaPorte Jr. City Park. The river is wadable across its entirety during low water, and the shoals extend for several hundred yards,

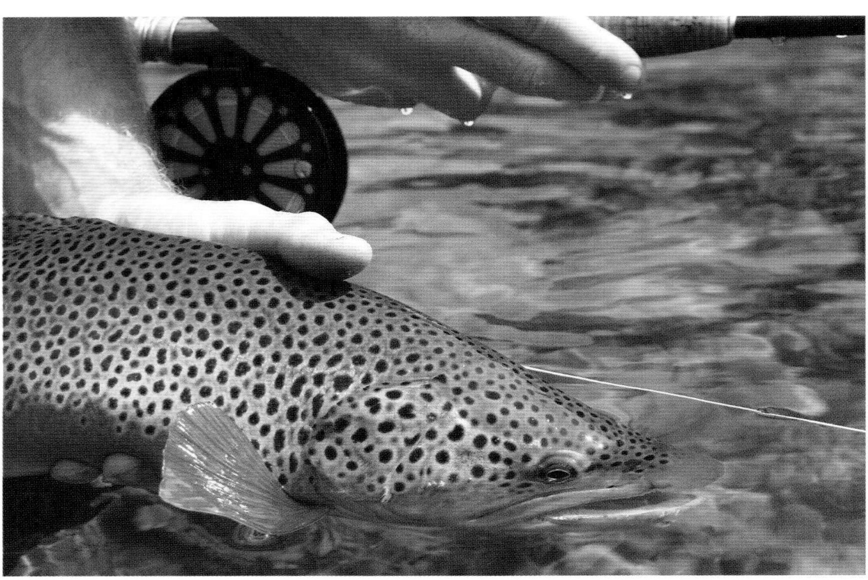

On the Watauga, small flies often equal big trout. Here, anything larger than a #18 is considered big, with smaller #20-22 nymphs being the better choice to fool brown trout like this one.

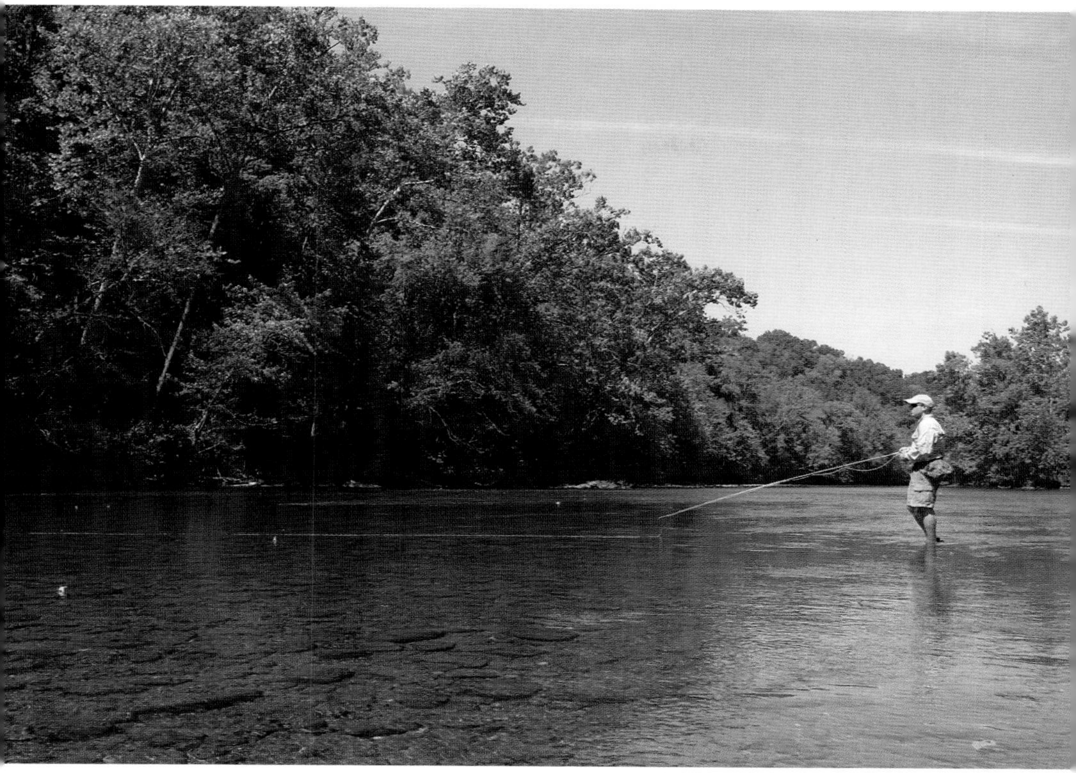

Slow, shallow stretches of water cloak scores of trout. Wade carefully and make your first cast count.

cutting around a midriver island before dumping off into a section of deeper water.

Downstream of Sycamore Shoals is a public boat launch and parking area off Blevins Road. There is a portion of water in front of the ramp and just upstream where you can wade, but it is fairly limited due to deep water just a short distance away. A better spot is located a few miles downstream at Persinger Bridge. From the shallow shoals below the bridge downstream until the river makes a large bend into deep water is a good stretch to fish for large trout, but you'd better spot them first. Hoping to hook up with a big trout here by blind casting doesn't work. Luckily, the boat traffic all but stops below the bridge, so if you're first on the water, your chance of finding cooperative trout multiplies.

Floating anglers can launch at the TVA ramp located at the base of Wilbur Dam. From there, you can float to the Hunter Bridge ramp just downstream of Siam. This section of river receives far less pressure than the trophy water downstream but can fish just as well as the famed trophy water.

From Hunter Bridge to the next public ramp off Blevins Road is a long way, but the float will take you through some gorgeous trout water and typically is not as crowded at the lower float below Blevins. The trout in this stretch can be cooperative, especially if the generators are on. Stripping streamers through this long stretch can yield some larger than average trout. Go with heavy sinking lines and big flies like Galloup's Fatheads or Stacked Blondes (#1/0-4) in yellow, black, white, and chartreuse to target the big trout that hold in the upper river.

Below Blevins Road, Persinger Bridge marks the next ramp useful to trout anglers. This is the last practical ramp for fly fishers, with a few floating below Persinger down to the slow water above the lake. This isn't classic fly water down low, so most folks avoid it and stick with floats between the dam and Persinger.

The Blevins-to-Persinger float is far and away the most popular on the entire river. It is a relatively easy float, but you'd best keep your wits about you or find yourself high-centered on a rock or worse. Drift boats are sunk in this stretch on something just slightly less than a regular basis, the rocky bottom channeling currents that, to the unfamiliar, are oftentimes too hard to read before it's too late. If you're going down for the first time, go with someone who knows the river, or better yet hire a professional guide. They cannot only get you into trout you'd probably never even see on your own, but can get you downstream safely while you concentrate on fishing.

With all the wade anglers, fun-float anglers, and guide boats, it is no surprise that the majority of trout are pretty hip to the game. Chances are if it's in a fly bin, these trout have seen it and probably know the more popular patterns by name. Brad Barnes, who guides out of Watauga River Lodge, told me that the secret to catching trout on the Watauga is to show them something they haven't seen before. Brad's advice was proven one afternoon as he proceeded to hook trout after trout on one of the most heavily fished stretches of the river. He was fishing just behind more than a dozen guide boats and two wading anglers, but still managed to hook up consistently into the evening with a simple beadhead nymph suspended under a nondescript terrestrial dry. After the trout have seen the same flies time and time again, for days on end, you sometimes have to shake things up a bit, showing them something new and fresh—especially if you are fishing through water that has already been covered by other anglers.

This is not to say the tried-and-true patterns of the river do not still catch fish, because they do. It is a good idea to call, or better yet drop in at either The Fly Shop of Tennessee or Mahoney's Sports, both in Johnson City, Tennessee, to find out what the week's hot fly is. Foscoe Fishing Company and Appalachian Angler are two other shops to check out. Located nearer to the headwaters than the tailwater stretch, both these shops have guides who work the Watauga on a daily basis and can offer fly suggestions as well as guided trips down the tailwater. Nothing compares to local knowledge, so use the expertise found in any of these shops to help plan your Watauga trip.

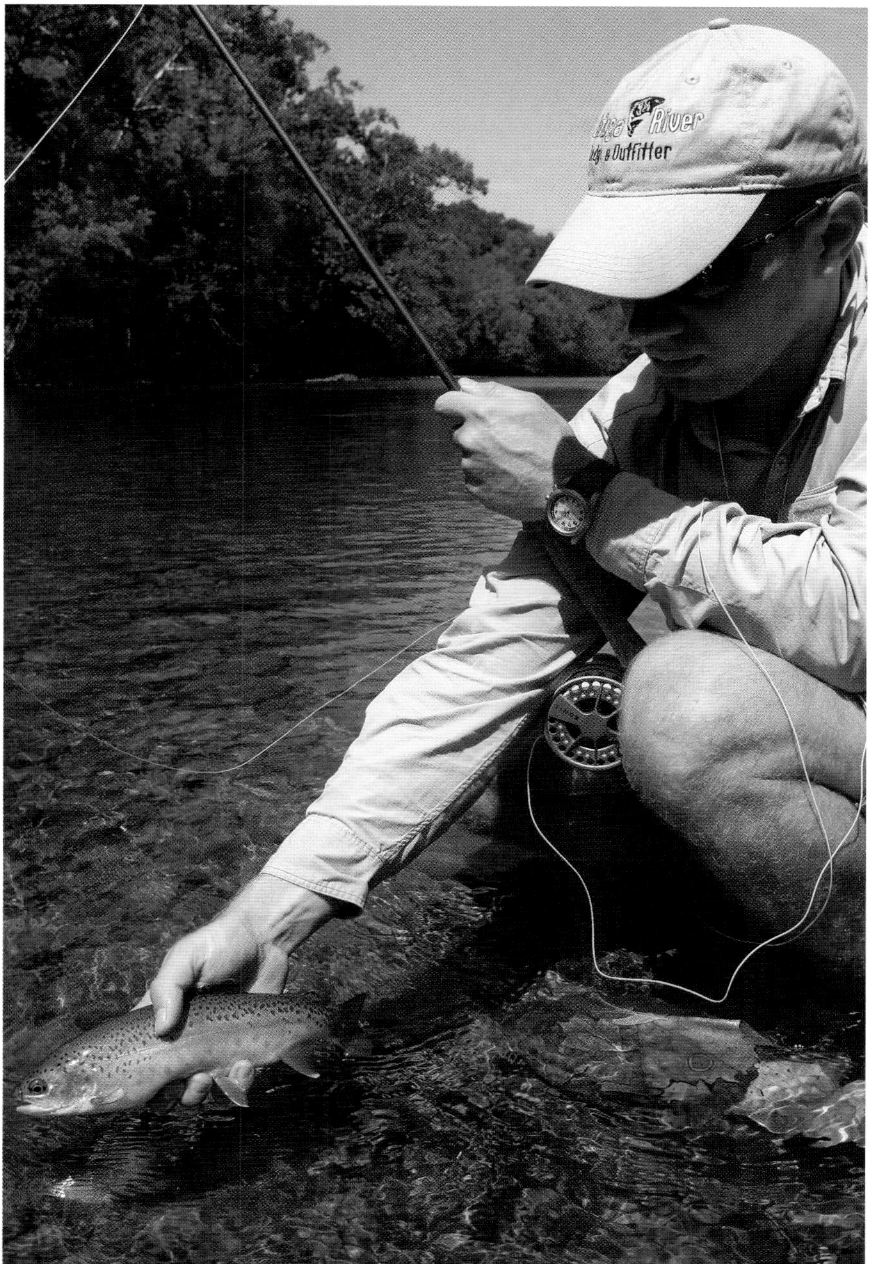

Although large trout are present in good numbers on the Watauga River, rainbows like this one are far more common. Don't let their size fool you, as they can be every bit as wary as their larger brethren.

As a general guideline for choosing flies when there is no hatch, you can't go wrong with variations on the big three: caddis, mayfly, and midge imitations. For the first two, don't be afraid to use something other than what you read on the posted fishing reports, because that is what most folks will be reading and you can bet the answer to "What are they bitin' on?" travels quickly throughout the Watauga community. Split Case BWOs, Thorax BWO Emergers, Mercer's Micro Mayflies (#18-20), Deep Six Caddis, and Stalcup's Bubble Caddis (#14-16), along with Zebra Midges, Cardinal Midges, and SLF Midges (#18-22) will work on any given day on the river, but as Brad said, keep an open mind and don't be afraid to break from the norm.

Hatches on the Watauga are a bit more predictable than on some other rivers in the South. In general, midges and Blue-Winged Olives can come off pretty much any time of the year, the latter hatching heavily on any given day between mid-October all the way through May. A smattering of midge dry flies in cream, black, and gray (#20-24) will cover you for the small bugs. For the Blue-Winged Olives, No-Hackles, Brooks's Sprouts, and Smith's Translucent Emergers (#18-24) have a proven track record at fooling Watauga trout. In low water, plan on fishing these patterns on long, fine leaders, and don't be discouraged if you get a few snubs from the trout. That's just life on the Watauga.

In the spring, the large black caddis, *Brachycentrus americanus,* begin hatching in early April near the lake, progressing upstream through the middle to the end of the month. As the caddis fill the air, anglers fill the river. The trout seem to let their guards down just a little, gorging themselves on the caddis. Just because so many trout are up during this hatch doesn't mean they are any less selective. Presentations must be spot-on, and you'd best have a good supply of dry flies with you to mimic this early caddisfly. A few patterns to keep in your box are Henry's Fork Caddis, Spotlight Caddis, CDC Bubble Back Caddis, and Harrop's CDC Caddis Emerger (#12-16).

Toward the end of the *Brachycentrus,* Blonde Sedges begin hatching in late April and continue through August. These caddis, not quite as large on average as the black version, continue to tempt fish on top. Also, a half-dozen other caddis species can come off during this time period along with the Blonde Sedges, so be prepared. Keep a watchful eye on which particular caddis the trout seem to be keying on and match it to size first, color second. Keep a well-stocked caddis box with blonde, brown, and gray caddis patterns similar to those used for the *Brachycentrus* hatch in #14-18. Put a few CDC Fertile Caddis (#14-18) in there to mimic the egg-laying females, and you should have the bases covered.

All this talk of caddis may get you to thinking they are the only things the trout eat during the spring. Not so, says Justin Shroyer, one of the most knowledgeable guides on the river. His familiarity with the aquatic world, coupled with rowing the river searching for big fish with clients, has given him a decisive edge when stalking trout on the Watauga.

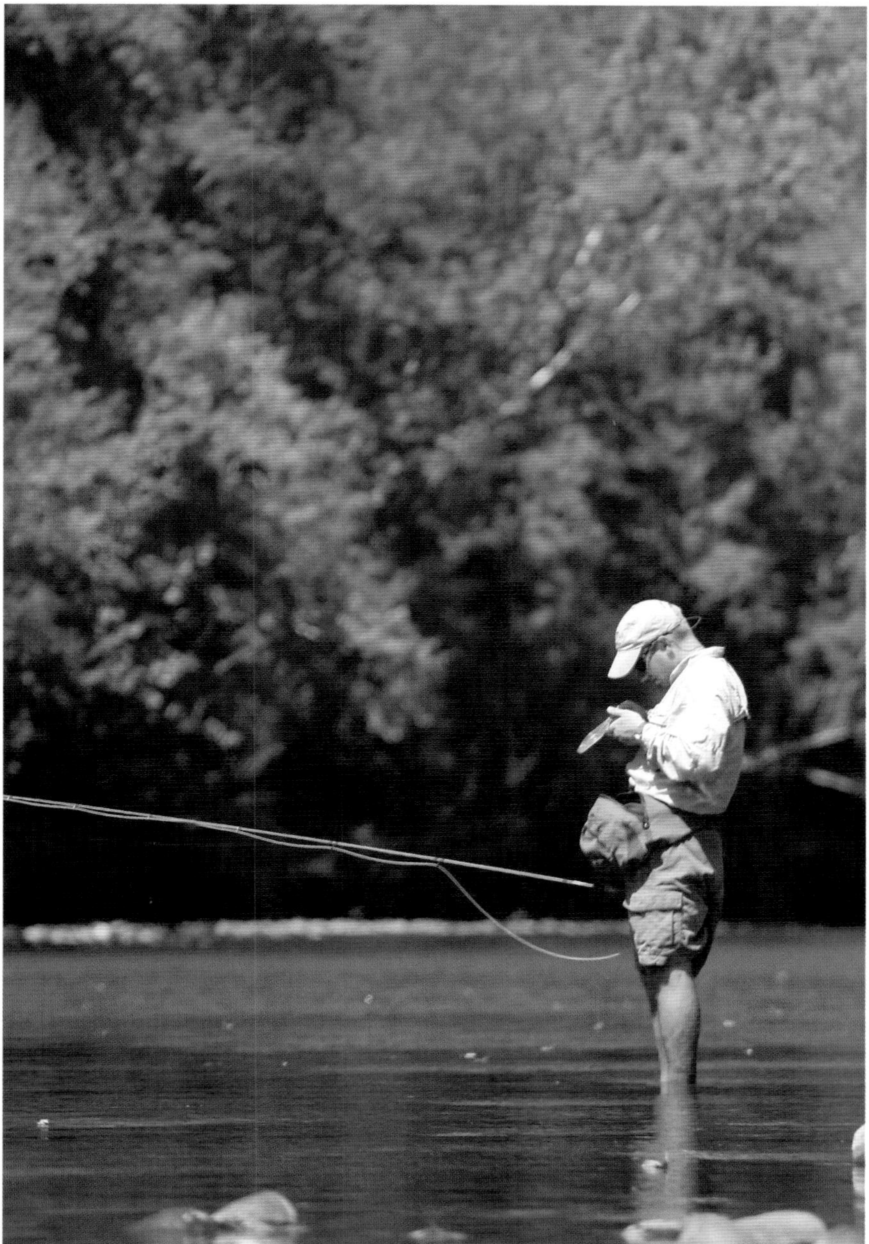

Pressured trout mean changing flies without hesitation. Oftentimes the secret lies in finding a pattern the trout have not seen before, so dig deep in your box if the trout are being stubborn.

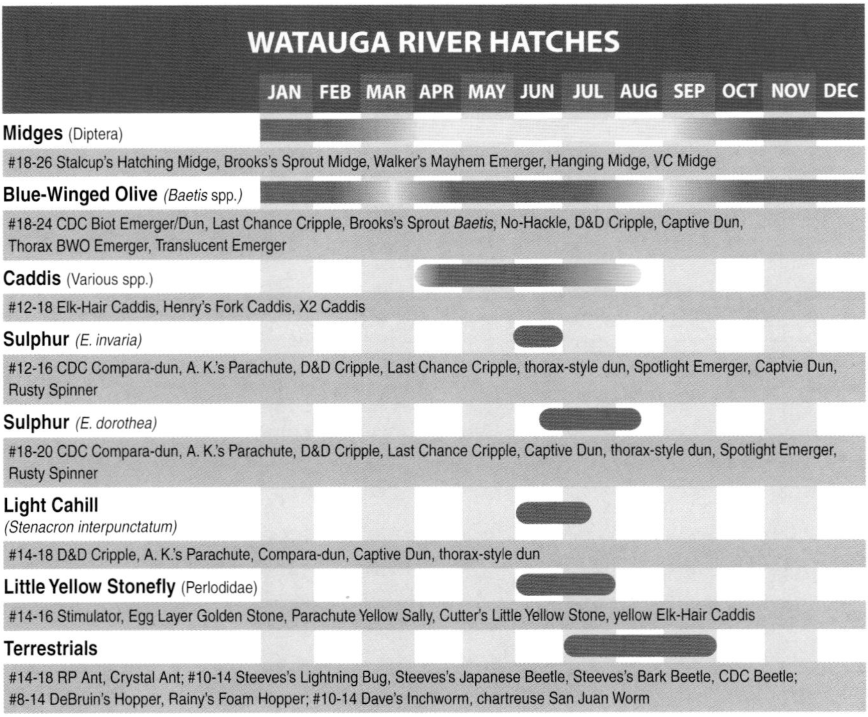
WATAUGA RIVER HATCHES
JAN FEB MAR APR MAY JUN JUL AUG SEP OCT NOV DEC
Midges (Diptera)
#18-26 Stalcup's Hatching Midge, Brooks's Sprout Midge, Walker's Mayhem Emerger, Hanging Midge, VC Midge
Blue-Winged Olive (Baetis spp.)
#18-24 CDC Biot Emerger/Dun, Last Chance Cripple, Brooks's Sprout Baetis, No-Hackle, D&D Cripple, Captive Dun, Thorax BWO Emerger, Translucent Emerger
Caddis (Various spp.)
#12-18 Elk-Hair Caddis, Henry's Fork Caddis, X2 Caddis
Sulphur (E. invaria)
#12-16 CDC Compara-dun, A. K.'s Parachute, D&D Cripple, Last Chance Cripple, thorax-style dun, Spotlight Emerger, Captvie Dun, Rusty Spinner
Sulphur (E. dorothea)
#18-20 CDC Compara-dun, A. K.'s Parachute, D&D Cripple, Last Chance Cripple, Captive Dun, thorax-style dun, Spotlight Emerger, Rusty Spinner
Light Cahill
(Stenacron interpunctatum)
#14-18 D&D Cripple, A. K.'s Parachute, Compara-dun, Captive Dun, thorax-style dun
Little Yellow Stonefly (Perlodidae)
#14-16 Stimulator, Egg Layer Golden Stone, Parachute Yellow Sally, Cutter's Little Yellow Stone, yellow Elk-Hair Caddis
Terrestrials
#14-18 RP Ant, Crystal Ant; #10-14 Steeves's Lightning Bug, Steeves's Japanese Beetle, Steeves's Bark Beetle, CDC Beetle; #8-14 DeBruin's Hopper, Rainy's Foam Hopper; #10-14 Dave's Inchworm, chartreuse San Juan Worm

Justin finds that when the caddis are hatching, so are the *Baetis*. "Most folks are fishing caddis in the evening hours, but the trout are really keying in on the BWOs." Justin says these tiny mayflies go all but unnoticed by many anglers who are intent on fooling trout with the same caddis patterns they've been using all day. It's not a masking hatch, but some trout do get off the caddis and turn on to Blue-Winged Olives, especially some of the big boys. When the sun begins dropping in the sky, clip off your caddis and tie on a Brooks's Sprout *Baetis*, CDC Biot Emerger, or Last Chance Cripple (#18-22) to test Justin's knowledge. I think you'll find he's right on the money.

During the caddis hatch, the river is a parade of boats dodging wading anglers, everyone trying to stay out of each other's way. Tempers occasionally flare, but for the most part, all anglers find their own little piece of paradise and become numb to the traffic.

Following the caddis, Sulphurs fill up the open airspace and give anglers yet another spring hatch to follow. Memorial Day marks the hatch, and what a time it can be. The area around Sycamore Shoals can see some heavy emergences of Sulphurs in the afternoons. If you're targeting the trout rising in the braided currents, tie on a Last Chance Cripple, D&D Cripple, Compara-dun, or Spotlight Emerger (#14-16). If you're trying to work a big fish in slow water,

Thorax BWO Emerger

Hook:	#18-24 Daiichi 1130
Thread:	Olive 8/0
Tail:	Olive turkey flat
Body:	Olive goose biot
Rib:	Olive Ultra Wire
Thorax:	Green dubbing over olive bead
Wingcase:	Medallion Sheeting

a Harrop's CDC Biot Emerger or CDC Compara-dun (#14-16) will do its job so long as you do yours.

From July to September, terrestrials become part of the trout's diet along with the caddis and mayflies. Sometimes the trout will take a floating beetle or hopper pattern over the hatch. This is not always the case, but it never hurts to tie one on after you've made several casts over a rising trout to no avail. Keep a few Steeves's Lightning Bugs, Japanese Beetles, and CDC Beetles on hand and don't be afraid to use them.

When the generators are on, nymphing and streamer fishing produce the greatest numbers of trout, but dry-fly fishing is not out of the question either. Floating is the only option when the turbines are online, as the water is too high and swift to allow safe wading. Use weight to get the flies down to the trout, and be ready for some of the larger fish to eat. It helps knowing where the big boys sit during high water, because they are difficult if not impossible to spot when the flows pick up.

Fall is a great time to fish high water with streamer patterns. The brown trout will be in their spawning colors and will aggressively take a large, bright streamer. Some anglers use this time of year to target the biggest browns of the season, knowing that the chances of hooking these fish are at their height.

Despite the crowds on the river, the Watauga can still give the feeling of an intimate river, not so large as to have anglers scratching their heads wondering where to fish. Exploring outside the norm, going up- or downstream from the heralded Quality Zone, is something few anglers choose to do, leaving those of us who do thankfully asking the question, "Why?"

Clinch River, Tennessee

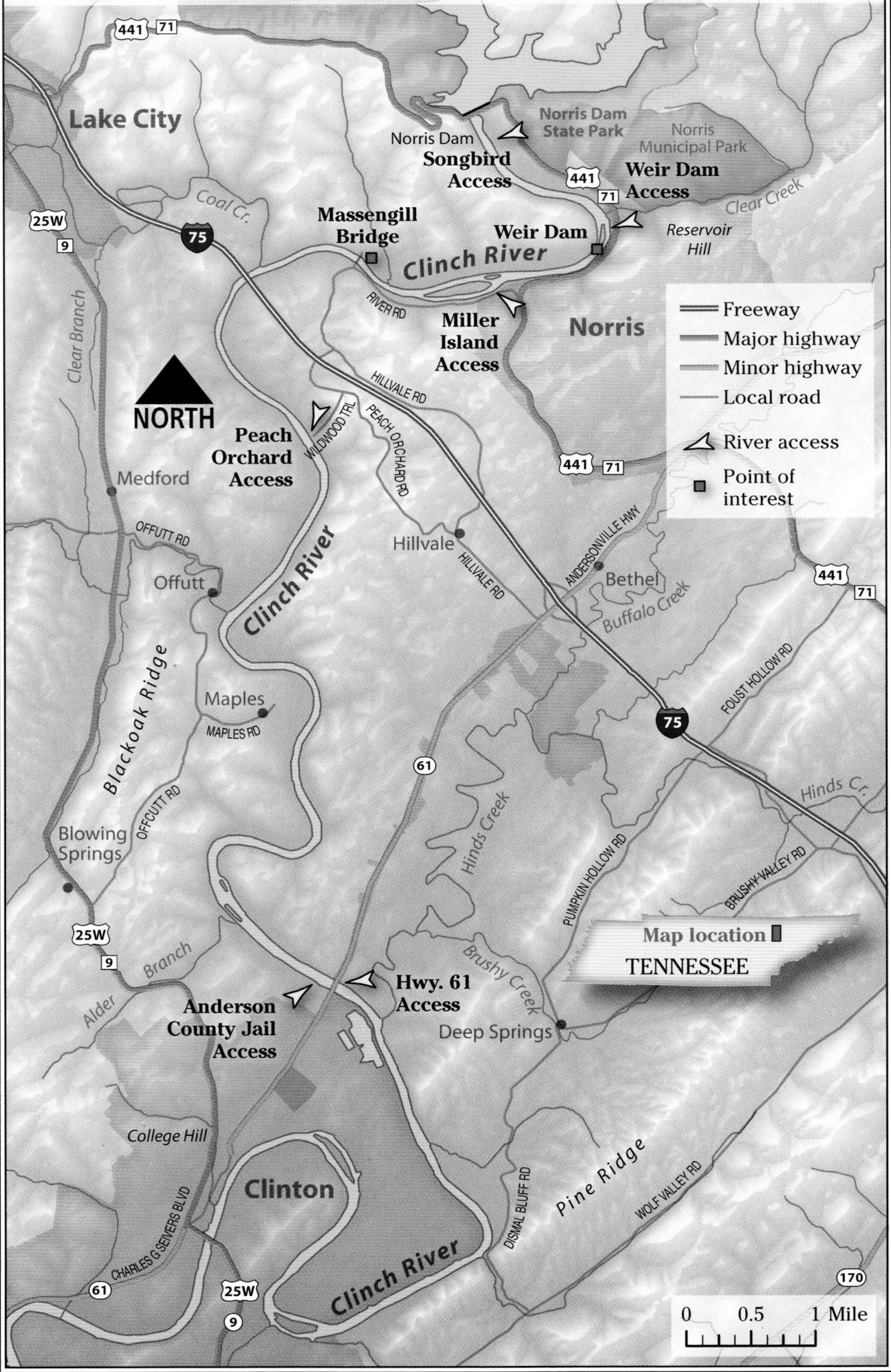

441
71
Lake City
Norris Dam
Norris Dam State Park
Songbird Access
Norris Municipal Park
Weir Dam Access
Clear Creek
Reservoir Hill
Coal Cr.
25W
9
75
Massengill Bridge
Weir Dam
Clinch River
RIVER RD
Miller Island Access
Norris
Freeway
Major highway
Minor highway
Local road
River access
Point of interest
Clear Branch
NORTH
HILLVALE RD
WILDWOOD TRL
PEACH ORCHARD RD
Peach Orchard Access
Medford
OFFUTT RD
Hillvale
ANDERSONVILLE HWY
Bethel
Buffalo Creek
Offutt
Blackoak Ridge
Maples
MAPLES RD
FOUST HOLLOW RD
61
Hinds Creek
Hinds Cr.
OFFCUTT RD
Blowing Springs
PUMPKIN HOLLOW RD
BRUSHY VALLEY RD
Map location
TENNESSEE
Brushy Creek
Alder Branch
Hwy. 61 Access
Anderson County Jail Access
Deep Springs
College Hill
Pine Ridge
Clinton
DISMAL BLUFF RD
WOLF VALLEY RD
CHARLES G SEIVERS BLVD
170
0 0.5 1 Mile

CHAPTER 15

Clinch River

Knoxville, Tennessee, when viewed from space, is a large, Creamsicle-orange spot in southcentral Tennessee. Everything here is orange: baseball hats, billboards, flags, automobile tags, dog collars. If someone made an orange fly rod and reel combo with a University of Tennessee logo on it, he could very well retire off the proceeds generated by Knox County alone.

High in southwestern Virginia, the Clinch is born. It flows for some 300 miles before finally emptying into the mighty Tennessee River. Along its entire length, the 14 miles downstream of Norris Dam near Clinton, Tennessee, receives the most fanfare. The first tailwater to be stocked with trout sometime in 1936, just three years after the dam was completed, the Clinch has ebbed as a trout fishery from the beginning. Early generation flows were inconsistent and would scour the river bottom several miles downstream of the dam. The fishery was already fragile and dangerously low flows during the heat of summer resulted in low levels of dissolved oxygen, which proved fatal for trout lying below the dam. The TVA began to establish more stable flows in the early 1980s, then in 1984 a weir dam was installed 2 miles below Norris Dam. The weir serves two purposes: it slows the onslaught of water to negate the scouring effect and aids in boosting the level of dissolved oxygen in the river. Further improvements were made when the TVA installed baffles on the dam's turbines, which trap air and mix it with the water when the dam is online. These improvements created a truly viable year-round tailrace, and the trout flourished.

Unfortunately, the regulations on the river have not always helped it realize its full potential. Beginning in 1993, quality fishing regulations were placed on a stretch of the Clinch, but these special regulations were hastily overturned just two years later. From 1995 through 2008, the river lay under general angling regulations. The river flourished for a time, during the quality

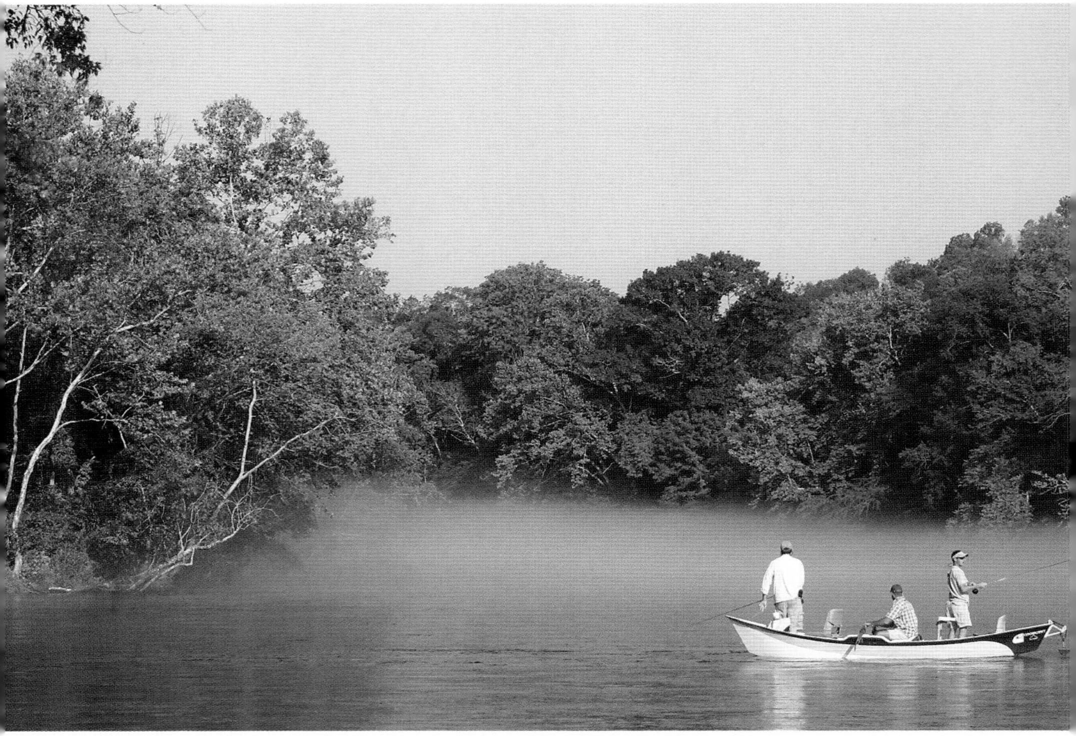

Clinch River guide Mike Bone floats two anglers in the morning fog. Floating the Clinch gives you access to water inaccessible to wading anglers and the chance to tangle with some large trout.

regulations period and for a few years afterward, with anglers catching many fish around 14 to 16 inches, and 20-inch or longer trout not being uncommon. Then the fish began shrinking, with the average trout around the 10- to 12-inch mark by the turn of the century. The Clinch continued to produce trout on the smallish side for several years, with the occasional gagger brown turning up on rare occasions.

Finally, in 2008, somebody woke up and the river was once again placed under special regulations. Now on the books, a catch-and-release slot limit maintains that all trout between 14 and 20 inches must be released in the section from Norris Dam downstream to Tennessee Highway 61 in Clinton. The implementation of a slot limit regulation was, like the 1993 quality fishing regulations, highly unpopular with some Clinch River anglers, however state biologists feel the new regulations will help grow larger trout in the river.

The Clinch River tailrace begins at the base of Norris Dam. At low water, when the majority of anglers come to fish, the river is clear and cold, and on weekends, crowded. Bait anglers, fly fishers, and everything in between descend on the Clinch in spring and summer to test the waters, looking for stockers and the elusive natives alike. They probe the waters with everything from worms to CDC midge emergers, some looking for just a strike, others looking for something more.

When the water is in low flow, the minimum maintained by the TVA is around 200 cfs. Very long, slow pools are interspersed with shallow riffles and rocky ledges, giving the river the feel of a large spring creek. Beneath the river's lazy currents, a vast supply of biomass is available to trout. Midges, mayflies, caddis, scuds, and several species of baitfish all provide the trout, and anglers, with a lot to choose from.

Once the turbines come online, floating anglers rule the roost on the Clinch, most wading anglers leaving the river due to its swift flows. Floating is also possible when the generators are offline, but from the weir downstream to TN 61, the river is difficult to navigate due to its shallow nature. Ideally, you would float the river on a single generator, which gives the trout enough water to lose some of their inhibitions. Trout will still rise during one-generator flows, and larger trout will oftentimes be out on the prowl. When two units are online, the river picks up speed and the trout drop to the bottom or slide into the banks to escape the powerful currents. Fishing isn't really all that good when two generators are going, and most fly anglers stay off the water. This is not to say that you cannot catch fish in high water, but figure your chances at slim.

Access to the river is plentiful, both for wading and floating anglers. Access points begin at the base of Norris Dam at the Songbird canoe access. From here to the weir dam about 2 miles downstream, the river pokes along, looking more like a large lake than a river in most places. The trout, some large, feed on an array of midges and scuds. Small patterns, long leaders, and fine tippets are the norm here. Midges can hatch pretty much any day of the year, bringing the trout to the top and giving anglers an eye test as they attempt threading a section of 7X through the eye of a size 24 (or smaller) midge pattern.

Floating anglers can launch canoes or drift boats at the Songbird Access, some floating only the short stretch of water between the dam and the weir. Others will opt for fishing the upper reaches, then taking a ride down the weir dam, a significant drop that, if hit wrong, will swamp a drift boat or capture a boat in the hydraulic. Be careful around this obstruction, and attempt it only if you are an experienced boater. The weir can be negotiated with one or two generators, but is far too shallow to clear during low water. Keep this in mind, and remember that the water just below the dam has little current. A day could be made floating this short stretch, head-hunting for large, selective trout, then rowing or paddling back upstream.

Below the weir, the scouring effects of the dam all but disappear, introducing larger populations of caddis and mayflies into the dense mix of scuds and midges. From the weir to Highway 61, the Clinch can see dense hatches near the many riffles and shoals that dot the riverbed along its path.

Wading anglers can look for trout at a number of access points, the most popular being the Weir Access, Miller Island, Massengill Bridge, and the shoals near the Anderson County Jail just upstream of TN 61. These areas offer plenty of shallow, wadable water adjacent to deeper seams and pools. The Weir Access, Miller Island, and the Anderson County Jail access offer the most water for wading anglers to spread out. Look for deep water just on the edges of shallow shoals, or microseams in long pools that will concentrate the trout in pods. Approach likely holding water slowly, watching for rises or the telltale flashes that betray feeding trout down below. Clinch River trout will not tolerate sloppy casting or presentations, so make every cast count.

Floating anglers have a lot to explore here. Float options include putting in at the dam, dropping over the weir, and taking out at the Miller Island access. For a longer float, you could float all the way to Peach Orchard, but this makes for a long day. A better option is one of the more popular floats on the river between Miller Island and Peach Orchard. This float can be made into a full- or half-day trip, depending on how quickly you want to move through.

Below Peach Orchard, the next takeout is downstream at TN 61. This is a full-day float covering several miles of water. From TN 61 upstream, nymphs, dry flies, and streamers are all equally effective depending on the day. For nymphs, make sure you have enough weight to get the fly down, especially in high water. Split-shot is your friend when floating during a single-turbine release, so don't be afraid to use it.

Below TN 61 to the end of the viable trout water at the US 25 bridge near Clinton, access is severely limited, with the best option being the Eagle Bend access. Fishing streamers on sinking lines in the lower reaches can bring out the big boys. Large brown trout use the deep, slow pools below TN 61 as their hunting grounds, especially when the turbines are running higher flows. A large fly and sinking line just may get you tied into one of these, but it will most certainly not be a daily occurrence.

Choosing flies on the Clinch can intimidate some folks, but there's no reason to fret over an open fly box all day long. My good friend Ross Cates, who has fished the Clinch for years, once shared with me an uncomplicated, astute observation I am sure he learned from someone else. "Ninety percent of the time, all you need to consistently catch fish on the Clinch is a Beadhead Pheasant Tail. Sure, the fish will eat other stuff, but they always seem to eat a Pheasant Tail. So I could run around changing my fly, trying to get a particular trout to eat something, or I could just fish a Pheasant Tail all day long and catch the fish that are eating what I have." Now, this could be said for a lot of rivers, but nowhere does it ring quite as true as on the Clinch. Trout both small and large seem to always have some love for the little nymph.

Even so, don't go thinking that a box full of Pheasant Tails will be all you need on the Clinch. You're best suited with an array of well-stocked fly boxes to cover any situation you find on the river. Year-round, nymphing with a midge pattern such as a Zebra Midge, Smethurst's Answer, UV Z-Midge,

Low water on the Clinch means spotting a good trout before making the first cast. The smooth, clear currents that typify this tailrace hide some large trout in nondescript current lines. Observing the water before making the first cast is imperative.

Disco Midge, or Rojo Midge (#20-24) will get your line tight with a trout. Fishing a tandem rig with something a bit larger up top, and trailing a small midge pattern is a widely popular tactic on the Clinch. Top flies could be a caddis, mayfly, or scud pattern, and many folks have their own special rigs, which are guarded probably a little closer than they should be. A number of patterns will work, including pink, gray, and orange scud imitations (#14-18), Lightning Bugs, Norris's Caddis Pupae, Split Case PMDs, Anatomical PMDs, and Skip's Ultimate Nymphs (#16-18) along with Mercer's Micro Mayflies and Split Case BWOs (#18-20).

Streamers also work well, pretty much anytime during the year. In low water, use floating and intermediate lines, especially when fishing above TN 61. Fly patterns should mimic baitfish and sculpins found in the river, but don't forget the crayfish either. Whitlock's NearNuff Crayfish and Stalcup's Crazy Dad (#6-10) tend to mimic the crayfish well enough. For baitfish, try a variety of patterns in variations of white, black, olive, and yellow. Be sure to take some Sculpzillas, Zoo Cougars, Bellyache Minnows, Woolly Buggers, and Shiela Sculpins (#6-10) for low water and in large sizes (#1/0-#4) for when the turbines come online.

In addition to going up a size or two in your streamer selection, sinking lines should replace the floating versions when fishing in high water. Heads with sinking rates of 3-8 ips (inches per second) will get the fly down. Some folks are using intermediate lines with great success to probe the shallower water along the banks, as many large trout will pull up within inches of the bank to escape the current and ambush prey. Whatever your preferred method, streamer fishing in high water can yield some of the largest trout in the river.

Hatches on the Clinch vary from heavy to sparse. Midges hatch year-round, and Blue-Winged Olives can emerge on any given day as well. Carry small dry flies such as Walker's Mayhem Emergers, Brooks's Sprout Midges, VC Midges, and Hatching Midges (#20-26), along with a variety of Blue-Winged Olive patterns including Brooks's Sprout *Baetis,* Last Chance Cripples, and CDC Biot Duns (#18-24) to match the tiny guys floating on top. Another proven tactic is to swing a Soft-Hackle Blue-Winged Olive in the riffles during even the lightest emergence. Clinch River trout will latch onto these swung patterns with uncontested zeal, breaking light tippets if you are not light-handed on the hook-set.

Guide Charity Rutter shows some love to a Clinch River rainbow. The cold waters below Norris Dam create a bug factory that gives the trout plenty of options, but midges are always a solid bet, as Charity has proven. IAN AND CHARITY RUTTER

CLINCH RIVER HATCHES

JAN FEB MAR APR MAY JUN JUL AUG SEP OCT NOV DEC

Midges (Diptera)

#18-26 Stalcup's Hatching Midge, Brooks's Sprout Midge, Walker's Mayhem Emerger, Hanging Midge, Griffith's Gnat, VC Midge

Blue-Winged Olive *(Baetis* spp.*)*

#18-24 CDC Biot Emerger/Dun, Last Chance Cripple, Brooks's Sprout *Baetis*, Hi-Viz Emerger, Thorax BWO Emerger

Caddis *(Brachycentrus* spp.*)*

#14-16 Elk-Hair Caddis, CDC Caddis Emerger, CDC Fertile Caddis, X2 Caddis, Stalcup's Parachute Caddis Emerger, Hemingway Caddis

Sulphur *(E. invaria)*

#12-16 CDC Compara-dun, A. K.'s Parachute, D&D Cripple, Last Chance Cripple, thorax-style dun, Spotlight Emerger, Captive Dun, Rusty Spinner, Hackle Stacker, Pullover Dun

Sulphur *(E. dorothea)*

#18-20 CDC Compara-dun, A. K.'s Parachute, D&D Cripple, Last Chance Cripple, Spotlight Emerger, Rusty Spinner, thorax-style dun, Pullover Dun, Hackle Stacker

Light Cahill
(Stenacron interpunctatum)

#14-18 D&D Cripple, A. K.'s Parachute, Compara-dun, thorax-style dun, Captive Dun, Spotlight Emerger

Terrestrials

#14-18 RP Ant, Crystal Ant; #10-14 Steeves's Japanese Beetle, Steeves's Bark Beetle, CDC Beetle, Monster Beetle; #8-14 DeBruin's Hopper, Rainy's Foam Hopper; #10-14 Dave's Inchworm, chartreuse San Juan Worm

Caddis hatch from March through June, but the hatches have been sporadic the last few years. Keeping slow-water caddis patterns in your box will put you ahead of the anglers throwing the generic Elk-Hair Caddis. Harrop's CDC Caddis Emerger, Fertile Caddis, Iris Caddis (#14-18), and other low-riding caddis patterns fool trout in the low-water periods, as well as when the turbines come online. If you can hit a heavy caddis hatch, the trout will be uncharacteristically cooperative when given the opportunity to eat a well-presented, low-riding pattern.

The Sulphur *(E. dorothea)* hatch is what most anglers think of when they imagine days of dry flies and rising trout on the Clinch. Beginning sometime in late March, the Sulphurs begin coming off in good numbers from the weir downstream to the TN 61 bridge. In low and high water, the mayflies will hatch and bring trout to the surface in what can be spectacular emergences. Again, like the caddis, Sulphur hatches have been a bit off the last few years. A theory for this is the near choking spread of *Didymosphenia geminata*. Commonly known as didymo or "rock snot," this invasive algae carpets sections of the river bottom. It is believed that there is a strong correlation between the spread of didymo and the decline in hatching insects on the river. Anglers visiting the Clinch should wash felt soles, or wear Aquastealth soles or a similar product to prevent the spread of didymo into other watersheds. Anglers who did not observe precautionary measures have infected many other tailraces with this noxious algae.

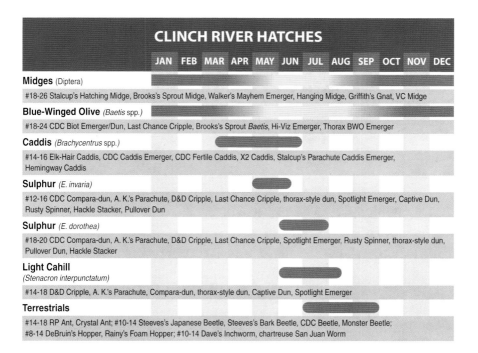

Although the Sulphur hatches have been on the decline over the past few years, there are still plenty of bugs out and about. Pattern selection should be along the lines of your caddis selection, low-riding patterns that present natural silhouettes to the fish below. CDC Compara-duns and A. K.'s Parachutes (#14-18) tend to work as imitations of the adults. It couldn't hurt to toss a few Last Chance Cripples, D&D Cripples, Captive Duns, and Lawson's Half-Back Emergers (#14-18) into your box for good measure.

In low water, look to the pools below the braided side channels around islands and midstream riffles for some large trout feeding on Sulphur emergers. They will not be easy to fool, and long leaders—over 12 feet—serve as added insurance for long drifts and überstealth presentations. High water requires getting a long drift in fast, complex currents, further necessitating long, fine leaders.

Following the end of Sulphur season, terrestrials fill the summer plate. Inchworms, grasshoppers, beetles, and ants could work on any day. Terres-

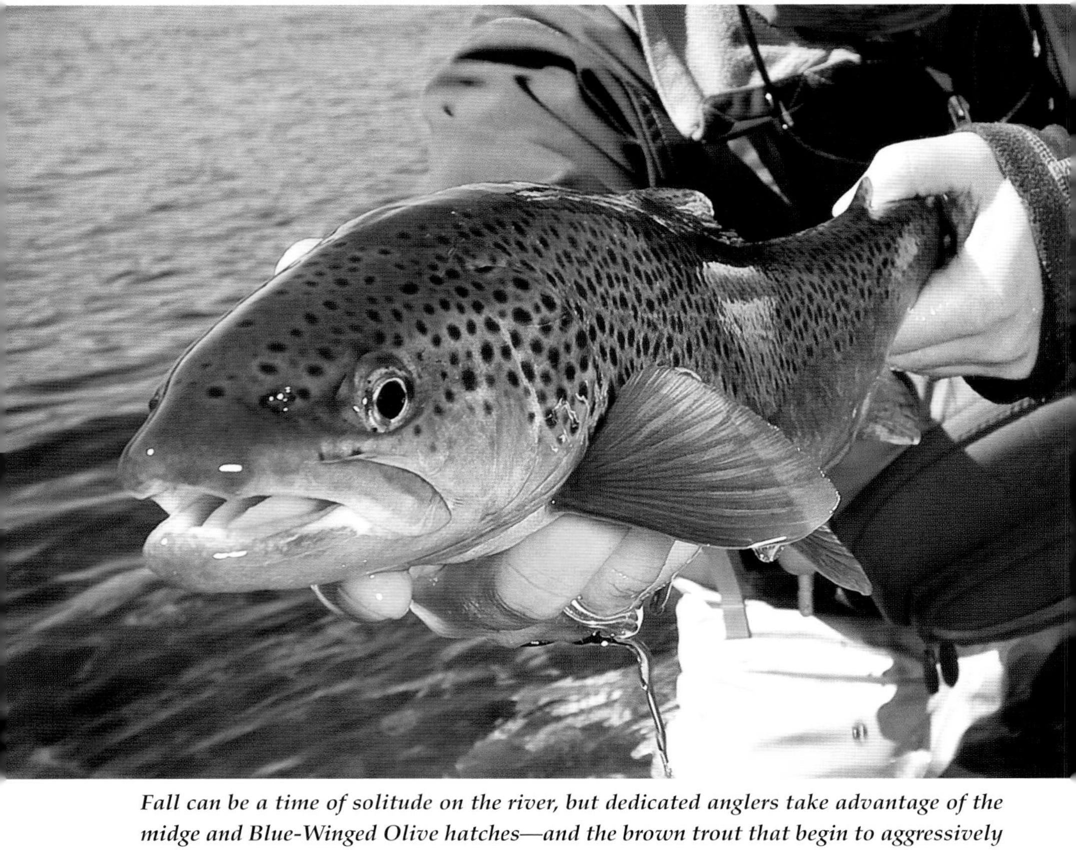

Fall can be a time of solitude on the river, but dedicated anglers take advantage of the midge and Blue-Winged Olive hatches—and the brown trout that begin to aggressively hit streamers. LOUIS CAHILL

UV Z-Midge

Hook: #18-22 Tiemco 2487
Bead: Black Cyclops
Thread: Black 8/0
Body: Thread to match natural
Rib: Small copper or silver wire
Thorax: Ostrich herl
Wing: Midge Krystal Flash

Last Chance Cripple

Hook: #12-18 Daiichi 1130
Thread: Yellow 8/0
Tail: Wood duck and Z-lon
Body: Yellow-orange goose biot
Rib: Copper Ultra Wire (extra small)
Thorax: Yellow-orange dubbing
Hackle: Cream grizzly
Wing: CDC

trial fishing along the Clinch River's banks can be sublime. Watching the bank to see what insects are available will aid in choosing the right pattern. Overhanging bushes tend to hold Japanese beetles from early in July through the end of the month, while fields just a few hundred yards downstream may be filled with hoppers. Switching your pattern to match the "hatch" generated by the riverside growth can make all the difference.

Fall can be a time of solitude on the river. Many anglers are off the water, either hunting deer or engaged in the region's other pastime, watching the University of Tennessee football team. Dedicated anglers take advantage of this time of year, fishing midge and Blue-Winged Olive hatches, the latter really picking up in November. Also, brown trout are beginning to display their spawning colors around the first of October, aggressively attacking bright streamer patterns. Following the prespawn, as the hen fish make their redds, some anglers choose to fish with egg patterns, harassing the trout as they attempt to propagate. Most anglers chose to leave the spawning browns alone, figuring that they'll be around after the spawn is over and that not walking on the redds will ensure more browns in following years.

Tellico River, Tennessee

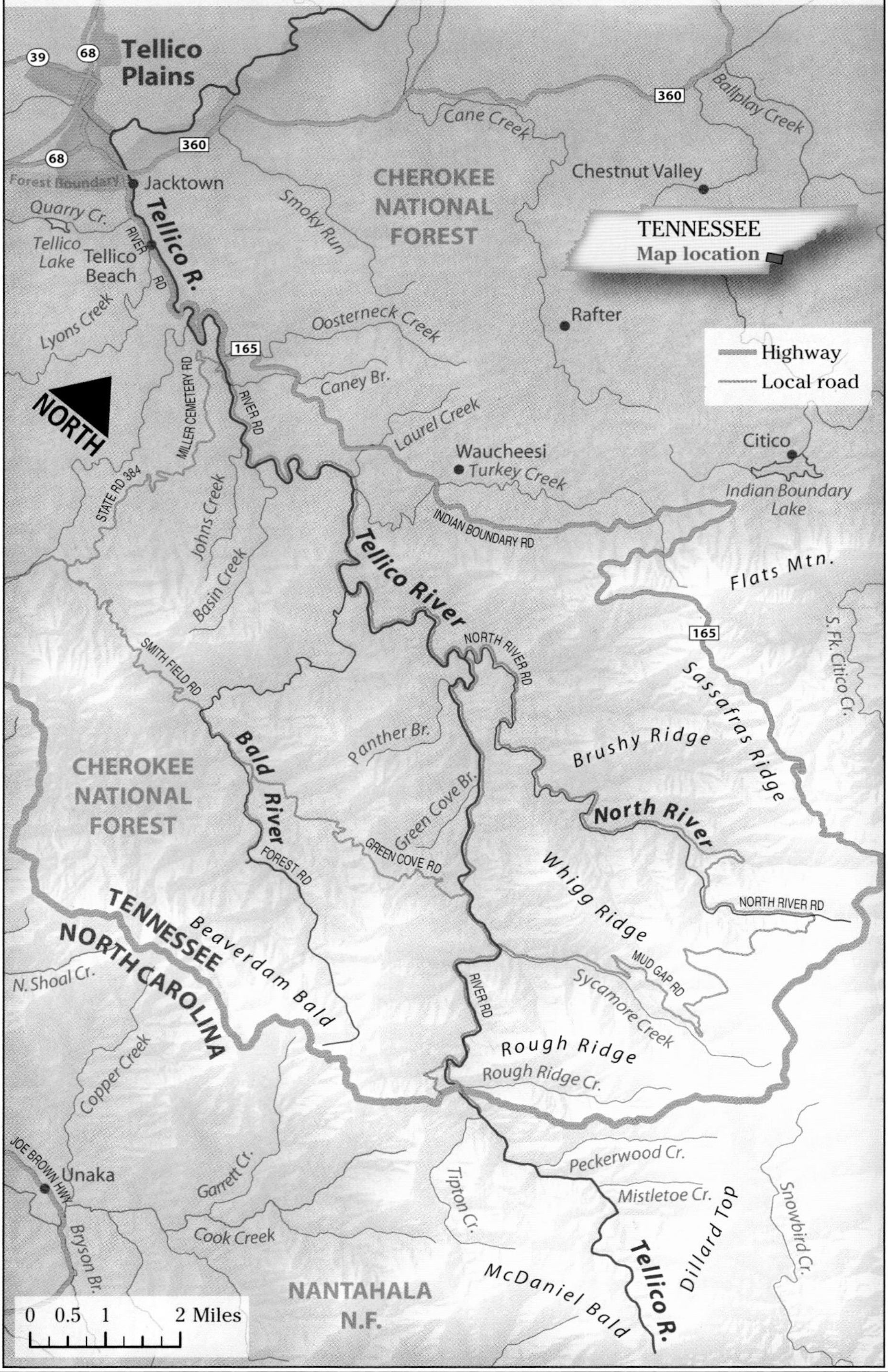
Tellico Plains
39
68
68
360
360
165
165
Forest Boundary
Jacktown
Quarry Cr.
Tellico Lake
Tellico Beach
RIVER RD
Tellico R.
Lyons Creek
Smoky Run
CHEROKEE NATIONAL FOREST
Cane Creek
Ballplay Creek
Chestnut Valley
TENNESSEE
Map location
Rafter
Oosterneck Creek
Caney Br.
Highway
Local road
NORTH
MILLER CEMETERY RD
RIVER RD
Laurel Creek
Waucheesi
Turkey Creek
Citico
Indian Boundary Lake
STATE RD 384
Johns Creek
Basin Creek
INDIAN BOUNDARY RD
Tellico River
Flats Mtn.
NORTH RIVER RD
S. Fk. Citico Cr.
SMITH FIELD RD
Sassafras Ridge
Brushy Ridge
Panther Br.
Bald River
Green Cove Br.
North River
GREEN COVE RD
FOREST RD
Whigg Ridge
NORTH RIVER RD
TENNESSEE
NORTH CAROLINA
Beaverdam Bald
MUD GAP RD
Sycamore Creek
N. Shoal Cr.
RIVER RD
Rough Ridge
Rough Ridge Cr.
Copper Creek
JOE BROWN HWY
Unaka
Garrett Cr.
Peckerwood Cr.
Tipton Cr.
Mistletoe Cr.
Dillard Top
Snowbird Cr.
Cook Creek
Bryson Br.
Tellico R.
McDaniel Bald
NANTAHALA N.F.
0 0.5 1 2 Miles

CHAPTER 16

Tellico River

including North and Bald Rivers

If you are from the South, heck, even if you're not from here it would be nearly impossible to avoid some sort of contact with a Tellico Nymph. This versatile fly can be found in the bins of almost any fly shop worth its salt in the Southeast. Its namesake is one of the most heralded freestone rivers in the region. The Tellico River isn't a big and burly river until it rains. Then it becomes a raging torrent, favored by kayakers.

The Tellico begins deep in the mountains of western North Carolina as a small creek, its headwaters flowing just south of the Great Smoky Mountains National Park before entering the Tennessee backcountry. It is not much of a stream up here, the narrow brush-choked flow hosting native brookies in familiarly tight quarters. Getting to the brook trout waters is no easy task, and many anglers forgo the upper Tellico in favor of easier hikes and better fishing elsewhere in the park. Besides, it is not the brook trout that have anglers flocking to the Tellico, and I do mean flocking.

Encompassing more than 140 miles of trout water, the Tellico River watershed is one of the largest free-flowing trout destinations in the Southeast. High in the mountains surrounding the maze of blue lines are 20 or so miles of native brook trout water, much of which is seldom explored. Find a blue line on a map, plot a course, and start hiking to what could be an entry into your secret brook trout file.

Despite the miles of water draining into the main river, it is the section of water on the main stem between Turkey Creek and the North Carolina state line that receives the majority of pressure. During the Tellico-Citico Permit season, which runs for half the year (March 15 through September 15), crowds can be nauseating. During this season, the TWRA releases 5,000 trout per

Stalking trout much like you would when big game hunting will pay off with larger than average trout on the Tellico.

week (yes, you read that right) into the designated waters, turning the river into something of a flea market for trout. If possible, avoid the river on any weekend or holiday, unless lawn chairs, Zebco 33 outfits, and stringers full of trout are your idea of nice scenery.

Weekdays see a bit less pressure, and the fishing can be good, but mostly for freshly stocked trout. If you're searching for wild trout and solitude, your best bet during this season is to explore the river's tributary system. Following the catch-and-keep season, Tennessee has placed delayed-harvest regulations on the river from Turkey Creek upstream to the mouth of the North River. The season begins shortly after the harvest season on October 1 and continues through March 14. During this time, fly anglers are in the majority, and the trout fishing becomes far more enjoyable.

Large for a Southern freestone river, especially below the confluence of the North River, the Tellico spills over granite boulders, forming deep green pools and cuts alongside towering rock walls, forming dark seams where trout love to hide. Although most of the river parallels Tellico River Road, upstream from the town of Tellico Plains there remains a sense of seclusion in the valley. Hemlocks and a dozen or more species of hardwoods flank the riverbanks, framing what can only be described as a perfectly sculpted home for trout.

Most anglers prefer to go subsurface when searching for trout. During the Tellico-Citico Permit season, Pheasant Tails, Lightning Bugs, Split Case PMDs, and the venerable Tellico Nymphs (#14-18) are standard fare. Streamers are also effective, with Rolex Streamers, Sculpzillas, and various Woolly Buggers (#8-12) working well when stripped across the river's expansive plunge pools early and late in the day.

Dry-fly fishing in the spring consists of a smattering of tan-brown mottled caddis April through May, but it is by no means reliable. You are just as likely to see the caddis hatching one day, then disappearing for a week before reappearing in decent numbers. The trout, lucky for us, remember the flailing insects and will attack a number of caddis imitations including the standby Elk-Hair Caddis, Hemingway Caddis, and CDC Bubble Back Emerger (#12-16). If you want to up the ante, tie on a pupa dropper or Soft-Hackle Pheasant Tail behind the dry.

Light Cahills and *Isoperla* stoneflies come off in late May or early June, usually lasting through July, and sometimes August. Drifting a parachute-style Yellow Sally (#12-14) or a Light Cahill Compara-dun (#14-16) anywhere along the length of the river would not be a bad idea, especially if you're in serious need of some dry-fly therapy.

Summer also means terrestrials, so keep plenty of ants, beetles, and inchworms in your box. Cinnamon ant imitations (#14-18), wood beetle patterns such as Steeves's Bark Beetle and Tiger Beetle (#12), and inchworm patterns such as Dave's Inchworm or a chartreuse San Juan Worm are pretty much all you need.

Once the delayed-harvest regulations get underway, the same nymphs you would use during the catch-and-keep season work equally well. Add a few brightly colored nymphs such as Y2K Bugs, San Juan Worms, and Rook's Blueberries (#14-16) into the mix, as it is a well-known fact that delayed-harvest trout like it bright and flashy.

Fall on the Tellico is a time of transition. The fishing will taper off sometime in late October as the weather changes, but once the season stabilizes, it's back to business as usual. This is also the perfect time to look for some aggressive brown trout. Stories of 10-pound-plus browns trickle into the general stores where photos of these massive fish lend credence to the anglers' fish stories. Some folks go for years, even a lifetime, without ever seeing one of these legendary trout, but they are there. As my father used to tell me: "If you know big fish are in the river, you know you have a chance of catching them."

Undoubtedly there are some Godzilla browns in the Tellico, so you might as well try your luck. Early and late in the day are the best times to fish for the larger browns, but it is also advisable to wait until the river first begins

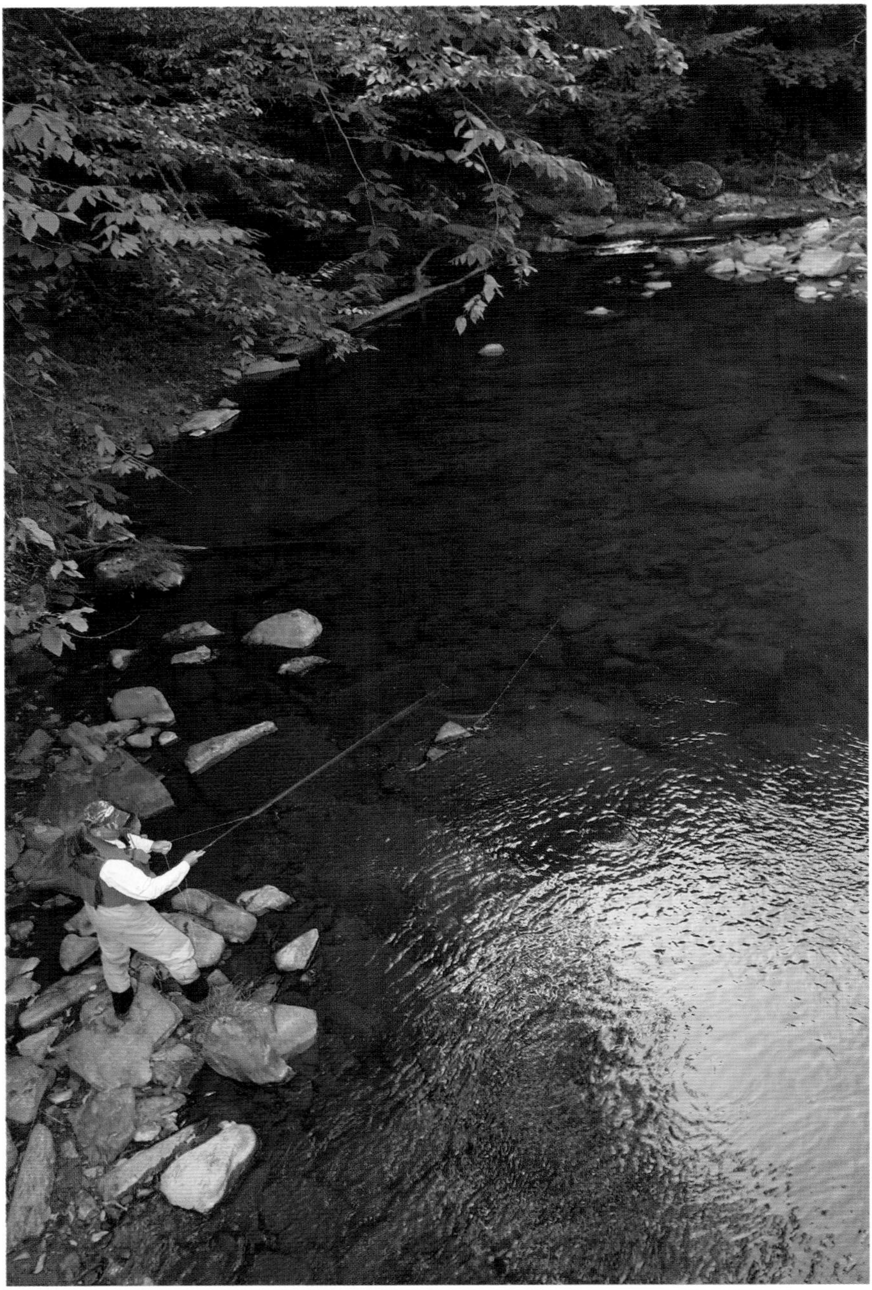

Anglers who explore the many tributaries of the Tellico River may very well discover their new favorite mountain destination.

clearing after a good rain. The water will be higher than normal, so wading might be a bit tricky, but the rewards can more than make up for the effort.

Perhaps the most effective way to fish this type of water is by using a short, heavy sinking tip around 6 feet in length tied to the end of a floating line. This will get the fly down into the meat of the river's larger pools, where the browns are more than likely holding. Stalk each pool as if you know the fish of a lifetime is lying in it, because it very well could be. Large streamer patterns such as Galloup's Zoo Cougars or Stacked Blondes, along with Beldar Buggers, Sculpzillas, and Zonkers (#1/0-4) may sound like a lot of meat on the end of your line, but when you think about it, if you're going after trout in excess of 5 pounds, the fly isn't really all that big.

The Tellico is the largest river in the area, but it is the main river's tributaries that often receive the most praise from fly fishers. It could be the wild trout holding in the tributary waters or the intimate, small-stream settings that call to anglers. Whatever the reason may be, the Bald River and North River hover dangerously close to eclipsing the Tellico in beauty and angling pleasure.

Bald River

High in the watershed, the Bald River cascades into the Tellico over Bald River Falls. The trailhead leading up the ridge and above the falls is a steep climb worth the short exertion. Above the falls, the Bald River flows through a gorge of the same name. You can see the water down at the bottom of the rocky, uninviting ravine. It tempts you from way down there, cascading over ledges into plunge pools, hiding what can only be imagined as huge trout far removed from the angling masses. The gorge section flows for nearly 5 miles up from the falls through the Bald River Wilderness Area and is paralleled by the Bald River Trail for its entire length. Anglers looking to fish the gorge should plan on making a day of it—partly due to the hike required to get to the gorge, but mostly because once you get there, you're not going to want to leave.

Upstream of the gorge, the Bald flows through a long flat known as Holly Flats. Thick laurel overhangs this narrow stream masquerading under a river's title. You can reach the upper stretch by taking Forest Service Road 126 to the Holly Flats Campground, but that will only give you a short section of park-and-fishing water. Less than a mile below the campground, the river leaves the road, making the only access a hike down Brookshire Creek Trail.

For the length of the river, nymphing during the colder months of November through February is the best method of fishing. Attractor nymphs like Lightning Bugs, Princes, and Tellico Nymphs (#14-16), along with smaller Pheasant Tails, Cased Caddis, and Drifting Caddis Pupae (#14-16) can work, especially in the gorge area. Don't be afraid to prospect with a dry fly on the warm days, as the trout will quickly turn on, feeding sometimes just as they would in the spring. Try drifting an Elk-Hair Caddis, Royal Trude, or Stimu-

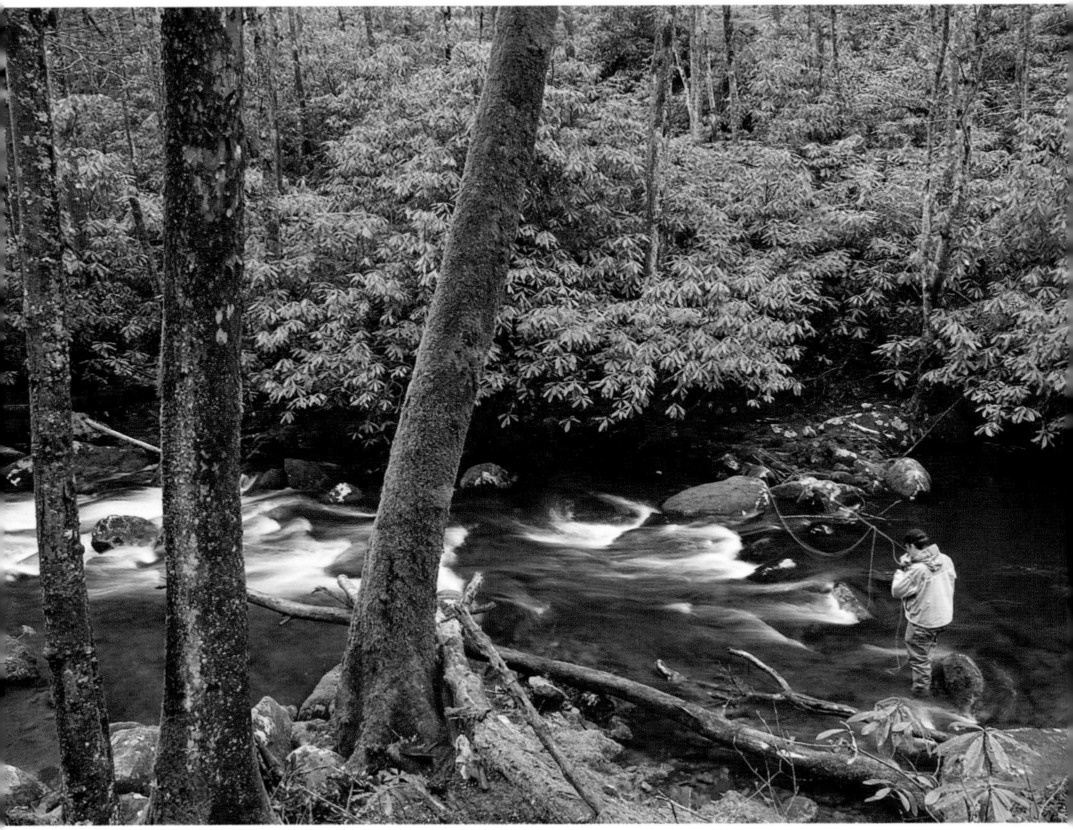

Hiking into the Bald River Gorge will take you away from the crowds that sometimes plague the lower Tellico River. ZACH MATTHEWS

lator (#12-16) through the pocketwater and the edges of faster water during a warm winter day.

Spring brings a few bugs up, but with no regularity. This is still considered a mountain stream, and hatches are, at best, sparse. A few Catskill ties mimicking March Browns, Blue Quills, and Light Cahills (#14-18) should be on hand and fished frequently during the spring and early summer. It is also advisable to have some Yellow Sally parachutes (#12-14) to match any *Isoperla* stoneflies, as they hatch in numbers great enough to get the attention of trout in the late spring.

Summer can bring low water to the Bald, so judge your trips into the wilderness area by the amount of recent rain and the condition of the water. If the water is low and clear, hold off until a summer rain, then head up the trail. A shot of fresh water will be all that is needed to give the trout a little kick in the tail. You could fish nymphs or streamers after the rain, but it is so

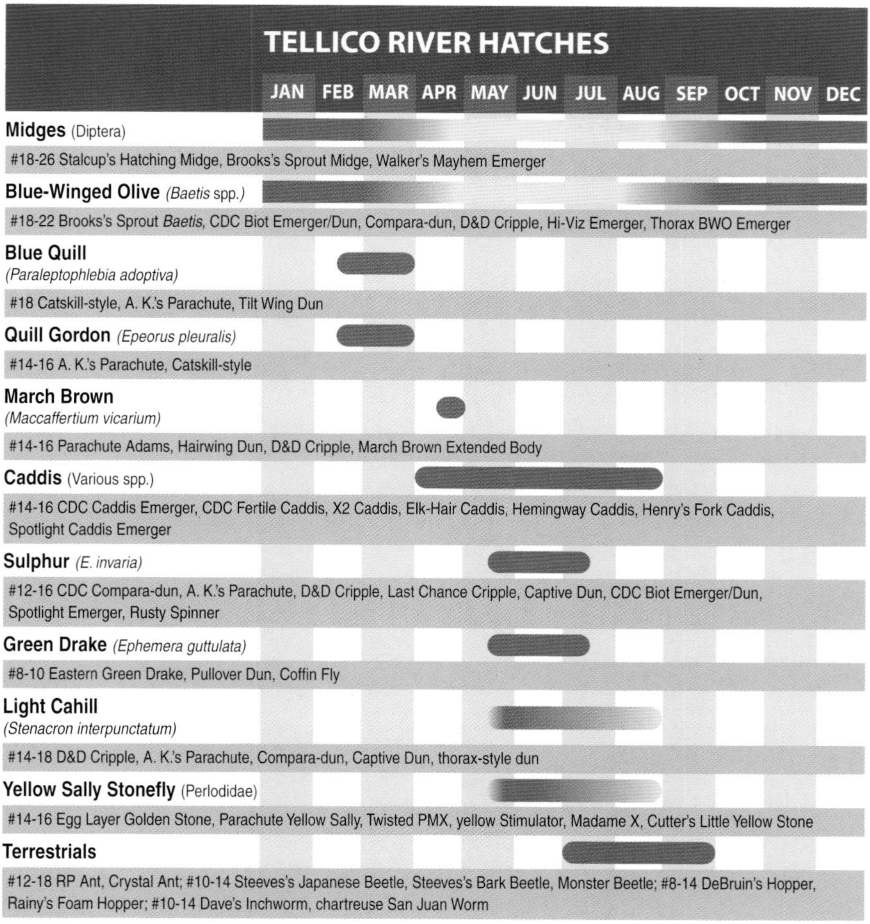
TELLICO RIVER HATCHES
JAN FEB MAR APR MAY JUN JUL AUG SEP OCT NOV DEC
Midges (Diptera)
#18-26 Stalcup's Hatching Midge, Brooks's Sprout Midge, Walker's Mayhem Emerger
Blue-Winged Olive (Baetis spp.)
#18-22 Brooks's Sprout Baetis, CDC Biot Emerger/Dun, Compara-dun, D&D Cripple, Hi-Viz Emerger, Thorax BWO Emerger
Blue Quill
(Paraleptophlebia adoptiva)
#18 Catskill-style, A. K.'s Parachute, Tilt Wing Dun
Quill Gordon (Epeorus pleuralis)
#14-16 A. K.'s Parachute, Catskill-style
March Brown
(Maccaffertium vicarium)
#14-16 Parachute Adams, Hairwing Dun, D&D Cripple, March Brown Extended Body
Caddis (Various spp.)
#14-16 CDC Caddis Emerger, CDC Fertile Caddis, X2 Caddis, Elk-Hair Caddis, Hemingway Caddis, Henry's Fork Caddis, Spotlight Caddis Emerger
Sulphur (E. invaria)
#12-16 CDC Compara-dun, A. K.'s Parachute, D&D Cripple, Last Chance Cripple, Captive Dun, CDC Biot Emerger/Dun, Spotlight Emerger, Rusty Spinner
Green Drake (Ephemera guttulata)
#8-10 Eastern Green Drake, Pullover Dun, Coffin Fly
Light Cahill
(Stenacron interpunctatum)
#14-18 D&D Cripple, A. K.'s Parachute, Compara-dun, Captive Dun, thorax-style dun
Yellow Sally Stonefly (Perlodidae)
#14-16 Egg Layer Golden Stone, Parachute Yellow Sally, Twisted PMX, yellow Stimulator, Madame X, Cutter's Little Yellow Stone
Terrestrials
#12-18 RP Ant, Crystal Ant; #10-14 Steeves's Japanese Beetle, Steeves's Bark Beetle, Monster Beetle; #8-14 DeBruin's Hopper, Rainy's Foam Hopper; #10-14 Dave's Inchworm, chartreuse San Juan Worm

much more fun to throw a small leaf hopper, ant, or beetle pattern. Look for any overhanging bush or likely holding spot near the bank, and cast a Rainy's Grand Hopper (#10-12), Monster Beetle (#10), or Parachute Ant (#14-18) to the trout that are hopefully looking up.

North River

Upstream of where the Bald River empties into the Tellico, the North River adds a significant amount of water to the main stem. Unlike the Bald, the North is not a wilderness river. North River Road parallels most of the river, which consists of the 6 or so miles below Meadow Branch downstream to the Tellico.

Numerous roadside pullouts make the North an easily accessible, park-and-fish stream. Look for trout anywhere among the river's pocketwater areas and plunge pools. There are some nice trout in the North, but expect to encounter mostly rainbows and browns in the 8- to 10-inch range. If you're looking for a big brown trout, fishing a streamer during the fall months could get you hooked up with one of the fabled Tellico browns that make their way into the Bald during the prespawn.

Fly selection for the North River should include the same patterns as you would have on the main stem of the Tellico and the Bald rivers. Much like the Bald, the North River is a great place to prospect for trout using a dry fly, pretty much anytime during the spring. The swift, high-gradient stream doesn't give the trout much time to inspect a fly, so keeping your casts accurate and getting a good drift is far more important than fly pattern selection.

Healthy populations of wild rainbows are found in nearly all tributaries to the Tellico River. Rainbow trout like this will readily attack bushy dry flies such as Wulffs and Stimulators. Keep a good assortment on hand for both the trout, and the bushes. LOUIS CAHILL

Tellico Nymph

Hook:	#10-16 Daiichi 1530
Thread:	Black 6/0
Tail:	Guinea body feathers
Body:	Yellow floss
Rib:	Peacock herl and copper wire
Back:	Turkey
Collar:	Brown hackle

Unlike the Bald, keep a few streamer patterns on hand during the fall when fishing the North. There is a good chance that some of the larger browns in the Tellico will make their way into the Bald once the spawning urge strikes. Use the same patterns as you would downriver on the Tellico, with a few smaller baitfish imitations such as Whitlock's NearNuff Sculpin and Sculpzillas (#8-10).

Finding trout on the Tellico's massive watershed isn't hard, and you don't have to hike in miles to find good fishing. But it can't hurt if you do. Whether your game is wild rainbow and brook trout or stalking big browns in the fall, the Tellico and its tributaries bring a lot to the table. Big trout do not come easy here, but if you are willing to put in the effort and have a little luck on your side, who's to say what could happen?

THE SOUTHEAST'S

PART IV

Brook trout have made an incredible recovery within Great Smoky Mountains National Park. Today, lower-elevation brook trout streams make reaching waters holding these precious creatures less arduous for anglers and have helped expand the range of brookies in the park.

BEST FLY FISHING

GREAT SMOKY MOUNTAINS NATIONAL PARK

Great Smoky Mountains National Park encompasses over 500,000 acres covering roughly 814 square miles. The park contains one of the most diverse ecosystems in the country, with over 130 species of trees and 4,000 species of plants thriving within its boundaries. Whitetail deer, wild turkeys, and black bears, along with myriad birds, reptiles, and aquatic species, call the park home. In addition to the already diverse wildlife population, elk have been reintroduced to the park and are now thriving in certain regions, most notably the Cataloochee Valley. Elevations range between 800 to 6,643 feet above sea level, making for a diverse ecosystem capable of producing an array of angling opportunities.

We should probably begin with a bit of history before jumping into the fishing side of things. Great Smoky Mountains National Park was chartered by Congress in 1934, officially dedicated by President Franklin D. Roosevelt in 1940. Before national park status, extensive logging operations all but obliterated the region's virgin timber stands. Only those lying in the most inhospitable areas were spared. The result was massive erosion and the displacement of the Southern brook trout, the region's only native trout species. Once the trees were gone, runoff and lack of canopy drove the brookies into the high country, where they remained for the most part until very recent lower-elevation brook trout fishery experiments proved successful.

Rainbow and brown trout were introduced and stocked in the park for several decades before stocking operations for nonnative species halted in 1975. To protect the brook trout, fishing for them was banned in the park for nearly 30 years. This has only recently been lifted, opening up over 130 miles of native trout water to anglers.

Rainbow and brown trout in the Smokies are small, and most of them are under 8 inches in length. Most of the park's trout live for only a short period of time, around four years or less. Brown trout tend to represent the park's

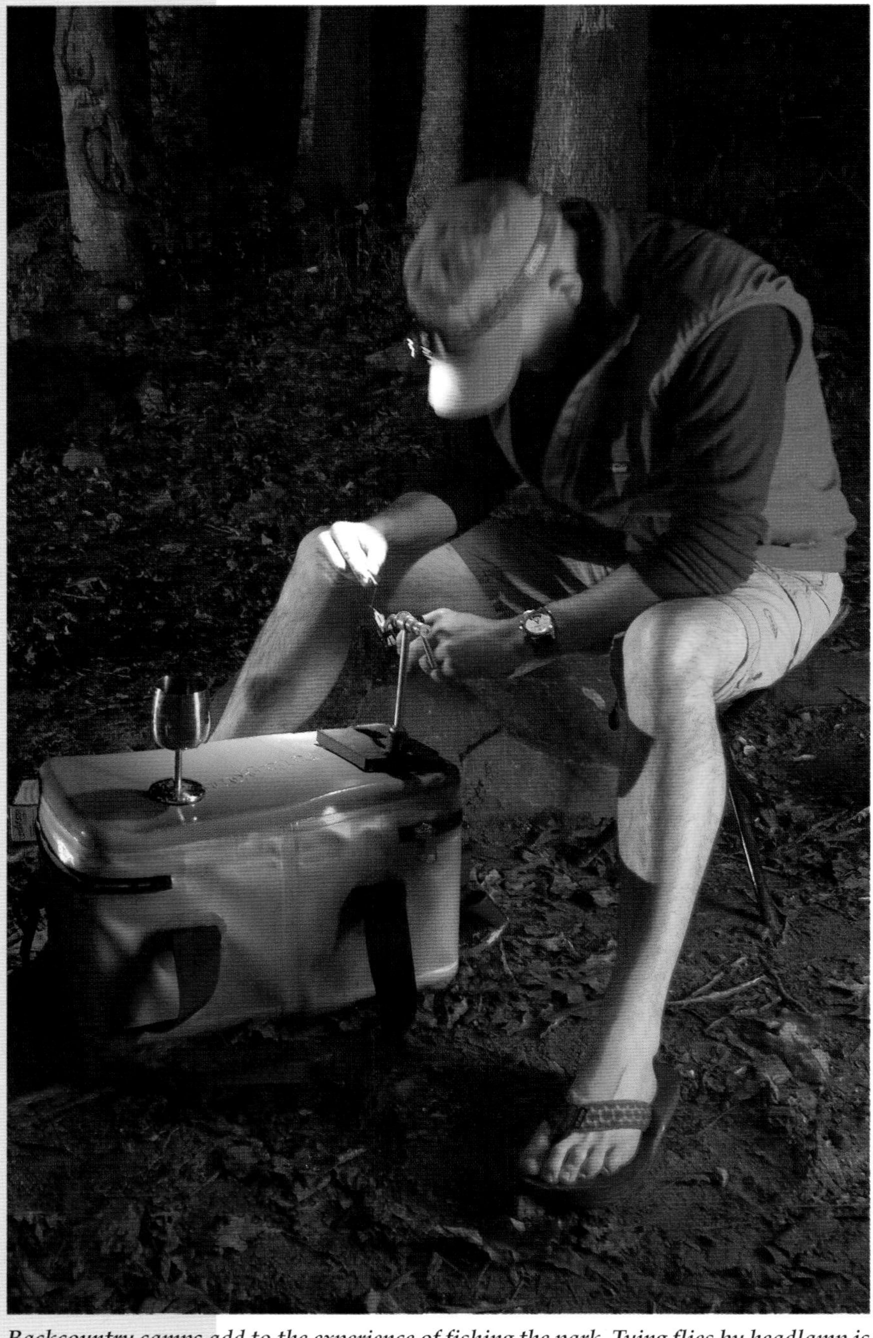

Backcountry camps add to the experience of fishing the park. Tying flies by headlamp is a great way to close out a day of fishing. ZACH MATTHEWS

largest trout, partly because once they reach 8 inches long, their diet begins turning to other fish. The larger trout in the park will usually be browns, but their wariness keeps them off the hook. In the park, big brown trout tend to show up in the most unlikely places. Just because a river may follow a road doesn't mean a large trout doesn't live there.

Most anglers come to the park to get away from the roads, but be prepared for the unexpected when venturing far off the pavement. Accessing the backcountry is never easy—even when a stream is within sight of the road or trail, it can be a monumental undertaking just to reach the water. The ridges and valleys of the Southern highlands are masters of deception, cloaking a jagged Picasso landscape under the serenity of a Monet overpaint.

Some anglers get so caught up in fishing that they forget to look around. The flora and fauna streamside and on the trip to and from the water are part of the experience. As they say, trout do not live in ugly places, and nowhere is this more evident than in the Smokies.

Brown, rainbow, and native Southern brook trout thrive in the park's waters, the majority being juvenile fish less than 6 inches long. Only a small percentage reach 12 inches or better, making the expectations of park anglers less intent on size and more in tune with the experience of catching wild trout in such a uniquely diverse environment. When you consider that most of the park's medium-size streams have around 2,000 trout per mile of river, one would assume visitors would have little trouble catching trout. This is not the case.

Many anglers figure the trout are dumb or easy, or that since so many inhabit such narrow confines, they will practically jump onto your hook. In actuality, the trout in the Smokies are wary, spook easily, and are by no means pushovers. This goes double for the larger fish, seldom caught due to their lower numbers and ability to ghost away at the slightest hint of danger.

One of the park's biggest draws for anglers lies in the small streams, most above 3,000 feet. Here, in the narrow, tumbling waters native Southern brook trout thrive, their brilliantly colored bodies blending in surprisingly well among the cobble and braided currents.

The brook trout are the only native trout species to the park, their predominance beginning during the Ice

Great Smoky Mountains National Park Fly Shops and Guides

FLY SHOPS AND GUIDES

Smoky Mountain Anglers
466 Brookside Village Way, Suite 8
Gatlinburg, TN 37738
(865) 436-8746

Little River Outfitters
106 Town Square Drive
Townsend, TN 37882
(877) 448-3474
littleriveroutfitters.com

Curtis Wright Outfitters
5 All Souls Crescent
Asheville, NC 28803
(828) 274-3471

Rolf Lanz Outdoors
8039 Ray Mears Blvd.
Knoxville, TN 37919
(865) 690-3200

Orvis of Sevierville
136 Apple Valley Rd.
Sevierville, TN 37862
(865) 774-4162

GUIDES

Mike Bone
Knoxville, TN
(865) 494-0972, (865) 567-7138
clinchguides.com

Ian and Charity Rutter
(866) 766-5935
randrflyfishing.com

An angler sneaks up on a pool in winter. Low water and cold temperatures make winter fishing challenging. Small flies such as Blue-Winged Olive nymphs and midge patterns are standard fare when the mercury drops.

Age, when northern char migrated south as their home range lay within a block of solid ice. After the glaciers retreated, the brook trout that remained were isolated from their northern brethren, the genetic code for Southern brook trout containing unique traits that separate them from those in the northern United States and Canada.

Life was not always easy for the brook trout in the park. Logging in the late 1800s and early 1900s destroyed most of the region's virgin forests, and the resulting lack of canopy protection and runoff decimated over 50 percent of the brookie's native range. Following the demise of the brook trout, rainbow trout were introduced into the low-lying streams, migrating into the brookie's range and displacing the less aggressive fish. In 1975, seeing a threat to this native species, park officials closed many native brook trout streams in an attempt to preserve this unique Southern resource.

After a lengthy moratorium just shy of three decades, the park reopened many brook trout waters, following intensive restoration projects that are still ongoing. Many streams remain closed while officials conduct surveys, complete restoration projects, and work to further expand the range of the brook trout within the park's boundaries. Numerous brook trout streams are open under standard park regulations. Some require a backcountry hike; others lie less than a mile from the trailhead. The streams that I write about represent only a tiny fraction of the brook trout fishing to be had in the park.

My suggestion to you is to find a blue line on the park's fishing map and strike out. This self-discovery will not only carry you through the dark forests and high mountain ridges of the park, but deliver you to crystal streams holding brightly speckled brookies so brilliant they seem to glow in your hand. Finding a brook trout on your own is much like unlocking a secret garden—you feel as though you are the only one who has seen the creek and the trout that swim beneath its surface. It is a glorious feeling that every angler should experience at least once. But I can assure you, once is never enough.

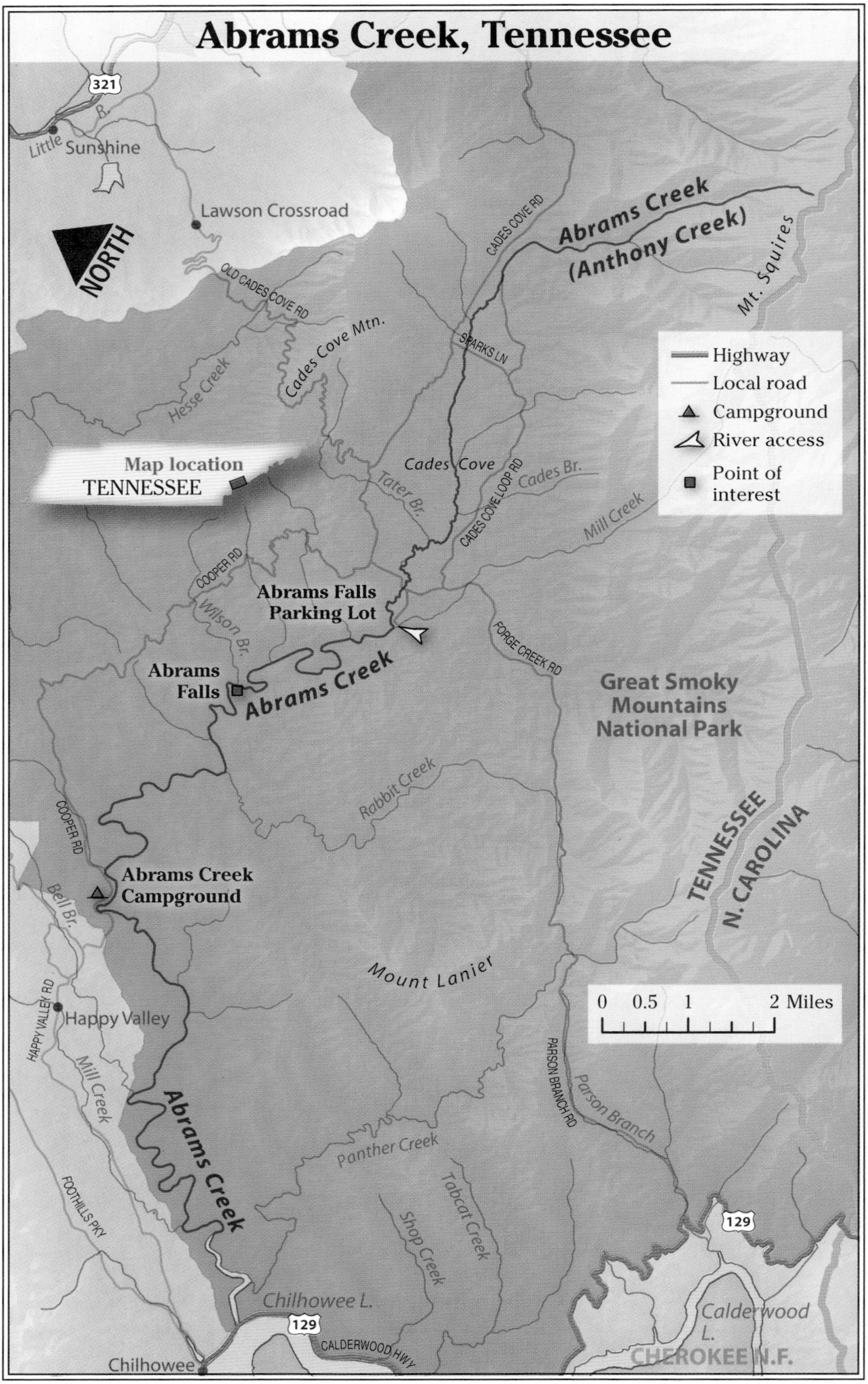

Abrams Creek, Tennessee

321

Little R. Sunshine

Lawson Crossroad

OLD CADES COVE RD

CADES COVE RD

Abrams Creek
(Anthony Creek)

Mt. Squires

NORTH

Hesse Creek

Cades Cove Mtn.

SPARKS LN

Map location
TENNESSEE

Cades Cove

Tater Br.

CADES COVE LOOP RD

Cades Br.

Mill Creek

	Highway
	Local road
▲	Campground
◁	River access
■	Point of interest

COOPER RD

Wilson Br.

**Abrams Falls
Parking Lot**

◁

FORGE CREEK RD

**Abrams
Falls** ■ **Abrams Creek**

**Great Smoky
Mountains
National Park**

Rabbit Creek

TENNESSEE

N. CAROLINA

COOPER RD

Bell Br.

HAPPY VALLEY RD

▲ **Abrams Creek
Campground**

Mount Lanier

0 0.5 1 2 Miles

Happy Valley

Mill Creek

Abrams Creek

PARSON BRANCH RD

Parson Branch

FOOTHILLS PKY

Panther Creek

Tabcat Creek

Shop Creek

129

Chilhowee L.

*Calderwood
L.*

129

CALDERWOOD HWY

Chilhowee

CHEROKEE N.F.

CHAPTER 17

Abrams Creek

If you read this and want to go to Abrams Creek, I hope you're not in a hurry. You see, there are only two ways to get to the trout water between Cades Cove and the lake. One is to park at the lower Abrams Creek Campground and hike upstream several miles through the forest. It's a long hike that takes several hours to complete, seriously cutting into your fishing day. The other way is to drive through Cades Cove just a couple of miles back to the Abrams Falls trailhead. From there, you get out, lace up your wading boots, and walk just a short ways before stepping into the water. The latter may sound easy, but there is a good chance that the time you save in hiking boots, you'll make up for with "windshield time" once in Cades Cove.

The drive through the cove is a beautiful one, the surrounding mountains and ridges framing an expansive valley where deer, black bears, and wild turkeys parade in the lush green fields. The wildlife is also the catalyst for the rush hour–style traffic you find when making the drive around the one-way loop that takes you to the Abrams Creek parking lot. Some folks will stop if they see a squirrel gnawing on a nut, but it takes a larger animal, usually a bear, to really lock things down. What would normally take only a few minutes can consume up to an hour.

Coming into Abrams from the Cades Cove side is what most folks do. From the parking lot, a short hike can put you into what can be a few hours' or a long day's worth of fishing. From where the creek crosses the bridge downstream to just below Abrams Creek Falls, the river comes into contact with the trail for only a short distance. The creek leaves the trail in two large, horseshoe-shaped bends, the upper bend nearer to Cades Cove winding away from the trail for more than a mile. To fish this horseshoe along its entirety, you'd best plan on a day's trip. The stretches at the top and bottom of the bend next to the trail receive a fair amount of pressure, but the farther you wade, the fewer people you see.

The upper horseshoe is a long single day trip so budget your time so you are not hiking out after dark, or plan on camping. Trying to cut cross-country through the dense undergrowth is nearly impossible and can easily disorient even experienced hikers. In some places along the creek, faint trails give only false hope, as they usually dead-end into impenetrable thickets or loop around back to the creek. Wading is also difficult, the rocks feeling like linoleum covered in industrial lubricant. Bring a friend just in case something bad happens. It's better to be safe than sorry, and you may need someone to hold the camera at the very least.

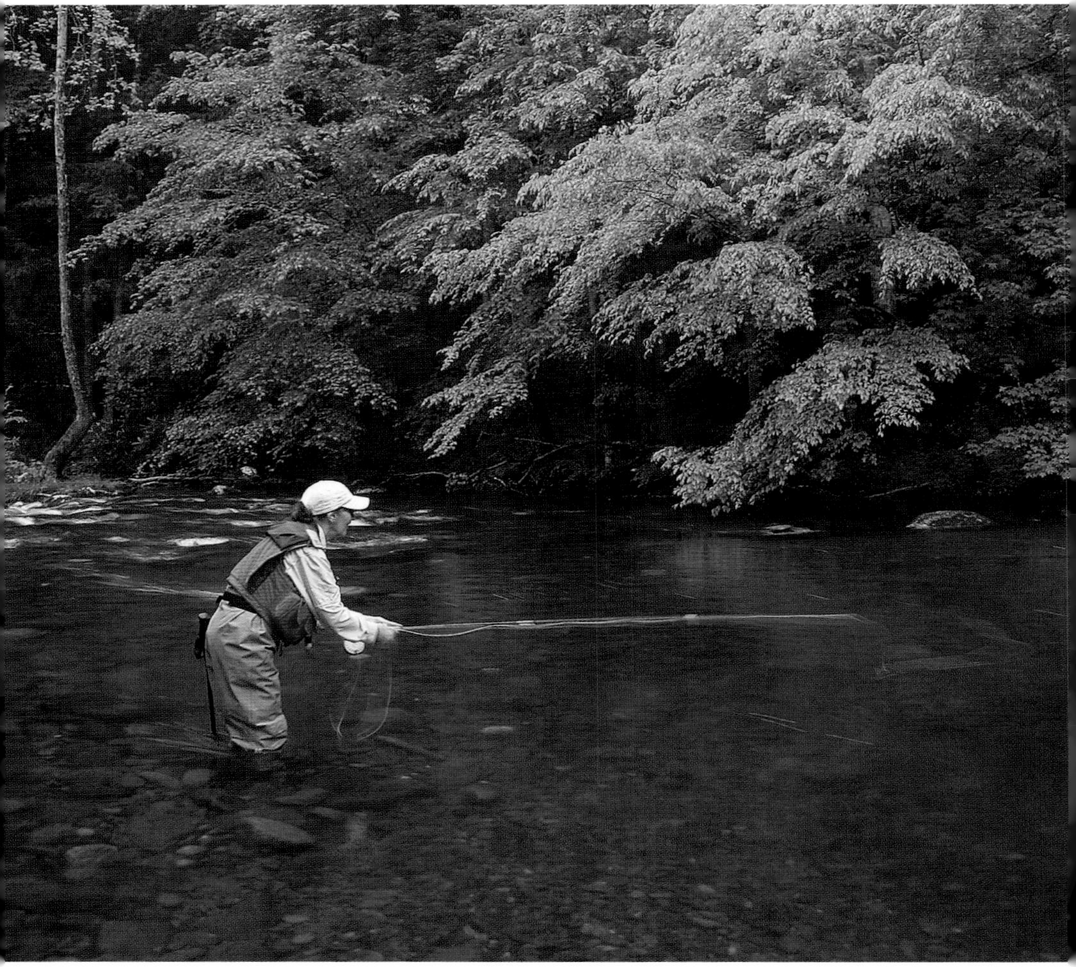

Access to Abrams Creek is not easy, but anglers will often be rewarded with solitude and a slick pool to cast a dry. ZACH MATTHEWS

Downstream, just below the first horseshoe, the river forms a smaller semiloop just above Abrams Creek Falls. The bend above the falls doesn't take you into quite as remote a location as the horseshoe farther upstream, but it does wind away from the main trail.

Below the falls, a massive plunge pool hides what all of us want to believe is some Godzilla trout that has managed to elude anglers' hooks. It is an inviting place to fish, especially with a streamer, but don't expect anything out of the ordinary. This is, of course, excluding the warmer months, when tourists come to the falls to swim in the creek's cold waters. After the summer sun begins warming the valley, the pool below the falls becomes a better spot for people watching and less of a trout hole.

After the creek passes over the falls, it is not long before the flow flattens considerably and you are left with a calm, slow-flowing, brush-choked stream. In the lower reaches, Abrams Creek warms quickly in spring, the trout migrating upstream or holding near a hidden spring to wait out the doldrums. Once the water temperature drops back into a comfortable trout range, some of the larger trout in the creek will hunt in the long pools. There are also rumors of larger rainbows living in Chilhowee Lake most of the year that run up Abrams Creek like faux steelhead in the winter and spring. The possibility of this is slim, but it is something to ponder on those cold days when nothing is going on.

From Chilhowee upstream nearly to Abrams Creek Campground, the river is not hospitable to trout anglers nor, for the most part, to trout. The creek deepens and creeps along at a numbing pace, with water temperatures too warm for trout. However, it is a fun paddle from the lake upstream into the creek. Just make sure that Chilhowee Dam is not generating, as the lake is much like a long, deep tailrace, complete with heavy currents when the turbines are on.

Since this is basically a limestone-based fishery for the first few miles after crossing the loop road inside Cades Cove, the dry-fly fishing on Abrams Creek can be spectacular. Mayflies and caddis can be seen fluttering above the surface, the diverse biomass creating similar conditions to a spring creek. The trout are not easy for this very reason. The slow, clear currents, combined with plenty of forage, make Abrams Creek trout cagey and not easily fooled by sloppy angling.

Stalking a rising or sighted trout is not always possible, so approach each piece of water with the care you would if a 20-inch rainbow was sipping the last of a spinner fall. Getting out of the creek to move up on a fish is not always possible, so slow, stealthy, in-stream stalks are usually required. If this all sounds like a lot of trouble, it is. The reward is far worth the effort. A hard-won Abrams Creek trout confers bragging rights for anyone who fishes the park.

When winter's hand looses its grip on the valley, Hendricksons begin hatching. Usually in late February or early March, these large mayflies begin

Abrams Creek Falls provides a dramatic backdrop to the fishing. The horseshoe bend above the falls can be one of the better stretches on Abrams, but always fish with a partner on this remote section. ADAM LITTELL

a winged ascent from the river, and you should be there if possible. The early-season hatch can bring some of the river's larger trout to the surface. Parachute and CDC Compara-dun patterns work best on Abrams, especially A. K.'s Parachutes (#14-16).

In April, caddis begin showing up in decent numbers, giving the trout more bugs to look at than the early mayfly hatches. Patterns that sit low in the water, such as Harrop's Fertile Caddis, Henry's Fork Caddis, and Stalcup's Parachute Caddis Emerger (#14-16) far outproduce traditional Elk-Hair Caddis and close varietals. Along with the caddis, early May brings Light Cahills, Little Yellow Stoneflies, and some Sulphurs. As with the Hendrickson hatch, patterns that have a realistic profile will prove far more valuable than Catskill ties.

CDC Compara-duns, Last Chance Cripples, and floating nymphs such as Lawson's Half-Back Emergers and Harrop's Captive Duns (#14-18) will all work for the Cahill and Sulphur hatches. Parachute-style Golden Stones and Fluttering Stones (#12-14) will work for the often light, but heavily fishy stonefly hatches.

Green Drakes begin coming off around Memorial Day. Well, it can be anytime around that time, the day being used as a common waypoint in the yearly hatch calendar. Sometimes the drakes come off in good numbers, while other days—even years—the hatch is a mere scrap of bugs flying about. In either event, parachute-style Green Drakes and a few extended-body versions (#8-12) should always be in your box.

As with most freestone streams in the South, when June wanes into July, the bugs on Cades Creek taper off and the trout begin feeding heavily on terrestrials. One of my favorite summer patterns on this creek is Harrop's CDC Beetle. This fly imitates a variety of beetles on the creek and can be fished wet or dry. Bring a few of these, along with flying ants (#14-18), Monster Beetles (#10), and Steeves's Fireflies (#14). The terrestrials will fish well into September until the temperatures drop and the beetles, ants, and other creepy-crawlies hunker down for a long winter.

There can be a few caddis fluttering around through the fall and winter, along with decent numbers of *Baetis* and midges. Most of your trout fishing, however, will be done subsurface, and this is no easy task. Blind-casting to likely holding water, drifting a BTS Nymph, Split Case PMD, or WD-40 (#16-20) under a greased line, tiny indicator, or subtle dry fly is typical during the colder months. Don't expect more than a few fish on even a good day at Abrams, but know that you earned them.

Aside from the deer and bear jams associated with Cades Cove, the valley is one of the most beautiful in the area, much akin to the region sur-

Rainbow trout now dominate the spring creek–like waters of Abrams Creek. Most successful anglers prefer to stalk trout from the banks, keeping out of the water to avoid sending ripples across the water's surface. LOUIS CAHILL

Monster Beetle

Hook:	#8-10 Daiichi 1260
Thread:	Black 6/0
Body:	Green Flashabou
Back:	Black foam
Post:	Orange foam
Legs:	Black rubber
Hackle:	Green grizzly

rounding Cataloochee Creek on the opposite side of the park. Deer will feed curiously close by as you wade the streambed, forcing you to question why the trout are not as tame. If you're ever curious about what is going on out at Abrams, a call to Little River Outfitters can save you a long drive. They are always abreast of the region's fishing and are eager to share info regarding what is hatching, water temps, and how the creek is fishing.

It is not a matter of if you will fish Abrams, it is a matter of when. This creek has a way of drawing anglers like no other piece of water in the park. Whenever you go, Abrams will surely pull your boots out from under you, the trout will snub even your most perfect drifts, and you may at the very least lose a fly or two in the bushes. On the drive home, you'll be smiling, missing the creek, and contemplating a return trip because this time, you think you've got it figured out. Yeah, right.

Little River, Tennessee

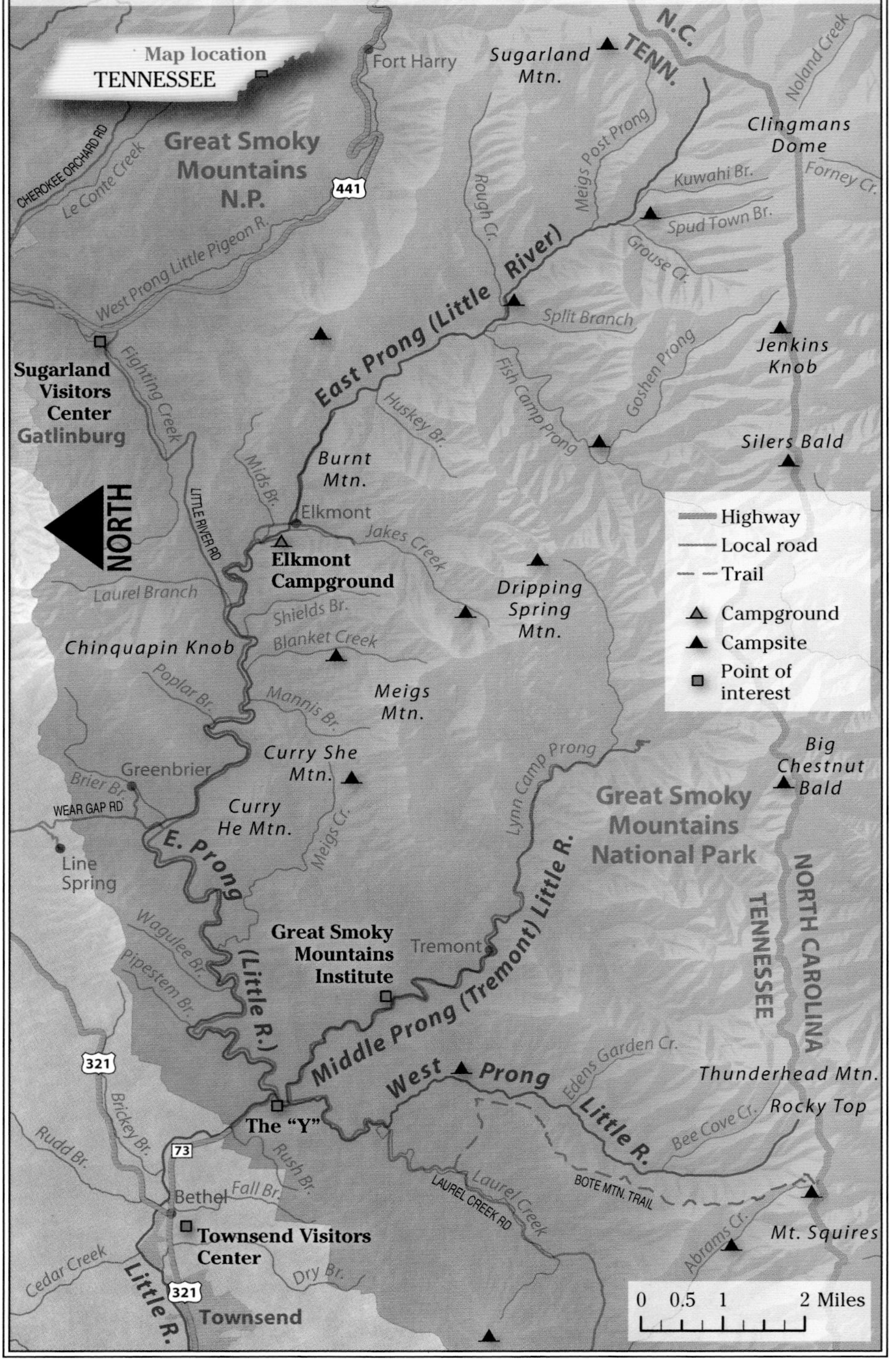

Map location
TENNESSEE
Great Smoky Mountains N.P.
Fort Harry
Sugarland Mtn.
N.C.
TENN.
Noland Creek
Clingmans Dome
Forney Cr.
Kuwahi Br.
Spud Town Br.
Grouse Cr.
Meigs Post Prong
Rough Cr.
441
CHEROKEE ORCHARD RD
Le Conte Creek
West Prong Little Pigeon R.
East Prong (Little River)
Split Branch
Jenkins Knob
Goshen Prong
Fish Camp Prong
Huskey Br.
Silers Bald
Sugarland Visitors Center
Gatlinburg
Fighting Creek
NORTH
Burnt Mtn.
Mids Br.
Elkmont
Jakes Creek
Elkmont Campground
LITTLE RIVER RD
Highway
Local road
Trail
Campground
Campsite
Point of interest
Dripping Spring Mtn.
Laurel Branch
Shields Br.
Blanket Creek
Chinquapin Knob
Poplar Br.
Mannis Br.
Meigs Mtn.
Curry She Mtn.
Curry He Mtn.
Meigs Cr.
Greenbrier
Brier Br.
WEAR GAP RD
Line Spring
E. Prong
(Little R.)
Lynn Camp Prong
Big Chestnut Bald
Great Smoky Mountains National Park
NORTH CAROLINA
TENNESSEE
Middle Prong (Tremont) Little R.
Tremont
Great Smoky Mountains Institute
Wagulee Br.
Pipestem Br.
321
Brickey Br.
Rudd Br.
The "Y"
West Prong Little R.
Edens Garden Cr.
Thunderhead Mtn.
Rocky Top
Bee Cove Cr.
73
Rush Br.
LAUREL CREEK RD
Laurel Creek
BOTE MTN. TRAIL
Bethel
Fall Br.
Townsend Visitors Center
Mt. Squires
Abrams Cr.
Cedar Creek
Little R.
Dry Br.
321
Townsend
0 0.5 1 2 Miles

CHAPTER 18

Prongs of the Little River

West, Middle, and East Prongs

There are over 2,100 miles of trout water within the boundaries of Great Smoky Mountains National Park. Of this expansive, seemingly endless parade of trout water, you would be hard-pressed to find a watershed receiving more fanfare than the Little River. It's one of the largest streams in the park, and the Little River and its prongs are perhaps the most heavily fished waters within the park's boundaries.

Sandwiched between the major tourist hub of Gatlinburg and the mountain city of Townsend, the three prongs of the Little River join just outside of Townsend to form the main stem. There is a lot of hubbub surrounding the area. During peak season, both fly shops servicing the northern end of the park look like the mall at Christmas. Anglers pick through the fly bins, the ubiquitous "What are they biting on?" is uttered dozens of times, and undoubtedly somebody buys a rain jacket after forgetting one at home—wherever that may be. Both Little River Outfitters and Smoky Mountain Fly Shop see their fair share of business during the spring and summer months. Many of these anglers are planning to explore some section of the Little River watershed, if only for part of their trip.

The Little River system can be divided into the main stem and three tributaries, the East, West, and Middle prongs. The main river flows for just a short distance past the "Y," where all three come together to form the main stem. The Little River proper flows a short distance through the park before leaving its boundaries, afterward becoming more of a warmwater fishery than trout water. The section in the park fishes well for trout only during the cooler months of the year, summer temperatures proving too much for the delicate trout, which either move upstream or perish in Darwinesque fashion.

Upstream of the "Y," each of the prongs possesses its own unique personality. All are tumbling mountain freestones with populations of brown and rainbow trout below the headwaters, and brook trout upstream. Access to any of the prongs is easy, accounting for some of the pressure anglers give

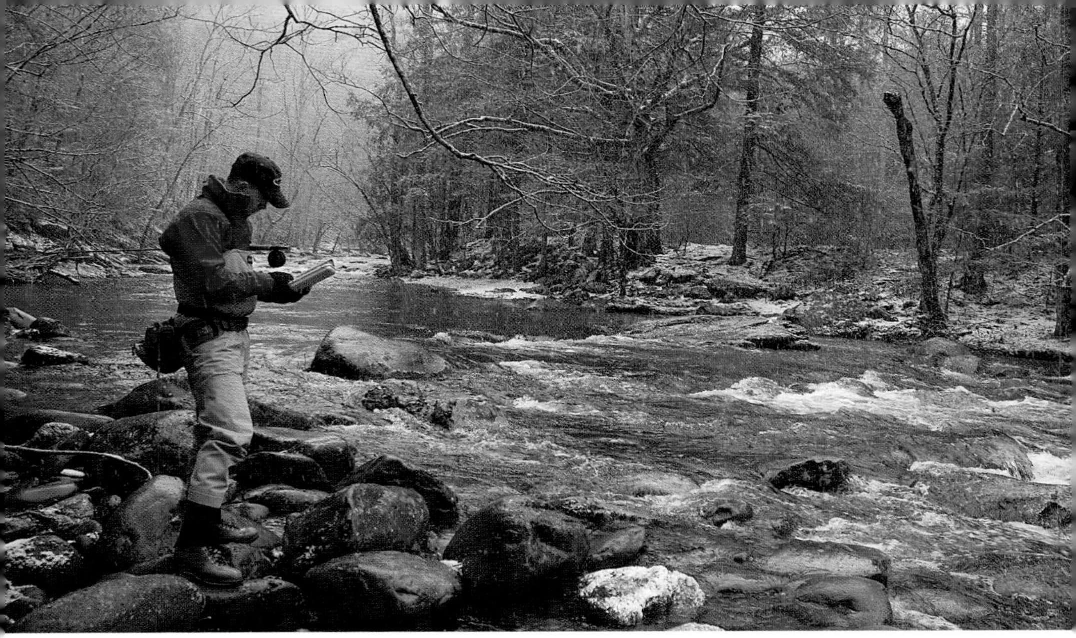

Cold weather doesn't deter some hardy anglers from fishing the Little River region, and fishing can be spectacular despite the frozen fingers. Zach Matthews

them. The other, perhaps more important contributing element to their popularity is the fact that they fish as well if not better than many streams in the park. These factors, combined with a certain *je ne sais quoi,* are what keeps anglers religiously making the pilgrimage to these creeks year after year.

West Prong

The smallest of the three prongs is the West. This small creek, in reality about average for much of the park's water, flows alongside Laurel Creek Road for around 2 miles before snaking into the tree line to its headwaters. Access is found alongside Laurel Creek Road on the lower reaches, with numerous pullouts to park and walk down to the creek. Brown and rainbow trout hold in the lower reaches of the creek, the browns thinning as the river's gradient becomes a bit too steep for their comfort. The average trout is 8 inches or smaller, but a few nice brown trout have turned up in the lower reaches.

To reach the upper sections of the creek, West Prong Trail offers an easy walk, putting you at the doorstep of gorgeous rainbow trout that seldom grow much past 8 inches. What they lack in size, they make up for in striking color and long, white-tipped pectoral fins.

The West Prong is often overlooked in favor of the East and Middle Prongs, but it can save the day if the other two are not fishing well. Depending on the time of year, the other two prongs could be either too crowded for some folks' liking or blown out after a heavy rain. The West Prong can prove to be a viable alternative to the two larger prongs, as well as Abrams Creek, which sits just across the gap.

Middle Prong

Known as Tremont, the Middle Prong of the Little River drops from the region surrounding Buckeye Gap near Cold Spring Knob. Its two major tributaries, Lynn Camp Prong and Thunderhead Prong, are stellar small-stream fisheries in their own right, but the long hike in would make camping at site #28 a good idea.

The waters on Tremont are fast and tumbling, the stream spilling over large boulders to form jade plunge pools that tail out in braided channels before repeating the process over and over again. This is a larger stream than the West Prong, paralleling the road that runs alongside the Great Smoky Mountains Institute at Tremont. After a short while, the pavement turns to gravel, continuing up alongside the Middle Prong. When the road ends, you'd best strike out in hiking boots and head up Middle Prong Trail if you want to get into some spectacular brook trout fishing on one of the river's tributaries.

Trout in Tremont run about the same as on the West Prong, perhaps slightly larger. But it is not the size of fish people come to the park for. To fish in such a natural environment for wild fish in the backcountry of one of the country's greatest national parks counts for far more than a few extra inches on the end of your line. The brown and rainbow trout that swim in Tremont are feisty and are due the same respect you would show a large rainbow sipping Rusty Spinners on one of the tailwaters. They are every bit as wary, despite their diminutive stature. Just ask some folks who head up and fish the cascading waters of Tremont and come back empty-handed.

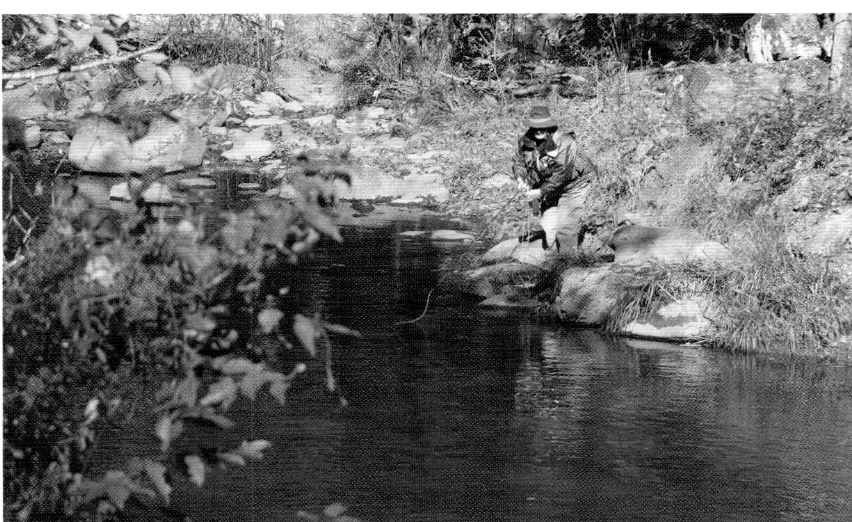

Keep a low profile and blend in if you want to be successful when fishing the Little River system.

East Prong

The East Prong is known as Little River, taking the name from the main stem to its headwaters above Elkmont. The longest and most complex of the three prongs, the East Prong is also the most heavily used. If you head to the East Prong during the late spring or summer, you're likely to see tubers floating the lower reaches, vastly outnumbering the anglers. The river can be broken down into five distinct sections from the headwaters to the "Y."

From Fish Camp Prong near the headwaters 4 miles downstream to Elkmont, the river is full of small, wild rainbows that eagerly take dry flies. If you're feeling like exploring, Fish Camp Prong can make a cool day trip. The river is fairly large below Fish Camp, narrowing considerably above the tributary. It is classic Smokies fishing, requiring little more than a dry fly on most warm days.

Below Elkmont to Long Arm Bridge, rainbow and brown trout appear in heavy numbers, but so do the anglers. This is one of the more popular stretches of water on the East Prong, with numerous pools, spillovers, and deep runs tempting anglers with the trout they hold. Downstream from Long Arm, the river continues to tumble and fall in like fashion until it reaches Metcalf Bottoms. In this section, large pools can hold some of the river's larger trout.

Metcalf Bottoms, a long stretch of low-gradient water, is located just above a falls in an area known as "The Sinks." The Sinks mark the line where summertime trout fishing begins on Elkmont. Downstream of here, the summer sun warms the river to levels unacceptable to the trout. They hunker down or find a nice cool spring to sit by until the night falls or the thermometer drops to a more civilized number.

The area around Metcalf can have some of the East Prong's heaviest hatches, ranging from caddis to Hendricksons, March Browns, Light Cahills, or Little Yellow Stoneflies. The fishing here is far more technical, requiring anglers to occasionally match the hatch, with selective trout feeding just as they would on a much larger river. This is not to say that hatches do not occur on other sections of this and the other prongs, but the consistency and intensity of hatches around the Metcalf area are usually greater.

Downstream from Metcalf Bottoms all the way to Meigs Creek, the water reverts to the tumbling nature of a true Smoky Mountains stream. During the fall months, this sec-

Large stonefly nymphs provide trout with a big meal and are why stonefly imitations are highly effective in freestone rivers. CHRIS SCALLEY

tion often produces some larger than average brown trout, a few so large I won't print them here because folks would surely call me a liar. For the most part, rainbows and browns will average 8 to 10 inches, as they do on much of the East Prong, with a few going a tad over.

Below the falls where Meigs Creek enters the river downstream to the "Y," the East Prong dumps into large, deep pools and flows part of the way through Little River Gorge. This lower stretch is the first to warm as soon as the temperatures begin rising in late spring, making it a fall through early spring fishery.

In the fall, especially after a rain, this is the place to hunt for large brown trout. Throwing streamers in the clearing water can provoke strikes from some of the park's largest brown trout. Some anglers target these fish with some success, but they should not be expected. As rare as a politician passing a lie detector test, the big browns are not only wary, but few in numbers. To catch one is a rarity, but they are there and you can't catch them standing at your car and wishing.

Fly selection on the river is fairly simple. During the colder months, nymphing with a Pheasant Tail, Tellico Nymph, Morris's Holy Grail, or Prince

Classic pocketwater on Little River begs to be fished with big, bushy dry flies. Attractor dry flies work well in the spring with many anglers tying on a beadhead dropper to double their chances. DAVID KNAPP

Gabriel's Trumpet

Hook:	#10-16 Daiichi 1120
Thread:	Yellow 6/0
Bead:	Gold metal
Tail:	Tan goose biots
Body:	Silver tinsel
Rib:	Red Ultra Wire
Thorax:	Cream/tan ostrich herl
Hackle:	Cream/tan
Wingcase:	Swiss Straw

Nymph (#14-18) is your best bet, getting the fly down to where the trout are holding. In the spring, add a few stonefly patterns to that selection. Stalcup's Tungsten Rubber-Legged Stone and Mercer's Epoxy Stone (#8-12) would be well-deserved additions to the mix. These nymph patterns should carry you though summer and into the fall, but feel free to add more because you can never have too many flies.

For the most part, hatches on the river are not all that heavy, but they do wake the fish up and get them looking to the surface. The first hatches to see the new year can come as early as February, but usually begin showing up in March. Blue Quills and Quill Gordons hatch, respectively, during the early spring following the first warm spells. Keep a few corresponding Catskill ties in your box in case you run into either of these hatches.

The month of May is a busy one, with Little Yellow Stoneflies, caddis, and Light Cahills all hatching. You'll want to drop in the fly shop to see what the fish are eating and maybe pick up a few flies to match whatever bug happens to be on the trout's menu. A few staples are brown and tan Elk-Hair Caddis (#14-16), Yellow Sally parachutes and yellow Stimulators (#12-16), along with a few Light Cahill parachutes (#14-18). The dry-fly action should continue through late June and possibly into July if the weather and water levels hold.

During the summer, move higher into the watersheds to find cold water and more responsive trout. It is time to break out the terrestrial box, which should have a smattering of black and cinnamon ant patterns (#14-18), Steeves's Fireflies (#14), green Rainy's Leaf Hoppers (#12), DeBruin's Hoppers (#12-14), and various beetle patterns (#14-16). A few inchworm patterns, both floating and sinking, will round out the summertime terrestrial box for the entire Little River watershed—and the rest of the park, for that matter.

You probably won't find solitude when fishing the Little River area during the peak season, but that's only a few pages in the calendar. The fishing in the spring and early summer makes it well worth a drive to this side of the park, despite a few extra folks on the water. Besides, we're all in this together, and you just may make a few new friends along the banks.

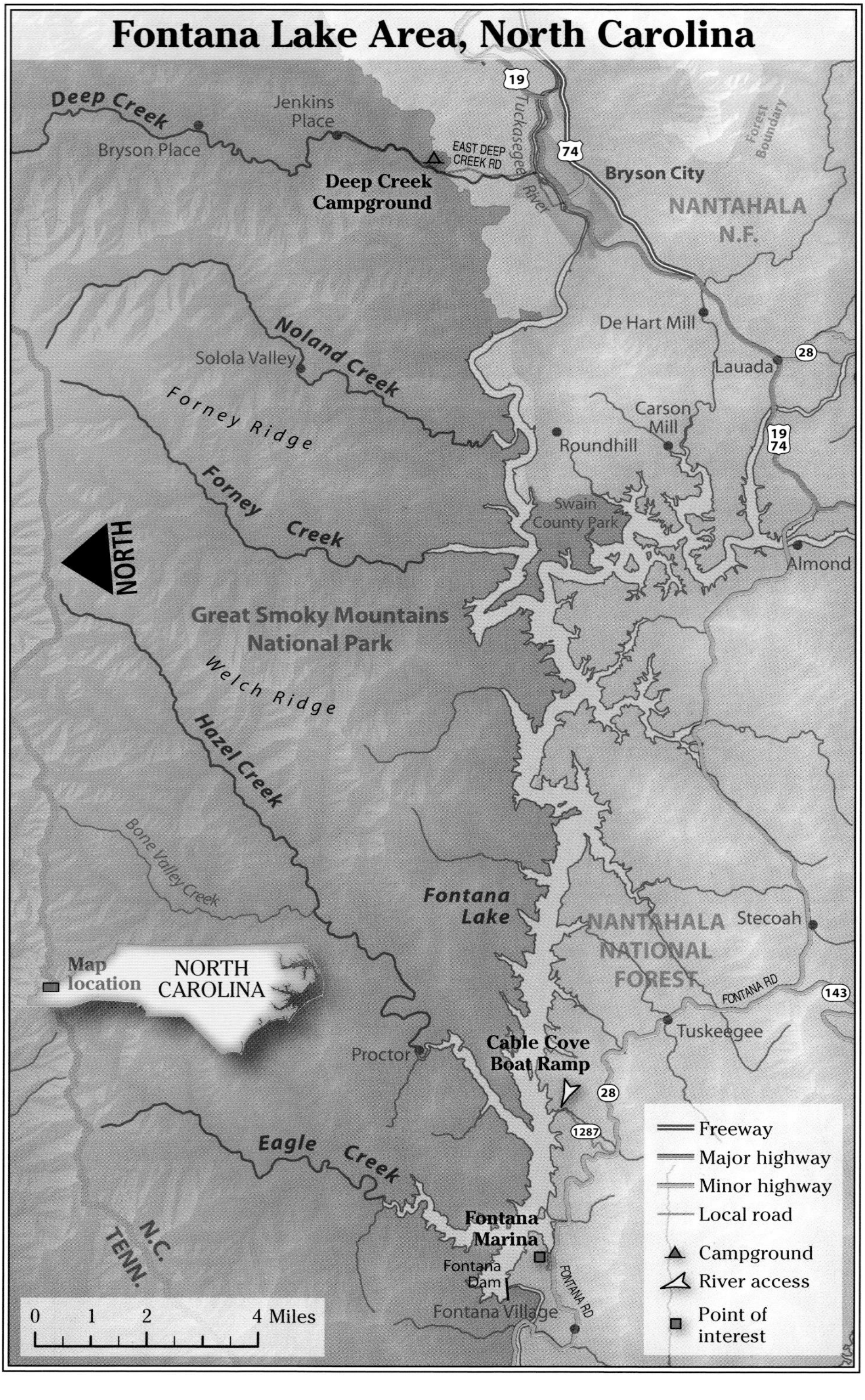
Fontana Lake Area, North Carolina
19
Deep Creek
Jenkins Place
Bryson Place
EAST DEEP CREEK RD
Deep Creek Campground
Tuckasegee River
74
Forest Boundary
Bryson City
NANTAHALA N.F.
Noland Creek
Solola Valley
De Hart Mill
Lauada
28
Forney Ridge
Carson Mill
Roundhill
19 74
Forney Creek
Swain County Park
Almond
NORTH
Great Smoky Mountains National Park
Welch Ridge
Hazel Creek
Bone Valley Creek
Fontana Lake
NANTAHALA NATIONAL FOREST
Stecoah
FONTANA RD
143
Map location
NORTH CAROLINA
Tuskeegee
Proctor
Cable Cove Boat Ramp
28
1287
Eagle Creek
N.C.
TENN.
Fontana Marina
Fontana Dam
FONTANA RD
Fontana Village
0 1 2 4 Miles
Freeway
Major highway
Minor highway
Local road
Campground
River access
Point of interest

CHAPTER 19

North Shore of Fontana Lake

Deep, Hazel, Forney, Noland, and Eagle Creeks

The area surrounding Fontana Lake in extreme western North Carolina is chocked with Southern angling history. Old cabins and camps still survive, telling the story of settlers past. Logging towns sprang up practically overnight in the region; their combined actions all but deforested the mountainsides in a time frame stretching from the late 1800s through the first decades of the 20th century.

In 1942, with the need for power rising to a critical level during World War II, construction of Fontana Dam was begun. It took only two years to complete the project, with nearly 5,000 workers working around the clock in three shifts. The completed project stands today as the highest dam east of the Rocky Mountains, nearly 480 feet high, spanning 2,365 feet across what was the Little Tennessee River. Fontana Lake stretches for 29 miles and impounds more than 10,000 acres of water surface, equating to around 240 miles of shoreline. Along the north shore of the lake, extending up into the Tuckaseegee River, five streams lay claim to a near cultlike following of anglers and conjure iconic images of fly fishing in the Smoky Mountains.

These are large creeks that fall from the most remote reaches of the Great Smoky Mountains National Park. Wild rainbow and brown trout hold in their currents, some reaching sizes that, for the park, require a photograph or notarized eyewitness account to believe. Four creeks—Hazel, Forney, Noland, and Eagle—make up the most notable tributaries of Fontana's famed North Shore. In addition, Deep Creek, which we'll look at first, is just around the corner, spilling into the Tuckaseegee River arm of Fontana Lake. For many, the North Shore typifies angling in the Smokies, where a long hike and a wilderness camp lead to wild trout in a setting that only God could create.

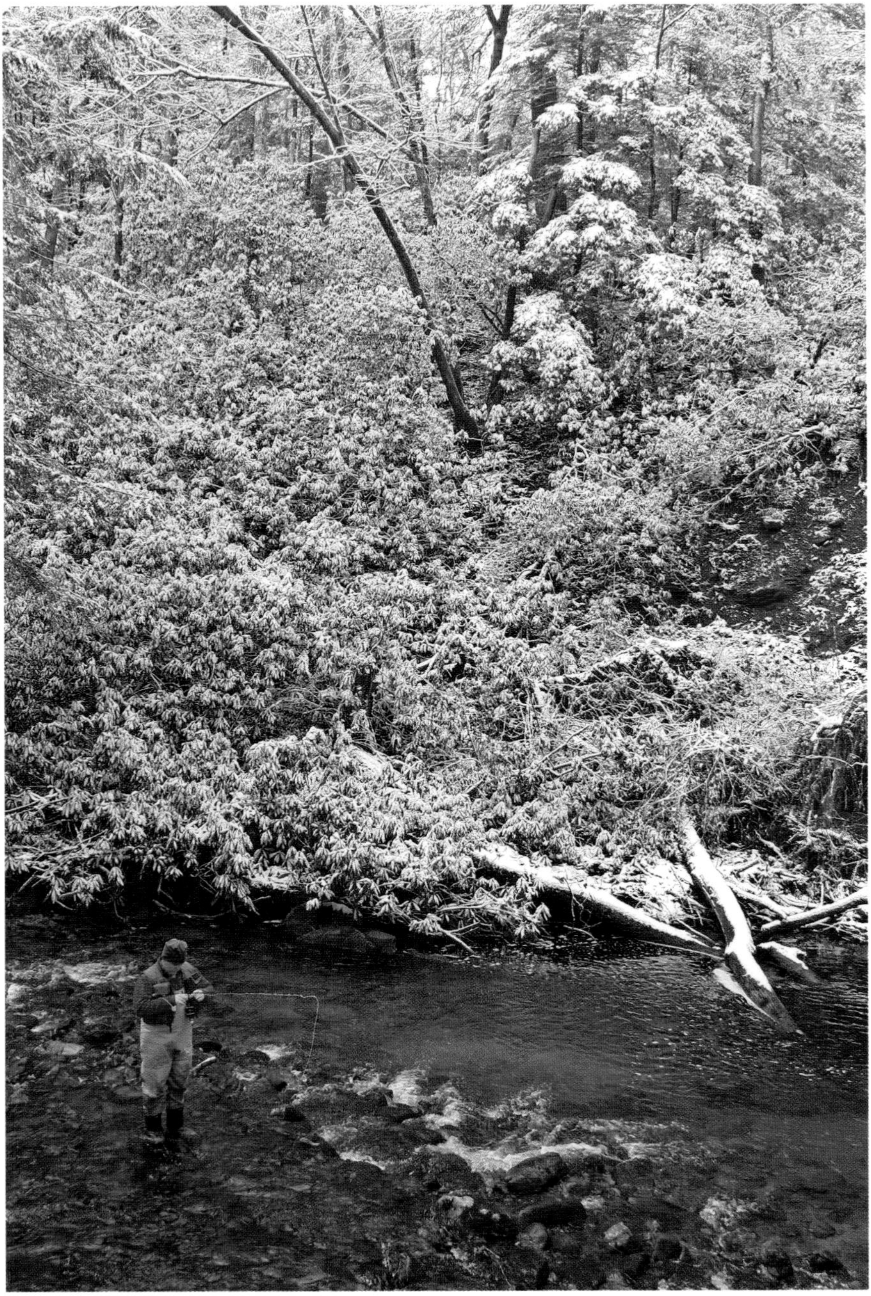

Winter fishing on Fontana's North Shore can be brutally cold, but the trout don't seem to mind. Watch the weather and be prepared if you are caught in the backcountry during a winter storm.

Deep Creek

If you're looking for big brown trout in the park, Deep Creek offers yet another option to explore. Not really considered a true North Shore creek, it empties into the Tuckaseegee River just a few miles before the river begins backing up into Fontana Lake. Access to Deep Creek is much easier than on most of the North Shore creeks, making it more popular with day hikers.

Along the creek, eight campsites can be accessed by hiking in along Deep Creek Trail off Newfound Gap Road on the north side, or via the trailhead near the ranger station on the south end. If you come in from Newfound Gap Road, it is a 2-mile hike to the river that makes for a great day hike for experienced hikers and puts you on some striking trout water. Coming in from Newfound Gap, you can chase brook trout as well as wild rainbows in the upper reaches. If you want to try for brookies in the upper reaches, you're going to need a tent, good hiking boots, and a strong set of legs to make the walk in and out.

Coming in from the south side, you can hike in to some big brown trout water on a day trip. If you're wanting to camp, hike to Site #59 or #60 to get a feel for some of the best water Deep Creek has to offer. This will get you away from the crowds and hopefully into some nice brownies. Below the trailhead parking lot from Indian Creek Falls downstream to the park boundary, tubers fill the creek, displacing anglers, but it's probably all for the best. The lower reaches become too warm for the trout during the warmer months, so the area is best left to the floating hordes.

The long, deep pools on Deep Creek hold some large brown trout, but they are just like any other big browns: wary and mostly nocturnal. Fishing early and late in the day will up your chances, but if you blow your approach to a trout's lie, the game is over before you even roll the dice.

Hazel Creek

Ask any veteran park angler to name the top five streams, and you can bet that at least two will be ones you've never heard of, and one will be Hazel Creek. The large, rippling creek falls from high in the park from the area around Welch Ridge and Jenkins Trail Ridge. For 18 miles, from the headwaters downstream to Fontana, Hazel has been the catalyst of more "big-brown-trout-in-the-park" stories than any other creek in the Smokies.

Rough and remote, the country around Hazel was home to the mountain settlement of Proctor, once a lumber town with nearly 1,000 residents by 1920. Like much of the park, the area was raped by lumber companies. Nearly 200 million board feet of lumber was removed from the valley and surrounding mountains before the operation was ended.

In 1944, the last residents of the valley left Hazel Creek for good as the Little Tennessee River slowly filled in to form Fontana Lake. The old road that led from Fontana to Hazel Creek now lies under many feet of water. Nowa-

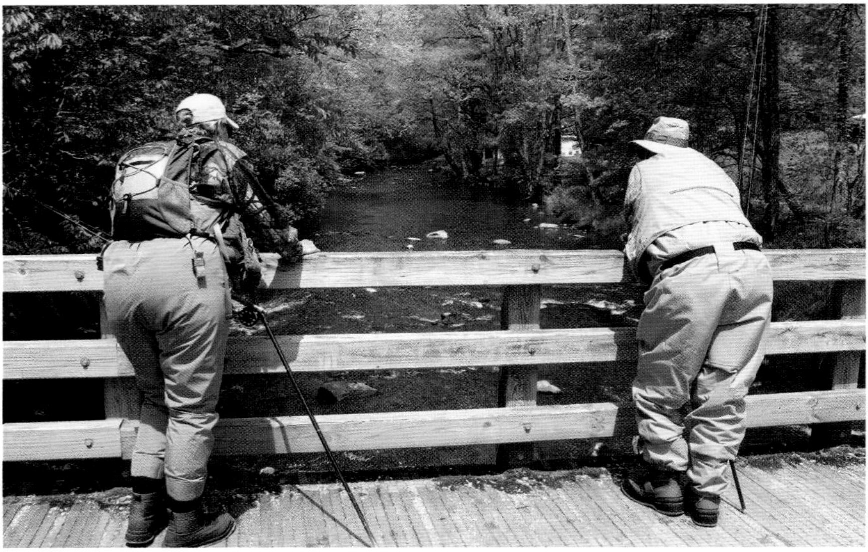

Two anglers survey the water on Hazel Creek near the historic settlement of Proctor. Aside from this last vestige of the early settlement, the region is as remote as anywhere in the vast Smokies. IAN AND CHARITY RUTTER

days, if you want to reach Hazel Creek, you paddle across the lake or saddle up for a 10-mile hike into the remote creek from Fontana Dam. Hiking in from Clingman's Dome is another option, as you can link up with Hazel Creek Trail, but you're not cutting down on the miles, as it is nearly just as far as the dam from the creek. The upside is that if you want to access the upper portions of Hazel, hiking in from Clingman's Dome will save you some time, but it is still at the least an overnight trip.

Needless to say, most folks choose either to make the short paddle across the lake from Cable Cove Boat Launch, or secure a shuttle for a nominal fee at Fontana Marina. It's only about an hour's paddle from Cable Cove to the landing at the Old Calhoun House. From the old settlement area, it is a little over 2 miles to Site #85, where many anglers choose to camp when fishing. Needless to say, the stretch between the lake and just above the campsite is the most heavily fished stretch of Hazel Creek.

Pressure on Hazel is relative, as its location, far removed from pavement, keeps many anglers at bay. During the spring, the campsites can become crowded, so make sure you get there early to get a prime spot, or simply hike farther upstream and reserve one of the campsites higher on the drainage. Site #84 (Sugar Fork) is around 2 miles past #85 and sits along an old road, making for an easy walk in.

Two more campsites sit along the river, the water above Site #82 holding brook trout in the cascading water. It is a long hike into the headwaters from anywhere, but it is something that any able-bodied Smoky Mountain angler should do at least once. It is true backcountry fishing and perhaps the closest you may come to experiencing the Smokies much as the famed author Horace Kephart did in the early part of the 20th century.

If you're not into totally roughing it on your own, Ian and Charity Rutter of R&R Guide Service offer hosted trips to Hazel Creek, complete with elaborate tent camps and backcountry gourmet cooking. This type of camp takes a lot of the logistical nightmares out of play for anglers who may not be that experienced in the art of backcountry angling. It is also nice to finish a day of fishing and not have to worry about who's cooking dinner, or if raccoons got into the freeze-dried beef stroganoff.

Forney Creek

You can reach Site #74 nearly as fast by hiking the 3 miles along Forney Creek Trail as you can by paddling a canoe across the lake from Swain County Park near the town of Almond. The river near this site is large for a park stream, holding brown and rainbow trout that require a great deal of stealth when approaching before you even make a cast.

The lower portion of the river below Huggins Creek is more easily accessible by parking at the end of Lakeview Drive, also known as the Road to Nowhere. As is true with all North Shore creeks, there is no easy way to get here, making access to the middle reaches an overnight ordeal.

Hiking in from Clingman's Dome on Forney Ridge Trail will put you into the headwaters of the creek and is a great jumping-off spot if you want some

North Shore creeks are larger than most Smoky Mountain streams, giving anglers room to roam and growing larger than average trout for the region.

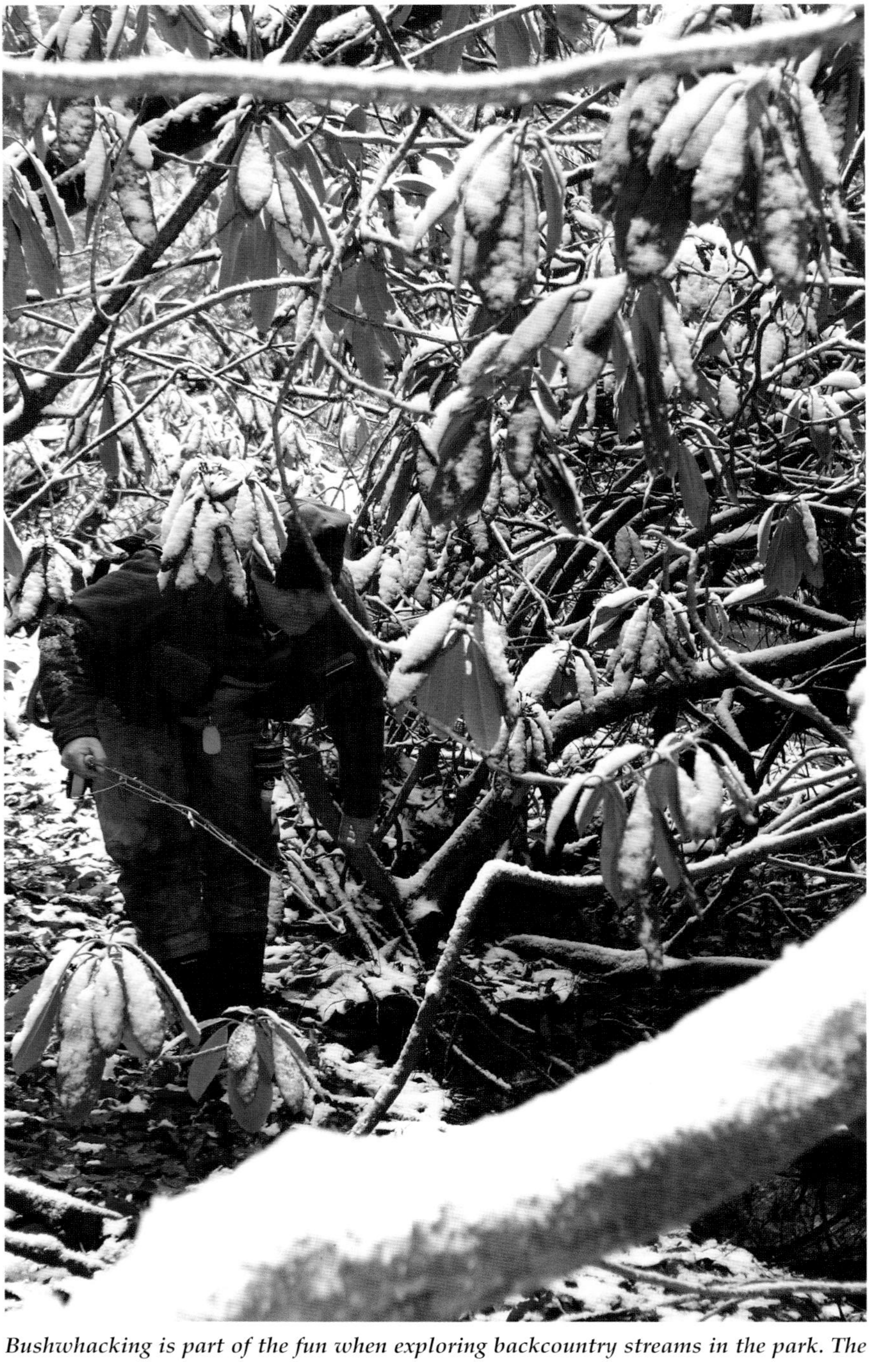

Bushwhacking is part of the fun when exploring backcountry streams in the park. The remote nature of these waters means making your own trail when traversing streamside.

tight quarters work when searching for wild rainbows and brook trout. Forney shrinks in size around Site #68, and the lower reaches fish better for larger trout. Most folks opt for camping on the lower reaches of the creek downstream of Site #71, preferring more casting room to the laurel thickets higher in the watershed.

At Site #70, Jonas Creek comes in, emptying into the main flow near the middle of the creek's length. This is a prime camping spot, allowing you to fish the lower reaches of the creek by hiking a few miles. You can also cruise up Jonas Creek Trail to find brook trout in this small tributary.

Noland Creek

Located on the far eastern side of Fontana Lake, Noland Creek drops through the valley from the area surrounding Andrews Bald, where it begins as a small trickle before quickly gaining size. The majority of the creek comprises pocketwater and its average trout are probably smaller in size than trout in the surrounding creeks. Nevertheless, Noland Creek is well worth exploring, as surprises can be found in larger rainbows and browns on any of the North Shore watersheds.

There are six backcountry campsites accessible by Noland Creek Trail off Lakeview Drive (The Road to Nowhere). The trailhead is about a mile upstream from the lake, and Site #66 sits near the creek's mouth. The stretch from Site #66 upstream to Site #65 is heavily fished, but there are some choice pieces of water sitting in this stretch, so don't always pass it by.

Above Site #65, pressure drops off as the trail winds up the river for 4 miles to Site #64 where Mill Creek enters the main flow. Camping here and exploring Mill Creek will put you deep in brook trout territory. The rainbows in the main stem are about the same size as the brookies you will catch on Mill Creek, so you might as well go for the more colorful brook trout if you hike this far.

Eagle Creek

Just to the east of Fontana Dam, directly across from Fontana Marina, Eagle Creek enters the lake, making it the westernmost North Shore creek. A 5-mile hike from the dam or a boat ride across the lake puts you on this remote Smoky Mountain stream. You can launch your own boat from Cable Cove, or pay the shuttle fee from Fontana Marina to reach the mouth of the creek and hike upstream to one of the four campsites located along the water's edge.

Site #90 is the most heavily used by boaters coming across the lake to fish, and it is the first campsite encountered by hiking anglers visiting the creek. The creek slips around large boulders into deep plunge pools under a canopy of conifers and oak stands. The trout on Eagle are on the smallish side, averaging around 8 inches, but there's always the chance of encountering larger trout, especially in the lower reaches near the lake.

Most anglers forgo Eagle Creek, preferring to head farther east to Hazel. It is true that Hazel holds larger trout, but the feisty rainbows in Eagle prove to be an inviting reason to make the boat ride across the lake or the long hike in from the dam.

Just as in the other North Shore creeks, brook trout can be found in the headwaters. Eagle Creek's major tributaries are deserving of some exploration. Tub Mill Creek and Gunna Creek are a pair of brook trout streams that seldom

Stonefly patterns are popular choices when probing freestone creeks during the colder months. Just watch your casting or you'll end up fishing in the bushes.

see anglers. Both are located about 5 miles up from the lake, making this an overnight or multiday excursion. Don't expect anything out of the ordinary when exploring these creeks. Even without the pressure, the brook trout simply do not grow larger than average. They are plentiful, and if you are a backwoods brook trout junkie, they should be on your list of creeks to explore.

Hatches can appear anytime during the warmer months on all the creeks. Keep a good supply of various Catskill dry flies to match the Hendricksons (#14-16), March Browns (#12-16), and Blue Quills (#16-18) that hatch in early March. The hatches will not be heavy, nor will they provide reliable dry-fly action, but enough trout take notice to make having a few in your box worthwhile.

Caddis begin hatching in April or May, depending on the year, with Little Yellow Stoneflies and Light Cahills later in the spring. Elk-Hair Caddis (#12-16), yellow Stimulators and Yellow Sally parachutes (#12-16), and Light Cahill parachutes (#14-18) should be packed in, along with your nymphs and streamers. It often takes little more than drifting a general attractor pattern like a Royal Trude, Thunderhead, or Humpy (#12-16) over a trout's head to elicit a strike. If they're really not on the dry or if the temperatures are too cold for you to feel comfortable going dry fly only, try dropping a Beadhead Pheasant Tail, Prince Nymph, or Lightning Bug (#14-16) off the back of the dry.

Winter fishing can be good, and a good dusting of snow can make for striking scenery, but early to late fall and spring to early summer encompass the prime seasons. There is no easy way to reach most of the water on the North Shore creeks, so it's best to try and plan your trip during the peak season. It is doubtful you will find enough anglers in the backcountry to spoil your trip, especially if you don't mind putting in some leg time.

Prepare for anything in the backcountry, especially if fishing in the fall or early spring. Temperatures can easily drop into the 40s even as late as May, and ice storms can creep in early in the fall. Pack accordingly so there are no surprises, and you should have many memorable trips exploring the North Shore.

Cataloochee Creek, North Carolina

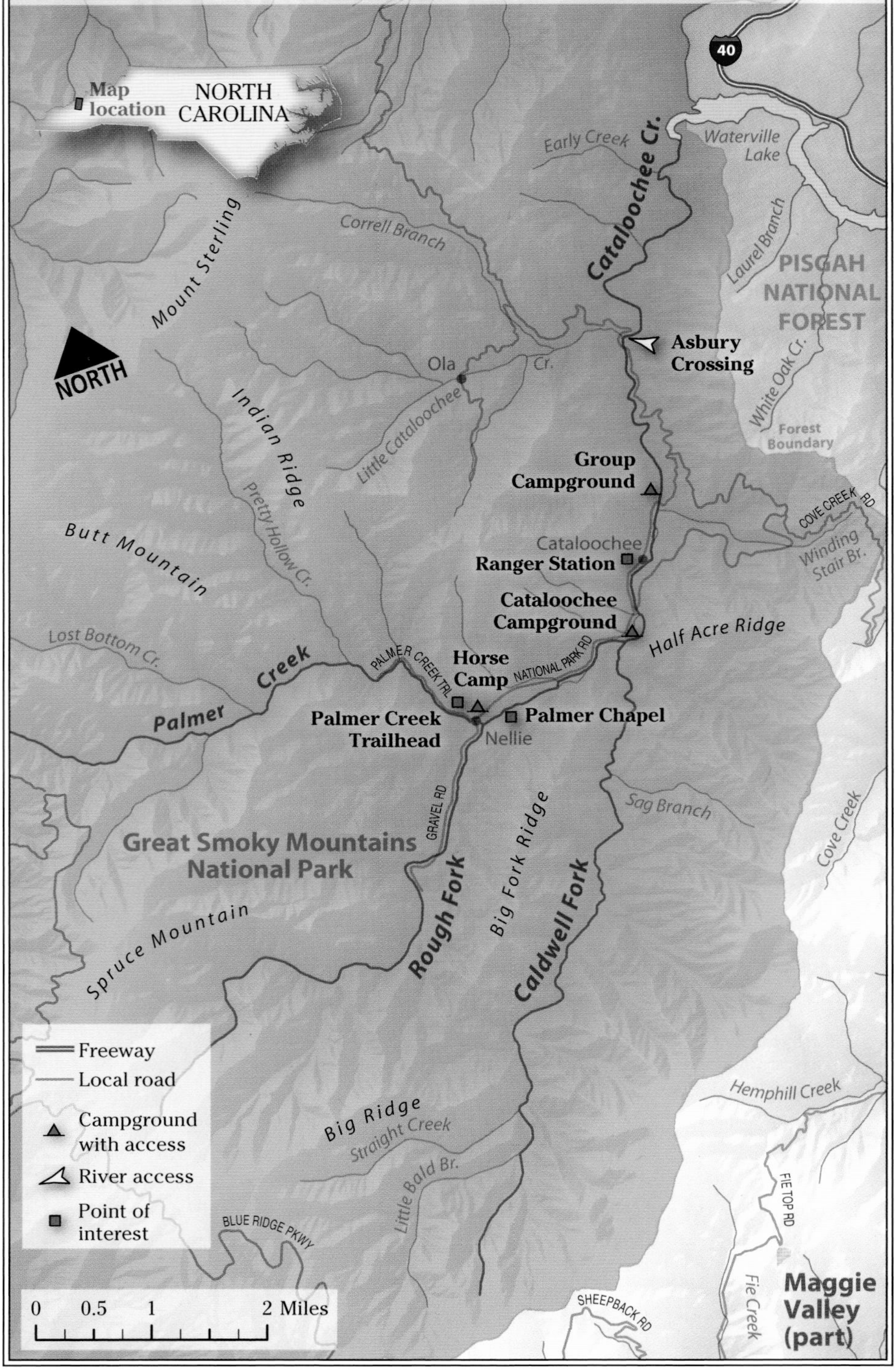
Map location
NORTH CAROLINA
40
Early Creek
Cataloochee Cr.
Waterville Lake
Laurel Branch
PISGAH NATIONAL FOREST
Correll Branch
Mount Sterling
NORTH
Asbury Crossing
Ola
Cr.
White Oak Cr.
Forest Boundary
Indian Ridge
Little Cataloochee
Group Campground
Pretty Hollow Cr.
COVE CREEK RD
Butt Mountain
Cataloochee Ranger Station
Winding Stair Br.
Cataloochee Campground
Half Acre Ridge
Lost Bottom Cr.
PALMER CREEK TRL
Horse Camp
NATIONAL PARK RD
Palmer Creek
Palmer Chapel
Palmer Creek Trailhead
Nellie
Sag Branch
GRAVEL RD
Big Fork Ridge
Cove Creek
Great Smoky Mountains National Park
Rough Fork
Caldwell Fork
Spruce Mountain
Freeway
Local road
Campground with access
River access
Point of interest
Hemphill Creek
Big Ridge
Straight Creek
Little Bald Br.
BLUE RIDGE PKWY
FIE TOP RD
Fie Creek
SHEEPBACK RD
Maggie Valley (part)
0 0.5 1 2 Miles

CHAPTER 20

Cataloochee Creek
and Tributaries

Nestled in the extreme southeastern corner of the park, over an hour's drive from the nearest town, the Cataloochee Valley appears seemingly out of nowhere among the high mountain ridges and thick forests. As Cove Creek Road descends from the mountains, the valley unfolds into expansive fields where deer, wild turkeys, and an ever expanding heard of elk roam. The valley is steeped in history with some of the first residents' homes still standing as they once did, a reminder of the early mountain pioneers who were members of one of the largest Appalachian settlements within the park's boundaries. Split-rail fences line the roads as you drive through the valley, flanking Cataloochee Creek and Rough Fork, a primary tributary of Cataloochee Creek, before ending at the Big Fork Ridge and Rough Fork trailheads at the southwestern corner of the valley.

The valley's namesake creek is one of the prettiest stretches of dry-fly water in the region. It has been compared to the classic trout waters of upstate New York, inspiring anglers who fish the remote waters in a near religiously fanatical manner to return every season. Even if the trout are not dimpling the gentle currents, the smooth glides that make up much of the river's character beckon to be fished with a dry fly, if for no other reason than it just feels like the right thing to do.

Cataloochee Creek is formed by the joining of the two headwater tributaries, Palmer Creek and Rough Fork. Both creeks are well worth exploring, and you would be doing yourself a great disservice by crossing them off your list in favor of fishing only the main stem. Camping for a night or two downstream of the confluence of these two creeks alongside the main stem of Cataloochee Creek will afford you the time needed to dutifully examine all the valley has to offer.

Less than a mile above the formation of the Cataloochee, Palmer Creek descends past the valley's horse camp. Parking at the horse camp and hiking upstream via the Palmer Creek Trail will carry you quickly into brook trout

The slick pools on the Cataloochee beg to be fished with a dry fly. The creek has been compared to the hallowed dry-fly waters of New England, so bring a well-stocked dry fly box.

territory. Narrow and steep, Palmer Creek offers classic plunge pool and pocketwater fishing for its entire length. Less than a mile upstream from the horse camp, about where Pretty Hollow Creek enters Palmer, expect to find brook trout 4 to 8 inches long holding in the softer pockets and plunge pools. The trail closely follows the creek for several miles, allowing you to easily jump from spot to spot. These trout do get pressure, especially in the summer months, but will still attack a well-presented dry fly. Several tributaries to Palmer also hold brook trout, but are narrow and brushy, making for some tighter than comfortable fishing.

Flowing past the old Caldwell homesite, Rough Fork parallels the uppermost field in the valley for a little over a mile. This stretch holds mostly rainbows, with a few brown trout from the tree line downstream to where it joins with Palmer to form the Cataloochee. Inside the tree line, the creek narrows quickly and isn't really worth further inspection unless you are just a small-stream junkie looking to explore new water. Rough Fork is not as tumbling and steep as Palmer Creek and is far easier to access, the road following the creek separating it from the large field. Don't expect to be alone here. Although most folks forsake Rough Fork for Palmer or Cataloochee, wildlife viewers will park alongside the road to watch as progressions of elk meander out of the forests and into the fields at dusk, creating miniature traffic jams on the narrow, dead-end road.

After Palmer Creek and Rough Fork meet to form Cataloochee Creek, the main stem flows roughly 8 miles before emptying into Waterville Lake on the Pigeon River. From the headwaters to the campground, the Cataloochee flows away from the road, but even then it is only a short walk. Parking alongside the road and hiking across the fields will put you on the creek in just a matter of minutes. Below the campground to the second bridge downstream, the creek runs close to the road, access being never more than just a few steps away. Below the second bridge at the group campground, the river is more remote, with no access except an easily dismissed trail, until it reaches Asbury Crossing. Below Asbury, trails are nonexistent and trout begin showing up with diminishing frequency until they are overtaken by smallmouth bass a mile or so before the river enters Waterville Lake.

The upper river, from the headwaters to the second bridge, is where the majority of folks fish. This area seems to hold the highest numbers of trout and is by far the easiest to access. The water is a decent flow from the get-go, but grows a bit larger when Caldwell Creek enters across from the campground. Casting is easy so long as you take inventory and know where your backcast is heading. The trout, a mixture of rainbows and browns averaging 6 to 10 inches, are not pushovers by any means, and at times are downright tough. Some larger trout, 12 to 14 inches, show up, usually browns, and are caught during the heavier hatches or on streamers in the fall before the spawn.

Past the second bridge, the river is a good-size stream by park standards and can be tough to wade in higher flows. Parking at the bridge or downstream at Asbury Crossing and hiking in will usually put you on some virgin water for the day. Trout are less plentiful here, but the stretch holds some of the bigger brown trout in the river. The browns will take dry flies in the spring and summer, or in the "off-season" if enough bugs come off to get their attention. However, as is true elsewhere in the park, streamers will consistently get more strikes, especially when the water is dropping after a heavy rain. Brown trout up to 16 inches have been caught here and below, but should never be expected. Expect to find the same size fish as you would upstream, with anything over 12 inches being a special gift.

The Cataloochee Valley is one of the few places in the South where elk can be seen roaming the open fields. These grand animals are part of an introduction program in the park and make nice background music during the rut in September.

Below Asbury, Cataloochee Creek flows just a few hundred yards before being joined by Little Cataloochee Creek. I encourage you to explore this little version of the main flow, as it may surprise you with the numbers of trout it holds in the lower reaches. You can either hike up the creek from the confluence, or drive out Old NC 284 and enter the creek from the road. If you're wanting to explore a bit higher up, take Little Cataloochee Trail until it crosses the creek and have at it.

The main Cataloochee below where Little Cataloochee flows in fishes well for only a short distance, then begins warming, and smallmouth bass begin displacing the trout. There are no trails, so a lot of bushwhacking is needed to access the creek as well, keeping most folks out. I should say that if a big brown trout were to pick his lie, it would be somewhere down in this transitional zone, but expecting such a thing would be setting unrealistic expectations on the creek.

From top to bottom, Cataloochee Creek produces some of the better hatches of any park stream. Springtime finds anglers chasing Hendricksons

Heavy canopy shelters Cataloochee Creek keeping it cool late—even into the summer. The canopy also acts as a large serving plate from which beetles, inchworms, and ants drop into the water. Don't forget that box of terrestrials!

CATALOOCHEE CREEK HATCHES

	JAN	FEB	MAR	APR	MAY	JUN	JUL	AUG	SEP	OCT	NOV	DEC
Midges (Diptera)			■	■	■	■	■	■	■	■	■	■
#18-26 Stalcup's Hatching Midge, Brooks's Midge Emerger, Walker's Mayhem Emerger, Griffith's Gnat, VC Midge												
Blue-Winged Olive (Baetis spp.)			■	■	■	■					■	■
#16-22 Compara-dun, CDC Biot Dun, Last Chance Cripple, A. K.'s Parachute, Hi-Viz Emerger, Thorax BWO Emerger												
Blue Quill (Paraleptophlebia adoptiva)				■								
#18 Catskill-style, A. K.'s Parachute, Tilt Wing Dun												
Quill Gordon (Epeorus pleuralis)			■	■								
#14-16 A. K.'s Parachute, Catskill-style, Quill Gordon spinner												
Hendrickson (Ephemerella subvaria)			■	■								
#14-16 Catskill-style, Parachute Adams, Last Chance Cripple												
March Brown (Maccaffertium vicarium)					■							
#12-16 Parachute Adams, Hairwing Dun, D&D Cripple, March Brown Extended Body, Brooks's Sprout Mahogany												
Light Cahill (Stenacron interpunctatum)					■	■						
#14-18 A. K.'s Parachute, D&D Cripple, Compara-dun, thorax-style dun												
Caddis (mottled brown/tan) (Ceratopsyche spp.)				■	■							
#14-16 Elk-Hair Caddis, X2 Caddis, Hemingway Caddis, Fertile Caddis, Translucent Emerger												
Little Yellow Stonefly (Perlodidae)						■	■					
#14-16 Stimulator, Egg Layer Golden Stone, Parachute Yellow Sally, Cutter's Little Yellow Stone												
Sulphur (E. invaria)					■	■						
#12-16 CDC and hairwing Compara-duns, A. K.'s Parachute, D&D Cripple, Last Chance Cripple, CDC Biot Emerger/Dun, Captive Dun												
Green Drake (Ephemera guttulata)						■						
#8-12 Green Drake Pullover Dun, Eastern Green Drake, Coffin Fly												
Sulphur (E. dorothea)							■	■				
#18 CDC Compara-dun, A. K.'s Parachute, D&D Cripple, Last Chance Cripple, Captive Dun, thorax-style dun, Spotlight Emerger												
Isonychia (I. bicolor)						■	■					
#10-12 Compara-dun, Sparkle Dun, Parachute Adams												
Terrestrials						■	■	■	■			
#10-12 CDC Beetle, Steeves's Japanese Beetle, Monster Beetle; #10-14 Rainy's Grand Hopper, DeBruin's Hopper; #14-18 RP's Ant, Crystal Ant, Dave's Inchworm												

and Quill Gordons beginning in March, then continuing into early April. Even if you do not see any bugs coming off, the trout are looking up after a long winter, so prospecting with a Parachute Adams, Ginger Quill, or A. K.'s Parachute (#14-16) should be Plan A.

Following the early mayflies, mottled brown and tan caddis begin hatching in early to mid-April and continue through the end of the month, oftentimes overlapping with March Browns, Blue-Winged Olives, Sulphurs, and

Light Cahills through April sometimes into May. Hatches here, while usually heavier than on other park streams, are just as unpredictable as on any Southern freestone. Keep an assortment of dry flies in your box to cover you for any occasion. Elk-Hair Caddis (#16) in tan and brown, Blue-Winged Olive parachutes (#16-18), Sulphur Compara-duns (#14-18), and the venerable Parachute Adams (#10-16) will fill your needs for any spring hatch.

One hatch receives more fanfare here (and elsewhere in the Smokies) than any other: the Green Drake hatch, which traditionally comes off sometime around Memorial Day. If you happen to be on or near Cataloochee when the Green Drakes begin coming off, call in sick to work and take a few days of vacation, because you have just won the proverbial fishing lottery. Anglers lucky enough to have caught the Green Drake hatch on Cataloochee come away with stories their grandchildren will surely hear about. Typically, word of the hatch spreads slowly, so by the time most folks hear of it, the hatch is all but gone. Large parachute-style Green Drake patterns and even traditional Catskill ties will both work, so long as your presentation is flawless.

Another notable spring and early summer hatch on Cataloochee is the Little Yellow Stonefly. It can begin emerging sometime in June and roll through the summer in decent numbers. There are never many of these bugs around, but the trout do remember their bright yellow bodies and the telltale profile on the water's surface. Yellow Sally parachutes and yellow Stimulators (#10-14) spark interest from trout looking for something big and yellow floating along in the river's current. The large dry flies also work well as indicators supporting a small bead-head pattern underneath.

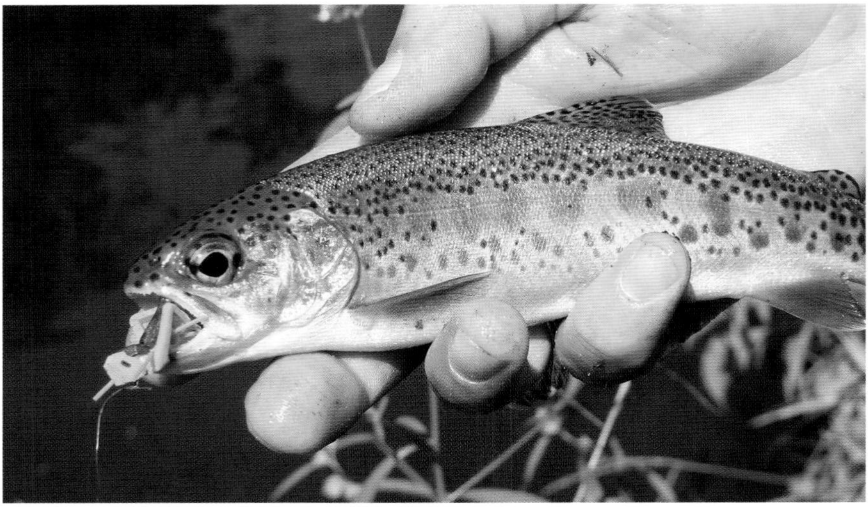

Hopper fishing in the summer is a favorite among Cataloochee anglers, not always so for the trout. High-floating grasshopper patterns tempt both small and large trout on the creek.

Rainy's Foam Hopper

Hook:	#8-14 Daiichi 1270
Thread:	Tan 6/0
Body:	Tan foam cut to shape
Wing:	Turkey coated in Softex
Underwing:	Krystal Flash
Thorax:	Tan dubbing
Legs:	Rubber

The summer months bring terrestrials, typically black ants and beetles, but on Cataloochee Creek, hoppers rule. This is especially true in the sections flanked by one of the fields that lie near or alongside the creek. Rainy's Foam Hopper, Schroeder's Parachute Hopper, and Cave's Hopper (#8-12) should be in your box if you visit the creek from June to August. These, along with a variety of beetle, inchworm, and ant patterns, should keep things interesting even on the hottest summer days.

In mid to late September, cool days signal the onset of autumn. Aside from the failing dry-fly action, fall is my favorite time to fish the Cataloochee Valley. Around September, the elk begin bugling, adding a cadence to the nip in the air that has you reaching for a sweater in the early morning. The brown trout are lit up like streetlights, becoming more aggressive as the days shorten and frost coats the valley floor. Overcast days are the best for casting streamers into deep pockets, near fallen logs, and behind large boulders, searching for browns. Going to a 7½-foot, 3X or 4X leader and casting a Galloup's Zoo Cougar, Whitlock's NearNuff Sculpin, or Shiela Sculpin (#4-8) is your best bet for stirring up something that you may not have seen during the spring.

Winter in the valley can be brutally cold or unseasonably warm. On the coldest days, the trout lie dormant, and not even a crowbar could pry them from the creek's bottom. When the mercury rises above 60, the river comes alive. The trout begin feeding on whatever is readily available at the time. If you can be on the water on these warm winter days, there's a good chance you'll be the only one on the river, perhaps in the whole valley.

The Cataloochee Valley is a special place, where elk roam and trout fin in the cold waters just as their ancestors did eons ago. The formerly tilled fields are now grasslands, and hollow buildings lie silent, reminders of those who came here long before us. Rich in history, steeped in Appalachian lore, Cataloochee Creek is more than just a simple angling destination, it remains a fixture in the Smoky Mountains and a symbol of what the park is there to preserve.

THE SOUTHEAST'S

PART V

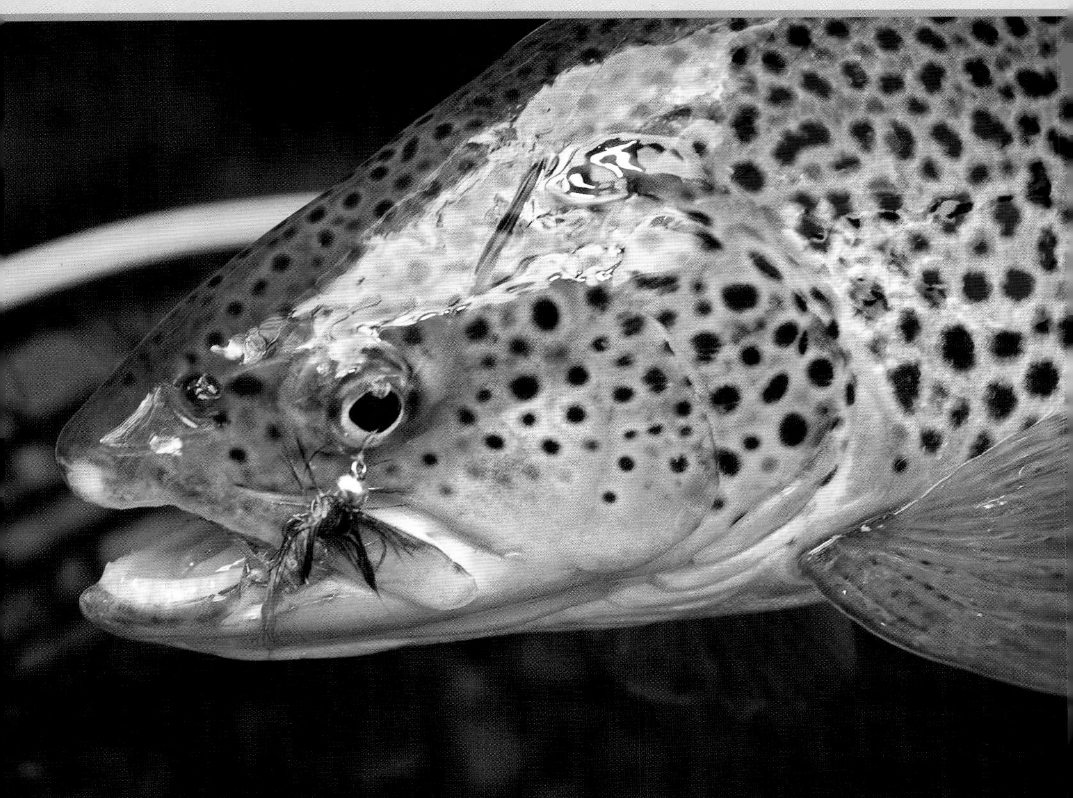

Fishing large nymphs and animated streamers are proven tactics for big browns on the Cumberland River and other tailraces. LOUIS CAHILL

BEST FLY FISHING KENTUCKY

Depending on whom you talk to, Kentucky can be lumped geographically into either the Midwestern or Southeastern portion of the United States. There are many things the Bluegrass State is known for, perhaps the most notable being smooth bourbon, fast horses, and Daniel Boone. When sportsmen think of Kentucky, white-tailed deer, wild turkeys, bass, and other warmwater species generally come to mind. Trout are somewhat off the radar.

Kentucky has never been thought of as a "trouty" state. Many of the state's waters are incapable of supporting self-sustaining populations of trout, due to water quality, average temperatures, and/or nutrient levels. Currently, 68 or so streams provide a touch over 300 miles of trout water in the state, around 90 miles being tailwater fisheries. When looking at the state's trout-fishing opportunities, only one stream rises to the top in terms of year-round sustenance, quality of angling, and overall appeal to anglers. The Cumberland may not be the only game in town, but it does without a doubt qualify as the state's premier trout-fishing destination.

Despite its scarcity of trout fisheries, Kentucky is undertaking efforts to restore brook trout in some regions, as well as maintain those last vestiges of the native fish. The state is also very progressive in terms of quality management for its trout fisheries. Several of the state's trout waters fall under some sort of special regulatory program designed to grow larger trout by limiting harvest, both by size and limit. The state's fish and wildlife officials have taken what is available and cultivated the limited resource to world-class standards.

In a region where put-and-take fishing is, by and large, the standard operating procedure, Kentucky has proven that proper management and restrictions on creel and size limits can create a trophy trout fishery like the Cumberland.

Kentucky Fly Shops and Guides

Cumberland River

FLY SHOPS AND GUIDES

Fly South
1514 Demonbreun Street
Nashville, TN 37203
(615) 251-6199

Strange Bait and Tackle
(270) 864-2248

GUIDES

Southeastern Anglers
(866) 55-TROUT
southeasternanglers.com

River Through Atlanta Guide Service
(770) 650-8630
riverthroughatlanta.com

Cumberland Drifters
Brandon Wade
(859) 272-9231

Mike Wlosinski
(859) 492-7906
cumberlanddrifters.com

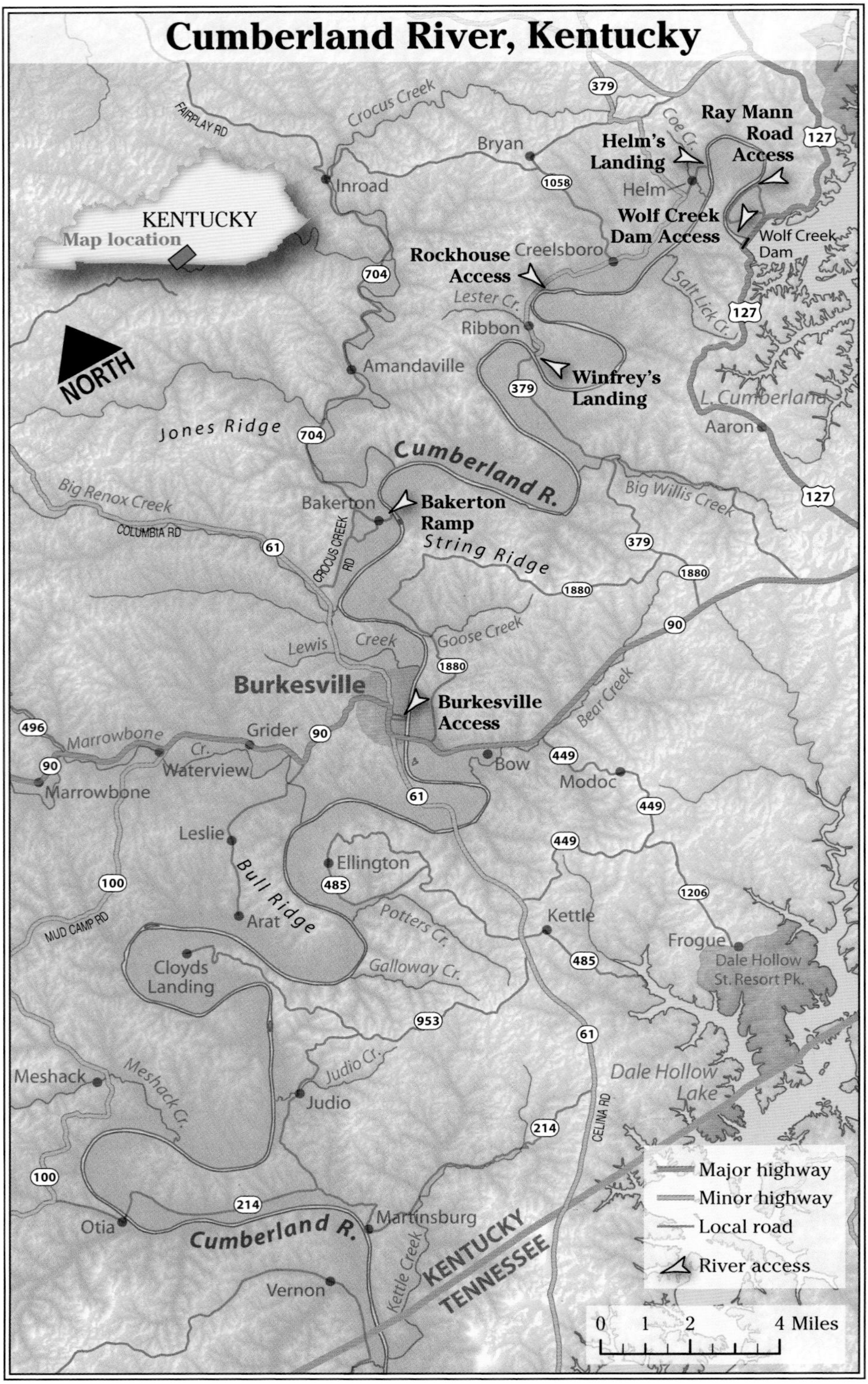

Cumberland River, Kentucky
KENTUCKY
Map location
NORTH
Crocus Creek
FAIRPLAY RD
Bryan
Inroad
379
1058
Helm's Landing
Helm
Coe Cr.
Ray Mann Road Access
127
Wolf Creek Dam Access
Wolf Creek Dam
Rockhouse Access
Creelsboro
704
Lester Cr.
Ribbon
Salt Lick Cr.
Amandaville
Winfrey's Landing
L. Cumberland
Aaron
Jones Ridge
Cumberland R.
Big Renox Creek
Bakerton
Bakerton Ramp
Big Willis Creek
COLUMBIA RD
61
CROCUS CREEK RD
String Ridge
1880
90
Lewis Creek
Goose Creek
Burkesville
Burkesville Access
Bear Creek
496
Marrowbone Cr.
Grider
Waterview
Marrowbone
Bow
449
Modoc
Leslie
Bull Ridge
Ellington
485
100
MUD CAMP RD
Arat
Potters Cr.
Kettle
1206
Frogue
Dale Hollow St. Resort Pk.
Cloyds Landing
Galloway Cr.
953
Meshack
Meshack Cr.
Judio Cr.
Judio
Dale Hollow Lake
214
CELINA RD
Otia
Martinsburg
Vernon
Kettle Creek
KENTUCKY
TENNESSEE
Major highway
Minor highway
Local road
River access
0 1 2 4 Miles

KENTUCKY

CHAPTER 21

Cumberland River

Only within the last few years has the Cumberland River below Wolf Creek Dam in southern Kentucky entered into the angling spotlight. For years before, the river sat shrouded in its foggy mist, hidden from the angling masses who dismissed rumors of the tailrace—that is, if they'd heard of it at all. Then, like a light switch being clicked on, the Cumberland River was a near overnight sensation that sat on the lips of what seemed like every fly fisher in the South. Well, it wasn't really overnight, but it sure seemed that way. Just as the Cumberland was gaining popularity, the wind was seemingly sucked from its sails when Wolf Creek Dam made the national news, in classic media worst-case-scenario fashion. The dam was going to fail, and all was lost—well, not quite. Essentially, the limestone base of the dam was beginning to fail, and a massive repair effort was required to restore the structure, which holds back around 63,000 surface acres of water at full pool. Current projections estimate that the restoration effort to put the dam back in good order won't bear fruit until around 2014 at the earliest.

In an effort to relieve pressure on the failing dam, officials dropped the lake level nearly 50 feet below full pool. This level is maintained through a combination of generation and sluicing, both of which draw water from the lower, cold reaches of the lake. The resulting flow downstream creates a nearly perfect water level for both trout and anglers. Before, water levels could fluctuate several feet, turning a nearly barren riverbed into a virtually featureless Mississippian torrent. Now the flows are, for the most part, relatively stable and should remain so, barring a very wet season and pending full repair of the dam. Consequently, the length of the downstream trout habitat was reduced, in effect cutting the coldwater fishery in half, confining it to the first 35 miles of river downstream from the dam. It's not all bad, and many folks are wondering what is going to happen to this now-blossoming fishery once the dam comes online and its multiple generators begin turning midway through the next decade.

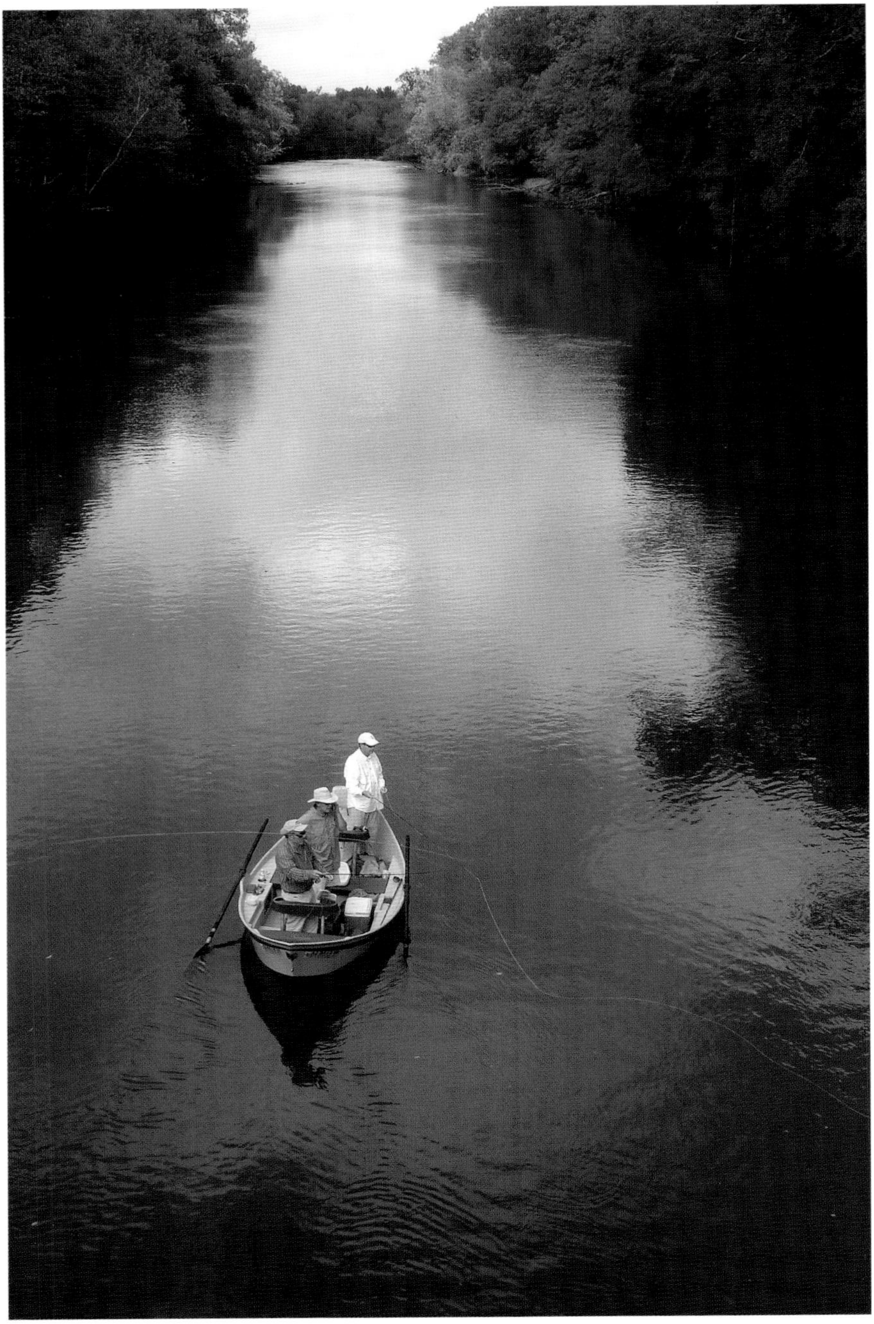

Long, deep stretches on the Cumberland can make for a long day floating, but the reward is well worth the extra time on the water. CHRIS SCALLEY

Brown trout like this are what every angler who visits the Cumberland dreams of. Fishing a nymph under an indicator in the tailouts of islands and in the deeper water adjacent to gravel bars is a preferred method of many Cumberland anglers. ZACH MATTHEWS

Until that time, the Cumberland is a haven for anglers seeking big trout by whatever means they choose to fish for them. Dry flies, nymphs, and streamers all prove equally effective, even on the river's larger trout. Since it is a tailwater, there is fishing to be had year-round. Add in the special regulations, which include a generous slot limit—mandating that all rainbow trout from 15 to 20 inches must be released, as well as all brown trout save one, which must be over 20 inches in length—and you have the makings of a world-class trout fishery.

On the Cumberland, access is limited for wading anglers. This is not due to the lack of public access—although that does play a part—but due to the river itself. Many of the large gravel bars that litter the Cumberland are found midstream, separated from the bank by a slough of deep water, precluding wading access. Boats are essential to see and fish the best parts of the river.

Wade anglers can find access at all boat launches and a few pullouts. Anglers fishing near the dam should pay very close attention to water levels, because with the generators and sluicing, water levels can rise to levels dangerous for those without boats. It's a good idea to keep an eye on a fixed object, marking the water level on that object and keeping an eye on it while fishing. If water begins creeping higher, get out to be on the safe side. Always have an escape route planned in case the water begins rising and you find yourself caught in the river. A personal floatation device (PFD) is a good idea. One of the self-inflating models that you wear like a fanny pack stays out of the way and will provide you that extra bit of insurance should things get dicey.

For those with boats, the Cumberland is a world to explore, miles of trouty water with each bend seeming to open up into another "perfect" stretch of river. Anglers typically use larger boats on the Cumberland. Drift boats and powerboats up to 20 feet, some larger, are the norm on this river. Personal pontoons and canoes are not as popular, partially due to the length of water you must cover, along with the possibility of high, fast flows where a larger vessel really comes into its own. Since there are only a few ramps that allow an easy day float, outboard motors are all but a necessity. Most anglers power up- and downstream from one of the various ramps, fishing the banks with streamers or side-drifting nymphs from the boat, then hopping out on the gravel bars to wade-fish obvious seams and tailouts. Not all the likely spots hold fish, but most do. However, there is a lot of water to cover, and you can find yourself burning hours probing what may look like an epic piece of water that is actually fishless.

Navigating the river and knowing which stretches the fish prefer, along with knowledge of subtle nuances in drift and presentation, really make a guide on the Cumberland one of the best investments you can ever make. This is especially true if you're new to the river or have little experience with running a boat in a river. Anglers not familiar with the latter have put more marine engine mechanics' kids through college than federal grants, and more than a few boats have found their way to the bottom of the mighty river.

A number of private boat ramps are scattered along the river from Wolf Creek Dam downstream to Burkesville. Finding one of these ramps is often as easy as asking a local gas station attendant or dropping into Strange Bait and Tackle, operated by Chuck Strange. Chuck's shop is one of the last vestiges of true Americana. Almost every angler who has fished the Cumberland owns one of his signature "Strange Bait" T-shirts or camouflage hats. If you've come off the river and for some reason think the stories of big trout in the Cumberland are just fish tales, a quick look at the photos around Strange Bait will make you book that cabin for another night.

Along with the private ramps (many of which, by the owners' choosing, are designed to keep their numbers out of the public eye for fear of being inundated by the masses), the state maintains a series of ramps from Wolf Creek Dam downstream to the state line. Still, most folks focus on the stretch between the dam and the town of Burkesville. These ramps are all improved, well-maintained, and can accommodate pretty much any boat you'd like to launch on the Cumberland.

Just below Wolf Creek Dam is the first ramp on the Cumberland. Downstream from here, two more ramps enter the river in rapid succession. The first of these is at Ray Mann Road, also known as Old Kendall Ferry Landing, which sits just under 2 miles downstream from the dam. From Ray Mann, it is only another 2.7 miles downstream to Helm's Landing.

Downstream from Helm's Landing, it is nearly 6 miles to the Rockhouse Access. Rockhouse is hard to miss: a massive natural rock arch can be seen from the river, giving testament to the powerful effects of water over thousands of years. Five and a half miles downstream from Rockhouse, Winfrey's Landing gives anglers yet another access point for both boats and boots. From there, it is a long, long way to the next ramp at Bakerton. The 11½ miles that lie between these two ramps can see some incredible hatches during the spring. Bakerton is not a state-maintained ramp and requires a small fee to access, but the price of admission is well worth it. Many anglers choose to motor upstream from here, floating back down to the ramp.

Floating down to the next public ramp in Burkesville from Bakerton without an engine is not really an option, since around 12 miles of water separate the two. The lower stretches between Rockhouse and Burkesville are where johnboats really come into their own, the stretches being too expansive to float and fish in a single day.

Just below Burkesville is the private ramp at Trace's. For a small fee, they will allow you to use the ramp, and they also offer johnboat rentals for those who want to explore the river on their own. A word of caution: Before venturing out into the Cumberland fog on your own, get to know the river very well, or you may find yourself the proud owner of a newly damaged boat!

After the ramp at Trace's, there are a few additional ramps where anglers launch large boats as well as smaller johnboats, many looking for striped bass rather than trout. Wade access also becomes nearly nonexistent below Burkesville.

Cumberland trout eat about what you would expect tailwater trout to eat, especially when fishing a few miles below the dam. Scuds, midges, blackfly larvae, and small *Baetis* mayflies make up much of the upper Cumberland's forage. Most effective near the dam, but equally useful for the length of the

Streamer fishing on the Cumberland can yield impressive results like this hefty rainbow. If you're wanting to target the river's largest fish, put away the light rods and bring out the 8-weight and 300-grain sinking heads.

CUMBERLAND RIVER HATCHES

JAN FEB MAR APR MAY JUN JUL AUG SEP OCT NOV DEC

Midges (Diptera)

#20-26 Stalcup's Hatching Midge, Griffith's Gnat, Brooks's Sprout Midge, VC Midge, Walker's Mayhem Emerger, Hanging Midge

Blue-Winged Olive *(Baetis spp.)*

#18 Brooks's Sprout *Baetis*, Biot Emerger/Dun, Last Chance Cripple, D&D Cripple, Translucent Emerger, CDC Compara-dun, A. K.'s Parachute, Thorax BWO Emerger, Hi-Viz Emerger

Gray Spotted Caddis *(Brachycentrus spp.)*

#14-16 CDC Fertile Caddis, CDC Caddis Emerger, X2 Caddis, Elk-Hair Caddis, Henry's Fork Caddis, Spotlight Caddis Emerger, Iris Caddis, Hemingway Caddis, Henryville Special

Sulphur *(E. invaria)*

#12-16 CDC Compara-dun, A. K.'s Parachute, D&D Cripple, Last Chance Cripple, CDC Biot Emerger/Dun

Terrestrials

#16-18 RP Ant, Crystal Ant; #10-12 Steeves's Japanese Beetle, Steeves's Bark Beetle; #10-14 DeBruin's Hopper, Rainy's Foam Hopper; #10-14 Dave's Inchworm, chartreuse San Juan Worm; #2-4 Rainy's Magnum Cicada, Criss-Cross Cicada, Elvira Cicada

river's trout water, are the workhorses on the Cumberland: UV Z-Midges, Zebra Midges, Rojo Midges, SLF Midges, and Split Case BWOs (#18-22), along with pink, tan, and orange scud imitations (#14-18), fished under an indicator with enough weight to get the fly down.

Farther downstream, larger stonefly patterns, such as Stalcup's Tungsten Rubber-Legged Stones, 20-Inchers, and Tungsten Terminator Stones (#8-12) are popular when looking for large trout in the deeper tailouts and seams. Mayfly patterns such as the Split Case PMD, Thorax BWO Emerger, Pheasant Tail, and Psycho Mayfly (#14-18) work well when fished alone or in tandem with one of the stonefly, midge, or scud imitations mentioned above. It would be a good idea to keep a few "trash" flies and a smattering of caddis imitations in your box to round out the nymph selection. Deep Six Caddis, Stalcup's Bubble Caddis, and Sparkle Pupae (#14-16) will help cover the caddis. Y2K Bugs, San Juan Worms, and the ubiquitous egg pattern in various colors can be filed inside your "just in case" fly box.

If you're wanting the biggest of the big, put up the bugs and ring the dinner bell with a nice piece of steak. The Cumberland is a "buggy" river, and large trout are routinely caught on nymphs and dry flies, but for those seeking the extraordinary, big rods and big flies mean go time on the Cumberland. Eight- and nine-weight rods rigged with sinking-tip lines in the 300-grain range should be in the big-fish quiver. Tip the lines with around 3 to 4 feet of 15- to 20-pound fluorocarbon leader and a pattern like a Galloup's Fathead, String Sculpin, or Double Bunny (#1/0-4). This is your big-fish rig. It may not sound like your average trout setup, but you're not looking for your average trout.

Nymphs and streamer rigs work well year-round and can be employed in conjunction with one another, fishing streamers as you float downstream

CDC Sulphur Compara-dun

Hook:	#14-18 Daiichi 1180
Thread:	Cream 8/0
Tail:	Dun Microfibetts
Body:	Sulphur orange goose biot
Thorax:	Yellow/orange dubbing
Wing:	Two dun CDC feathers

through the deeper stretches, then fishing the nymphs in the riffles and tailouts of gravel bars or shallow shoals. This is, of course, unless you see trout feeding on top, at which point the game changes a bit.

Midges, mayflies, caddis, and terrestrials all bring Cumberland trout to the surface. Most of the heavier mayfly and caddis hatches are found between Helm's Landing and the first 10 or so miles below the town of Burkesville. The 5 miles above Helm's Landing is mostly midge country with a few Blue-Winged Olives mixed in, but the caddis and larger mayflies are all but absent. Dry-fly hatches are also heavily affected by water generation, high water putting off the hatches and the trout. With the current situation surrounding the dam, only very wet periods will create high-water events when large amounts of water must be released from the dam to relieve pressure as the lake fills.

Midges and Blue-Winged Olives can hatch any day of the year, especially during late fall through early spring. If the midge hatch is heavy enough, the trout will set up in feeding lanes, and you can target some of the larger trout as they rise to pluck tiny flies from the surface. Stalcup's Hatching Midge, Brooks's Sprout Midge or Brooks's Sprout *Baetis,* or a Walker's Mayhem Emerger (#18-24) fished on a long leader will test your eyes as you drift the tiny offerings over rising fish. Flies for the Blue-Winged Olive hatch should include Harrop's CDC Biot Emergers and Duns, Brooks's Sprout *Baetis,* and Compara-duns (#16-22), the size depending on the brood. A strong Blue-Winged Olive hatch on the Cumberland can rival caddis and Sulphurs for the "big-trout-on-a-dry-fly" picture.

Around Mother's Day, caddis begin appearing on the Cumberland, sending the trout into a near frenzy as the hatch picks up. For the slow stretches so familiar to Cumberland anglers, CDC Caddis Emergers and Fertile Caddis (#14-16) are good choices. For braided tailouts, try a Mathews's X2 Caddis or standard Elk-Hair Caddis (#14-16), dropping a Deep Six Caddis, Soft-Hackle Pheasant Tail, or Sparkle Pupa (#14-18) off the back.

The Sulphur mayflies arrive in the latter weeks of May. The Sulphur hatch is so prolific that Georgia fishing guide Chris Scalley of River Through Atlanta

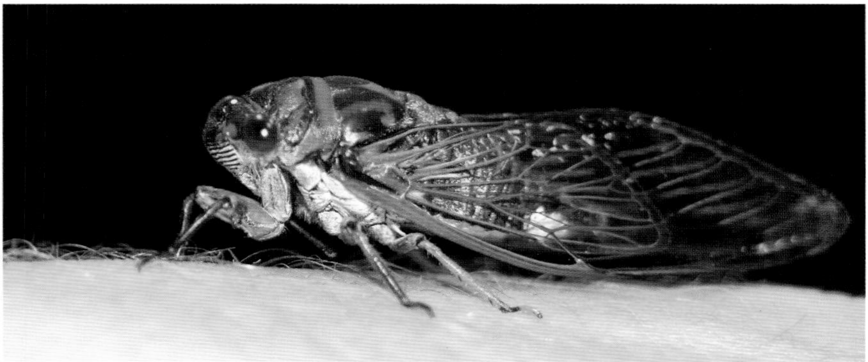

Cicadas! The word can bring a smile to even the most stoic curmudgeon. When these oversized bugs are singing in the trees, head to the Cumberland River. There is no better time to catch big trout on a dry than during the Cicada "hatch", especially on the Cumberland.

Guide Service travels to the Cumberland to fish and guide the Cumberland's Sulphur hatch. Scalley believes that the Sulphur hatch on the Cumberland creates the best dry-fly fishing in the Southeast and could be one of the best in the country. Trout—some of them very large trout—rise to the yellow-orange mayflies from June through August. Popular patterns for the Sulphur hatch include CDC Compara-duns, A. K.'s Parachutes, D&D Cripples, and Last Chance Cripples (#12-18). Long leaders are often required on the Cumberland during the Sulphur hatch, or for any dry-fly work for that matter.

Cicadas! Once this big, animated bug begins singing in the trees around the Cumberland, word spreads quickly. Fly shop dudes take vacation days, anglers call in sick to work, and guides begin furiously tying big, foam creations late into the night. Large and rather ominous, the cicada is a big meal for any trout, especially those that make you dig for the camera in the bottom of your tackle bag. Very large patterns are required to tempt Cumberland trout, but when "splatted" on the surface, the big bugs can move trout from several feet away. Enter the dry-fly underground with a Rainy's Magnum Cicada, Criss-Cross Cicada, or Elvira Cicada (#4-6) when these bugs hatch sometime in July. Your best bet for keeping tabs on the hatch is by calling Fly South in Nashville. Jim Mauries has the uncanny ability to predict this hatch like no one else and can offer blow-by-blow insight to anglers visiting the Cumberland.

It would be pessimistic to speculate that the Cumberland will not fish this well after the repairs to Wolf Creek Dam are complete, but the fact is we just don't know. All hope lies that the newly repaired dam will, along with its primary purpose of power generation, maintain some type of minimum flow to ensure that the trout habitat and superb angling remain intact. Through the conservation efforts of Kentucky wildlife officials, proper water regulation, and responsible anglers, the Cumberland will remain in the top ranks of trout destinations in the Southeast.

INDEX